COMPUTER LOGIC

PRENTICE-HALL ELECTRICAL ENGINEERING SERIES

W. L. Everitt, Editor

■ + ■ – ■ + ■ – ■ + ■ – ■ + ■

IVAN FLORES

Consultant
Norwalk, Connecticut

COMPUTER LOGIC

The Functional Design of
Digital Computers

Prentice-Hall, Inc.

Englewood Cliffs, New Jersey

■ × ■ ÷ ■ × ■ ÷ ■ × ■ ÷ ■ × ■

First printing.........October, 1960
Second printing.........May, 1961

Library of Congress Catalog Card Number: 60-16719

PRINTED IN THE UNITED STATES OF AMERICA
16567—C

PREFACE

This book considers computers first at the overall or highest level of organization and proceeds later to the lower levels of detail. We emphasize the organization and functional interrelationship of the fundamental units. These relationships are discussed from the viewpoint of necessity— they are not dependent upon mathematical logic or Boolean algebra, and they are not arrived at by circuit theory. They are, instead, discussed from the point of view of operational necessity.

A minimum is required of the reader in the way of engineering and mathematical background. The work should be comprehensible to those of some scientific training. Problems have been included to provide a means of acquiring facility with computer theory.

It is the method of the first part of the book to examine computers from the air down—a first look, a bird's-eye view from the air, is taken to see how the computer fits into the overall system of scientific investigation and business enterprise. The characteristics and specifications, then the relationship between the problem and the computer are examined. The structure and organization are investigated with regard to the large functional units, their interrelation, interdependence, and control, and an examination of programming is included. The function and composition of each unit are then pursued. The analytic approach in the first part of the book will help the reader to understand at each step the overall pattern. The second half continues, by synthesis, to build up larger and larger functional units with the goal of a complete and unified machine concept.

The interplay between design and application is emphasized. A design which keeps the user, the programmer, and the applications in mind cannot help but be superior. Similarly, the programmer who is aware of how the computer operates to carry out his instructions is able to make use of the machine.

How is each process initiated and controlled and what are the methods of coordinating the varied activities of the units which comprise the computer?

Programming is considered from the point of view of the programmer, the functional units of the computer, and the type of problem to be handled by the computer and the designer. The job of the programmer and the art of doing it are explained by programming a fictitious machine. The flow diagram is used as a tool. The techniques of tallying, comparison, subroutines, branch points, cycle indices, sentinels, iterations, decision making and automatic program alteration are the programming background required for effective computer design.

The computer performs arithmetic by addition, complementation, and shifting. How these are used to do subtraction, multiplication, and division is explained with examples in the decimal system so that the reader may follow with ease.

A thorough background of counting and number systems is developed in order to bring an understanding of how arithmetic is performed by the computer in its own language. This understanding is expanded to a perception of arithmetic and translation within and between different number systems. The other languages used by machines, the machine codes, and the means for performing arithmetic in machine code are discussed.

Manipulation of five kinds of elements is used to present the process of symbolic logic: propositions, geometric areas, letter symbols, functional blocks, and components. Symbols proposed by the Institute of Radio Engineers' Standards Committee are adopted. After an introductory treatment, logical methods are discussed and the binary half-adder and adder are derived; examples of its use are given. Boolean algebra is summarized. *Nor* circuits are given attention as logical blocks, along with examples of their incorporation in a computer logic.

The logical construction of functional units and operational units from elementary logical units is considered, including a discussion of serial, serial parallel, and parallel adders for different codes and counting systems, accumulators, shift registers, comparators, complementors, coding units, and control units. This material comprises a fund of "unwritten art" in the computer field.

Here is where the *synthesis* approach really pays off. Starting from simple logical elements, large functional units are built up; a simple symbolic block is used to represent each large functional unit. When constructing still larger operational units it is thus possible to see and understand the relationships among the functional units because each is represented by a single block. There is not a welter of symbols all over the page to confuse the reader and obscure and complicate the reasoning.

The section on arithmetic capitalizes upon this principle. The functional and logical blocks are combined before the reader's eyes to make operational units to do each of the arithmetic operations. Before each construction, the reasoning and the elementary steps required of each unit are explained both verbally and with subcommand operational flow charts. The generation of the sign of the result is also covered.

Nothing could be more important to the computer than how its functions are controlled! A chapter is devoted to the previously neglected topic of control unit operation—where the asynchronous decentralized computer control is dissected for the reader. The plan of action for the control unit is presented verbally and with operational flow charts; then each subdivision of control is analyzed. Finally, the logic to supplement the control is presented and discussed; centralized control is also examined here.

The operation of the memory is dependent largely upon the characteristics of the components comprising it. These components are investigated first and the logic necessary for memorizing and remembering follows. More attention is given core and drum memories than others because of their importance in modern computers.

Input and output equipment have received the greatest slight in the computer literature, at least in the aspect of the logic associated with them. Maybe the author has gone overboard in his coverage of this area. But there has been so little available elsewhere that an extensive treatment is necessary to tie things together. Much mechanical detail has been included which may seem expendable. Yet, to appreciate the symbiosis of the mechanical and electronic aspects of the equipment one must comprehend its mechanical function as well as the logical principles involved. The kinds of direct communication to and from the computer are catalogued and control panels of current computers are used to demonstrate these general principles.

To encapsulate the ideas which pervade the book, a problem is presented in the last chapter. A complete analysis is made of what happens from the time the problem is given to the computer programmer until he returns the answer to whomever posed it.

The Glossary which follows the text has been culled from a number of glossaries published by the various professional computer societies. To these extracts have been added a number of definitions not found elsewhere, and some of the published definitions.

I would like to express sincere gratitude to those who have made this venture possible. First, to my wife Helen, who courageously and devotedly waded far afield into the morass of computer technology. Next, to the small band of associates, Saul Teichman, Andre Godefroy, Tom Cull, and Ralph Townsend, who painstakingly read each draft to point out where the text became unintelligible and obscure. Then to the alert and untiring efforts of the stenographic force, notably Virginia Kirchhoff and also Alice Bennett and Evelyn Davison. Lastly, to all my friends who have gracefully accepted my hibernation for the duration of this project.

I. F.

CONTENTS

CODING (*Continued*)

FUNCTIONAL UNITS (*Continued*)

COMPUTER LOGIC

ONE

INTRODUCTION

1.1. WHAT IS A COMPUTER?

Anyone who has sufficient interest in computers to search out a book on that topic must have some idea of what one is. But somehow a fresh look at this question before plunging into a detailed study may be an advantage.

A computer, whether analog or digital, is a device for solving problems automatically. The word "automatically" indicates that there is as little human intervention as possible. Modern computers can solve problems so quickly because they are electronic devices. The types of problems computers can solve are discussed in the next section.

An important consideration is the language used by the computer. It is obvious that the computer doesn't use the same language as we do, either for receiving the problem or for solving it. If it did, we could merely tell our problem to the computer and it would answer us in spoken English.

The computer uses a unique language for solving problems. A different language may be required to get information into the computer. Thus, we may have to contend with three different languages: the English language we speak; the intermediate language used to convey information to the computer, such as the language of the holes on punched cards; and the language the computer uses for the information and for solving the problem. Let's hope this language barrier is not too great for the reader!

1

The computer can perform certain *operations* upon the information furnished it. If these operations are repeated in various sequences, different *problems* can be solved. Each *application* requires the solution of one or more problems. Thus a hierarchy exists: a few operations can solve many problems, and sets of these problems make up the applications.

In the next section the problems are discussed in answer to the question, "What can the computer do?" The operations the computer performs are discussed in Section 1.3. Section 1.4 mentions a number of applications.

1.2.   WHAT CAN THE COMPUTER DO?

Computers in general can do a number of different things. The list we are going to make may lie beyond the capabilities of any one computer, but there are single computers that can do several of the things listed below. The more kinds of jobs we wish to have the computer do, the less efficiently it will be able to do any single job. On the other hand, if we only wish the computer to be able to do a few jobs, it may be able to do each in less time. In other words, more diverse requirements for the machine result in its taking a longer time to solve a given problem. Examples of tasks that various computers can do follow.

Mathematical Problems

Solutions can be found for linear equations, linear differential equations, matrices, partial differential equations, polynomials, and so forth.

Simulation

An important function of a computer is to act as, or to create, a model of an experimental or practical situation. This can be done in two fashions:

REAL-TIME SIMULATION. Here, whatever should happen in a laboratory or in the field must appear to happen at the *same rate* within the computer.

SCALED SIMULATION. Here the rate of time of simulation within the computer may be foreshortened, so that what would normally take a week or a month to transpire in the field would happen within a few moments in the computer. Or, conversely, the computer may perform in the period of an hour what happens within a split second in actual practice.

Both these forms of simulation are very important, and great pains may be required to get the proper scaling (ratio of computer time to actual time). An example of real-time simulation may help the reader visualize what is meant.

Take the case of a nuclear reactor. Of course, the computer does not simulate the physical characteristics of the reactor—it does not look like it, nor does it in any physical sense act like the reactor. What it does do is produce numbers which represent the energy being generated by such a reactor. The operator of the computer can then note at any moment the state of the reactor and his own capacity to control it as limited by his reaction time. He can find out how the reactor would operate, for instance, if the control rod were fully withdrawn and the reactor went critical. In the field the reactor might blow up; the computer responds by producing a very large number. If the operator at any time wished to examine closely what was happening in a short period of time, he would use scaled simulation instead of real-time simulation.

Control

One of the great accomplishments of computer science is its enabling computers to control things. Not only can a computer control processes and movement outside itself, but it can also control itself!

Some of the areas of control follow.

PROCESSES. Information is supplied to a computer about the functioning of, say, a chemical plant by describing in quantitative form the pressure, temperature, rate of flow, and other data. The computer can then, by the various formulas incorporated within it, determine what adjustments should be made in each of these variables so that the processing is carried on under the proper environmental conditions. It will send back information in the form of currents and voltages or mechanical movements in order to provide compensations in such things as actuators, valves, relays, heating elements, and so forth, and thus effect a control of the processes. The use of such devices and computations provides precise chemical mixtures to produce the delicate fibers required for some of the inexpensive but beautiful fabrics manufactured today.

MOVEMENT. By the same means—by reporting to the computer information on location and rate of movement—we can have the computer produce outputs that control movement. An example of such control can be found in the new "electronic elevators" which have computers that operate to schedule them during periods of even the heaviest traffic in the world's largest skyscrapers. Also, the mechanism that enables the much-talked-about guided missiles to reach their targets is a calculator which can compensate for the various physical phenomena which impinge upon the missile as it flies its path.

ITSELF. The ability of the computer to control itself enables it to follow a given course of action until it has found a particular kind of result and then to adjust its behavior accordingly. The ability to make decisions is what makes the more advanced computer particularly effective.

Record Keeping

One of the sections of a computer which we will discuss in more detail later is its memory or storage facility. Some computers can store large amounts of information in a small physical volume and in a form quickly accessible to the computer. The computer can insert and withdraw information from storage within an extremely short time. This enables the computer to be used for tasks such as keeping track of large inventories for commercial installations or of the entire accounts receivable or accounts payable of a vast organization.

Construction of Tables

Modern computers can perform many arithmetic operations in extremely short periods of time. This computational speed makes it practical and, nowadays, customary to use a computer for the calculation of mathematical and physical tables. The computer exercises control over itself by continuing to change the various look-up variables it uses in calculating the entries for a table.

Language Translation

Because of its ability to store large amounts of information, a big computer can be and is used to translate from one language to another. In order that this translation be more than literal, various complex rules of syntax and grammar must also be stored in the memory of the computer. At the present time it is possible to translate foreign languages by computer for less than it would cost for a human to translate them. But this is so only when the input cost is not included. That's the catch! It is almost as expensive to have an operator enter the material into the machine as it is to have a person translate it!

The high-speed computer is being used now on the immense job of compiling and indexing each and every word in the recently unearthed Dead Sea Scrolls. Many of the scrolls are merely fragments. With this index containing every context in which a word appears, it is possible to do the heretofore unapproachable job of reconstructing these fragments into cogent texts; this work is now in progress.

Function Plotting

The output of a computer can be displayed in graphic form. Thus, in addition to the normal output of the computer which might take the form of printed records or tables or the control of physical phenomena, output can be obtained on a visual basis.

Synthesis and Analysis

An important form of drudgery taken over by the computer calls upon its ability to find the functional relation that exists within raw data. The computer can find the curve which most closely fits given data as long as it is provided with some criterion (such as "least squares") for evaluation. It can go even further than that—it can optimize variables existing in a given problem. This is done for many power companies. A power company has several generators, power lines, and busses; at any time during the day there are different loads on the different lines connected to the generators. Several different makes of computers have been put into use for the power companies to calculate which generators should be running and at what per cent of their maximum rate.

Limitations

It might appear that the computer is a modern magic genie. Press the button and the imp ferrets out your problem and solves it. Not so! There is much hard work involved in systematizing and translating the problem into the computer's limited language and in "telling" the computer just what and when to do things. This will be clarified in the next two chapters.

1.3. HOW DOES IT WORK?

What the computer does to the information it receives is called *processing*. Processing is defined by enumerating the operations which are so classified.

One function of the computer is to *store information*. Computers have provision for temporary storage as well as for long-term storage.

The computer is capable of *altering the information*. This is done in two ways, known as *editing* and *arithmetic* (discussed further below).

The computer is able to *move information about*. Movement takes place from the input device to the computer, from the computer to the output device, and within the computer to the various sections of the computer where storage, editing, and arithmetic take place.

Arithmetic—What Is It?

Because we are all so familiar with how arithmetic is done, it may be difficult to put into precise terms what we require of a computer when we wish it to do arithmetic. For that reason space is devoted here to an explicit statement of what is meant by arithmetic in general.

Arithmetic can best be described in terms of symbols. Symbolically, arithmetic may be represented as "$a \otimes b = c$" where $\otimes$ represents one of the four arithmetic operations (addition, subtraction, multiplication, or division) and a, b, and c are information elements acceptable to the computer. The computer can deal with certain elements only. These restrictions will be discussed subsequently.

Arithmetic can be considered as a mapping relationship. For any two acceptable elements, a and b, and a process, $\otimes$, a third element is determined, c. The relationship is referred to as mapping because one dimension (c) is used to represent three dimensions (a, b, $\otimes$).

We are more familiar with maps representing a three-dimensional locality in two dimensions. On such a map a building is represented by a dot or square. This symbol represents all the floors and ceilings and the roof and basement of the building; it also represents the pipes and the sewers below it and maybe even the subway station below them. Thus, all these things are "mapped" into one symbol. This is called a many-to-one mapping or relationship. Each of the many items (floors, ceilings, and so on) we map into one symbol (the dot or square); and conversely, the symbol stands for many different height levels.

Arithmetic is a many-to-one relationship. Thus the elements 3 and 5 and the process of addition yield the resulting element 8; the elements 4 and 4 and the process of addition yield the element 8; the elements 2 and 4 and the process of multiplication yield the element 8. There are many different possibilities or combinations of choice for the elements a and b and the process $\otimes$ that would yield the same result, 8. It may be said that these various combinations are mapped into the element 8.

Many-to-one relationships exist when there are many combinations of elements and processes that have but one resulting element associated with them, and, conversely, when one result is associated with many different combinations of elements and processes.

Arithmetic—How Is It Done?

The mapping view may be simplified a little if we fix a value in the process dimension and say that for a given process, any two elements may be mapped into a third element. Thus two dimensions (the numbers) are mapped into one dimension. This mapping can be performed by the use of a table. To compute by this method would require four tables, one for each of the processes of arithmetic.

Let us examine how a table would be composed to form addition. At the head of each column would appear one of the numbers to be added; along the side of the rows would appear another list of possible numbers to be added. One would perform addition by finding the column headed by the first number to be added and the row bearing the label of the second number to be added. The sum would be found where these two intersect. Such a procedure could be followed in the adding of small numbers, but think of the size of the tables that would be required to add the numbers used in arriving at the national budget!

The other method of performing arithmetic is to incorporate some rule or procedure for generating the result within the machine. This rule would not depend upon the size of the elements a and b and hence would not impose size restrictions upon the machine.

The Elements Used in Arithmetic

When the elements a, b, and c discussed above are restricted to the integers, the numbers used in counting with signs attached, the computer is called a *digital computer*. When the restriction that the elements be integers does not exist, that is, when the elements used may be "real" numbers or even the complex numbers, the computer is called an *analog computer*. Chapter 7 discusses bases and counting, and the concept of integers is developed there. The above definition is quite precise, but it does not transmit the practical limitations and advantages of each system.

The outstanding quality of the integers is discreteness: there is a big gap between the values of any two consecutive elements which are used by a digital computer. Analog computers use real numbers which have the property of continuity: between any two elements it is always possible to find another element. There is no guarantee, of course, that the analog computer can distinguish this intermediate element from its neighbors.

As an example, consider the input to a computer to be a shaft rotation. The angular position would be read by the computer as one of the elements a, b, or c above. For an analog computer the shaft could rotate to any angular position without restriction and hence could occupy an infinite number of positions. For a digital computer the shaft could stop only at discrete (distinct) positions. This input would be similar to a rotary switch with positive detents at a number of positions so that the shaft can assume only one of the positions for which there is a detent. Increasing the range of the digital computer would consist of increasing the number of switch positions for one rotation of the shaft or of gearing several shafts together. No matter how much the number of positions was increased, these positions or position combinations would still be countable and not infinite.

Editing—What Is It?

One phase of editing is the removal or addition of information to data. For instance, the computer might deal with an employee's pay of $40.00 as 0004000. Before this is written out in the final document, the initial three 0's must be removed and a decimal point inserted between the 40 and the 00. Similarly, it may be desired to print out the date of transaction, even though this was not included in the input data to the computer. This information may be entered into the computer once each day and then printed out with the other information as desired.

The second phase of editing is translation. Information is often handled within the computer in the form of code numbers or letters. Thus, an item in an inventory problem may be referred to in the data-handling operation of the computer by a part number. When the computer writes out information about this part, it must refer to it by name rather than by number. Similarly, during the calculation of the payroll of an employee, he may be referred to by clock number rather than by his name. In writing out his paycheck, it is necessary to refer to the employee by his name. The computer does this task of interpreting as part of the editing.

1.4. WHAT JOBS ARE COMPUTERS USED FOR?

In Section 1.2 a computer's functions have been discussed. In this section we will classify computer applications, some of which were mentioned earlier.

Commercial

High-speed computers can be used for all kinds of accounting and bookkeeping applications; notable among these are accounts receivable, accounts payable, payroll, and inventory. In these applications it is customary to keep the full records within the computer. At any time, at the accountant's discretion, a status report can be made giving the present standing of the company. During normal operation periodic reports are produced for the various accounting and executive branches of the company.

Scientific

Any engineering or scientific enterprise runs across many applied mathematical computational problems, such as the solving of differential equations, matrices, or simultaneous equations. When a computer is available, it can be used to solve these problems.

The computer can be used as part of experimental situations. It can act as a model in either of the modes discussed previously—real-time or scaled-time operation.

The computer can be used to control and monitor experiments by incorporating relays and mechanical switches, thermostats, and so forth. A complete experiment can be automatically performed.

Industrial

Computers find application in industries wherever long, tedious, and repeated calculations must be made. Such use arises in design problems where complicated formulas are involved or where solutions by approximation are necessary. Trial-and-error methods can be "programmed" on an automatic computer, so that the computer will work without human assistance until it reaches the solution, at which time it will stop and announce its mission complete.

In industry there is also much use for a computer as a control and simulation element.

Government

One important application of a highly accurate, very compact and durable computer is in the missile guidance field. Here the computer must be sufficiently accurate to determine the compensations required for the various forces acting upon the missile, compact enough to fit into the small space allotted to it within the missile, and hardy enough to withstand the extreme temperatures and forces of acceleration applied to the missile before it reaches its target.

Air traffic control is an application where the human being has already reached his maximum performance. Here the problem concerns a number of airplanes approaching a landing field at the same time, each having a limited amount of gasoline and therefore able to stay aloft a limited time. A definite landing schedule must be allotted to each. The path of each plane must be assigned and monitored, so that as it circles the field it will not collide with other airplanes. Also, there is a take-off schedule for planes departing from the field which must be adhered to as closely as possible. Further, when emergency landings become necessary they must be given first priority and the schedule adjusted accordingly. When the problem reaches the size of that encountered at an airport as congested as La Guardia, for instance, it is impossible to remedy the situation with human operators alone within the time required for the safety of the air-

planes aloft. Additional traffic-control personnel do not seem to help—
they only get in each other's way.

Still another application is in the early warning systems which gather
information from throughout the continent to determine what friendly
and enemy airplanes are in the area and what defense measures should be
taken if enemy airplanes are sighted. Interceptors must be dispatched
and monitored, anti-aircraft alerted, and so forth.

Logical and Tactical

The areas of operational research, linear programming, and game
theory have become sophisticated disciplines which require advanced theoretical background. Here, problems of marketing, logistics, and warfare
can be solved on a mathematical basis but with complicated formulas
best solved by trial-and-error technique. Hence they lend themselves to
computational methods.

Statistical and Analytical

Computers can be used for complicated analyses of experimental,
psychological, or sociological data. Multidimensional techniques of handling such data, which formerly took months of hand computation, can
be done in a short time on a computer. It is also possible to connect the
computer directly to the source of data.

1.5. ANALOG *vs* DIGITAL

In order to bring home the practical differences between analog
and digital computers, a brief mention will be made of some of these
distinctions.

Quality of Information

The analog computer uses information which is continuous; that is,
between any two possible readings, another reading can always exist. The
digital computer uses discrete information, and it is possible to have two
input readings between which no other input computer reading is found.

Kinds of Units

It might be profitable to mention some of the kinds of units which
might be used by each type of computer. If electricity were the information-bearing medium, an analog computer would examine the amplitude

of the voltage; a digital computer would examine the spacing and arrangement of pulses that exist above a given minimum voltage. In considering weight, an analog computer would derive information from total weight, whereas a digital computer would consider the number of objects with a weight greater than a given minimum. With rotation, as considered previously, the analog computer would use an angle; the digital computer would consider the number of steps required to make that rotation.

Processes

The digital computer can perform directly only the processes of arithmetic. The analog computer can also differentiate and integrate directly.

The Limit of the Size of the Numbers Handled

With a digital computer, the size of the numbers dealt with is limited by the number of digits which comprise the largest datum. In an analog computer the limitation is due to the range of linearity of the components. Amplifiers have such limitations. A linearity range of ten thousand to one is large, but this must be compared with the smaller digital computers which can handle with ease numbers like 9,999,999,999 (not quite ten billion).

Accuracy

The digital computer may be provided with means for automatically detecting some types of errors it could make. The analog computer is limited by the effective noise present in its amplifiers; this noise determines the smallest increment in signal which can be positively recognized. The analog computer is also limited by the stability of the circuits which comprise it as it is subjected to power-line variation, environmental changes, and age. Component failure haunts both camps!

Decisions

The digital computer can make binary, ternary, and multiple-branch decisions and can alter its behavior accordingly without intervention. The analog computer depends entirely on diodes to make simple yes-no (binary) decisions. It is limited to elementary decisions which it makes on a digital basis.

T W O

FIRST PRINCIPLES AND
DEFINITIONS

This chapter will acquaint the reader with the first principles of computers, and it will introduce a large amount of terminology.

Each technical discipline has its own jargon; someone becoming acquainted with a new field will often have difficulty because its terms are completely alien to him or because a common word is used in a new and special sense. For this reason several references to glossaries are given. A comprehensive glossary (to which the reader is invited to refer frequently) has been compiled by the author and appears in Appendix A. The glossaries from which this one was compiled are listed there.

The definition of terms is emphasized because each represents a distillation of the principles encountered. Establishing a precise usage of terms early in this book permits later development to flow at a more rapid and even pace.

2.1. STRUCTURE

The structure of the computer, the interconnection of the various components, the choice of the components, and the plan of operation of the computer are determined by several factors. The three factors that most

12

influence the structure of the computer are language, storage, and arithmetic.

Language

Language is the form or means by which information is communicated.

The language used by the computer is not the same as that used for communication between human beings. The efficiency of the computer is greatest when the language used for manipulating information and performing arithmetic is one that conforms to the properties of the components used to construct the computer. The structure of machine languages is discussed in Chapter 8. It is important to note here that the machine language is different from human language and therefore poses the problem of translation.

Translation is necessary to change the information from human language into machine language. Direct translation from human language to machine language is often complicated and costly. Therefore, one customary sequence of operation is to translate human language into an intermediate language used by equipment in direct communication with the computer. A second translation is then made between this equipment and the computer.

The typewriter can be used to communicate with the computer. An operator uses a specially constructed typewriter such as that described in detail in Chapter 15, and performs the operation of translating English language data into key strokes. The key strokes are translated into machine language within the typewriter.

Sometimes a further intermediate step is inserted. An operator may interpret English language into key strokes which are translated into an intermediate language, and the information is temporarily stored in a punched card in the form of punched or unpunched holes (an unpunched hole being *no* hole at all). Equipment that reads the hole positions in the card is then attached to the computer, and the information is translated into machine language for computer consumption.

Magnetic tape is also used for temporary storage after translation of data. Here the information is transcribed into the intermediate language upon the magnetic tape and is retrieved by the computer using suitable magnetic reading devices.

Of course, taking information from the computer and putting it into an output medium such as punched paper tape or magnetic tape is the complementary process and is also required in most systems. Equipment which puts information into the computer or receives information from the computer is lumped into one category referred to as **input/output equipment,** or simply **in/out equipment,** or even more simply **I/O.**

Storage

Devices that hold information temporarily or permanently for later recovery are called **storage.** Such devices are sometimes classified by the length of the normal storage period. Long-term storage is called a **memory;** intermediate storage is referred to as a **buffer;** short-term storage is called a **register.** The quantity of information stored in a device is usually proportional to the time for which it may be stored. The *memory* holds a large quantity of information; the *buffer* holds a moderate amount; the *register* holds just enough for current use. The kind and quantity of such storage has an influence on the structure of the computer and its capacity and efficiency.

Arithmetic

Arithmetic is explicitly defined for the computer as addition, subtraction, multiplication, and division of the integers. The means used to perform arithmetic is related to the structure of the computer. A machine performing arithmetic using a table look-up will be constructed quite differently from one generating the answer by direct construction.

The arithmetic operation is also dependent upon the computer language and the arrangement of the data within the computer.

2.2. DATA STRUCTURE

The data handled by the computer almost invariably represent human language data. Since the data we use in communication can be broken down into words and characters, we might expect that the computer's internal language would lend itself to a similar breakdown.

Characters

The character is the smallest unit of the written, English-language word. The word is the symbol for the unit of written-language intelligence. The character is the "atom" from which the "molecular" words are formed. Two kinds of characters may be considered—numbers and letters. Both may be used in human-language *coded* information. Thus, 5U4 is a human-language code for a particular type of vacuum tube and is composed of numbers and letters.

Machine Coding of the Character

Presently the computer is not able to recognize or manipulate the written number or letter symbol. Therefore, it uses its own set of symbols to compose and represent these characters. The set of symbols used by the computer to represent the written symbol is called a **code.** The symbols the computer uses to compose this code conventionally consist of "yes" or "no" information. Information of this sort bears a similarity to the properties of the devices used to fabricate a computer.

The most popular, reliable, economical, and rapid components used in computers have two stable states and are hence called **bistable** devices. Such devices as relays (energized—unenergized), gas tubes (conducting—nonconducting), magnetic cores (magnetized in one of two directions), and flip-flops (a pair of vacuum tubes or transistors, one and only one of which is conducting) are examples of bistable devices.

A piece of "yes-no" information is called a BInary digiT, often contracted to "bit."

The machine character code for the written character symbol is most often constructed of bits. Machine character codes which have five possible "yes-no" positions are called five-bit characters. The principles of construction and manipulation of the machine codes and languages are discussed in Chapters 7 and 8. Machine character codes for written character symbols are simply referred to as **machine characters.**

Words

Machine characters are assembled to form computer "words" which are not usually the same as written-language words. They are the unit multiples of machine characters. Some computers are restricted to handling words of a fixed size and are called **fixed-word-length computers;** others not having such restrictions are called **variable-word-length computers.**

FIXED WORD LENGTH. All transfer, processing, and editing of data or arithmetic in a fixed-word-length computer is done with groups of characters of fixed length.

VARIABLE WORD LENGTH. The groups of characters manipulated are not fixed in length. Some means of distinguishing the end of one word and the beginning of the next is required. Distinction may be made by

1. the position of this information with respect to the rest of the data,
2. a special symbol between the two words that delineates them, or
3. a space or blank between the words.

In such a computer a part number may be a 20-character word and the part type or classification may be a one-character word.

The variable-word-length computer does have a maximum length which no word can exceed, determined by the physical structure of the computer.

The Block or Blockette

It is handy to have a unit of information larger than the word. Such a unit is called a **block** (or sometimes a **blockette**). A block in a fixed-word-length computer consists of a fixed number of words. Thus a 12-word block in a computer having a word size of ten characters will consist of 120 characters. In a variable-word-length computer a block of information is again of fixed length. Since the words are not of a fixed length, the block must be designated in terms of characters. Thus, a variable-word-length computer could also have a block of length 120 characters.

Field

When space is not at a premium, it is desirable in a fixed-word-length computer to use one word or a multiple of words to represent each "package" of information. Sometimes space is scarce and it is required to pack the information as closely as possible. The result is that packages of information may overlap from one word to the next. Thus, a 12-character part number would require two words in a fixed-word-length machine of word size ten; therefore eight character spaces would go to waste in the second word. Often another package of information of eight characters, such as the number of the department making the part, is inserted. A package of information that is a fraction (proper or improper) of a word length is referred to as a **field.**

A field might be considered to be a variable-word-length word in a fixed-word-length computer.

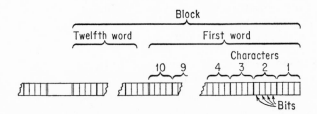

FIGURE 2.1.   Data structure.

Figure 2.1 shows a 12-word block with ten-character words and four-bit characters. The first (right-hand) word contains field A of five characters. Field B spans two words.

2.3. STORAGE

Memory (Long-Term)

The memory may be used to store large quantities of information. It is handy for holding such things as reference tables; it can store vast amounts of information required during processing; it can accumulate information until enough is collected to be sent to the output equipment; it can be used as an integral part of the machine, as in bookkeeping or inventory applications.

The entire inventory of a large company may be kept in a large memory. Each day the contents of this memory may be adjusted by subtracting withdrawals and adding new items received. The output required of a computer for this application consists of various records needed by management and orders for items in insufficient supply in the inventory. These records may be produced directly from memory.

Memory is rated, as are other types of storage, by the number of words or the number of characters that it will hold.

Buffers (Intermediate)

In large computers where the processing of information constantly requires reference to the memory, it would often be inconvenient to stop processing in order to take out or put information into the memory. To prevent this kind of slowdown, an intermediate storage unit, often called a **buffer,** is used. Big blocks of information can be transferred quickly from the memory to the buffer or from buffer to memory without detracting from the processing in the main computer. The input or output operation can go on between the input or output equipment and the buffer without interfering with computer operation.

Registers (Short-Term)

Information must be quickly available to the computer during processing. A word or field of information is held in a **register** while it is operated upon; the operation performed may be arithmetic or editing. A word or field which is operated upon, or with, is called an **operand.** Two numbers are added together directly from registers.

Registers operate much like a roundhouse in a railroad yard. They take the data (locomotives) out of storage (yard houses) and get them on the right track.

The length of a register is a single word for a fixed-word-length computer. In a variable-word-length computer it must hold a word of the maximum length used in the computer. The time required to place information in the register or to take it out of the register is called one **word time.**

Address

A storage medium of any consequence will be able to store a plurality of pieces of information; thus some means must be available to refer to the site of a particular datum. An **address** is the label for the physical location within the memory where the information is stored. Each storage position has a unique address. Directions can be given to the computer to find information or to store information by reference to the address. The address is a set of coordinates defining a memory cell. In practice it is usually a multidigit number.

Access

The means by which information may be entered or withdrawn from storage is referred to as **access.** The sequence in which this is done classifies memories into three types: (1) **serial,** (2) **arbitrary,** or **random,** and (3) **random sequential.**

SERIAL. The information is entered into or withdrawn from memory in a prescribed sequence for a serial memory. The addresses must be examined in a fixed sequence. If a datum is stored in the middle of a serial memory, then all preceding data must be reviewed before the desired information can be extracted. Information is stored serially on magnetic tape since it is written on or read from the tape in a fixed order.

ARBITRARY. A memory which does not require a fixed sequence of reference is called **arbitrary.** Although "random" is the more prevalent term, "arbitrary" better conveys the idea that access is independent of the previous choice of address and does not imply that this or any other choice of address is determined by chance. Information is available in the same length of time regardless of where it is stored in the memory. Thus information stored in any array of cores is immediately available by reference to its address.

ARBITRARY SEQUENTIAL. Arbitrary sequential memory requires two coordinates of reference to locate information. One coordinate of reference is found immediately, whereas the other must be searched for sequentially.

Such is the case with the magnetic drum memory, where a choice of heads and tracks is made immediately but the finding of the information on the track awaits the rotation of the drum and therefore is sequential.

Access Time

Access time refers to the time required to insert information into or retrieve it from the storage medium. For arbitrary storage, access time is fixed; no matter where the information is, the time required to enter or withdraw it does not vary substantially. For sequential storage the access time depends upon the relative location of the information desired. **Maximum access time** is the time required to retrieve information stored in the position where it is most difficult to locate. (In a tape this would be at the other end of the tape.) The **average access time** is the time required on the average to remove information. (In the case of the tape this would be the time required to go halfway through the tape.)

Memorization and Remembering

There is a definite similarity between the computer's memory and our own. Memorizing material is quite different from recalling it. Think of all the trouble we went to in high school to memorize *that poem*. How many times we read it over, saying it out loud, even writing it down. Stop a moment and try to recall it and back it comes (maybe).

The components used for memory (long-term storage) today are almost entirely magnetic and their properties can be spoken of as a group.

Entering information into a memory location must destroy the information previously stored at that address. Two pieces of information cannot occupy the same storage location at the same time. (Some authorities believe that the human memory has so many virgin addresses that it is never necessary to use an occupied location.)

To "remember" the information is a different story. **Remembering** may or may not destroy the information. When the recall process annihilates the information, a computer has a **destructive** read-out. When remembering does not affect the memory the computer has **nondestructive** read-out.

Word Time

The **word time** for a register is the amount of time required to withdraw or enter one word into the register. The word time for a magnetic drum memory is similarly defined and is discussed in Chapter 13.

2.4. ARITHMETIC

The method by which arithmetic is performed depends on a number of things. Most important of these is the coding of information. A written number symbol is represented in the machine by a fixed binary code (such as 0100 for 4). The code that is chosen for each number will affect the manner in which arithmetic is performed. The rules of performing addition with the coded numbers depend on the coding. The coding used depends upon whether arithmetic or some other function, such as editing is the primary consideration.

Subtraction, multiplication, and division can be done using only addition and one other machine function, **complementation.** However, there are different ways these three processes can be composed, and the speed and functioning of the computer will depend upon the method of composition.

Logic

The computer consists of electronic components—tubes, transistors resistors, diodes, capacitors, and so forth. These components are combined to form **logical elements.** These logical elements, in turn, are combined to make **functional units** which perform more complicated logical functions. Functional units and logical elements are then grouped together to carry out one of the computer's arithmetic or editing operations. These larger configurations that perform a single computer operation are called **operational units.** The computer is composed of overlapping operational units.

The way in which the logical elements and functional units are associated to do the arithmetic and processing required of the computer is termed **logic.** The method of associating the units together actually comprises the method of reasoning of the computer and therefore can be reasonably referred to as the logic of the computer.

The coding, the logic, and the logical building blocks comprise a team and each must be chosen to assist the other.

Speed

Historically and currently the speed of processing and of performing arithmetic in the computer depends for the most part on the access time of storage in the computer. This includes access time to registers, buffers, and the main memory.

Arithmetic time is vitally affected by the time required to do addition. Addition time depends on the system of coding used and the logic used for addition, which, in turn, is interrelated with the choice of components. The register word time affects the addition time because operands and intermediate results must be entered into and withdrawn from registers during addition.

The time in milliseconds or microseconds or in word times specifies the speed of addition. In most modern machines, addition is independent of the numbers being added. The time required for subtraction, multiplication, and division depends on the addition time, and on the logic used. These processes are rated in word times, addition times, absolute time, or by a formula. A formula relating the size of the digits in each operand for multiplication and division is often required to determine the time necessary for these processes. This makes more difficult the estimation of the computer time required to solve a problem. Hence, time estimates for computation must sometimes be done on an average basis.

The editing speed is also dependent upon storage speeds.

2.5. TIMING

Timing here refers to the rate at which the "microscopic" processes in the computer occur. It is not the word or character but the bits used to code each character that interest us now.

Form of the Information

Characters coded in the form of "yes-no" information are conventionally represented electronically by a train of pulses. The presence of a pulse indicates a "yes" and the absence of a pulse indicates a "no" (or, less frequently, the reverse). The time at which the information-bearing waveform is examined to determine if a pulse is present or absent is called the **bit time.** If we examine the waveform over a sequence of bit times, we are able to read the character from the code represented by the pulse train.

Rate of Handling Information

The reciprocal of the interval between the two bit times is the **pulse repetition rate** or the **bit rate** of the computer. It is also referred to as the **clock rate.**

The clock rate is the frequency or rate of handling pulses which are the coded representation in electronic form of the characters comprising the information to be processed. PRR is used to abbreviate the term pulse repetition rate or clock rate.

Synchronism

This is a term applied to the relation to one another of the periods allotted to the operations performed by the computer. Multiplication and division may be of variable duration. If a fixed time is allotted for each such function, the computer is termed **synchronous.** This fixed time, of course, would have to be the largest time required for any operation to be completed. Enough time must be allotted to complete the longest operation. If the computer completes an operation before the time allotted, it waits until the period has completely expired.

This type of operation is inefficient since time is frequently wasted just waiting for the allotted operation period to elapse. Still, it simplifies the design and construction of the computer as a whole and may result in a cost saving in the initial purchase of the equipment and in increased ease of programming.

If, on the other hand, the computer starts the next operation immediately after the completion of the current operation, the computer is termed **asynchronous.** This type of operation increases the initial cost of the computer, but increased efficiency may result in more profitable use of the computer.

Some computers fall between these two extremes, doing some chores synchronously and others asynchronously.

2.6. MEANS OF INSTRUCTING THE COMPUTER

It would not be wise to design a computer which could only do one problem unless that was all that would ever be required of it (missile guidance, for example). To make a computer versatile, it is necessary to break down a problem into tasks. These tasks are unit operations which the computer performs. The original problem solution can be assembled with these tasks. Other problems can be tackled as they arise. A sequence of tasks is chosen to solve the largest universe of problems.

Tasks which are subdivisions of a problem are called **instructions, commands, operations,** or **orders** (used interchangeably in the text). The sequence in which these instructions are performed is called the **routine.** The person who sets up the sequence of commands is called the **programmer** or **coder.** What he does is called **coding** and **programming.** The **program** is the entire activity required to solve a problem on the computer; the coding reflects the sequence of operations performed by the computer. Chapters 5 and 16 are devoted to the techniques of coding and programming.

Here is a good place to pause a moment to note the prevalent ambiguous use of the term "code." We first encountered this term in connection with the language used within the computer. Here "code" conveyed the machine representation of a human-language symbol. As now encountered, "code" means a symbolic representation, which calls for a machine order or instruction. This instruction code may take two forms: the human-language instruction code is a letter and/or number combination that conveys to the coder or programmer the instruction to be performed at a given relative time by the computer; the machine language translation of the instruction code or the "coded code" is the machine language datum that causes the computer to perform the instruction desired by the coder or programmer. To illustrate this, the instruction code for the instruction *Add* for the Datatron 205 is 74; the coded code or machine language instruction code for *Add* for the Datatron 205 is 0111   0100. More detail on this point appears in Chapter 4.

The routine composed by the coder may be stored within the memory of the computer, just as the information or data to be processed are stored. The computer can then "get its orders" by referring to its memory; it is said to be **internally programmed.** In all other cases the computer is said to be **externally programmed.**

2.7. CHECKING

Information is manipulated, edited, and moved about from place to place within the computer. It is of prime importance that this information be kept correct at all times. Information may be damaged at any time during processing or transfer by the dropping of a pulse or the picking up of an extra pulse. Such damage must be detected at the earliest opportunity. A detected error should be corrected if possible, or the solution so far completed discarded as worthless. There's no sense in finishing the problem with an error present, is there?

Checking Arithmetic

When one number is added to another the result may be checked by subtracting one of the numbers added from the sum. The result should be the other number. To check we perform the complementary arithmetic process. Here we refer to addition and subtraction as complementary; multiplication and division are also complementary. An example is shown in Figure 2.7.1.

Problem	*Check*		*Problem*	*Check*
2319	10060		2319	6
+7741	−2319		+7741	1
10060	7741		10060	7

FIGURE 2.7.1. Checking by performing complementary arithmetic.

FIGURE 2.7.2. Casting out nines.

An old method of checking arithmetic which you might remember from elementary school is known as "casting out nines." This method may be found in an arithmetic book or a text on number theory. An example is given in Figure 2.7.2.

Information Corruption

In transferring information, one of the bits may be corrupted and a zero misread as a one, or a one misread as a zero. The coding used may offer a means for checking the information. Checks are of two kinds.

ERROR-DETECTION CODING. The corruption of one bit of such a code can be detected. The machine will recognize this type of corruption by the presence of a forbidden code.

ERROR CORRECTION. By means of more elaborate codes, not only may the presence of an error be detected, but also the exact bit which was corrupted. The corruption can thus be completely eradicated.

PROBLEMS

1. Draw a block diagram showing the various *language* translations which might take place in entering data into and retrieving data from the computer.

2. Show how the message below might be entered into a variable-word-length computer using asterisks as separators; into a fixed, ten-characters-per-word computer without spanning two words with one field.

    (a) Felt brake-drum cover 39R1.
    (b) Azimuth 39.17, elevation 72.38.

3. (a) Draw a triangle illustration of the hierarchy of the computer. Include functional units, operational units, circuit elements, logical elements.
    (b) What is computer logic?

4. Do and check by casting out nines and by complementary arithmetic:

    (a) 258×381 \qquad (b) $109,153 \div 3851$ \qquad (c) $3457 - 1085$

5. Contrast long-term, intermediate, and short-term memories for (a) size, (b) name, (c) use, (d) access.

    Contrast the ways in which access is made to each kind of memory.

T H R E E

SPECIFYING THE COMPUTER
FOR THE PROBLEM

3.1. INTRODUCTION

In this chapter business applications are emphasized. We discuss what happens from the time a company discovers that there are problems that might suitably be solved by a digital computer installation to the time when that installation is working satisfactorily on the problems.

There are five major phases in the procedure, each of which is discussed in a separate section of this chapter. We may list the phases as follows:

1. State the problem in such a way that the applicability of computer methods may be determined.
2. Make an initial analysis, setting forth in a general way how a computer would solve the problem, and go on to determine the computer characteristics that the problem requires.
3. Decide whether the computer should be bought, leased, or constructed. A consideration of the important features of design and construction enters here.
4. Analyze the application of the chosen computer to the problem—this is similar to the initial analysis, but is pursued to greater depth and a specific computer is kept in mind.

5. Develop operating procedures, and set the computer to work on the problem!

Of course, a project of this size—establishing a computer installation—is one that requires the skill of several people of specialized and diverse backgrounds. *People* will set up and run the project. Therefore, throughout this description, the reader should bear in mind the great amount of consideration needed for the proper acquisition, training, and utilization of personnel and consultants. This item is frequently neglected in the planning with the result of considerable delays in getting the installation into operation and sub-optimum performance once it is started.

Note also that along the way valid reasons may appear for abandoning the use of an automatic digital computer; at this point management must choose the path to be taken.

3.2. THE PROBLEM

A computer system (by "system" we mean the computer and its associated equipment) may be required to solve a single problem, or a set of problems of a similar nature, or problems that are dissimilar in nature and which make quite broad demands upon the computer.

We will consider the case where the kind of problems to be solved is known.

Initial Statement

A simple statement of the problem gives three of its features: the output required, the input data supplied, and the method of processing. The following three questions must be answered for the **initial statement** of the problem: (1) What results are desired and what form will the results take? (2) What kind of information is necessary in order to solve the problem? (3) What must be done to the information to get the output results?

Other Requirements

Other features that must be considered before a system can be proposed are speed, cost, accuracy, and pre- and post-problem processing.

SPEED. How fast must information be processed in the computer? How quickly must results be produced? How fast must the input mechanism be able to "consume" the data?

COST. The cost of the equipment may be broken down into several factors: the initial cost (purchase price); installation cost; the normal cost of operation, including the salary of the personnel in attendance while the machine is solving the problem; computer maintenance. If maintenance interferes with normal operation, it can become an expensive factor. The cost of space for housing a large computer is considerable. The temperature and humidity of this space might have to be controlled, requiring air conditioning. For large vacuum-tube computers the normal electrical facilities are inadequate, since they consume a large amount of power.

ACCURACY. Errors can arise at several points in the computer solution of a problem: the input, the translation, the processing, the movement of information, or by an incorrect program or insufficient word size.

The *input* introduces errors because the transcription is done by human operators. Even with uncommon diligence it is impossible to enter or type vast amounts of information without an occasional error. In some installations it is common to enter the data twice and check the places where inconsistencies arise.

Translation, transportation, and processing of the data, once they have been properly entered into the computer, are constantly verified by the use of error-checking and error-correcting codes.

The *programming* is checked for correctness by comparing the results of a trial run-through. A sample problem done on a hand calculator is compared with one done by the computer.

The *word size* of the computer can limit the accuracy of results. One instance is astronomical calculations, which depend on the difference of two large numbers. If the two numbers are identical in their first ten digits, a ten-character word machine will show a zero difference between the two numbers; what is needed here is either a machine of larger word length to give the required number of digits, or double-precision coding which furnishes twice as many digits in the answer at a small sacrifice in computing speed.

The accuracy and precision required must be weighed against resources. The customer must decide if he can afford to pay more to decrease the possibility of errors, maybe errors that he accepts currently in a nonautomatic system.

PREPARING THE DATA FOR THE COMPUTER. Often the input data must be handled manually or by other machines before it is entered into the input equipment to the computer. The form the original data take may not be a human language and may require preliminary translation before secondary translation into the machine input language. The items listed on a sales slip must be put into a standard format before thay are fed into a computer for inventory control. The information must then be punched into cards or paper tape, or written into a similar medium for the input equipment translation.

Sometimes processing such as sorting or ordering is required before data enter the computer. For example, entering items into inventory may require the corresponding records to be sorted in order of part number, so as to match the master inventory tape kept in part-number order.

Another type of pre-processing is editing—necessary for some computers that require full computer words. Thus, "40 hours" must be written as 00040000, because blank spaces are not tolerated by this computer.

The method of collecting and transmitting data is also considered to be pre-problem processing. The original source of the data, the means by which the data are collected, and the means by which they are transmitted and received by the equipment depend on the needs of the input equipment. For instance, for automatic distillation of gasoline from crude oil, information is collected by transducers on the oil and gasoline tanks, on the flow meters, and on the temperature and pressure gauges. This information is converted into telemetering signals which are transmitted by long telegraph lines to the computer site. The computer is not intended to serve only one oil field—it processes information from many fields. The data are then converted into the input language of the computer.

POST-PROBLEM REQUIREMENTS. Not only the answer to the problem, but also the form in which the answer is written is important. The last statement is a pun, because information can be placed on "cut forms" or "continuous forms." **Continuous forms** consist of long reels of paper on which the output information is printed and possibly aligned. A continuous form may be later cut into individual records. **Cut forms** are used for telephone or utility bills and are single documents sent to the subscriber. In any case, the relative position of each word on the form, called **format,** may be very important. If the format is wrong, the clock number might appear as the amount on the employee's pay check!

Editing and sequencing are other kinds of post-computer processing. Thus, items which leave the computer in order of part number might require sorting by the purchaser's name. Or perhaps the output documents must be separated into batches (*e.g.,* pay checks to be distributed to each department.)

3.3. PROBLEM ANALYSIS

A sample problem is used to illustrate how a problem is worked through its initial analysis. The inventory system of a large company using a computer with punch card input and output is examined. A description of the problem precedes the analysis.

Problem Description

Reduced to barest essentials, the inventory problem is to determine (1) by how much the stock on hand was depleted yesterday, (2) what new items were received yesterday, and (3) what orders for stock should be issued today. This is shown diagrammatically in Figure 3.3.1.

A mathematical approach to inventory control sets the reorder point and reorder quantity by usage, item cost, storage cost, reorder cost, shortage cost, and average time to procure the item. When and how much to reorder is a function (ideally) of how often an item is withdrawn from stock, its cost, the costs associated with stocking the item, the cost to the firm for not having any of the item on hand, and the time it takes to get the item. These calculations are done on a periodic basis; the method used does not concern us here. Suffice it to say that the results of these calculations are now stored in the computer.

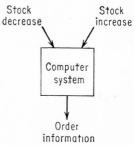

FIGURE 3.3.1. The inventory system.

With the proper constants in computer storage, the whole problem consists of examining and storing the proper portions of the stock-change information and producing the output information.

Systems Analysis

For our sample problem we have a computer with a sequential storage. To enter information efficiently, it is necessary to order (sort) it beforehand. It is most efficient to take it out in the order produced.

The job of the **system analyst** is to set up the general methodology for handling information and getting it into and out of the computer. His emphasis is on input and output and pre- and post-processing. The analyst makes a diagram of the system like that in Figure 3.3.2 (a typical punched card system diagram).

Document Flow

The documents that come from various departments of the company are in handwritten form (See 1, 2 in Figure 3.3.2). They must be translated onto punched cards. They are then put in the proper input sequence

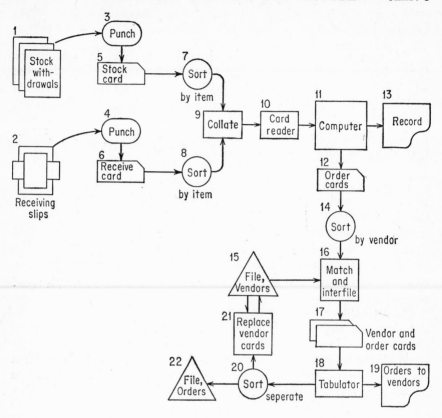

FIGURE 3.3.2.   A computer-tabulator inventory system.

(3, 4). The stock withdrawal cards (5) and receiving cards (6) are sorted by item number (7, 8). These cards are merged together, the stock cards being placed behind the corresponding receipt card (9). This merged batch of cards is now placed in the card reader, the computer input device (10). The computer (11) reads the first set of item cards. It scans its memory sequentially until the item record is found. Calculations are made to see if an order must be issued. If so, an order card is punched (12) containing the item number, description, quantity to be ordered, price each, total price, and vendor. After all the cards have been read and the order cards punched, the summary records are produced (13) to keep management informed of the inventory situation. Summary records might list back-ordered items, overshipped items, emergency-status items, and out-of-stock items.

Before any order is printed, all the items to be purchased from the same vendor should be grouped together. This is done by sorting the order cards by vendor instead of by item as produced (14). The name and address of each vendor are kept on a vendor card in the vendor file (15). The sorted order cards are matched with the vendor file. In front of each set of order cards for one vendor is placed the proper vendor card (16). This stack of interleaved vendor and order cards (17) is placed into a tabulator (18) which prints the orders (19) to be mailed. Each order contains the vendor's name and address and the items to be purchased from him. The stack of order and vendor cards must then be sorted (20) to separate the two kinds of cards. The vendor cards are replaced (21) by a collator into the vendor file. The order cards may be filed and compared with the incoming orders if desired.

Calculations

Each datum on the output document must be accounted for. It may arise from direct transfer from an input document; it may be an edited input datum (output $40.00—input 00004000); it may appear automatically on all output documents (order card punch to distinguish order cards from other types); it may be calculated from input and stored data.

For inventory we will discuss one of the required calculations. The symbols used are:

H = quantity now on hand
W = quantity withdrawn from stock
R = quantity received
P = reorder point (reorder when stock falls below P)
Q = reorder quantity (reorder enough so that Q will then be on the shelf)
N = quantity for new order (difference between reorder quantity and what is now on hand)

Now to calculate N we have that

$$\text{if}\quad P < H - W + R \qquad N = 0, \text{ (do not punch output card)}$$
$$\text{and if}\quad P \geqslant H - W + R \qquad N = Q - H + W - R$$

Notice that W and R are input data, $H, P,$ and Q are stored data, and N is an output datum.

Data Flow

When all the required calculations are performed and the edited information is collected, the data flow can be planned. During this phase, the origin and destination of each piece of information must be determined as well as the sequence in which the processing will best be performed, together with the decisions required at each step of the processing. This stage of data processing is discussed in detail in Chapters 5 and 16.

The programming is done after the data flow is determined.

Coded Routine

The data flow is usually specified as a number of tasks done in sequence. Each task in the data flow can then be converted into one or several program steps. Thus in the data flow the statement, "Calculate the order quantity N," will become several commands for computer operations in the routine.

Both the data flow and the programming are different for different computers; they can be examined only in a preliminary manner in the initial analysis since a choice of computer has not been made.

3.4. THE COMPUTER

Build, Buy, or Lease

With the general specifications of the required computer now at hand, the decision to be made is threefold: should we build, buy, or lease the equipment? To most firms not specifically in the computer business, the choice narrows down to buy or lease. Since leasing offers a tax advantage and a choice of newer equipment when it becomes available, the question may be settled on a fiscal basis. However, buying is usually cheaper than leasing. Further discussion of this important topic is inappropriate to this volume.

The next steps apply when construction is the chosen course of action. Otherwise the steps of Section 3.5 follow.

Design

The computer design is affected by a number of factors. Some of these are imposed by management and some by the restrictions of the physical installation. Other restrictions are imposed by specific problems that the machine will solve, by the general requirements for the predicted use of the computer, and by the sequence in which the component choice is made—e.g., the choice of transistors over vacuum tubes means that low-voltage power supplies and components are also used.

Limiting Factors

Some of the limiting factors have been discussed previously. One of the main problems, of course, is price. This enters the realm of computer design when the costs of designing the equipment or buying it outright must be evaluated and compared. In any case, the cost of using and maintaining the equipment must also be considered.

The space available for the equipment, the power supply, and the environment may prove limiting factors in computer design. Training the operators and programmers is another consideration.

Specific Problem Requirements

The conditions which must be met to perform the problems quickly and accurately will now be discussed.

SPEED. Depending on the structure of the problem, the point at which handling must be most rapid might be the input, the output, the processor, or the access to the memory. Thus, in the inventory problem, the bind will come on the input equipment because it is necessary to get information most rapidly into the computer. Processing requirements are few, and very fast access to the memory is not required.

In a scientific problem the calculations may present the greatest need for speed. In a sorting problem, access to the memory is the main concern.

ACCURACY. Accuracy can be achieved by increasing the number of digits per word or per item in the calculations and by making frequent positive checks.

CAPACITY. The limitations in capacity can be felt in problems such as inventory and record keeping when the number of items to be kept track of becomes large. Capacity then refers to the amount of storage available. One can also refer to the capacity of the system by the number of documents it can accept information from or produce as output in a given unit of time (such as 300 checks per hour in an automatic banking system).

General Requirements

In a general-purpose computer one has the problem of designing equipment for maximum versatility. Because it may be called upon to do so many jobs, it may be used for a large percentage of the full day.

VERSATILITY. Versatility can take many forms. When applied to input or output equipment it refers to the number of different pieces of equipment which can be tied into the system. Thus a system can have data entered by means of a typewriter, punch card reader, punched tape reader, a magnetic tape unit, or by direct keyboard entry. Output versatility can be specified similarly.

Versatility also applies to the kind and number of commands the computer can perform. If a large number of different instructions are available to the programmer, he can construct programs with greater ease.

The concept of versatility also applies to the type, amount, and accessibility of available storage. A large quantity of storage can be in the form of slow-access memory. The ability to obtain information quickly can be furnished by the presence of a fast-access buffer memory system. This allows information to be taken out of the slow memory in big chunks and placed into the buffer for quick reference. Separate storage facilities may be available for different kinds of data and for the program as separate from the data.

There are other special features which add versatility to the computer. One example of such a special feature is the display medium. Some computers have facilities for displaying the contents of many of the registers. There may also be alarm displays to attract the operator's attention and wake him up if emergencies should arise.

DUTY FACTOR. The fraction of time a computer is in working order and could be used to solve a problem is termed the **duty factor.** This is interrelated with the maintenance time required for the computer. It is customary that a general-purpose computer be active or its services called for a large part of the day. If it is not usable when needed, the duty factor suffers.

Design Factors

The design of the computer requires consideration of components, language, and logic.

COMPONENTS. In choosing the components one must weigh several characteristics. Cost is usually most important, unless the computer is being developed for military use, where other specifications such as environment or reliability take precedence. Speed may necessitate the use of components and circuitry capable of fast action. Of course, reliability of the components will affect the reliability of the computer. Because so many components are required, and the probability of a machine failure is a function of the number of components and the probability of failure of each component, it is necessary to use components which are extremely reliable. Environmental conditions impose further restrictions upon the components. The designer can compensate for component mortality by error-detecting circuitry, information redundancy, duplication of logic, and multiple-level logic system, but he must always be aware of the threat of multiple component failure.

LANGUAGE. The machine language used internally by the computer must incorporate a means for checking the data to insure accuracy of results.

Sometimes a machine language is chosen to give maximum calculation speed at a sacrifice in the speed of input and output translations. This is the case with scientific problems, where few data are put into the machine but many calculations are made. The opposite is true in business applications. Here many data are handled but little calculation is done. Then the choice is for a machine language that is easy to translate.

LOGIC. The logic, the interrelation of the functional units, is determined mostly by the kind of functional unit used, the components that comprise these units, and the machine language. There is still some latitude left to the "logical designer."

Computer Construction

The designer and fabricator of the computer have at their disposal two methods of construction. For simplicity and quick maintenance, a modular unit which may be quickly replaced and used interchangeably is most frequently used. With such modular construction the designer may use plug-in units, turret design, "Tinker Toy" units, printed circuits, or other kinds of packages. It is still possible, though, to consider seriously a unified construction if few computers are to be produced.

There is also a choice as to whether the subassemblies are purchased or assembled by the manufacturer or subcontractor.

3.5.   ANALYSIS FOR THE SPECIFIC COMPUTER

It is now assumed that a computer has been designed and constructed and is to be incorporated into the data processing system. We must re-evaluate the initial analysis with the specific computer in mind. This will be discussed in the same order as in Section 3.3.

System Analysis

What modifications of the system analysis are required for the chosen computer?

FORM OF THE DATA. Is the former assignment of data to each document still correct? It might be necessary or desirable to incorporate in one document the information previously stored in several documents. Or, conversely, it might be necessary to separate into several records what was formerly on one input source document.

INPUT. The way the information is entered into the computer must be re-examined. It may be found desirable to use an intermediate storage medium such as punched cards. Pre-computer editing may now be necessary. The time factor should be reconsidered. Should information be entered immediately or should it be accumulated and entered when a sufficient quantity is on hand?

PROCESSING. The input requirements have been firmed up. Now what editing is required within the computer to obtain the necessary output? Determine what calculations are to be made, in what order they are to be made, and how they should be broken down into steps to correspond to the facilities available within the computer.

OUTPUT. The kind of output equipment unit to be used is determined. The number of such units must be set. Thus, once the speed of input and processing is known, it is possible to foresee the number of paper tape punch units required to handle the full output required of the machine. The format control necessary so that placement of information in the output documents will be correct is set up for the output equipment.

Physical Document Flow

The system analysis makes it possible to plan the flow of documents through the peripheral (pre-processing) equipment into the input unit, through to the computer input, and thence into the files. The flow of output documents is now planned as they leave the computer and go through the peripheral equipment to the ultimate "consumer" of the documents and reports. The kind of documents used and the quantity required in *each* operation is now stated. The format, and the rate of handling of each document is determined.

Calculations

The basic nature of the problem has not changed since the initial analysis; therefore the calculations required will be the same.

Data Flow

The sequence of entering the data into the computer from the documents is determined from the document format. The jobs done upon the data and the order in which the jobs are performed are decided in laying out the data flow occurring within the computer. A flow chart of the data flow is prepared just before the programming is done. This procedure is discussed in Chapter 5 and a simple flow chart is shown in Figures 5.4.2 and 5.4.3.

Programming

Now we can make a program of detailed instructions to the machine to be used in working out the specific problem or set of problems.

3.6. COMPUTER OPERATION

We have reached the final phase: putting the computer into operation. We have just about solved the problem on paper; now it is time to find out if our solution can be put into practice.

Computer Construction Debugging

Before the computer becomes part of a system, it is necessary to find out if it is working properly. All kinds of things can happen between computer design and the working computer. Because of human failings, errors in wiring are inevitable. Since it is impossible to predict where these errors will occur, it is necessary to ferret them out after the computer is constructed. There will also be errors in the logical design, and possibly even in the circuitry although one would expect that circuitry problems would have been eliminated in the laboratory. Often circuits that work well on the bench present unpredictable difficulties when interconnected together within a machine. Only with the close cooperation of engineer and technician can these random problems be uncovered and (hopefully) eliminated.

Program Debugging

Of course, before any errors in a program can be discovered, it must be presumed that a properly working computer is on hand. Again, through human failings, it is possible to construct a program into which errors have crept. At the end of the problem solution, for example, it may be found that the total price calculated for an item is incorrect. Possibly the cause is that the unit price or the number of items was not properly provided. It is then necessary to find out whether the programmer happened to use the part number instead of the unit price, or the shipping address instead of the number bought. Program debugging is more complicated when done with a newly designed computer, since reliability of the circuits used in the computer is not a foregone conclusion. It is difficult to separate programming faults from computer wiring faults.

Operating Procedure

With a properly working computer and program, it is next necessary to outline instructions to the operating personnel. It is important to determine whether a single operator will be able to insert punched cards in the input, take out punched cards from the output, get the printing paper aligned properly on the printing mechanism, operate the control console, and so on. (What should the operator do first and when can he sit back and relax?)

Change-over

In a scientific problem such as solving a set of differential equations there will be no change-over necessary. Here it is a simple matter of converting a problem into a program, entering the program and problem into the computer, and then running the problem on the computer. On the other hand, if a computer is to take over the handling of the entire inventory of a manufacturing plant, it cannot do this all at once. Thirty or forty people might be engaged in doing the inventory process manually and all the records they are working on cannot be transcribed in the wink of an eye. It is therefore necessary that the machine take over a little at a time, a step requiring much thought and consideration. The employees who have been working on the tasks now to be done by the computer must also be considered.

Systems Operation and Modification

With the computer and program working, the operating procedure set up, and the change-over completed, some difficulties may still arise. "Special" cases which were formerly handled by human judgment may again arise, and some method of handling these must be devised. What happens when the automatic inventory system orders 50 items and 60 are shipped, billed, and invoiced by the vendor? However, if the system operates without a hitch for a few weeks after the change-over, it is usually evident that the system is acceptable and any difficulties that might arise will be minor.

PROBLEMS

1. Make an analysis flow diagram to encapsulate Sections 3.1 and 3.2 showing the processes and decisions necessary to decide whether or not a computer is needed and what computer to buy.

2. Make an operational flow diagram of how a problem is set up for the machine to solve.

3. Make up a checklist form a special-purpose computer manufacturer may use to determine the specifications (capacity, etc) required by his client. Devise a scale to go with it to rate each specification.

4. Draw a document flow chart for a payroll system. Include inputs for employee time cards (have a block there for this and other inputs to be punched into punch cards), new-employee data, changes in employee data. The outputs are the employee's checks, his deductions, receipts, the payroll journals, and the tax journals.

5. Add to the payroll system a means for labor distribution. One employee can charge his time to several accounts; the computer then accumulates the *cost* for each employee (time $\times$ rate) for each account. This is then printed out by department onto a labor distribution journal.

6. Consider a computer to handle accounts in a savings bank. The first run enters deposit and withdrawal data onto the computer memory. All withdrawals must be previously checked by the teller on the spot to prevent the account from being overdrawn. The second daily run prints a journal of all activity. The third run calculates the interest accrued and adds it to the account.

Draw document flow diagrams for the savings bank system. How are new and canceled accounts handled? Is input to the system required to be in order?

FOUR

THE FLOW AND CONTROL
OF INFORMATION

4.1. THE PLAN OF THE COMPUTER

Let us take another look at the computer organization. An enlarged pictorial representation appears in Figure 4.1. The input records (1) are fed into an input translator (2). Information from the record is stored in the buffer (3) until called for. It is then transferred from the buffer into the memory (4). Here it is available for processing at the request of the processor unit (5). Processed information may be transferred to the output buffer (6) during periods when the processing unit is otherwise engaged. Information may be translated by the output unit (7) into the output record (8) at the convenience of the output unit. Notice that there is another buffer (9) between the memory and the processor, in order to make information more quickly available to the processor so that it can work at its own rate.

The last functional unit in Figure 4.1 is the control unit (10). It is this unit that coordinates the activity of the computer both internally and in regard to the external stimuli (input data) and responses (output records). It must keep track of the scheduling of operations [note the clock in (10)], and it must communicate with each unit [the loudspeaker in (10)]. The schedule of activities is available to the control unit in the form of the program. It may be referred to in the memory (for internally programmed computers) or externally [the clipboard (11)].

You will remember that the program is a series of commands. Most of these commands are for the computer to manipulate information in some way; *reflexive commands* apply to the computer only, such as "STOP" or "LOOK FOR ANOTHER COMMAND AT ____!" This chapter is concerned with information-processing commands; reflexive commands—those which

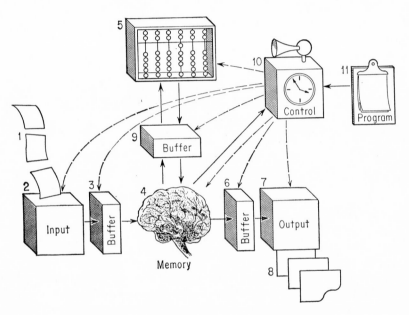

FIGURE 4.1. Organization of the computer in pictorial form.

augment the operation of the computer but do not affect the data directly —are discussed in the next chapter.

The specific processing tasks the control unit performs are now soberly delineated. The control unit directs the procurement of the information from its source as referred to in the command under consideration. It supervises the processing of the information and any checking operations while the information is transported from one section of the apparatus to another. When only a portion of the source information (fraction of a word) is processed, the control unit must determine that this portion is correct in quantity and position. Lastly, the control unit directs the processed information to a destination.

4.2. OPERATION OF THE CONTROL UNIT

The purpose of the control unit is to oversee each operation of the sequence of computer operations required to solve the programmed problem. To study these operations, we must break down this sequence into the smallest possible unit. This unit is called the *order*.

The order (also called command, operation, instruction) is a label describing what the computer is doing during a given period in its operation. Each order specifies where the information is to be obtained, what happens to it, and where the information will go when its processing is complete. Sometimes the source and destination of the information are permanently associated with an order. It is only necessary to mention the process (see the shift orders below) to convey the source and destination information to the control unit.

The cycle of operation of the computer for a given problem is determined by the sequence in which the orders are performed. The machine cycle is divided into a number of time periods known as **steps**. The step is the time period required to perform an order (any order).

To each step in the cycle of operation of the computer is assigned one and only one order. On the other hand, an order may be used for many steps. Thus the add operation may be performed several times in the machine cycle but, if the add order is specified at a given step, no other order can be performed at that step.

The length of time required to perform a given order, the **step time,** may be fixed or variable, according to whether the machine is **synchronous** or **asynchronous.**

The complete sequence of operations for a given problem, the specification of an order for each step, is a **routine.** The making of routine, the assignment of an order to each step, is called **coding.** Special training is given (usually by the computer manufacturer) to those whose task it is to write these routines.

4.3. COMMUNICATION BETWEEN THE PROGRAMMER AND THE COMPUTER

How does the control unit know, or how is it told, what order to associate with what step in the computer operation? There are three chief methods by which the programmer can communicate this information to the computer.

Permanent programming is used when the job to be done by the computer is immutable; it will never have to do anything different. The program is hence permanently wired into the computer. Such computers have no versatility, since they have but one program and so can solve but one problem. Only special-purpose computers designed to do a specific task and do it most efficiently have this permanent kind of programming. Permanent programming provides short-cuts for machine solution of a single problem which would not be possible with general-purpose computers. An example of permanent programming is found in the guided-missile digital computer. It will never do a different job!

External programming is so called because the program is set into the machine by adjustment or manipulation of wires of components which are physically part of the computer but are not part of the computer memory. The most popular means for effecting such programming is the plugboard. At the completion of the operation assigned to a given step, a signal appears at a connector or hub of the plugboard numbered to correspond with that step. This output is connected by an external wire to the input hub corresponding to the next order desired in the programmed machine cycle. By wiring from the program-step output hub to a given order input hub, this order is associated with this step. The actual information flow takes place through the plugboard or program board. The routing of information is therefore directly available to the programmer. He can decide the flow of information for each problem by the placement of the wires on the program board. The control unit is the agency by which these program instructions are interpreted to the computer, causing it to carry out the proper commands.

A simplified program plugboard is illustrated in Figure 4.3. There is only one hub for each program step number, but there are several hubs for each order. All the hubs for one order are connected together so that each order hub may be wired to several step hubs. The signal which accompanies the completion of the order specified at step 5 energizes the step 6 hub. The step 6 hub may be connected to any order hub to cause that order to be done next.

A big advantage of the plugboard is that it may be removed from the machine and immediately replaced by a different plugboard previously wired to do a completely different job. A number of large and complicated programs may thus be kept on hand ready to be used at a moment's notice.

Switches can also be used to direct the flow of information into one of several paths. A separate rotary switch can be used for each step. Each of the switch positions then specifies one of the possible orders available in that machine. No external inserts are necessary. There are no plugboards to be mislaid. A plugboard might have wires pulled loose causing the computer to function improperly, and it would take valuable time to track down the trouble and fix it. But with switches, set-up time is required whenever a different program is used, and the switch settings must be scrupulously checked each time the program is changed.

Punched paper tape can specify the sequence of orders by the place-ment of the holes in the paper tape. Each time the paper tape is advanced, a new order is set up to be performed by the computer. This is called external programming only if the paper tape is reread each time a new machine cycle occurs to process new data. If the information on the paper tape is read and stored within the machine and this stored information is

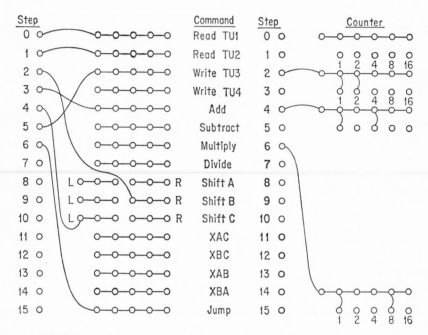

FIGURE 4.3.   A simplified plugboard showing a sample problem wired in.

referred to as the program, this is internal programming—because the external source, the tape, is not used during the computer operation, but rather its stored image.

Internal programming is the most modern, rapid, and versatile method of machine programming. The entire information associating orders with steps is entered and stored within the memory of the computer. The pro-gram is no longer physically accessible to the programmer as in the plug-board. But it is completely available to the machine and, in fact, may be altered by the machine. This ability of the machine to alter the program is indeed useful. It makes the machine extremely adaptable. Since it already possesses the ability to make decisions, the machine can adjust its behavioral pattern to the situation by treating its instructions like data. In processing these commands, a new sequence of operation is developed which the computer then follows. It has thus modified its own behavior! The machine examines the successive memory locations the program is stored in to review the program sequentially.

4.4. THE REGISTER

The register is a unit which stores information temporarily during processing. In the course of a single operation, several numbers may be manipulated. It is necessary to have some place to hold these data as they are shuttled about.

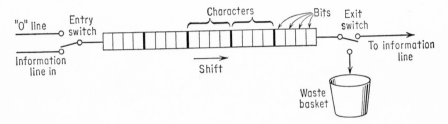

FIGURE 4.4.1.   Representation of a serial-bit serial-character register.

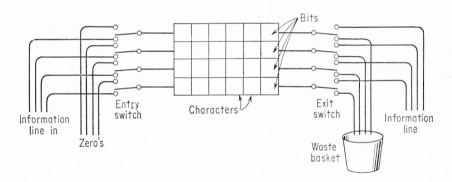

FIGURE 4.4.2.   Representation of a parallel-bit serial-character register.

The register illustrated in Figure 4.4.1 consists of a number of storage cells. Each of these cells stores one character of an information word. Each character is further subdivided into bits.

The register shown in Figure 4.4.1 is a serial-bit serial-character register. A word is inserted into such a register a bit at a time.

A parallel-bit serial-character register is shown in Figure 4.4.2. Here the bits of each character are entered simultaneously and the word is entered a character at a time.

The register has means for moving the information from one cell to the next, called **shifting.** The register has an entry switch which permits or refuses the entry of information. It also has a two-way exit switch which permits or refuses the exit of information. If the exit switch is closed, information may move out towards its destination; if the switch is open and information is moved by the shifting operation, the information is pushed into the "waste basket" and is destroyed. The shifting operation, with the exit switch open, will eliminate information character by character, starting with the first character pushed out.

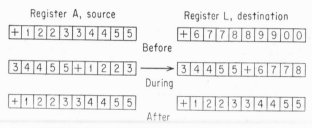

FIGURE 4.4.3.   Transferring a word from A to L.

The operation of moving a word from a source register to a destination register is pictorialized in Figure 4.4.3. The top line shows the registers before any action has taken place. In the "during" phase, the right-hand five characters at the destination register have been shifted out (into the "waste basket"); the left-hand five characters of the destination register have moved to the right-hand side; the right-hand five characters of the source register have moved into the left-hand side of the destination register; 0's or blanks or other characters are moved into the source register on the left-hand side. The bottom line of Figure 4.4.3 shows the registers after completion of the operation; the number previously in *A* is now also in *L*.

In order to control a register, it is necessary to control the exit switch, the entry switch, and the shifting process for that register.

The register is hooked into the system as illustrated in Figure 4.4.4. Here you see the information appearing on a common line. Register A, which we will suppose is the source register, has its exit switch closed connecting the output to the main line. It has its shifting process activated so that the information will be pushed through it and out the closed exit switch into the main line. Register B is the destination register. Its entry switch is closed, allowing information to pass through it. The shifting process is activated for that register so that information can be moved along it. Its exit switch is open so that old information in the register will be pushed through it and out into the waste basket.

Note that in Figure 4.4.4, the entrance switch to register A is closed. This allows the information coming out of the exit switch to go through the main line and re-enter register A through the entrance switch. Thus you see that if a complete word is to be transferred from register A to register B, that word can be re-entered into register A. At the end of the operation, the word which originally was in register A alone, is now in both register A and register L. This accounts for the ability of the computer to maintain information in a source register while transferring that information elsewhere.

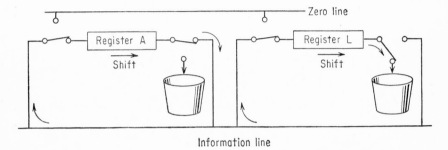

FIGURE 4.4.4.   Register interconnection for a transfer of data from **A** to **L**.

Information is withdrawn from or entered into the memory in the same fashion via the main information line. The ability to duplicate a datum from a register to memory or from memory into a register is analogous to the duplication of information from one register to another. This discussion is an oversimplification of memorizing and remembering; the details are discussed in Chapter 13.

4.5. STORAGE OF INFORMATION AND INSTRUCTIONS IN COMPUTER MEMORY

The memory of the computer may be thought of as a number of pigeonholes, each with a label (referred to in computer parlance as its **address**). Each of these pigeonholes or locations may hold a quantity of information. In general, this quantity of information is one word. A word thus stored at any location can be used as an operand in any process the computer is capable of performing. Any word may be examined by the control unit for use, either as an order or as a datum. Only certain combinations of characters are recognizable by the control unit as proper orders. It is up to the programmer to be sure that all words examined by the control unit are admissible orders and that the control unit is not examining a location for instructions where a data word is stored.

An instruction word can be used as a datum. It is by this kind of handling that the computer is capable of altering instructions. On the other hand, it is not desirable to examine a datum word for use as an instruction. If such an occasion arises (by accident), the operation called for by the datum word, if it is an admissible combination of characters, must be carried out by the control unit. This almost invariably results in altering valuable information stored in other locations in the memory. If the word is not an acceptable operation code, the computer grinds to a halt. Neither alternative is a happy one. It is up to the programmer to prevent such "accidents" by seeing to it that only instructions are stored at locations examined by the control unit.

If we were able to examine each word in each memory location, we could not tell whether a word was an instruction or a datum. We could only tell whether a given word was capable of being used as an admissible instruction.

The arithmetic process is characterized as the mapping of two numbers (or operands) and a process into a third number. For a given arithmetic operation, the computer must know where to find the two operands and where to store the results of the operation. It must, of course, also know what operation is to be performed. In some computers the operands and the result may all come from or go into registers. In other machines, part of the instruction word includes memory locations of both operands and the location in which the result will be stored.

Computers are classified by the information the instruction word carries. The command specifying the kind of processing the computer must do is part of the instruction word in all address systems. Single-address systems have only one other piece of information in the instruction word, the address of one operand. The location of the result and of the other operand used for the order are not part of the instruction word. These locations are usually specific registers permanently associated with the order. The next instruction word is stored at an address one greater than the address of the order being done, i.e., after performing the command at location 497, the computer uses the word stored at 498 as the next instruction.

The "1 + 1" address system instruction word is the same as in the single-address system except that it additionally contains the address of the next instruction. Here "+1" shows that the address of the next instruction is included in the instruction word.

Another popular system is the three-address system. The instruction word indicates the location of both operands and the destination of the result but not the next instruction, which is at the successive location.

Other possibilities exist: two-address system—specifying the two operands; 2 + 1—two operands and the next instruction; 3 + 1—two operands, the result, and the next instruction.

The three-address system has the advantage that a program can be crowded into a few steps. Only one three-address order is required to take two numbers from memory, add them, and replace the result into the memory. The one-address system requires three orders to do this. On the other hand, a single order in the three-address system takes longer to perform and sometimes time and effort is wasted. In adding a string of numbers, for instance, the three-address machine will place the result of each addition into the memory. The result will have to be withdrawn again for the next addition. It is quicker and more efficient to store the intermediate results in a register.

For any internally programmed computer, the instruction word or order must *always* contain the process to be performed, *usually* contains the memory location of at least one operand, and *sometimes* contains additional information pertinent to the order. This information must use no more characters than those contained in one word—the same length as for a datum. This is simple to achieve and some computers store two or more instructions in a single word.

4.6. ILLUSTRATIVE MACHINE*

It is much easier to explain and to understand the operation of computers in general by postulating a computer with certain characteristics and rules. The machine we will use to illustrate these principles will incorporate some of the features of several machines on the market. There is no feature in this machine that is not present in one or another currently available computer. We refer to this machine familiarly as the *Polyvac*. Since it has its roots in many computers, it is polygenic (or polygenetic); because it incorporates many attributes of the other machines, it is a variform automatic computer. Thus this polygenic variform automatic computer is called the Polyvac.

The Polyvac has several one-word storage registers. These are called the A register, the L register, and the Q register; the symbols, A, L, Q, are associated with these registers. The machine has a drum memory with a capacity of 1000 words. The memory is referred to as M in orders to be described, and a memory location is designated by MMM.

The Polyvac is a single-address machine with a ten-character data

---

* This section and several that follow are devoted to an explanation of the characteristics of the illustrative machine, the Polyvac. The more advanced reader may find it sufficient to refer to Appendix C, in which the Polyvac's characteristics are summarized.

and/or instruction word. This is illustrated in Figure 4.6.1. The first three characters of the instruction word, PRO indicate the process requested by the order; the next three characters MMM indicate the memory locations of one operand. The next four digits CBXX are not used in the simple order. The Polyvac data word has ten characters—a sign and nine digits. The character on the extreme left is the sign.

The implementation of the programming lies in the repertoire of commands. A minimum number of commands is basic to all machines. Additional commands facilitate editing, which is a fundamental activity of a computer for commercial applications. Other commands help in scientific computers whose application requires many repetitive operations.

| + | 3 | 7 | 2 | 8 | 5 | 4 | 1 | 1 | 3 | Data

| P | R | O | M | M | M | C | B | X | X | Command

FIGURE 4.6.1.   The polyvac data and command structure.

Our illustrative machine combines the commands used for commercial and scientific applications, which explains the large number of instructions available. Although not all are used in the sample programs discussed, they are covered in the exercises at the end of Chapters 4, 5 and 16.

The order is completely described by specifying the source, route, and destination of the information and what processing is done en route. To describe these commands several methods may be used: the mnemonic, the order code, the symbolic description, and the written description.

The mnemonic for the Polyvac is a set of three letters, which is an abbreviation of the command to be performed. The letters are chosen for easy recall of the order description. For instance, the letters XAM are used to describe the transfer order which takes information from the A register and places it in the memory. The "X" indicates that a transfer process is taking place; "A" indicates that the A register is the source of the information; "M" indicates that the memory is the destination for the information.

A code number is usually associated with each order. This is the number the programmer puts down on his code sheet (the list of steps and the instruction code orders associated with each). This will later be transferred into machine language and will be stored in the memory as the official process number that the machine reads and uses to select the proper switches to open or close. In the Polyvac, to simplify the programming discussed in the next chapter, the mnemonic and the instruction

* See Glossary.

code coincide. Examples of instruction code numbers for three machines are given below:

Add order, Polyvac   Mnemonic: ADD   Code: ADD
Add order, Univac I   Mnemonic: —   Code: A00
Add order, Datatron   Mnemonic: AD   Code: 74

A symbolic description sometimes conveys the process performed by the computer more vividly. The order, XAM, might be written symbolically as

$$\text{XAM} \qquad (A) \longrightarrow M$$

The parentheses distinguish between the content of a register or memory location and the actual register or memory location. "(A)" indicates the *content* of register A. The destination "M" does not have parentheses about it above because it is the memory location M that is the destination of the information, not the content of that memory location. The arrow ($\longrightarrow$) indicates the movement of information. The symbolic description graphically shows that the content of the A register is copied into location M.

A fourth method of describing the order, used at the beginning of the section, is to discuss what occurs during performance of the order.

For order description intended primarily for the programmer, the intermediate steps in the process are often omitted. As an example of this, the add order is

$$\text{ADD:} \qquad (A) + (M) \longrightarrow A$$

Here, to the content of the A register is added the content of memory location M, and the result is then placed in the A register. To perform this order, the information in memory location M is first placed in the L register. The operands are then taken simultaneously from their registers and added in an accumulator. From there the result is placed in the A register. The above process works simply by specifying the order code or symbolic description but the programmer must be aware of how. Otherwise he might store a datum in the L register which would be destroyed in the course of the ADD order.

The Polyvac has a memory of one thousand words. Each word location is referred to by an address which ranges from 000 to 999. This cell number is represented by M (the three-digit number MMM in the order description).

The Polyvac has three addressable one-word registers. If it is desired to specify a register as a source or destination in an instruction, the register's address is used in "M" instead of a number from 000 to 999. The address of the A register is 00A; of the L register, 00L; of the Q register, 00Q.

Some of the orders will now be described. A complete list for reference is found in Figure 5.7, page 76.

TRANSFER ORDERS. If the first letter of an order is an "X," a transfer is to take place. The second letter indicates the source of information and the third letter indicates the destination in the order code. The contents of the two registers concerned are illustrated before, during, and after a typical register transfer order, XML 00A in Figure 4.4.4. This requires transfer of the word in 00A (the A register) to the L register.

The following transfers are defined:

XAM:	(A) $\longrightarrow$ M		XML:	(M) $\longrightarrow$ L
XMA:	(M) $\longrightarrow$ A		XQM:	(Q) $\longrightarrow$ M
XLM:	(L) $\longrightarrow$ M		XMQ:	(M) $\longrightarrow$ Q

In these transfer orders the information at the source is *always* preserved; the information at the destination is *always* destroyed, because new information replaces the old in a destination register. The information is preserved at the source when it is a register by using the method previously described, replacing the information at the beginning of the register as it is passing out of the register.

SHIFT OUT. It is sometimes necessary to process information within a register—to round off numbers and to adjust decimal points. The "shift out" command moves the word with respect to the register, but maintains the order of the characters within the word. The "shift out" commands have a direction associated with them—the direction in which the word moves in relation to the register. As the characters at the end of the word reach the end of the register, they pass out and into the waste basket. This is the reason for using the term "shift *out*." During this command the register is caused to shift in the proper direction but neither of the switches, exit or entrance, is connected to the information line. No information is entered from the main line. To make up for the information shifted out or destroyed, "zero" characters are entered into the "source" end of the register. After the shift-out operation, valid characters will still occupy the register.

The kind of operation performed (shifting) is indicated by the first letter of the command word; the direction of the shift is right or left, if the second letter is R or L, respectively; the register to be shifted is determined by the third letter, A or L. The place in the command usually reserved for the operand address (M—there is none associated with this command) is used to indicate how many characters are to be shifted. To

Shift the A register Right three characters, the command is SRA003.
Four shift orders are given below.

$$\text{SRA:} \quad 0 \xrightarrow{\text{M}} A$$

$$\text{SLA:} \quad A \xleftarrow{\text{M}} 0$$

$$\text{SRL:} \quad 0 \xrightarrow{\text{M}} L$$

$$\text{SLL:} \quad L \xleftarrow{\text{M}} 0$$

Notice here that the "M" indicates that M digits have been shifted.
Since the symbolic description shows that 0's are put into one end of the
register, it is evident that M characters are pushed out. The direction of

Register A

| + | 1 | 2 | 2 | 3 | 3 | 4 | 4 | 5 | 5 |
Before

| + | 0 | 0 | 0 | 1 | 2 | 2 | 3 | 3 | 4 |
After

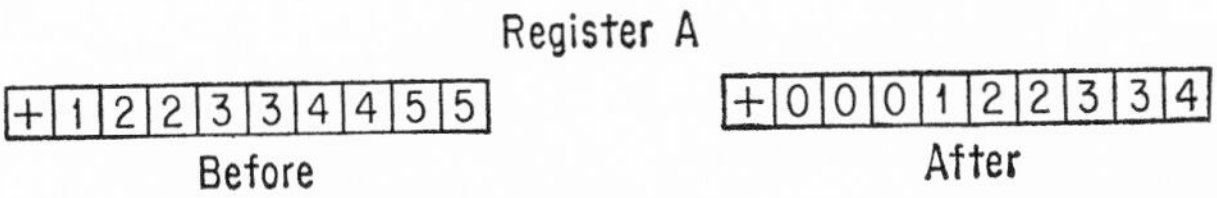

FIGURE 4.6.2.   The shift out order, SRA003.

the arrow shows the direction of shifting. The order SRA003 is illustrated
in Figure 4.6.2.

END AROUND SHIFT. Sometimes in a shift operation it is preferable to
have the digits leaving one end re-enter the register at the other end.
This is done when information is transferred from one register to another.
But in that case, the full word is simply replaced in the register. It is now
desired to move the beginning of the word to the end of the register and
replace the end of the word in the beginning of the register (which has
been vacated). This is termed **end around shift,** because the characters
that leave one end go around and re-enter at the other end. The number
of characters moved externally—those which pass out one end and in the
other—is given by M; the number of characters which are shifted within
the register is therefore $9 - M$. Four end around shift orders are

$$\text{ERA:} \quad (A) \xrightarrow{\text{M}} A$$

$$\text{ELA:} \quad A \xleftarrow{\text{M}} (A)$$

$$\text{ERL:} \quad (L) \xrightarrow{\text{M}} L$$

$$\text{ELL:} \quad L \xleftarrow{\text{M}} (L)$$

The "E" is for end around shift; the other two letters are used as in the
shift-out order. Notice the arrow indicates that the characters leave one

end of the register and enter the other end and the direction of the shift. The M again indicates the number of digits to be shifted. The order ERA003 is illustrated in Figure 4.6.3.

Register A

| + | 1 | 2 | 2 | 3 | 3 | 4 | 4 | 5 | 5 |

| + | 4 | 5 | 5 | 1 | 2 | 2 | 3 | 3 | 4 |

Before   After

FIGURE 4.6.3.   The end around shift order, ERA003.

LONG SHIFT. The long shift might be thought of as an end around shift using two registers. It is indicated as

$$\text{LSR} \qquad (A) \xrightarrow{M} L; \quad (L) \xrightarrow{M} A$$

The word in the A register is partially shifted into the L register and at the same time the word in the L register is partially shifted the same number of characters into the A register. This is shown in order LSR004 illustrated in Figure 4.6.4. This order is associated with multiplication, which

Register A   Register L

| + | 1 | 2 | 2 | 3 | 3 | 4 | 4 | 5 | 5 | Before | + | 6 | 7 | 7 | 8 | 8 | 9 | 9 | 0 | 0 |

| + | 9 | 9 | 0 | 0 | 1 | 2 | 2 | 3 | 3 | After | + | 4 | 4 | 5 | 5 | 6 | 7 | 7 | 8 | 8 |

FIGURE 4.6.4.   The long shift right order, LSR004.

is discussed below. Some computers other than the Polyvac use a shift out for a long shift. This is shown symbolically as

$$\text{LSR (non-Polyvac)}: \qquad 0 \xrightarrow{M} L; \quad (L) \xrightarrow{M} A$$

ARITHMETIC. What the programmer must know about arithmetic is delineated in the order description as listed,

ADD: $(A) + (M) \longrightarrow A$

SUB: $(A) - (M) \longrightarrow A$

MUL: $(M) \times (L) + (A) \longrightarrow A \cup L$

DIV: $(A)/(M) \longrightarrow Q, \quad \text{Remainder} \longrightarrow A$

ADA: $(A) + |(M)| \longrightarrow A$

SBA: $(A) - |(M)| \longrightarrow A$

The mnemonics for the first four are self-explanatory; the third letter, A, in the last two mnemonics indicates they are used for adding or subtracting absolute values. The start and finish of a sample machine addition are shown in Figure 4.6.5.

In the multiplication order, it should be remembered that the product of two ten-digit numbers is a 20-digit number. Therefore, the product will occupy two registers. The product will be found with its most significant half in the A register and its least significant half, the units, tens, and so forth, digits in the L register. "A ∪ L" symbolically conveys the use

Register A
Memory location 139

| + | 0 | 0 | 0 | 0 | 3 | 0 | 1 | 2 | 5 | Before | + | 0 | 0 | 0 | 0 | 1 | 2 | 3 | 4 | 5 |

| + | 0 | 0 | 0 | 0 | 4 | 2 | 4 | 7 | 0 | After | + | 0 | 0 | 0 | 0 | 1 | 2 | 3 | 4 | 5 |

FIGURE 4.6.5.   The addition order, ADD139.

Memory location 773   Register A   Register L

Before | + | 0 | 0 | 1 | 1 | 1 | 1 | 1 | 1 | 1 | 1 | | + | 0 | 0 | 2 | 2 | 2 | 2 | 2 | 2 | 2 | 2 |

After | + | 0 | 0 | 1 | 1 | 1 | 1 | 1 | 1 | 1 | 1 | | + | 0 | 0 | 0 | 2 | 4 | 6 | 9 | 1 | 3 | | + | 5 | 5 | 5 | 3 | 0 | 8 | 6 | 4 | 2 |

FIGURE 4.6.6.   The multiplication order, MUL773.

Memory location 401   Register·A   Register Q

Before | + | 0 | 0 | 0 | 0 | 0 | 5 | 1 | 0 | 0 | | + | 0 | 0 | 0 | 0 | 0 | 0 | 3 | 5 | 9 | 5 |

After | + | 0 | 0 | 0 | 0 | 0 | 5 | 1 | 0 | 0 | | + | 0 | 0 | 0 | 0 | 0 | 0 | 0 | 2 | 5 | | + | 0 | 0 | 0 | 0 | 0 | 0 | 7 | 0 | 0 |

FIGURE 4.6.7.   The division order, DIV401.

of two registers. An example is shown in Figure 4.6.6. Here MUL773 requests the computer to multiply the content of memory location 773 by the content of register L, add it to the content of the A register and place the result in the combined A and L registers. A long shift is sometimes required to adjust a decimal point at the end of the multiplication.

A division order generates both a quotient and remainder. The supplementary quotient register, Q, is used to store the quotient; the remainder is to be found in the A register. A sample division order is shown in Figure 4.6.7.

4.7.   THE CONTROL OPERATION

Let us take a brief look at the over-all picture of what happens during the first few steps of a program. Let us assume that the program and the data have been loaded into the memory. When the start button is pressed, the first instruction word is taken from memory location 000 and is placed into the control register, C. This register stores the instruction word for reference during the processing of that instruction. The process to be performed (PRO) is examined and the proper switches are opened or closed—the flow of information is set up so that the operation will take place as required. Next, if required, the operand location, M, is used to obtain the operand from the memory or addressable register. When this is completed, the requested operation is set into motion. While it is taking place, a control counter that keeps track of the step number of the instruction being performed is advanced by one. It now contains the location of the next order. (In the case under consideration, this is 001.) This location is used to procure the next order from the memory and to store it in C. Upon completion of the original process (the one at 000), the new instruction word in C is examined. The same sequence of events is then repeated. When the process listed in the instruction word is STP, the computer will stop operating and wait for further instructions from the keyboard or manual entry unit.

As an example of the very simplest operation, consider how the computer might be programmed to add two numbers, X_1 and X_2, located at 500 and 501 respectively, and to put the result into location 502. The programmer's list would be:

Step	PRO	MMM	Explanation
000	XMA	500	$X_1 \longrightarrow A$
001	ADD	501	$X_1 + X_2 \longrightarrow A$
002	XAM	502	$X_1 + X_2 \longrightarrow 502$
003	STP	. . .	✋

PROBLEMS

1. The process of making a coded routine for a computer is analogous to many other activities we, or other specialized personnel, do in pursuing vocations or avocations. For instance—

   (a) Devising a *dance* with fundamental *dance forms*.
   (b) Composing a musical piece with notes.
   (c) A shop project such as constructing a bookcase.
   (d) Finding your way to a friend's house.

   In each case, distinguish clearly between *steps* and *orders* in the analogy with the computer program. Show how each such entity should be defined. What are the similarities and differences between the program and the analogy —for instance, the notes which the composer uses vary in two qualities, tone and duration (any others?) while the *commands* differ in only one specification.

Make up a typical routine for at least (c) and (d). Show in all—(a) through (d)—where loops might exist. Create at least three more analogies and repeat the analysis for each.

2. Of what kinds of devices is the register composed? Conjecture on the composition of a register.

3. For the programmer's list on p. 56, what part of the listing is contained in each command word? What do the four instruction words look like? (Fill up each word on the right with 0's.) For each address system below,

   (a) $1 + 1$ (b) 2   (c) $2 + 1$ (d) 3   (e) $3 + 1$
   (1) show what the instruction word might look like;
   (2) rewrite the list on p. 56;
   (3) write the instruction words corresponding to the list above, in order.

4. Let's incorporate another register, the Z register, into the Polyvac. Examine the top third (I) of Figure 5.7 and augment it with orders to accommodate the Z register.

5. Go through Figure 5.7(I) and augment the orders as would be required by a 2- and a 3-address computer. Amalgamate the orders whenever possible, e.g., include a shift with a transfer, if you can. Include orders for the Z register.

6. With U, V, W, X, Y, and Z respectively at 500, 501, ... 505, code these operations:

   (a) $U - W \longrightarrow 506$ (b) $VX \longrightarrow 507$ (c) $Y/Z \longrightarrow 508$
   (d) $(Y/Z)(U - W) \div VX \longrightarrow 509$ (e) $(UV - WX)(Y - Z) \longrightarrow 510$
   (f) $(UV + W)/(XY - Z) \longrightarrow 511$ (g) $(Z + (UV - X)/YW \longrightarrow 512$
   (h) $X(W(U + V) + Z) \longrightarrow 513$

7. Assume that U, V, ... Z are stored in a fashion which requires correction by shifting before use: U, W, and Z should be shifted right three characters, V and X right two characters, and Y right one character. Do Problems 6(a) through 6(h) above, shifting the result once to the left before storing.

8. Do the preceding problem using the 3-address code which you devised in Problem 5.

F I V E

CODING

5.1. THE TECHNIQUES OF CODING

The method or system for assigning orders to each step is important not only to the programmer, but to the computer designer, the user, and the prospective purchaser of the computer. The designer who is aware of the needs of the programmer can improve the design of the computer so that coding will be easier and the routine itself shorter. The prospective user who knows how to program and code a computer is aware of its limitations and also its advantages over other machines. He will not require it to do problems done more easily on other machines. On the other hand, he will be aware of the unique coding facilities it affords. The buyer will know how his problem will fit in with the capabilities of his contemplated purchase.

For the computer to perform a given task, the programmer may choose a routine that will excel others for one of many reasons. He may compose a routine because it is the quickest and easiest to construct, even though it takes longer to run. He may compose a routine that takes the least amount of time to run. He may compose a routine which checks the results for accuracy and consistency of information at many points along the way, and consequently takes longer both to compose and to run. The routine may require the machine to stop and deliver intermediate results which the operator may check against a simple problem he has done by hand calculation, providing a check of the routine rather than the results. The routine may have to meet various physical limitations. The capacity of the memory of the computer, the type of orders the computer can perform, or the number of program steps available to the programmer present limitations to coding.

After a certain amount of experience, the programmer will understand the relationship between the problem at hand and the computer available to do the problem. This involves two kinds of knowledge. The first concerns the computer. The programmer must be fairly familiar with its capabilities and limitations. The second concerns the programmer's experience in converting a problem into a routine. He must be able to see how the problem can be subdivided into small sequences of steps or calculations that can be considered as a programming unit.

Some routines are composed of groups of operations to do a specific task or calculation, such as taking a square root. This group can be regarded as a unit and is called a **subroutine.** The square-root subroutine consists of a set of commands performed upon the number contained in a given memory location yielding, on completion, the square root of that number. Subroutines can be further divided into portions called **cycles, loops,** or **iterations,** which are performed many times during one subroutine. Adding a group of numbers together is a loop that could be used to compose an integration subroutine. The hierarchy of programming is: a library of programs, the program, the routine, the subroutine, the loop, and the command (the atom).

The experienced programmer sees the problem as a number of familiar subroutines and a number of unfamiliar tasks. If he can discern all the subroutines that can be used for a given problem and computer, then he is a good programmer for that machine and that type of problem.

The designer must be aware of how to build the computer so that it can perform routines and subroutines with facility and with as few program steps as possible. This requires that he be familiar with some of the techniques involved in programming and coding. It also requires that he be familiar with commands facilitating programming and with the "logical" structures within the computer associated with flexible programming (such as cycle counters, discussed at the end of this chapter).

5.2. THE FLOW DIAGRAM

The large routine is divisible into smaller sections. Perhaps these sections may be classified as subroutines; on the other hand, they may be unfamiliar to the programmer and may simply be tasks for which a programming procedure must be set up. The programmer starts with the single concept of the problem the machine must solve, and from it he must develop the many hundreds of steps which a large program requires. This is an immense job and requires some plan of action to coordinate the programmer's efforts. An intermediate approach towards constructing a program is setting up a "flow diagram." This diagram indicates what happens to the information being processed at different intervals. These intervals may cover one or several program steps.

The flow diagram may be compared to a block diagram, familiar to the engineer as an approach to understanding the makeup of electronic equipment. Such a diagram shows the connections among various large sections of the equipment and enables one who is unfamiliar with the equipment to visualize the interrelations of the large functions of the machine. He is then able to study in more detail the operation of one function within a designated section of the equipment. Similarly, the flow diagram is a means for visualizing the program by breaking it down into functional units and indicating the interrelation between these program units as well as the way they correspond to the different sections of the problem.

A typical flow diagram may be seen in Figure 5.3.3, page 65. Each geometric form represents a different process to be carried on by the computer and facilitates the reading of the flow diagram. These geometric forms have not been standardized, although some consistency does exist among programmers. The common symbols and some extra ones used by the author are described in the paragraphs which follow.

The Function Box

The function box illustrated in Figure 5.2(A) is a rectangle used to indicate arithmetic functions or the transfer of information from one section of the computer to another. Note that in the box is written the function to be performed. An arrow enters the box from the box representing the last operation performed by the computer. An arrow leaves the box proceeding to the box representing the next function to be performed.

Comparison

When a comparison is to be performed, it is indicated by a diamond or rhombus, illustrated in Figure 5.2(B). Within the rhombus are the two words to be compared; a colon between them indicates the order of comparison. An arrow enters the box from the last operation performed and there are several lines leaving the box, representing the different results that can be obtained from the comparison of the two words. In doing "$a:b$," the line with the "$>$" on it indicates the condition "$a > b$." The

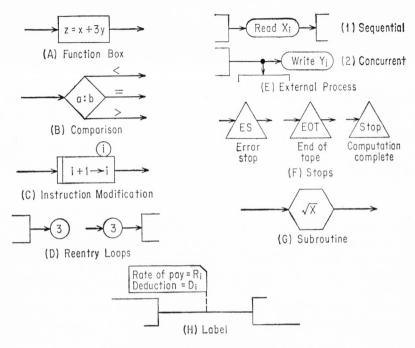

FIGURE 5.2.   Flow-chart symbols.

lines are the alternate routes the program will take as a result of the comparison. In a comparison all alternatives must be provided for.

Instruction Modification

When an instruction used in another part of the program is modified by the computer, the modification is shown in the flow diagram by a rectangle with an extra line on its left-hand side, as shown in Figure 5.2(C). Within the box is indicated the index or address that is changed. If the index or address is increased by 1, this is indicated by

$$i + 1 \longrightarrow i$$

which is interpreted as "$i + 1$ should be used now wherever i appears." The index or address that is changed may be inserted in a little circle placed on top of the rectangle to call attention to the modification.

Re-entry Loops

When a flow diagram grows large, it is often inconvenient to draw a line from the end of a routine to the point at which the flow re-enters the program; these lines would only complicate the diagram. Therefore, a given series of steps may end with a circle with a number in it, indicating to the reader that he should look for a similarly numbered circle to re-enter. This is shown in Figure 5.2(D).

External Processes

During the course of the program, information may be read into the computer from outside sources, or may be rewritten as output onto magnetic or punched tape. To set this off from the rest of the flow chart, a rectangle, two sides of which have been curved, is used as in Figure 5.2(E1). Some computers can communicate with the input or output equipment and simultaneously perform calculations. This is indicated by an arrow going to two places—the in/out operation and the next processing operation as in Figure 5.2(E2).

Stop

Several things should cause the computer to stop: an error may be detected in operation, such as arithmetic which does not check; the input or output operation may be unable to continue—for instance when the magnetic or paper tapes run out in the input or output equipment; the computer is done—it has finished the computation. All these are indicated by triangles with an arrow leading into them. Inside the triangle the cause of the stoppage is indicated. An arrow may lead out of the box if the equipment is to be started up from this point. Examples are shown in Figure 5.2(F).

Subroutines

Sometimes a subroutine has been programmed elsewhere and/or flow-charted elsewhere. The entire subroutine may be represented by a hexagon with a process to be performed written inside. As in the function box, one arrow leads in and one leads out to indicate the sequence of operations. This is illustrated in Figure 5.2(G).

Labels

Along the flow of information, little flags may be drawn in which are indicated prevailing conditions useful for the reader to know, but not essential to the flow of information. These little flags are connected to the flow of information by dashed lines. The flags are rectangles with one of their corners missing. There is no arrow entering or leaving these labels. A label is illustrated in Figure 5.2(H).

5.3. CODING THE ADDITION OF A SET OF NUMBERS

Let us suppose that we have a very simple problem to solve on our Polyvac. In the memory at locations 100 to 149 there are 50 numbers. It is desired to add these numbers together and to place the sum in memory location 150.

The programmer first makes the flow chart and then finds the steps that would make a proper program. Since we are not familiar with the flow chart technique yet, we will first work out this program and then see what the flow chart should be to go with it.

First, get the first number (in memory location 100) in position so that the next number may be added to it. The add operation adds the number at a given memory location to what is stored in the A register. Therefore, the first number should be placed in the A register. Our first step is stored at address 000 (or simply 0) and is listed as

Step	Process	Operand	Description
0	XMA	100	$X_1 \longrightarrow A$

The first three columns contain information to be entered into the machine; the last column helps the programmer keep track of what's going on. When the start button is pressed, the control unit takes its first instruction from the location 000. This command transfers the first number (X_1) from location 100 to the A register in preparation for addition. The next order is (omitting the column headings):

$$1 \quad ADD \quad 101 \quad X_1 + X_2 \longrightarrow A$$

This order adds the second number (X_2) to the first number and stores this partial sum in the A register. The next order is

$$2 \quad ADD \quad 102 \quad \Sigma + X_3 \longrightarrow A$$

where "Σ" is used to indicate the sum of previous numbers which is located at A. Step 2 adds the next number to the sum-so-far and places

64 CODING • CHAP. 5

this new partial sum back into the A register. The additions continue until all the numbers have been added together and the result stored in the A register. The step which adds in the last number is:

$$49 \quad ADD \quad 149 \quad \Sigma + X_{50} \longrightarrow A$$

Now, all that is left to be done is to place the result into the memory location 150. The next two orders are, therefore,

$$50 \quad XAM \quad 150 \quad \Sigma \longrightarrow 150$$

$$51 \quad STP \quad \ldots \quad \text{✋}$$

Our completed program appears in Figure 5.3.1.

Step	Process	Operand	Description
0	XMA	100	$X_1 \longrightarrow A$
1	ADD	101	$X_1 + X_2 \longrightarrow A$
2	ADD	102	$(X_1 + X_2) + X_3 \longrightarrow A$
. . . .			
48	ADD	148	$(X_1 + X_2 + \ldots + X_{48}) + X_{49} \longrightarrow A$
49	ADD	149	$(X_1 + X_2 + \ldots + X_{49}) + X_{50} \longrightarrow A$
50	XAM	150	$SUM \longrightarrow 150$
51	STP	. . .	✋

FIGURE 5.3.1.   Program (long) to add fifty numbers.

The flow chart for this program appears in Figure 5.3.2. It uses a separate box for each addition which takes place, and is self-explanatory.

The method described above is very simple to understand, to code, and to use. But where the problem involves the addition of, say, a thousand to even five thousand numbers, you can see how the programmer

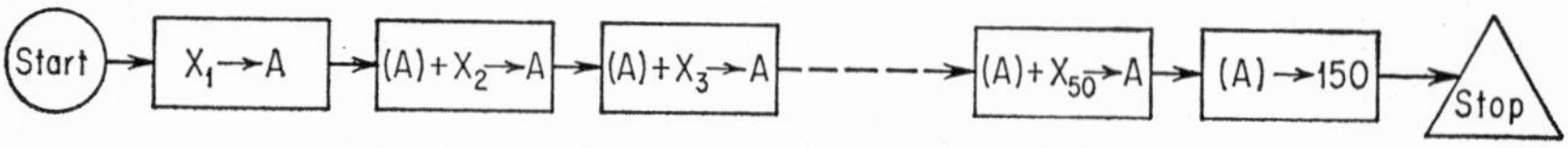

FIGURE 5.3.2.   Flow chart—add fifty numbers (long).

would get tired of writing down the same order at each step. Not only that, this routine requires more steps than there are numbers to be added. This means that the routine, which is stored in the memory, uses up many valuable memory locations. The whole routine may be simplified if we use the technique of modifying the operand address as described below.

An order for processing has a specific operand address as part of the instruction word. To allow this order to be re-used, the operand address must be changed according to some simple rule (if the operands are stored sequentially, which is customary).

The computer will perform an order. It will then modify the address of the operand as it appears in that order. It will then go back to the step in the program where the order is called for and perform the order using the address it has just modified. This is fine, except that somewhere along the line we must be able to get the computer out of its rut and make it stop. We know how many operands must be processed. We check the number of times the process was done after each operand is processed.

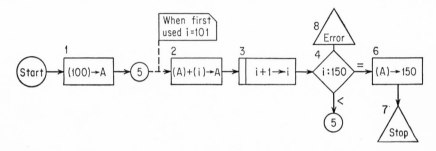

FIGURE 5.3.3. Flow chart, address modification to add fifty numbers.

An easy way to do this is to check the operand address. Whether the last operand has been processed is determined by examining the operand address in the processing order. When the operand address in that instruction is the address of the last operand to be used, this loop is complete.

We now have a method for getting the computer to repeat a process with different operands and to stop the process when the last operand has been processed. This is best illustrated by use of the flow chart.

The flow chart to perform the problem of this section by address modification appears in Figure 5.3.3. From the start circle we go to the first box. Here the first number (stored in memory location 100) is put into the A register. Next we go to circle marked "5." This is for re-entry into the system at a later date and no action by the computer takes place here. In box 2 we add to the A register the content of address i. The i is a variable index which indicates that the operand address keeps changing. The first time that it is used, i is 101. This is indicated in the label on the flow chart. After the add order has been done, the operand address is changed in box 3. Here the variable index i is increased by 1. Before we go on adding, we check to see if we have used up all the addend numbers by comparing the newly adjusted index with 150. When the memory location used in box 2 is 149 (the last addend location), then the newly adjusted index will be 150 and we have completed our processing; if i is less than

150, we continue our processing. These two eventualities are shown as the two arrows leaving the comparison box, box 4. The third alternative should never arise unless an error occurs and so the error stop for "$>$." If processing is to continue, we leave box 4 by the arrow with the "less than" sign adjacent to it. This arrow leads to re-entry loop 5. That means that we go back via the circle marked "5" and follow the processing flow as before. We do another addition, address modification, and another check to see if we are done.

If we have finished our processing, i is equal to 150 and we leave the comparison box by the "equal" line. Then, all that remains to be done is to put the result in memory location 150 and stop the computer. These operations occur in boxes 6 and 7 respectively.

In order to implement this flow chart with a suitable program, it is necessary to propose a few more orders for the computer.

5.4. FURTHER ORDERS

To perform the decision-making functions by which the computer may alter its own behavior some new orders are defined.

The comparison order compares the content of register A with content of the memory location M. The order is also used to compare the content of register A with that of another register. This is possible because the registers are addressable. Two examples of the comparison order are

$$\text{CMP309} \quad (A):(309)$$

$$\text{CMP00L} \quad (A):(L)$$

The result of the comparison is stored in a single-character register, called a **comparison box.** This box has three possible states. The plus state (P) indicates that the content of register A is greater than the other comparand (that with which it is compared). The equal state (E) indicates that the content of register A is equal to the other comparand. The minus state (M) indicates that the content of register A is less than the other comparand. The setting of this comparison box is used in conjunction with the jump orders discussed below.

The **jump order** tells the computer whether to look for its next instruction in the next memory location $I + 1$ as it normally would, or to look for its next instruction in memory location M. This depends upon the setting of the comparison box. The four jump orders are listed here,

$$\text{JOP:} \quad (A) > (M') \Rightarrow M, \qquad (A) \not> (M') \Rightarrow I + 1$$

$$\text{JOM:} \quad (A) < (M') \Rightarrow M, \qquad (A) \not< (M') \Rightarrow I + 1$$

$$\text{JOE:} \quad (A) = (M') \Rightarrow M, \qquad (A) \neq (M') \Rightarrow I + 1$$

$$\text{UCJ:} \qquad\qquad\qquad \Rightarrow M$$

The jump-on-plus order (JOP) indicates that the next instruction will be found in location M if the comparison box is set to P. The next instruction will be found at memory location I + 1 (where I is the memory location of the present instruction) if the comparison box is not set to P. M′ is the comparand of the comparison performed most recently. The address, M, following the double arrow ($\Rightarrow$) is where the next instruction is located. The jump-on-minus order (JOM) is similarly interpreted: the minus refers to the M in the comparison box. Jump-on-equal (JOE) is used to test for an E in the comparison box. The unconditional jump order requires the computer to examine the content of M as its next instruction without any if's!

The comparison box is also set by the results of an arithmetic order if an S is placed in an auxiliary position of the instruction word. It is set to plus (P) for a positive result, minus (M) for a negative result, and equal (E) when the result is zero. The conditional jump orders apply as above. JOP then means jump to M if the box is set to P, and to I + 1 if not set to P.

The stop order tells the machine to stop. The machine must be manually started after a stop order. It may be started using as the next instruction that which is located at M, or it may be started from the beginning of the program. This is determined by which start button is pressed.

STP: Stop; go to M
                                 when restarted

5.5. ANOTHER ROUTINE TO ADD 50 NUMBERS

Now that we have the orders necessary to implement the flow chart of Figure 5.3.3 we can make up a routine to perform this task. You may follow the completed routine shown in Figure 5.5. The first box after the start circle requires that the content of memory location 100 be loaded into the A register. This is done by the order stored at 000.

Step	Process	Operand	Description
0	XMA	100	$(100) \longrightarrow A$

Box 2 requires that the next number be added into the A register. The label tells us that the first time this order is used, that location will be 101. This is done by

| 1 | ADD | <u>101</u> | $\Sigma + (i) \longrightarrow A$ |

The underline under the operand location indicates that this location will be modified later in the routine. The "Σ" indicates the sum accumulated so far. Box 3 indicates that the variable index i is to be increased by 1. This comprises the address modification just discussed. In order to add

1 to the address, known as a *tally operation*, the A register must be used. The result of the tallying will appear there.

While the address modification is taking place, it is necessary to store temporarily the sum that we have accumulated. This is done by

$$2 \qquad \text{XAM} \qquad 150 \qquad \Sigma \longrightarrow 150$$

Now the order to be modified is placed into the A register. We have stored the program steps at memory locations corresponding to the step number. The add order, step number 1, will be found at location 001. It is placed in the A register for modification by

$$3 \qquad \text{XMA} \qquad 001 \qquad (001) \longrightarrow A$$

Next, 1 is added to the address portion of the order. To do so, a number is used that, when added to the instruction, will increase the address section by 1, but not affect the rest of the order. Such a number is stored, say, in location 50 as

050	000	001	0000

The tallying operation which adds 1 to the operand location in the add order (001) now in the A register is

$$4 \qquad \text{ADD} \qquad 50 \qquad i + 1 \longrightarrow i$$

Have all the numbers been added? To determine this, the add order with the modified address is compared with a similar order for which the address is 150. After the last number is added, the order is, "ADD 149." When modified this becomes, "ADD 150." A dummy "order" is used for the comparison. This is its sole purpose. It is never examined by the control unit as an order and is called a *dummy* since it is really not an order. Our dummy will be stored at 51,

$$51 \qquad \text{ADD} \qquad\qquad 150$$

The add order is compared with the dummy by

$$5 \qquad \text{CMP} \qquad 051 \qquad i : 150$$

This compares the address in the just-modified add order with 150 to determine if all the numbers have been added.

The result of this comparison is stored in the comparison box as P, E, or M. It remains there until another arithmetic or comparison order is performed. Before we use this result, the modified order is replaced at its original location (001),

$$6 \qquad \text{XAM} \qquad 001 \qquad (A) \longrightarrow 001$$

Also, before continuing we withdraw the partial sum that we have accumulated and place it back into the A register.

$$7 \qquad \text{XMA} \qquad 150 \qquad \Sigma \longrightarrow A$$

Now completely prepared, we go back and do another cycle of addition and address modification (steps 1 to 7), if the result of the comparison is favorable; that is, if the new i is less than 150. M is stored in the comparison box if the additions continue—the "less than" condition. To go back to the add order (001), we do

$$8 \qquad \text{JOM} \qquad 001 \qquad i < 150 \Rightarrow 001$$

If the problem has been completed, the comparison box will be set to E (not M) and the computer will look at memory location 009 for the next order. This is a stop order.

$$9 \qquad \text{STP} \qquad \ldots \qquad \text{🖐}$$

Notice that the completed sum is stored in location 150 back at step 2 (002) of the last addition cycle. Therefore, nothing has been left undone—there is no step required for box 6 of the flow diagram, Figure 5.3.3.

Here, in Figure 5.5, is the completed program together with the tally and sentinel.

				DESCRIPTION	
Box	Step	Process	Operand	Symbolic	Verbal
1	000	XMA	100	$(100) \longrightarrow A$	Take first number.
2	001	ADD	101	$\text{SUM} + (i) \longrightarrow A$	Add next number.
3	002	XAM	150	$\text{SUM} \longrightarrow 150$	Store sum.
	003	XMA	001	$(001) \longrightarrow A$	Take add order.
	004	ADD	050	$(A) + 1 \longrightarrow A$	Modify add order.
4	005	CMP	051	$(A):(51)$	Check if done.
	006	XAM	001	$(A) \longrightarrow 001$	Replace add order.
	007	XMA	150	$(150) \longrightarrow A$	Replace sum.
5	008	JOM	001	$i < 150 \Rightarrow 101$	Start new cycle.
7	009	STP	$\ldots$	🖐	Stop when done.
	050	000	001		Tally
	051	ADD	150		Sentinel

FIGURE 5.5. Program, add fifty numbers, address modification.

5.6. CYCLES OR LOOPS

When a process is performed a number of times with different operands, it is called a **cycle** or **loop.** These arise many times in the course of programming.

Sometimes the same cycle or subroutine is called for several times during the course of one routine, and it is then possible to make use of the same set of program steps. This is discussed in Chapter 16 on advanced programming.

Now let us consider the construction of a cycle. The number of data to be processed corresponding to the number of cycles to be done is known and is called the **cycle criterion.** The location of the first data word is known, and it is assumed that successive data are stored in successive locations. Some command (or commands) is required to be performed upon the contents of several addresses. This prototype command will simply be referred to as PRO. This command, PRO, might stand for addition or comparison, and so forth.

The first step in the subroutine will start at some location, say S. The command at S is to process the first datum word,

$$\text{S:} \qquad \text{PRO} \qquad [\underline{X_i}] \qquad \text{Process } X_i$$

Here the memory location of the first data word is indicated by $[X_i]$. The square bracket means "the address of." By this means we can construct the program before knowing the exact memory assignments for the data. The variable index i is called the **cycle index.** When a variable location appears in a routine, it will be underlined. The address will be altered later in the program.

Having processed our data word, we must now alter its address. To do this, our partial result must be stored temporarily. Let us store it in memory location M,

$$\text{S} + 1 \qquad \text{XAM} \qquad \text{M} \qquad \begin{array}{l} \text{Store partial} \\ \text{result at M} \end{array}$$

The processing order must be brought into the add register.

$$\text{S} + 2 \qquad \text{XMA} \qquad \text{S} \qquad \text{"PRO } X_i\text{"} \longrightarrow \text{A}$$

It must then be altered or tallied,

$$\text{S} + 3 \qquad \text{ADD} \qquad [1] \qquad i + 1 \longrightarrow i$$

Here "[1]" means the address where "1" is stored, in proper form to modify the address. Note that [1] is a fixed address, but $[X_i]$ is a variable address because of the index i.

Next, we must find out if the processing of the data is complete. Such is the case if the cycle index has been increased often enough so as to equal the cycle criterion N. Here N is the number of data words to be processed. To check this, the memory location specified in the order at step S (modified each time the order is used) is examined. This order, now in the A register, is now compared with the cycle criterion dummy (simply indicated as [N]),

$$S + 4 \quad CMP \quad [N] \quad i:N$$

The dummy is really

$$[N] \quad PRO \quad [X_N]$$

Since further processing may be done, the processing order is replaced in its former location, S,

$$S + 5 \quad XAM \quad S \quad \text{"PRO } X_i\text{"} \longrightarrow S$$

The partial result is withdrawn from the memory and replaced into register A,

$$S + 6 \quad XMA \quad M \quad \text{partial result} \longrightarrow A$$

We are now ready to continue processing, if there is more to be done. To find out what the story is,

$$S + 7 \quad JOM \quad S \quad i < N \Rightarrow S; \quad i = N \Rightarrow S + 8$$

A complete prototype program is shown in Figure 5.6.1. Notice that the eight steps, S through $S + 7$ are repeated for each datum, X, to be processed.

Step	Process	Operand	Description
S	PRO	[X_i]	Process X_i.
S + 1	XAM	M_1	Store results at M_1.
S + 2	XMA	S	Take process order.
S + 3	ADD	[1]	Modify process order.
S + 4	CMP	[N]	Check for end of process.
S + 5	XAM	S	Replace process order.
S + 6	XMA	M_1	Replace partial result.
S + 7	JOM	S	Start new cycle.
S + 8	. . . .		Start new routine.

FIGURE 5.6.1. Prototype subroutine.

Cycle Index Registers

Cycle registers, often referred to as cycle counters, index registers, or B-boxes, are used to facilitate the construction of cycles. These, together with a number of appropriate orders, simplify immensely the task of making up a program. These extra registers are used for keeping track of the number of times each cycle is done. There are nine cycle registers in the Polyvac, and they are referred to as CY1 to CY9.

The cycle register works like this. When an order is withdrawn from memory and a number is present in the C portion of the order, the content of the cycle register corresponding to that number is added to the address portion of the command. For example, suppose the order being withdrawn from memory is, "Add the word at location 100," and suppose that cycle register number 1 has 17 in it. Then 17 will be added to 100 as the order is given to the control unit. "ADD 117" is the instruction which will be performed *if* the stored order is ADD 100 1, and 17 is in cycle register 1. The content of the memory location from which the order was drawn is unaffected. The unaltered add order "ADD 100 1" is still found there.

Each of the cycle registers is addressable: CY1 through CY9 are the addresses of cycle registers 1 through 9. To move the three least significant digits of the A register to cycle register 3, we use the order XAM CY3.

The cycle register is also used to initiate a jump. This will become clear in discussing the extra orders used to implement the cycle register.

The first order transfers the address portion of the memory location listed in M into the tally register.

$$\text{XMI:} \qquad \text{(M)} \longrightarrow \text{CYI}$$

Here I refers to the number of the cycle register called for. Since the cycle register only modifies the address portion of the instruction word, only the first three characters transferred are stored in CYI—the units, tens, and hundreds digits. A number may also be entered into the cycle register directly from the program. This is done by

$$\text{XPI:} \qquad \text{M} \longrightarrow \text{CYI}$$

This command inserts the number M into cycle register I. Note here that M does not have parentheses around it. This indicates that M is the number to be put into the cycle register and *not* (M) (the data word stored in location M). Information can also be withdrawn from the cycle register by

$$\text{XIM:} \qquad \text{(CYI)} \longrightarrow \text{M}$$

To use the cycle register for tallying we have

$$\text{TMI:} \qquad \text{(CYI)} - 1 \longrightarrow \text{CYI} \qquad \text{(CYI)} > 0 \Rightarrow \text{M}$$
$$\text{(CYI)} = 0 \Rightarrow \text{I} + 1$$

This order subtracts 1 from whatever is in cycle register I. It then checks to see if the cycle register has become zero. If not—that is, if there is still a positive number sitting in the cycle register—then the next order will be found at location M. When the cycle register contains zero, the next instruction is found in the next memory location, I + 1. This order makes it possible to tally down (subtract 1 from the memory location of the operand) and at the same time determine if processing is complete.

To tally up, a number is used to determine when the tallying operation is finished. This number, to be useful, must be stored in another register— the Q register is used for this, since it is the least used of the registers. This does not interfere with normal operation except when multiplication and division are required. In that case, tally up must be avoided. The tally up order is

$$\text{TPI:} \quad (\text{CYI}) + 1 \longrightarrow \text{CYI} \quad (\text{CYI}) < (\text{Q}) \Rightarrow \text{M}$$
$$(\text{CYI}) = (\text{Q}) \Rightarrow \text{I} + 1$$

In this order, 1 is added to the content of the cycle register. If the number in the cycle register is then smaller than the address portion of the word in the Q register, the next order is found in memory location M. When the content of the cycle register and the content of the address portion of the Q register are equal, the next order is found in the succeeding memory location, I + 1.

To facilitate the use of the Q register for tally operation, we may use

$$\text{XPQ:} \quad \text{M} \longrightarrow \text{Q}$$

Note again the absence of the parentheses around M, indicating that the number M is inserted into the address portion of the Q register. Sometimes the following order is helpful:

$$\text{XIQ:} \quad (\text{CYI}) \longrightarrow \text{Q}$$

It requires that the content of cycle register I be inserted in the address portion of the Q register.

Prototype Address Modification using the Cycle Registers

Let us see how these orders facilitate our prototype processing. First, zero must be entered into cycle register #1,

Step	Process	Operand	C	Symbolic
S	XP1	0	0	$\longrightarrow$ CY1

Then the number of data words to be processed is inserted in the Q register.

| S + 1 | XPQ | N | N | $\longrightarrow$ Q |

The first operand is processed.

| S + 2 | PRO | [X₁] | 1 | Process X_{1+i} |

This location is determined by adding the content of the cycle register to the address in the processing order. This is indicated by 1 in the cycle register column to the right of the operand column. The first time around it is desired to process the first operand. Therefore, the address of the first operand is used in the processing order. After the process is performed, the cycle register is checked.

Step	Process	Operand	C	Symbolic
S + 3	TP1	S + 2		$i < N \Rightarrow S + 2$

First, 1 is added to (CY1). Next, (CY1) is checked to see if it is equal to the number stored in the address portion of the Q register. If not, processing continues by jumping to the location of the processing order, S + 2. When processing is completed, the rest of the program continues. The whole program appears as Figure 5.6.2.

Step	Process	Operand	C	Description
S	XP1	000		Clear tally.
S + 1	XPQ	[N]		Enter sentinel.
S + 2	PRO	[X₁]	1	Process next number.
S + 3	TP1	S + 2		Tally and recycle.
S + 4	. . . .			Start new routine.

FIGURE 5.6.2. Subroutine with tally up.

To tally down, the program would run just a little differently and one step shorter (three steps in all). The first thing we do is to put the cycle criterion N into cycle register 1.

S	XP1	N		$N \longrightarrow CY1$

Next, we process the operand,

S + 1	PRO	[X₁] − 1 1		Process X_{1+i}

Notice here that the nominal address used in this order is one less than the address of the first operand; when the content of the cycle register is added to this, the result the first time is the address of the first operand used, X_N. Next we adjust the cycle register,

S + 2	TM1	S + 1		$i > 0 \Rightarrow S + 1$

We subtract 1 from its content. The next time around, instead of adding N to the data word location, we will add N − 1. That means the data word address will decrease by 1. The second time around we will use the next-to-the-last word; the third time around the (N − 2) data word, and so on. This tally order says that if we have not finished processing, we should go back to the process order at location $S + 1$. The last time around, there is 1 in the cycle register. The processing is performed on X_1 because $[X_1] - 1$ plus 1 in the cycle register yields $[X_1]$. At step $S + 2$, the cycle register is tallied down to 0 which brings a finish to this loop.

We are then ready to perform the rest of the program. This whole prototype subroutine only takes three steps as shown in Figure 5.6.3. Notice that for both cycles using the cycle register, only two instructions are used for processing any but the first operand.

Step	Process	Operand	C	Description
S	XP1	N		Sentinel ⟶ Tally.
S + 1	PRO	$[X_1] - 1$	1	Process next number.
S + 2	TM1	S + 1		Tally down, recycle.
S + 3	. . . .			Continue program.

Figure 5.6.3.   Subroutine with tally down.

When this method is applied to the problem of adding a set of numbers examined earlier in the chapter, the resulting program is as illustrated in Figure 5.6.4. The flow chart for this figure is also Figure 5.3.3., for the information flow has not been changed by the simplification resulting from the use of the cycle register.

Step	Process	Operand	C	Description
000	XPQ	049		49 ⟶ Q
001	XP1	000		0 ⟶ T
002	XMA	100		(100) ⟶ A
003	ADD	101	1	(A) + (101 + i) ⟶ A
004	TP1	003		Tally up, recycle.
005	XAM	150		Result ⟶ 150
006	STP			✋

FIGURE 5.6.4.   "Add fifty numbers" using tally up.

5.7. SUMMARY

A repertoire of computer orders has been acquired (except for the input/output orders to be introduced in Chapter 16). These are listed and symbolically described in Figure 5.7.

Type	Mne-monic	Symbolic Description	Mne-monic	Symbolic Description
I. Transfer	XAM	$(A) \longrightarrow M$	XMA	$(M) \longrightarrow A$
	XLM	$(L) \longrightarrow M$	XML	$(M) \longrightarrow L$
	XQM	$(Q) \longrightarrow M$	XMQ	$(M) \longrightarrow Q$
Shift Out	SRA	$0 \xrightarrow{M} A$	SLA	$A \xleftarrow{M} 0$
	SRL	$0 \xrightarrow{M} L$	SLL	$L \xleftarrow{M} 0$
End Around Shift	ERA	$(A) \xrightarrow{M} A$	ELA	$A \xleftarrow{M} (A)$
	ERL	$(L) \xrightarrow{M} L$	ELL	$L \xleftarrow{M} (L)$
Long Shift	LSR	$(A) \longrightarrow L; (L) \longrightarrow A$		
Arithmetic	ADD	$(A) + (M) \longrightarrow A$	ADA	$(A) + |(M)| \longrightarrow A$
	SUB	$(A) - (M) \longrightarrow A$	SBA	$(A) - |(M)| \longrightarrow A$
	MUL	$(L) \times (M) + (A)$	DIV	$(A) \div (M) \longrightarrow Q$
		$\longrightarrow A \cup L$		Remain $\longrightarrow A$
II. Decision	CMP	$(A):(M)$	STP	✋ $\Rightarrow M$
	JOP	$(A) > (M') \Rightarrow M$	JOE	$(A) = (M') \Rightarrow M$
		$(A) \not> (M') \Rightarrow I + 1$		$(A) \neq (M') \Rightarrow I + 1$
	JOM	$(A) < (M') \Rightarrow M$	UCJ	$\Rightarrow M$
		$(A) \not< (M') \Rightarrow I + 1$		
Cycle	XMI	$(M) \longrightarrow CYI$	XPI	$M \longrightarrow CYI$
	XIM	$(CYI) \longrightarrow M$	XPQ	$M \longrightarrow Q$
	TMI	$(CYI) - 1 \longrightarrow CYI$	TPI	$(CYI) + 1 \longrightarrow CYI$
		$(CYI) > 0 \Rightarrow M$		$(CYI) < (Q) \Rightarrow M$
		$(CYI) = 0 \Rightarrow I + 1$		$(CYI) = (Q) \Rightarrow I + 1$
	XIQ	$(CYI) \longrightarrow Q$		
III. Input/Output*	LOD	$(PT) \longrightarrow M$	ULD	$(M) \longrightarrow PT$
		$(PT) \longrightarrow M + 1$		$(M + 1) \longrightarrow PT$
		. . . .		
		$(PT) \longrightarrow 999$		$(999) \longrightarrow PT$
		$\Rightarrow 000$		$\Rightarrow I + 1$
	RED	$(PT) \longrightarrow M$	PUN	$(M) \longrightarrow PT$

* For description see chapter 16.

FIGURE 5.7. Polyvac commands.

The technique of programming, together with the tool of the flow chart, has been explained. The program is built with coding units called routines, subunits called subroutines, and cycles or loops composed of individual steps. The method of constructing the subroutines with normal orders and with the convenience of the tally orders was shown.

The technique using the tally and the cycle register should bring home to the designer the importance of one or more supplementary cycle registers. This is the area where the needs of the programmer and the user are reflected in the work of the designer. At a very slight cost in equipment and engineering development, a tool of inestimable power is given to the programmer and the consumer. This kind of predictive engineering can often "sell" a computer.

PROBLEMS

1. With U_0 in 100, U_1 in 101, ... U_{99} in 199, and V_i, W_i, X_i, Y_i, and Z_i in $200 + i$, $300 + i$, $400 + i$, $500 + i$, and $600 + i$, respectively, code the following problems making flow diagrams first.

   (a) $U_i - W_i \longrightarrow 700 + i$
   (b) $V_i X_i \longrightarrow 700 + i$
   (c) $Y_i/Z_i \longrightarrow 700 + i$
   (d) $(Y_i/Z_i)(U_i - W_i) \div (Y_i - Z_i) \longrightarrow 700 + i$
   (e) $(U_i V_i - W_i X_i)(Y_i - Z_i) \longrightarrow 700 + i$
   (f) $\dfrac{U_i V_i + W_i}{X_i Y_i} - Z_i \longrightarrow 700 + i$
   (g) $Z_i + \dfrac{U_i V_i - X_i}{Y_i W_i} \longrightarrow 700 + i$
   (h) $X_i(W_i(U_i + V_i) + Z_i) \longrightarrow 700 + i$

2. Recode the above, this time aligning the operands and results as below.

   Result: Shift one place left when stored.
   U's, W's, Z's: Shift three places right before use.
   V's, X's: Shift two places right before use.
   Y's: Shift one place right before use.

3. Make a routine to solve

   $$C_n X_i + C_{n-1} X_i + \ldots + C_1 X_i + C_0 = Y_i$$

   where the X_i's are stored in locations from 200 to 299 at $200 + i$; the Y's are to be stored at $300 + i$; and for $n = 9$, the ten C's are stored at $190 + n$. Note that for computational simplification the above formula may be written as

   $$X_i(\ldots X_i(C_n X_i + C_{n-1}) + C_{n-2}) + \ldots + C_1) + C_0 = Y_i$$

4. The Newton-Raphson method for finding the square root Y of X by iteration requires an initial guess for U, say Y_1. Further approximations of Y, Y_{i+1}, are

based on the current approximation, Y_i. Using this relation

$$Y_{i+1} = Y_i + \frac{1}{2}\left(\frac{X}{Y_i} - Y_i\right)$$

Let us store a best-guess factor b at [b] and a test factor t at [t]. The latter is used to stop the computation when $(Y_{i+1} - Y_i) \leqslant t$. The former makes a best-guess $Y_0 = bX$.

Devise a routine to find the square root of the numbers stored at 100 to 199, returning the answers to these locations. Flow chart first!

5. When a complicated function of a variable is to be used, it may be stored in the computer as a table. Consider $Y_i = F(X_i)$ with

$$0 \leqslant i \leqslant 99 \quad \text{and} \quad [Y_i] = 200 + i.$$

Further, let $X_{i+1} - X_i = \Delta X$ for all i, so that

$$X_i = X_0 + i\Delta X.$$

Store ΔX and X_0 at 300 and 301, say. Now for any given value of X, say X_α it is desired to find Y_α if X_α is within the range of X, i.e., if

$$X_0 \leqslant X_\alpha \leqslant X_{99}.$$

In such case a linear-mean interpolation formula is used to find Y_α, viz.

$$Y_\alpha = Y_n + \frac{X_\alpha - X_n}{\Delta X}(Y_{n+1} - Y_n)$$

where $X_n \leqslant X_\alpha \leqslant X_{n+1}$

Devise a routine which will (a) determine if X_α lies within the tabled values, (b) find the closest lower tabled value to X, X_n, (c) determine if X_α is tabled, viz. $X_\alpha = X_n$ for some n (then no interpolation is necessary), (d) otherwise calculate Y_α by the linear interpolation. Enter 99 ... 9 as the answer for X_α outside the range of X. The routine should look up X's stored between 400 and 514 and store the answers at the address from whence X's came. Flow chart first!

6. Find a series approximation for $y = \sin X$. Set this up as a subroutine with the proper testing and scaling factor in appropriate locations. Flow chart first!

7. Incorporate the square root subroutine (Problem 4) into a routine to find, for ten values of W (call them W_i's),

$$R = \frac{X + \sqrt{W^2 + VW + Z}}{Y}$$

8. Devise a routine to solve a quadratic equation using the formula

$$X_i = \frac{-b_i \pm \sqrt{b_i^2 - 4a_ic_i}}{2a_i}$$

for one hundred each of a_i, b_i, and c_i; one word for the real and imaginary parts of each root. This will require a different loop according to whether there is an imaginary part to each root.

MACHINE ARITHMETIC

6.1. INTRODUCTION

The processes of arithmetic are represented by the mapping $a \otimes b = c$. The result c can be found either by looking up the two operands in a process table, or by using the two operands to generate the result by some rule incorporated within the machine.

A computer is able to add, subtract, multiply, and divide. Usually, it is much too expensive to incorporate complete tables to generate these functions within the machine. It is, therefore, desirable to find a means of generating the result once the computer is aware of the two operands and the process to be performed. It turns out that if the machine is capable of performing addition, complementation, and shifting, then subtraction, multiplication, and division can be synthesized. This chapter will discuss how a computer performs arithmetic by using sequences of addition, complementation, and shifting.

Our discussion of arithmetic proceeds by examining first how the human performs each process and then how the machine can most easily and economically perform the same process.

The decimal system is used in all the examples—because it is familiar to us and makes the explanation easier. The reader should therefore keep in mind that although a machine may not deal with decimal numbers,

the numbers that it does use will be handled in a manner similar to that
discussed here.

Although these methods are typical and representative, this chapter
does not pretend to be an exhaustive treatise on current machines.

6.2. ADDITION

How do we normally do addition? It seems like a very simple question but the answer is hidden in a whole habit structure that we have
built up. Let us start from a simple case and reconstruct the action.

One-Digit Addition

When you or I add two one-digit numbers, we refer to our "mental
addition table." If we were to write out such a table, it would appear as
in Figure 6.2.1. Thus, to add 5 and 4, we do something mentally anal-

	0	1	2	3	4	5	6	7	8	9
0	0	1	2	3	4	5	6	7	8	9
1	1	2	3	4	5	6	7	8	9	0C
2	2	3	4	5	6	7	8	9	0C	1C
3	3	4	5	6	7	8	9	0C	1C	2C
4	4	5	6	7	8	9	0C	1C	2C	3C
5	5	6	7	8	9	0C	1C	2C	3C	4C
6	6	7	8	9	0C	1C	2C	3C	4C	5C
7	7	8	9	0C	1C	2C	3C	4C	5C	6C
8	8	9	0C	1C	2C	3C	4C	5C	6C	7C
9	9	0C	1C	2C	3C	4C	5C	6C	7C	8C

FIGURE 6.2.1.   Add table, no carry.

ogous to looking down the 5 column, across the 4 row and finding the
answer, 9. Of course, this is done as a single mental association. Since 5
plus 4 is the same as 4 plus 5, it does not matter whether we enter the
table with the row or the column first. Similarly, to add 7 and 6, we enter
the table and find the result, 3, with a C next to it. The table has been
set up for many-digit addition, and the C here indicates a carry. For use
with a one-digit number the 3C is interpreted as 13.

Many-Digit Addition

Next, let us see what happens when we add numbers of more than one
digit—for instance, add 1244 to 3456. First, examine the right-hand digit

of each number. Enter the addition table and note that 4 and 6 make 0 with a carry. The 0 is written down as the right-hand sum digit. The next digit of each number (proceeding to the left) is added. Mentally we say, "5 + 4 and 1 from the carry makes 10." This is equivalent to entering the "carry-sum" table, a table to be used in adding two digits if the previous addition yielded a carry. Such a table appears in Figure 6.2.2.

	0	1	2	3	4	5	6	7	8	9
0	1	2	3	4	5	6	7	8	9	0C
1	2	3	4	5	6	7	8	9	0C	1C
2	3	4	5	6	7	8	9	0C	1C	2C
3	4	5	6	7	8	9	0C	1C	2C	3C
4	5	6	7	8	9	0C	1C	2C	3C	4C
5	6	7	8	9	0C	1C	2C	3C	4C	5C
6	7	8	9	0C	1C	2C	3C	4C	5C	6C
7	8	9	0C	1C	2C	3C	4C	5C	6C	7C
8	9	0C	1C	2C	3C	4C	5C	6C	7C	8C
9	0C	1C	2C	3C	4C	5C	6C	7C	8C	9C

FIGURE 6.2.2. Add table, carry.

Entering this table we see that 5 plus 4 is 0 and a carry is created. We can proceed down the line (to the left) in the same manner using the appropriate table, according to whether the last addition has produced a carry or not.

It is left to the reader to analyze into its component parts the process of adding several one-digit numbers together and the more complicated problem of adding several many-digit numbers together.

Machine Additions

Let us see how a machine can be constructed to add *two* many-digit numbers. The first approach is to construct a machine that functions exactly as a human. It would consider each pair of digits and find the sum in one of the two built-in addition tables. It would add the digits in pairs, proceeding from the right-hand side of the numbers consecutively towards the left. Because the digits are added one after the other, this is called **serial addition.** Many machines currently use serial addition and function well where speed is not of the essence.

To hasten the addition process it is better to add all digits simultaneously; the only obstruction to such a process is the creation of the carry. In Figure 6.2.3 appear two numbers as one might add them normally.

In Figure 6.2.4 the digits are added simultaneously, using the table of Figure 6.2.1; the carries created are noted underneath. Let us now add in the carry and see what happens. When the carry is added to the 9 in Figure 6.2.4, another carry is created. The new sum has been written in the line below, and the carry is indicated one line further down. The

```
                              3456
                              1244
                              ____
                              4690   First sum
                                 1   First carry
           3456               ____
           1244               4600   Second sum
           ____                  1   Second carry
           4700               ____
                              4700
```

FIGURE 6.2.3.   School board addition.   FIGURE 6.2.4.   Simultaneous digit addition followed by successive carry additions.

complete process consists of (1) the initial addition—adding each pair of digits by use of the non-carry add table to get a partial sum and (2) the finishing process—adding in the carries generated by (1) until the complete sum is obtained. Each time a new carry is created in this "finishing" operation, it must be added into the sum-so-far. This may continue down the line (to the left). It is conceivable that there will be almost as many steps to the "finishing" operation as there are digits in the numbers

```
     3456
     1244
     ____
     4690   First sum
        1   Carry
     ____
     4700   Final sum
```

FIGURE 6.2.5.   Ripple carry.

we are handling. If there are many 9's in the "unfinished" sum, this "add and carry" will seem to ripple down the line. This is sometimes referred to as a **carry ripple.** The processing by this method has really not shortened the over-all time.

It is desirable to find a method of adding all the digits of two numbers together simultaneously, and then in a single step to effect the complete carry operation. The use of a simple rule will make this method possible. Let us add our two numbers of Figure 6.2.4. This is done in Figure 6.2.5.

Note the carry underneath the 9. The rule we are going to use to expedite the carry is, "If a carry is to be added to a digit which is not a 9, that digit is increased by 1 and written below; if the carry is to be added to 9, then the 9 is changed to a 0 and the carry process is applied to the next digit to the left." Two more examples are shown in Figures 6.2.6 and 6.2.7.

4321098			919435	
478902			89565	
4999990	First sum		998990	First sum
1	Carry		1 1	Carry
5000000	Final sum		1009000	Final sum

FIGURE 6.2.6. Ripple carry.   FIGURE 6.2.7. Ripple carry.

A machine based on the rule considered above is able to perform addition by two operations; corresponding digits of the addend and augend are added simultaneously using a single built-in adding rule; the carries generated by this operation are then applied to the "unfinished" sum and the result, the sum, is then obtained.

To add several numbers together, the machine must perform several additions. The first two numbers are added together (including carry of course), the next number is added to this result, the succeeding number is added to this result, and so forth. This is accomplished by programming the successive additions.

The human adds several numbers together in a different way. He uses his memory for a temporary storage operation. The reader may find it useful to work out how he adds a sequence of single-digit numbers; from this he can then work out the rules for adding several many-digit numbers.

6.3. SUBTRACTION

Manual

Two single-digit numbers are subtracted by using mental subtraction tables, such as illustrated in Figures 6.3.1 and 6.3.2. Notice that it is important in either table to look up the minuend in the column (vertical) and the subtrahend in the row (horizontal), because in subtraction it is important which number is being *subtracted from* and which number is being *subtracted with*. Thus, 3 from 5 is 2, but 5 from 3 is −2. A certain amount of symmetry still remains, though.

When a larger number is subtracted from a smaller number, a *borrow* is created. The value of the difference is the same as though the smaller

Subtrahend	Minuend									
	0	1	2	3	4	5	6	7	8	9
0	0	1	2	3	4	5	6	7	8	9
1	9B	0	1	2	3	4	5	6	7	8
2	8B	9B	0	1	2	3	4	5	6	7
3	7B	8B	9B	0	1	2	3	4	5	6
4	6B	7B	8B	9B	0	1	2	3	4	5
5	5B	6B	7B	8B	9B	0	1	2	3	4
6	4B	5B	6B	7B	8B	9B	0	1	2	3
7	3B	4B	5B	6B	7B	8B	9B	0	1	2
8	2C	3B	4B	5B	6B	7B	8B	9B	0	1
9	1B	2B	3B	4B	5B	6B	7B	8B	9B	0

FIGURE 6.3.1.   Subtraction table, no borrow.

Subtrahend	Minuend									
	0	1	2	3	4	5	6	7	8	9
0	9B	0	1	2	3	4	5	6	7	8
1	8B	9B	0	1	2	3	4	5	6	7
2	7B	8B	9B	0	1	2	3	4	5	6
3	6B	7B	8B	9B	0	1	2	3	4	5
4	5B	6B	7B	8B	9B	0	1	2	3	4
5	4B	5B	6B	7B	8B	9B	0	1	2	3
6	3B	4B	5B	6B	7B	8B	9B	0	1	2
7	2B	3B	4B	5B	6B	7B	8B	9B	0	1
8	1B	2B	3B	4B	5B	6B	7B	8B	9B	0
9	0B	1B	2B	3B	4B	5B	6B	7B	8B	9B

FIGURE 6.3.2.   Subtraction table, borrow from previous digit.

had been subtracted from the larger. With two single-digit numbers, the borrow is interpreted as a minus sign.

To perform the subtraction of two many-digit numbers, it must be first noted which is the larger. The value of the difference is obtained by subtracting the smaller from the larger. The sign of the difference is obtained by noting whether the minuend or subtrahend is larger.

To Subtract the Smaller Number from the Larger Number

One begins by examining the right-hand digit of each number. The subtraction table is entered by finding the larger number in the column and the smaller in the row. The value of the difference is recorded as the rightmost digit of the difference. The next digit to the left in the minuend and subtrahend is now examined. The table to be entered depends upon whether a borrow has been created in the previous digit subtraction. The borrow or no-borrow table will be used. (This is analogous to the carry or no-carry table used in addition.) The borrow-subtraction table is illustrated in Figure 6.3.2. The two-digit subtraction continues toward the

$$
\begin{array}{r}
4791 \\
\underline{1234} \\
3557
\end{array}
$$

FIGURE 6.3.3. School board subtraction.

left. The proper table is entered, depending upon whether or not the previous subtraction has created a borrow. This is clear when we examine a typical problem as in Figure 6.3.3, together with the tables in Figures 6.3.1 and 6.3.2.

Machine

There is no reason why a machine could not be constructed to perform subtraction in the same manner as done by a human being. As with the human method for addition, it would require the incorporation of tables within the machine. With the use of the process of complementation described below, subtraction can be reduced to addition.

The **9's complement** (or simply **complement**) of any digit is defined as the difference between 9 and the digit. Thus, the complement of 3 is 6. The complement of a number consisting of more than one digit is the complement with respect to 9 of each digit considered separately. Thus, the complement of 71 is 28. It is necessary to specify "9's" only when confusion might arise. In the computer, the complement of a number is taken with respect to the full word length of a register. For a number in a ten digit register, for instance, all ten digits of the word must be complemented. Thus, if the number to be complemented is 47, it is stored in the register as 0000000047, and its complement is 9999999952.

Let us see how the complement can be used in subtraction. First, it must be noted that when two words are added and the sum is greater than the capacity of the register, only the last digits corresponding to the word length of the register will be stored in the register. The computer will perform such an addition as shown in Figure 6.3.4. Call W the largest

Ten-digit register

$$
\begin{array}{ll}
9876543210 & \\
8765432109 & \\
\hline
18641975319 & \text{Correct result} \\
8641975319 & \text{Machine result}
\end{array}
$$

FIGURE 6.3.4.   Big word addition.

word which can be stored in the register. Then

$$W = 999\ldots 99 = 10^N - 1 \tag{6.3.1}$$

where N is the word length in digits. The word $W + 1$ or 10^N is recorded in the register as $000\ldots 0$. Any word larger than W will be recorded incorrectly. Thus $W + 1 + A$ or $10^N + A$ is stored in the register simply as A.

Suppose it is desired to subtract S from M, that is, find $M - S$. We will use the property of the register just mentioned—namely, that the quantity $10^N + M - S$ is stored as $M - S$. This may be stated as

$$M - S \approx M - S + 10^N \tag{6.3.2}$$

where " $\approx$ " means "recorded as." This is restated as

$$M - S \approx M - S + (W + 1) \tag{6.3.3}$$

Or, rearranging,

$$M - S \approx M + 1 + (W - S) \tag{6.3.4}$$

Let us remember how we construct the complement of a word, say S. We subtract each digit of S from 9 to form the corresponding digit of the complement. The complement of S is $99\ldots 9 - S$ or $10^N - 1 - S$ or $W - S$. Then $M - S$ is found by adding $(W - S)$ to M and adding 1 to that. In words, *non-negative subtraction can be performed by adding the minuend to the complement of the subtrahend and then adding one more.*

Machine Example

Let us see how the machine would do the problem of Figure 6.3.3. To the minuend is added the complement of the subtrahend; to this result is added 1. This is shown in Figure 6.3.5, using a ten-digit register. The overflow—the eleventh digit to the left—cannot be stored, of course.

The means by which "adding one more" is performed is derived from the fact that a valid non-negative subtraction by addition always causes an overflow. Subtraction is performed by using the relationship of (6.3.4) above. It leads to the result shown in (6.3.3) which is always larger than

0000004791	Minuend	4791
+ 9999998765	Subtrahend complement	8765
1 0000003556	Partial difference	⌐3556
0000000001	Add one more	⌊→1
0000003557	Difference	3557

FIGURE 6.3.5. Machine subtraction by addition.

FIGURE 6.3.6. Machine subtraction schematic representation.

$W + 1$ or 10^N for all $M > S$. This overflow is the indication that a number larger than W was presented to the register. It can be used to cause the computer to add the extra unit.

Machine subtraction may be represented more schematically, as in Figure 6.3.6. Notice that it is not necessary to write the full ten-digit word.

Subtrahend Larger Than Minuend

Sometimes the problem is to subtract a larger from a smaller number. The human must determine whether this is the case. He then subtracts the smaller from the larger, attaching a minus sign to the difference, as in Figure 6.3.7. The machine can be constructed to do exactly the same

35		−71 Larger
−71		35 Smaller
−36		−36

FIGURE 6.3.7. Subtraction with negative difference.

FIGURE 6.3.8. Machine subtraction with larger subtrahend, I.

thing using a comparison operation. This test fixes the sign of the difference. The value of the difference is found by machine subtraction of the smaller number from the larger. This is shown in Figure 6.3.8. This is also done when $M = S$.

An alternate machine method is to disregard the sign and perform the required subtraction by complementing the subtrahend and adding it to the minuend. When the subtrahend is larger than the minuend, the difference will be stored in the accumulator as the complement of the answer, as in Figure 6.3.9. A negative or zero is evidenced by the absence of an

$$
\begin{array}{r}
35 \\
+28 \\
\hline
63
\end{array}
$$
Complement of
difference

FIGURE 6.3.9. Machine subtraction with larger subtrahend, II.

end around carry. When it is desired to write out the difference, it may be complemented and the minus sign affixed when it is transferred to the output equipment.

6.4. MULTIPLICATION

One-Digit Numbers

As before, a table can be constructed for multiplication whereby the multiplier and multiplicand are looked up and the two-digit product is found.

Many-Digit Multiplication

The human being performs multiplication by using many mental memory locations in a manner which would be difficult for a machine to duplicate. Since the machine method is entirely dissimilar, it would not serve much purpose to put into words for the reader what he has been doing by rote for, lo, these many years.

The reader may find a challenge in trying to put into words the simple problem of multiplying two numbers.

Machine Multiplication

Multiplication may be interpreted as repeated addition. Thus, 24 × 378 means to perform additions using 378 as the addend. We have to be careful here when we state how many additions are to be performed. These statements are both correct:

"Add 378 to 0, 24 times"

"Add 378 to itself, 23 times"

A simplification can reduce the number of additions required. Multiplication by powers of ten can be done by shifting to the left a number of positions equal to the power of the number. Thus, 598 × 100 is 59,800. The shift-left order of most computers introduces zeros on the right-hand side of the register.

An example of machine multiplication is shown in Figure 6.4.1. At

Multiplier register		Multiplicand register		Product register	
123	(1)	598	(1)	0000000	(1)
1				598	
122	(3)			598	(2)
1				598	
121	(5)		.	1196	(4)
1				598	
120	(7)			1794	(6)
12	(8)	5980	(8)	5980	
1				7774	(9)
11	(10)			5980	
1				13754	(11)
				59800	
10	(12)			73554	(14)
1	(13)	59800	(13)		
1					
0	(15)				

FIGURE 6.4.1. Multiplication of 598 by 123.

the start, the multiplier and multiplicand register hold their respective numbers, and the product register has been cleared to zero. The multiplier is tested to see if the rightmost digit has been cleared to zero (1). It has not. The multiplicand is added once to the product register (2) and 1 is subtracted from the multiplier (3). The multiplier is tested for zero again. Another multiplicand addition (4), multiplier tally down (5), and zero test are done. This continues (6), (7), until after (7), the right-hand digit of the multiplier is zero.

Now the multiplier is shifted right and the multiplicand left (8). More sets of multiplicand additions, multiplier tally downs, and zero tests are done (9), (10), (11), (12) until the rightmost multiplier digit is zero. Another shift operation is done (13).

The operation continues like this; the process is complete when the multiplier has been tallied down to zero (15). The answer, the product, is in the product register; the multiplicand, now shifted, is in its register; and the multiplier has been reduced to zero. Notice that the multiplicand has been shifted once less than the number of digits in the multiplier.

Notice that the number of additions required is only six. In general, the number of additions is equal to the sum of the multiplier digits.

6.5. DIVISION

There is some similarity between manual and machine division. Again, an explanation in words of the manual division procedure would not clarify the machine process. However, it would pay the reader at this point to take pen in hand and do a simple long division problem noting, at each step of the way, what he is doing.

Machine Division

Many computers have a rule in the division process that the divisor must be larger than the dividend. In that case it is up to the coder to make sure that the divisor *is* larger—otherwise the machine will stop in the middle of the problem. Such a rule assures simple and foolproof operation. We shall consider a computer with such an operating requirement.

Division is performed by a sequence of repeated subtractions, tests, shifts, and tallies. Separate registers are allotted to the divisor, the dividend, and for totaling the quotient. A sample problem is illustrated in Figure 6.5.1, division of 6759 by 21100.

The divisor, 21100, is stored in the divisor register (not shown). The first step, step 0 which is not shown, is to verify that the divisor is larger than the dividend: This being the case, the divisor is realigned by shifting it once to the right. Thus in our example 2110 will now be used for the subsequent subtractions required for division. To do these subtractions the machine uses the method of complementation and addition—a fact which does not affect the present explanation.

The 2110 is subtracted from the dividend, 6759, in step 1. The difference, 4649, is tested to determine if it is positive or negative. Since it is positive, this subtraction indicates that 6759 contains at least one multiple of 2110. The subtraction has been tallied or counted in the quotient register, which now holds the partial quotient, 1. The subtract, tally, and test procedure is repeated twice more. At the end of step 3, three subtractions are completed without the dividend register going negative; the quotient register stores a 3; the dividend register has 429 in it.

In step 4, a fourth subtraction is made. It causes the dividend register to go negative. This means that too many subtractions have been made. Although 6759 contains 3 × 2110, it does not contain 4 × 2110. The dividend and tally registers must be restored to their readings at the end

Dividend register	Quotient register	Description		What happened
6759	0			
−2110				
4649	1	(1) First Subtraction		$6759 > .1 \times (21100)$
−2110				
2539	2	(2) Second "		$6759 > .2 \times (21100)$
−2110			First	
429	3	(3) Third "	Series	$6759 > .3 \times (21100)$
−2110				
98319	4	(4) Fourth "		$6759 < .4 \times (21100)$
+2110		and Overflow		
429	3	(5) Quotient Restoration		
4290	30	(6) Shift		
−2110				
2180	31	(7) First Subtraction		$6759 > .31 \times (21100)$
−2110				
70	32	(8) Second "	Second	$6759 > .32 \times (21100)$
−2110			Series	
97960	33	(9) Third "		$6759 < .33 \times (21100)$
+2110		and Overflow		
70	32	(10) Restoration		
700	320	(11) Shift		
−2110				
98600	321	(12) First Subtraction	Third	$6759 < .321 \times (21100)$
+2110		and Overflow	Series	
700	320	(13) Restoration		
7000	3200	(14) Shift		
−2110				
4990	3201	(15) First Subtraction		$6759 > .3201 \times (21100)$
−2110				
2880	3202	(16) Second "		$6759 > .3202 \times (21100)$
−2110			Fourth	
770	3203	(17) Third "	Series	$6759 > .3203 \times (21100)$
−2110				
98660	3204	(18) Fourth "		$6759 < .3204 \times (21100)$
+2110		and Overflow		
770	3203	(19) Restoration		$6759 = .3203 \times (21100)$

FIGURE 6.5.1. Division.

of step 3. This is accomplished by *adding* the divisor to the dividend register and tallying down the quotient register (instead of tallying up). Step 5 looks the same as step 3. The difference is that the test procedure has been completed and a new series of subtractions will soon start.

Before that, shifting takes place; both the dividend and quotient registers are shifted to the left. This multiplies the remainder and the quotient by 10 and is equivalent to dividing the divisor by 10. This allows the next quotient digit to be tallied. Shifting left places 0's into the right-hand side of the register.

The second series of "subtraction, tally, and test" takes place in steps 7 through 9. The minuend is the remainder of the last series multiplied by 10; the subtrahend is the divisor. The third subtraction causes the dividend register to go negative. It and the tally are restored in step 10. A shift left then takes place for the quotient and dividend registers.

Further series of "subtraction, test, and tally" are continued. When the number of series completed equals the number of digits in the dividend, the division may be considered finished. This is arbitrary, however, and depends on the machine. Here the dividend of the sample problem contains four digits; division is finished after four series are done. The division stops after the fourth restoration, step 19. The quotient has been tallied in the quotient register; the remainder is left in the dividend register. We have not bothered with decimal points or significant digits, but the programmer must be constantly aware of them.

Machine Division, Second Method

There is another method of performing division which eliminates the need for restoration of the dividend register in the subtraction process. It is best explained by referring to an example; Figure 6.5.2 illustrates this method.

Here it is desired to divide 560 by 3100. After alignment and testing a first subtraction is performed in step 1. Since the dividend register did not go negative, another subtraction may be made. This is done in step 2.

The second subtraction results in an overflow of the dividend register, indicating that the dividend register now contains a negative quantity. Instead of restoring the dividend register and the quotient register, this step is omitted.

Step 3 consists in shifting the divisor and the quotient register. But, now, instead of subtracting the shifted divisor, it is added. Since we have reversed the method of processing, we must also reverse our tallying; we tally *down*.

Step 4 demonstrates what has happened after the first addition. The dividend register is increasing and thus going in the positive direction. On the other hand, the quotient register has been tallying down.

In step 5 the second addition causes the dividend register to *change signs*. Here, changing signs indicates that the determination of this quotient digit has been completed. In the simple problem illustrated the answer has now been reached. In the quotient register is the quotient, 18, and the remainder in the dividend register is 2.

Dividend register	Quotient register	Description	What happened
560			
−310			
250	1	(1) First Subtraction	560 > .1 × (3100)
−310			
9940	2	(2) Second " and Overflow	560 < .2 × (3100)
+31	20	(3) Shift	
9971	19	(4) First Addition	560 < .19 × (3100)
+31			
0002	18	(5) Second Addition	560 = .18 × (3100)

FIGURE 6.5.2.   Division, second method, example.

In problems involving large numbers, the quotient will have more than two digits. The division process will alternate then between subtraction and addition. The tallying process will alternate between tallying up and tallying down.

This method eliminates the need to restore the dividend and quotient registers. Comparison of the two methods shows that the shorter method depends on the problem and is determined by whether alternate quotient digits or their complements are larger. However, the average of a large number of division problems there is a definite saving with the second method.

More equipment is required to do division by the second method, and the additional cost of the machine must be balanced against the small saving in time.

PROBLEMS

1. In the fashion of the examples of this chapter, show in detail how machine arithmetic is done on the following cases:

(a) 98765 + 43210
(b) 98765 − 43210
(c) 43210 − 98765
(d) 43210 × 98765
(e) 43210 ÷ 98765 (First Method)
(f) 43210 ÷ 98765 (Second Method)

2. Derive a formula for the machine time required for multiplication in terms of the number of digits of the multiplicand or multiplier using A for the add or subtract time, S for the shift time, 0 (nothing) for the digit check time, X_i for the digits of the multiplicand, and Y_i for the digits of the multiplier.

3. Do the same for division for both methods.

4. Multiplication of X by 28 (for example) can be done by subtracting the multiplicand twice from zero, shifting the multiplicand X to the left and adding it three times to the product-so-far. This yields $30X − 2X = 28X$. Show how this could be built into a machine using a chart similar to Figure 6.4.1, accurately describing same.

5. Derive a time formula for Problem 4 using the method described in Problem 2.

SEVEN

NUMBER SYSTEMS
AND COUNTING

7.1. INTRODUCTION

The concept of counting and numbers is easy to grasp intuitively and to use in everyday situations. A more intensive examination of this concept is in order before we attempt to investigate automatic methods of calculating. This will help us understand the functioning of the computer, which depends so heavily on numbers and counting.

The most primitive people are able to use the principles of counting in their daily dealings with one another. Some of the higher animals especially primates, can distinguish among different numbers. Here it is noted, then, that the concept of counting and its use does not depend on mathematical justification. However, we are interested in installing a counting system into a computer and so we must be aware of these mathematical foundations.

The concepts of group and individual essential to numbers and counting are now discussed.

Groups

Number is the property of a **group,** set, or plurality of individuals. The property of fiveness is common to a bunch of five bananas, a committee of five senators, or the sides of a pentagon. The delineation of the group depends, for its clarity, upon the delineation of the individuals or units that are the members of the group. The boundary distinguishing one **individual** from another must be clear.

In the examples of the last paragraph, the name of the group and the name applied to the members of the group can become confused. The group of senators is called the *committee*. It is this group, the committee, that has the property of fiveness *if* the committee consists of five senators. The name of the five-sided figure is the *pentagon;* the group with the characteristic of fiveness is "the sides of the figure called the pentagon."

The individuals encountered are of two types. The **primary** or **elementary unit** cannot be subdivided without losing its identity. Thus, neither the senator, the banana, nor the pentagon side can be cut up without losing its identity as a whole senator, banana, or side. On the other hand, a **secondary unit,** such as the committee or bunch, can be divided to form two committees or bunches. These secondary units must be defined further by some delineating property such as "the committee on finance for the Eighty-first United States Congress" or "the bunch of bananas I just bought." This delimits the secondary unit so that it cannot be partitioned without losing its identity. This applies to tertiary groups, which are groups whose members are groups of primary units, and to even higher groups which have as members lower-order groups.

In the banana business, a "stem" is the term applied to an ensemble of bananas that grew on the same branch of the banana tree. A stem will have several bunches or "*hands*" as the banana merchant calls them. A hand is a group of bananas growing from the same point on the branch. Here the "stem," "bunch," and "banana" are the names respectively of a tertiary group, a secondary group, and an individual.

Two stems of bananas may contain twelve hands which, in turn, comprise a total of three hundred fifty-eight bananas.

The person with an accounting background will recall his experiences with subtotals (secondary groups), totals (tertiary), and grand totals (fourth-order groups).

Philosophy and Definition

The concept of the individual is one with far-reaching consequences. Would you expect this idea to have ramifications in biology, law, and ethics? The definition of the individual is important in every phase of life. Here are a few examples.

The biologist is concerned with distinguishing a live individual from its dead environment. He must determine whether a virus should be included in the definition of live individual.

The lawyer is interested in delineating the individual from the environment too. If you swallow an apple, it will become part of you in a short time. If you swallow a diamond, it will never be absorbed by your body. Can you see the legal implication?

When is a human being first to be thought of as such? Is it at the moment of conception? of birth? or some time in between? This is a case, you will note, of determining when there is one and when there are two individuals. This is a moral, religious, philosophical, and legal problem, and on it hinges society's jurisdiction over the new being.

In any case, let us consider a group composed of a single delineated individual. We do not consider the individual, but the group which he comprises. The group of people who wrote this book has but one member—namely, me. A group of this sort is said to have *one* member.

Counting

When a secondary group can no longer be divided and maintain its identity, it is a group of one. Such groups are unit groups having but one member. They have in common only the aspect of **"oneness."** Such a concept presupposes an adequate definition of the individual. The concept of two can be visualized operationally as the process of **"adding one"** applied to an already established group. "Adding one" consists of opening the group boundary and inserting a new valid member within it. The group is now a group of "two." The concept of three is similarly described operationally as the process of augmenting the group of two by one more individual or "adding one" to a group of two. The extension to further numbers is immediately apparent. The **successor** of group A is the group obtained by "adding one" to group A. Thus, 4 is the successor of 3.

The process of "adding one" is acceptable on an intuitive level. When another person walks into the room, the group of people in that room has increased by one. Similarly, when another fruit is picked from the tree, it is "added" to the basket.

The essential points in understanding numbers are the delineation of the individual and the process of "adding one"—the concept of successor. Note here that all the numbers used in counting can be generated from these two concepts. These numbers—the ones used in counting—are called **natural numbers.** Possibly this term was applied because these numbers sprang up naturally without any theoretical background.

7.2. NATURAL NUMBERS

Man first became aware of the importance of counting many thousands of years ago and, in so doing, made use of the "natural numbers."

When communication between people first appeared, it was a necessity to communicate in terms of quantity. Men wanted to keep track of their animals, wives, and food—to count their wealth. A different symbol was used for each natural number. At this stage both the symbols and the counting process were limited. People conceived of counting only to a limited number—mainly because they did not need to count further. The Mayans could count up to twenty. They had a symbol for each number and a symbol which represented any amount over twenty. Such a system of counting with a symbol for each number is called a **baseless system.** This is contrasted with systems with bases to be discussed later in the chapter. A parallel to the baseless number system is found in the Chinese language. The Chinese use a different symbol for each spoken word and hence for each concept. They do not have an alphabet, which is in a sense the language equivalent of a base system. This explains why no practical Chinese typewriter is available today.

All the natural numbers can be generated by the process of "adding one." Also any two natural numbers can be "added" together. "Add A to B" means that the process of "adding one" is to be applied to the number B a number of times equal to A. We must find the successor of B, the successor of the successor of B, and continue to find successors until this has been done A times. The result is the sum of A and B. Thus, **add** 3 to 5 means find the successor of 5, 3 times: the first successor of 5 is 6; the second successor of 5 (the successor of 6) is 7; the third successor of 5 (the successor of 7) is 8, the result of adding 3 to 5. The process of adding two natural numbers is termed "closed." This means that if *any* two natural numbers are added together, the result is another natural number. In general a set is said to be **closed with respect to a process** if, when this process is performed on two members of the set, the result is also a member of the set.

7.3. NEXT LOGICAL STEP

We have discussed the method for increasing the size of groups. Next, it would seem natural to find a method of decreasing the size of groups. This concept was not completely thought out historically until more logically advanced concepts had been developed. To maintain a logical flow of ideas, we shall next consider the process opposite to "adding one" and call it **"taking one."** Thus, "adding one" changes the group from 5 to 6 and "taking one" changes the group from 6 to 5. Of course, what we are now defining is subtraction. But the stumbling block arises when we wish to apply the "take one" process to "1." What happens when we take one individual from a group of one? Well, we are left with nothing. The concept of **zero** is very difficult for people to accept. After all, if there are no individuals, how can there be a class? The property of zero can be applied to "no apples" just as well as "no senators." In the case of zero, the philosopher's question, "What is there zero of?" The whole argument seems rather esoteric, because we are all so familiar with manipulating "zero." But it was an uphill fight for the proponents of zero!

To go one step further means to apply "taking one" to "zero." This generates negative natural numbers, indicated by adding the minus sign to the natural numbers, thus: -1, -2, -3, and so on. Somehow this was easier to grasp than the zero concept. It could be put into more practical terms. Merchants and shopkeepers understand the notion of profit and loss or credit and debit. To them, the sign indicates the direction of the passage of goods or money—whether it was owed the merchant or whether he owed it to someone else.

The "taking one" process generates all the negative natural numbers. The entire set of numbers thus formed, the positive and negative natural numbers and zero, makes up what is known as the **integers.**

The natural numbers are not closed with respect to subtraction. But the integers are closed with respect to both addition and subtraction. This means that the sum or difference of any two integers is itself an integer. A basic property of the digital computer is that it deals only with integers. This might appear as a severe limitation, but by means of scaling and programming, it is able to handle decimals and fractions.

Multiplication and division are derived from addition and subtraction. **Multiplication** of A by B is defined as *the addition of A to zero, B times.* Zero is used here because otherwise the definition would have to be stated as the addition of A to itself $(B - 1)$ times—somewhat unwieldy. 3×5 means adding 5 to 0 three times. Notice that the natural numbers are closed for multiplication—the product of two numbers is itself a natural number. After a simple rule for dealing with signed numbers is incorporated (learned in high school as "a plus times a plus is a plus," "a plus times a minus ... ," and so on), it is also found that the integers are closed to multiplication.

Division is defined a bit circuitously. **A divided by B** requires that a number be found such that, when it is multiplied by B, the product will be A. It is seen by examining a few problems in division that neither the natural numbers nor the integers are closed with respect to division for the quotient of two integers is not always an integer. Thus, 5 divided by 3 does not yield an integer. The digital computer can do division only by giving as an answer a quotient and a remainder. Thus, the computer says that 5 divided by 3 is 1 with a remainder of 2; it can answer only in terms of integers.

The process of division generates what are called *rational numbers—* all numbers which can be expressed as the quotient of two integers. By further algebraic manipulation, the irrational numbers, such as $\sqrt{2}$, can be generated. Such numbers were accepted historically long before the concept of zero was accepted. In ancient Greece old Pythagoras found that $\sqrt{2}$ was the hypotenuse of an isosceles right triangle with unit sides.

7.4. BASES AND BUNDLES

Now that we have a system of counting and further, a system of integers and a *symbol* for many of them, we find that we are still limited. In order to use a variety of numbers, we require a large vocabulary of symbols to represent these numbers. To remove this limitation, a system of counting using a base was developed. To pictorialize this concept, we will think of combining units in bundles or packages.

The Principle of Bundles

To represent a number by means of bundles, we must first fix the size of the bundle. We will illustrate this by first using a bundle of size twelve. Twelve is chosen because it will divorce us from the decimal system which we are now used to (the word "twelve" does not carry the decimal implications of another number such as thir*teen*), but it will also be familiar to us because of the English system of counting in dozens.

We now have a bundle of size twelve. We will therefore count in dozens. To represent a number, say seventeen, we will first count out a unit of a dozen and see what is left over. In this case we will have 1 dozen plus 5. To represent the quantity thirty-two, we would count out our bundle of a dozen twice and have seven units left over. Thus, thirty-two will be represented in our "dozen" system by 2 and 7, or $(27)_{12}$, where $(\quad)_{12}$ indicates a base of 12 and $(\quad)_B$ would indicate the base B.

This system of representing a quantity by a number of bundles and the number of units left over works fine, but we are limited when we get to larger numbers. We must improve our concept of bundles.

The concept can be elaborated by compounding it. Thus, having considered bundles, we can conceive of "bundles of bundles." Now, if our original bundle size was called a dozen, the "bundle of bundles" would then be a dozen dozen, or what we call a gross.

We can apply this principle by examining the given quantity and counting out bundles of twelve. When we have twelve of these bundles of twelve, we have made up a gross. We continue to count out our bundles of twelve until we can no longer make up such a bundle. Our quantity is then broken down into grosses, dozens, and units. Thus, the decimal number three hundred five is represented as 2 gross, 1 dozen, and 5, or $(215)_{12}$.

The principle may be compounded further and we may discuss "a bundle of bundles of bundles" which, in the example, would be a dozen gross or in the garment trade, a great gross, and further to "bundles of bundles of bundles of bundles," or gross gross and so on, as you may well imagine.

The size of the bundle is called the base. In our example the base is twelve. Compounding of the base is actually raising of the base to a power. Thus, a dozen is (twelve)^1; a gross is (twelve)^2; a great gross is (twelve)^3 and a gross gross is (twelve)^4.

Any natural number except 1 can be used as a base in a counting system. We are familiar with the use of ten as a base and have a specific name for the system using it—the decimal system. A common base used in most digital computers is the number two and the system is called the binary system. The system of twelve used above is called the duodecimal system.

7.5. DECIMAL SYSTEM

We are all familiar with the decimal system, which uses as a base the number ten. The various bundles are formed by taking the powers of ten.

To simplify our terminology, instead of referring to a bundle of bundles, we will simply call this a **2-bundle.** Similarly, a bundle of bundles of bundles will be called a **3-bundle.** In the decimal system a 2-bundle refers to hundreds (10×10, or 10^2), a 3-bundle refers to thousands ($10 \times 10 \times 10$, or 10^3), and so on. In general, in the decimal system n-bundle stands for a bundle with 10^n units.

Now a quantity can be written in the decimal system by placing at the right the number of units left over after all the bundles have been made up. The next digit to the left will represent the number of 1-bundles that are left after making 2-bundles. The next digit to the left indicates how many 2-bundles are left over after making up 3-bundles, and so on.

In such a fashion the number 3467 is used to represent the quantity defined by

$$3 \cdot 10^3 + 4 \cdot 10^2 + 6 \cdot 10^1 + 7$$

or $$3000 + 400 + 60 + 7$$

One may wonder why, of all the admissible bases, the base ten was chosen. One can conjecture that since we possess ten fingers, this may have something to do with the origin of this base. Also, the term "digit" was derived from the Latin word for finger.

7.6. OTHER BASES

Since we now realize that it is possible to write numbers with any base and know how to interpret these numbers, we can translate a quantity written in any base to the decimal system. For example, if we know that the base being used is 8, we may translate the number 743 into the decimal system by the rules of the previous section. Thus, $(743)_8$ means

$$3 + 4 \cdot 8^1 + 7 \cdot 8^2$$

or
$$3 + 32 + 498 = (532)_{10}$$

Note that the subscript and parentheses in "$(743)_8$" tell us that this number is written in the base 8.

Observe now that in using any base B, there is a separate symbol for each of the quantities, 0, 1, ..., $B - 2$, and $B - 1$. The quantity B is always represented in a system of base B as 10. That is, in a system of base B, there is no single symbol for the quantity B; it is always represented by the two-digit symbols 1 and 0 combined as "10." In the decimal system there is no single symbol for ten; it is always written as 10. Similarly, in the octal system (base 8), there is no symbol for eight; it is written as 10. The only digit symbols used in the octal system are 0, 1, ..., 6 and 7. Conversion from a system of any base B, to the decimal system may be accomplished as done in the example above. To write this in mathematical terms, consider the number N, whose digits are, from right to left, b_0, b_1, ..., and written as b_n, b_{n-1}, ..., b_1, b_0. In the base B, this number stands for the quantity,*

$$b_0 + b_1 B^1 + b_2 B^2 + \cdots + b_{n-1} B^{n-1} + b_n B^n$$

This provides a rule for conversion from a system of any base B to any other base B'. In the example below, B is five and B' is seven:

EXAMPLE:
Convert $(324)_5$ to base 7.

	Addition, base seven
$(324)_5 = 4 + 2 \cdot 5 + 3 \cdot 5 \cdot 5 \quad [= (89)_{10}]$	135
$\quad = (4)_7 + (13)_7 + 3 \cdot (34)_7{}^*$	13
$\quad = (4)_7 + (13)_7 + (135)_7$	4
$\quad = (155)_7$	155 (total)

Check: $(155)_7 = 5 + 5 \cdot 7 + 1 \cdot 7 \cdot 7 = (89)_{10}$

* Multiplication base seven: $5 \cdot 5 = (34)_7$.

Note the addition on the right in the base seven; we say "5 plus 3 plus 4 is fifteen, put down 5 and carry 1" and so forth.

* For the mathematically oriented, $N = \sum\limits_{i=0}^{n} b_i B^i$

There is another method for conversion which is valuable, especially for conversion of numbers of base ten to another base. Below the number 468 base ten is converted to base seven.

$$
\begin{array}{r|r|l}
7 & 468 & 6 \\
\hline
& 66 & 3 \\
\hline
& 9 & 2 \\
\hline
& 1 &
\end{array}
$$

Read up along arrow.

The method uses the principle of making 1-bundles and finding the remainder in units, and then making 2-bundles of the 1-bundles and finding the remaining 1-bundles and so forth.

The first step is to make as many 1-bundles as possible. Divide 7 into 468; the result is 66 with 6 remaining. There are the 66 1-bundles in 468 with 6 units left over. Next, divide 66 by 7. The result announces that there are 9 2-bundles in 468 with 3 1-bundles and 6 units left over. The last step shows that there is 1 3-bundle in 468 with 2 2-bundles and so on, remaining. Thus, 468 is 1236 in the base 7.

The successive quotients are listed under the previous quotients; the remainder is listed at the right of the dividend; the divisors are continued until the last quotient is no longer divisible by the base; the result is read by following the arrow.

7.7. THE BASE TWO—THE BINARY SYSTEM

The base two is most important to understand in the study of computers. The reason is that electronic devices are available which have two possible stable states, called **bistable devices.** Examples of such devices are the relay which can be energized or de-energized, the magnetic core which can be saturated in either of two directions magnetically, and the multivibrator circuit for which one tube (or transistor) may be conducting and the other nonconducting.

For any given number system there are symbols for every quantity not exceeding one less than the base. This means that for the base two there are symbols only for the quantities zero and one: 0, 1. Of course, these two symbols can be used to represent the two possible states which might exist in bistable devices and are sufficient for the purpose.

A **binary number** of any size consists only of 0's or 1's; each digit of the binary number is either a 0 or a 1. This binary digit, either 1 or 0 has a special designation. It is called a **bit.** A five-digit binary number is thus called a five-bit number.

Any quantity can be represented in the binary system if sufficient bits are available. To put it a different way, every decimal number has a binary equivalent.

The binary number may be translated into the decimal system by

TABLE 7.7 BINARY NUMBERS AND THEIR DECIMAL EQUIVALENT TO FORTY-NINE

Decimal	Binary	Decimal	Binary
0	000000	25	011001
1	000001	26	011010
2	000010	27	011011
3	000011	28	011100
4	000100	29	011101
5	000101	30	011110
6	000110	31	011111
7	000111	32	100000
8	001000	33	100001
9	001001	34	100010
10	001010	35	100011
11	001011	36	100100
12	001100	37	100101
13	001101	38	100110
14	001110	39	100111
15	001111	40	101000
16	010000	41	101001
17	010001	42	101010
18	010010	43	101011
19	010011	44	101100
20	010100	45	101101
21	010101	46	101110
22	010110	47	101111
23	010111	48	110000
24	011000	49	110001

using the method of the previous paragraph. Thus the number $(1001101)_2$ stands for

$$1 + 0 \cdot 2^1 + 1 \cdot 2^2 + 1 \cdot 2^3 + 0 \cdot 2^4 + 0 \cdot 2^5 + 1 \cdot 2^6$$
$$1 \qquad + 4 \quad + 8 \qquad\qquad\qquad + 64 \quad = (77)_{10}$$

and consequently represents the decimal number 77. Similarly, by the method of the previous section, a decimal number may be converted into the binary system. To convert the number 77 into its binary equivalent, we perform the process below. The first few steps are shown separately:

$$
\begin{array}{r|r|l}
2 & 77 & \\
\hline
 & 38 & \\
\end{array}
\qquad
\begin{array}{r|r|l}
2 & 77 & 1 \\
\hline
 & 38 & \\
 & 19 &
\end{array}
$$

| | Start | | 1st Division | | 2nd Division | | 3rd Division |

2| 77 |
  38
Start

2| 77 |1
  38
  19
1st Division

2| 77 |1
  38 |0
  19
2nd Division

2| 77 |1
  38 |0
  19 |1
   9
3rd Division

2| 77 |1
  38 |0
  19 |1
   9 |1
   4 |0
   2 |0 = 1001101
   1

Complete

A list of the binary numbers from 0 to 49 appears in Table **7.7**.

Binary Arithmetic

A table could be constructed for binary addition, but it would have only four entries:

$$0 + 0 = 0 \qquad 0 + 1 = 1 \qquad 1 + 0 = 1 \qquad 1 + 1 = 10$$

or

+	0	1
0	0	1
1	1	10

Here is an example of binary addition:

```
13:  01101
21:  10101
34: 100010
```

Subtraction can be done directly,

```
34: 100010
21: 010101
13: 001101
```

or with complements as the computer would do it:

$$
\begin{array}{rl}
34: & 0100010 \\
\text{complement (21):} & 1101010 \\ \hline
\text{add} & 0001100 \\
\text{carry} & 1 \\ \hline
13: & 0001101
\end{array}
$$

Notice that the complement of a binary number is formed by substituting 1's for 0's and 0's for 1's.

Multiplication is done by shifts and addition using the multiplication table:

21	10101
13	01101
63	10101
21	10101
273	10101

×	0	1
0	0	0
1	0	1

$$100010001 = 256 + 16 + 1 = 273$$

Let us next divide 150 by 13 after translation into binary. The result should turn out to be 11_{10} with a remainder of 7:

$$
\begin{array}{r}
1011 \\
1101\overline{)10010110} \\
1101 \\ \hline
1011 \\
0000 \\ \hline
10111 \\
1101 \\ \hline
10100 \\
1101 \\ \hline
111
\end{array}
\qquad
\begin{array}{r}
11 \\
13\overline{)150} \\
13 \\ \hline
20 \\
13 \\ \hline
7
\end{array}
$$

7.8. ARITHMETIC WITH OTHER BASES

Arithmetic in number systems with bases other than two or ten simply requires tables of addition, subtraction, and multiplication. With a little practice skill can be acquired. Let us examine a couple of systems with other bases.

The Duodecimal System

We require two new symbols and names for them. Let us use # for ten and call it dec (pronounced "deck") and * for eleven and call it elf (like

an imaginary man). We count in the duodecimal system, "one, two, ...,
nine, dec, elf, ten, eleven, ..., nineteen, decteen, elfteen, twenty, ...,
twenty-nine, twenty-dec, twenty-elf, thirty, ..."

Let us add two numbers:

$$385*$$
$$79\#6$$
$$\overline{}\ 12$$
$$*645$$

As we add we say, "Six and elf is fifteen; put down five and carry one.
Five and one is six and dec is fourteen; put down four and carry one.
Eight and one is nine and nine is sixteen; put down six and carry one.
One and three is four and seven is elf."

Subtraction and multiplication follow the same pattern. The problems at the end of the chapter provide practice.

The Quinary System

We have all the symbols we need for the system of base five. Remember there are now no symbols used for five, six, seven, eight, and nine.
Let us try multiplication in this system.

$$243$$
$$324$$
$$\overline{}\ 5$$
$$2132$$
$$1041$$
$$1334$$
$$\overline{201442}$$

As we multiply we say, "Four times three is twenty-two; put down two
and carry two. Four times four is thirty-one and two is thirty-three; put
down three and carry three. Four times two is thirteen and three is
twenty one. Next, two times three is eleven; put down one and carry one.
Two times four is thirteen and one is fourteen; put down four and carry
one. Two times two is four and one is ten." After we find the last line
(1334) we add the three lines: "Put down two; one and three is four. One
and four is ten and four is fourteen; put down four and carry one. One
and two is three and three is eleven; put down one and carry one. One and
one is two and three is ten; put down zero and carry one. One and one
is two."

You see, it's just a matter of knowing the addition and multiplication
tables.

PROBLEMS

1. Describe the various systems of measure as multiple-base systems:

    (a) English length   (b) time   (c) angles
    (d) fluid measure   (e) weight   (f) British currency

2. The Romans had a system of number notation which might be called biquinary, using letters (I, V, X, L, C, D, M). State rigorously the rules for writing any number in the Roman number system. State the rules for addition and subtraction in this system. And for multiplication. Translate and perform, in Roman:

$$137 \qquad\qquad 791 \qquad\qquad 256$$
$$+963 \qquad\qquad -498 \qquad\qquad \times 32 \qquad\qquad 16\overline{)1024}$$

3. Give several instances in the practical world where the use of $(+)$ and $(-)$ are obvious with reference to:

    (a) time   (b) distance   (c) magnetism   (d) electricity

    How is the assignment of $(+)$ and $(-)$ made? Try to define right and left without pointing. Refer to the dictionary.

4. Are the natural numbers included in the integers? What is the difference between "inclusion" and a "one-to-one correspondence"?

5. Incorporate the concept of *sign* into the definition of multiplication; of division.

6. Think a little more about the concept of the individual as applied to the human. Characterize the bodily functions in respect to the boundary of the individual: eating-excreting; inhaling-exhaling. What can be said about the alimentary canal and the respiratory system in this respect? How would you define an alien body in regard to the human being?

7. Give examples of hierarchies of groups (primary, secondary, and so forth) using

    (a) Written-language elements (letters, ...)
    (b) Spoken-language elements
    (c) Field-army elements (soldier, ...)
    (d) Life elements (cell, ...)

8. Translate to base 10.

    (a) $(100110011)_2$ (b) $(1202121)_3$ (c) $(313121)_4$ (d) $(522415)_6$
    (e) $(423132)_5$ (f) $(381)_7$ (g) $(76153)_8$ (h) $(817423)_9$
    (i) $(887\#31)_{11}$ $[\# = 10_{10}]$ (j) $(*\#3971)_{12}$ $[* = 11_{10}]$

9. Translate to systems of base 2, 3, 4, 5, 6, 7, 8, 9, 11, 12 $[\# = 10_{10}, * = 11_{10}]$

    (a) 95   (b) 371   (c) 4238   (d) 5555
    (e) 78137   (f) -1932

    Perform on each base (2, 3, etc.) above:

$$a + b \qquad\qquad d - c \qquad\qquad f - a$$
$$b + c \qquad\qquad e + f \qquad\qquad b - f$$

109

10. Multiply in each base

$b \times c$ $\qquad\qquad$ $a \times b$ $\qquad\qquad$ $b \times c$

Divide in each base

b/a $\qquad\qquad$ c/g $\qquad\qquad$ c/d

11. Make one table each for $+$, $-$, $\times$, $\div$ for the base 6.

12. Show machine subtraction in the base 6 for

(a) $531 - 135$ $\qquad\qquad$ (b) $135 - 531$

E I G H T

MACHINE LANGUAGES

8.1. INTRODUCTION

Let us review the three languages used in dealing with computers. The original input document and the final reports the machine produces are written in **human language. Intermediate language** is used to expedite the input and output of information. Finally, all the data handling and processing occurs within the computer in *machine language*. It is this machine language which will concern us now.

The machine language found exclusively in modern computers uses "yes-no" information—*bits*. The way in which these bits are associated to represent characters is called a **code** and this code constitutes the machine language.

Codes* are chosen with different aims in mind. One code is constructed so that a check is constantly kept on information as it is transmitted from one section of the computer to another; another is chosen to check processing and arithmetic; a third, to simplify and expedite the calculations which the machine performs; still another is made for simplicity of translation from intermediate or human language into code. One code may possess several of these qualities.

---

* The reader might review here the distinction made on page 22 between "code" as applied to machine language and "code" as applied to the language representation that calls forth a given machine order.

The Binary Number System as a Code

It is a common practice in scientific computers, where the task is mainly calculation, to use the binary number system (discussed in Chapter 7) as the machine coding for information. Human-language code cannot be translated *simply* into binary coded words. On the other hand, a high efficiency in calculation and manipulation results using natural binary *numbers*, since fewer bits per word are required than in just about any other code. But note that there is no *character-to-character* correspondence between the human-language word and the binary coded word, only a *word-to-word* correspondence.

As an example, remember that the number 347 translates into the natural binary number, 101011011. That may be called its **natural binary code.**

To determine the number of bits, N', necessary in the natural binary coded word to translate an N-character numerical human-language word, the following relationship is used:

$$2^{N'-1} < N \leqslant 2^{N'} \tag{8.1.1}$$

Since $256 < 347 < 512$ or $2^8 < 347 < 2^9$, nine bits are required to encode 347 in natural binary code:

$$101011011$$

8.2. BINARY DECIMAL CODES

The difficulty in translation for natural binary coding (the name used to distinguish the binary number system when used as a code) results from the absence of a character-to-character correspondence between the human language and the code. If we sacrifice the efficiency of arithmetic in the natural binary coding, we may gain by the ease of translation in using binary decimal codes. A **binary decimal** code uses binary digits so that there is a correspondence between a decimal character and a set of bits. Translation from the human language is done very simply because, for *each* character in the human language, *one* set of bits is substituted in the machine language. A word of N human-language characters is translated into N bit sets in the machine language.

Another advantage to setting up this character to bit-set correspondence is that it can be easily adapted to encode alphabetic characters. This can be done either by using more bits per character or by using two digits to represent an alphabetic character (see Section 8.7).

Natural Binary Decimal Code

A unique code using binary numbers is assigned to each decimal digit. This requires a minimum of four bits; a three-bit code has only eight possible combinations.

The code using a four-bit binary combination to represent each decimal digit is shown in Figure 8.2.1. These are called natural binary coded decimal numbers (NBCD) because they use one of the first ten binary counting numbers as the code for each decimal digit. The other six combinations are not used and are called **forbidden combinations**; when one of these is observed it is due to an error or an uncorrected partial result in arithmetic.

Digit	Code	Digit	Code	Digit	Code	Digit	Code
0	0000	3	0011	6	0110	9	1001
1	0001	4	0100	7	0111		
2	0010	5	0101	8	1000		

FIGURE 8.2.1.   Natural binary coded decimal.

To code an N-digit decimal number we require N four-bit binary code sets. The number 347 is thus coded as 0011 0100 0111. Spaces are inserted between the code sets only for convenience in reading.

The computer is concerned with processing information coded in this form. How is it able to perform addition with these natural binary coded numbers? Let's see what happens when different pairs of digits are added.

Suppose the sum of the two decimal digits is nine or less. The rules for binary addition work fine. Try adding the NBCD digits 3 and 5 in Figure 8.2.2.

		Using binary rules	*Desired*
0011		1001	1001
+0101		+0010	+0010
1000		1011	1 0001

FIGURE 8.2.2.   NBCD addition.   FIGURE 8.2.3.   NBCD addition of 2 and 9.

Next, suppose that the sum of the two digits is greater than nine. The desired *coded* result is a coded sum digit and a carry. The result of adding coded 2 (0010) to coded 9 (1001) should be coded 1 (0001) and a carry. This is shown at the right side of Figure 8.2.3. The result, using binary addition values, appears on the left in Figure 8.2.3. Note that the result is a forbidden combination (a code for which there is no corresponding digit).

If we make a list of all possible digit additions, it becomes apparent that the forbidden combination is a natural binary *number* just ten greater than the proper code. The coding forms a counting system of base sixteen. The code for the proper sum digit may be generated by subtracting the code for ten (the *decimal* base) from the binary code obtained from the binary addition rules. It is equivalent to adding the binary code for six (six is the difference between the two bases, ten and sixteen; six is the sixteen's complement of ten). This will always create a carry (adding a number greater than nine to six in a counting system of base sixteen always produces a number sixteen or larger and hence creates a carry).

Figure 8.2.4 shows both methods applied to the example of Figure 8.2.3. Notice the carry created by the second method.

Subtracting ten	Adding six	Uncorrected	Corrected
1001	1001	1000	1000
+0010	0010	+ 1001	1001
1011	+ 0110	1 0001	+ 0110
−1010	1 0001		1 0111
0001			

FIGURE 8.2.4. NBCD addition of 2 and 9 and correction.   FIGURE 8.2.5. NBCD addition of 8 and 9 with and without correction.

When the sum of the two decimal digits is sixteen or greater, the sum obtained by using the rules of binary additions creates a carry, but the sum digit is not correct. It is corrected by the same means—adding the code for six. Since a carry was created in the first addition, the correction does not create a second carry. This is illustrated in Figure 8.2.5 (with and without correction).

Notice now that if correction is required, the coded sum using binary addition will generate a carry when a binary coded six is added to it and not otherwise. A rule by which the computer can determine what correction is necessary is now stated.

Rule for Adding Natural Binary Coded Digits: Add the two coded digits using the rules of natural binary addition; if this generates a carry, or if the result is a forbidden code, add the code for 6 to the sum of the codes; otherwise the result is correct.

The three examples cited are done using this rule in Figure 8.2.6.

3+5	*9+2*	*8+9*
0011	1001	1000
+0101	+ 0010	+ 1001
1000	1011	1 0001
	+ 0110	+ 0110
	1 0001	1 0111

FIGURE 8.2.6.   NBCD addition using the Rule.

8.3.   EXCESS THREE BINARY DECIMAL CODE

This code is formed by adding the natural binary decimal coding for three to the natural binary decimal code of the decimal digit being coded. This is shown in Figure 8.3.1. It is familiarly referred to as *XS3*.

		9's
Digit code		*Complement code*
0	0011	9 1100
1	0100	8 1011
2	0101	7 1010
3	0110	6 1001
4	0111	5 1000

FIGURE 8.3.1.   XS3 code.

The arrangement of the listing makes it obvious that a digit and its 9's complement have complementary coding.

The number 347 is coded in XS3 as 0110 0111 1010.

XS3 coding has four advantages: it is simple to translate; arithmetic may be performed in this code with ease; a digit and its 9's complement are complementary in this code; the representation of the decimal digit zero does not consist of four 0's—in fact no decimal digit is coded as 0000.

Addition of XS3 Digits

Figure 8.3.2 shows several examples of addition of two XS3 digits and the correction necessary to obtain the proper sum digit code. Since each digit code is three more than the natural binary code for the digit, when the XS3 codes are added using the rules of binary addition, the result is a code which is six greater than the natural binary code for the sum of the two digits. When the sum of the digits is nine or less, the sum of the XS3 codes is fifteen or less and no carry is generated. To correct this sum, which is three more than it should be, a binary three (XS3 coded 0 or 0011) is subtracted from it. The diminished result is then three more than the natural binary code of the sum and is, hence, the XS3 code of the sum. Examples of this are shown in Figures 8.3.2(a) and 8.3.2(b). The sum of the codes is six more than the proper binary sum and the

(a) *1+2*	(b) *3+5*	(c) *9+2*	(d) *8+9*
0100	0110	1100	1011
+0101	+1000	+0101	1100
1001	1110	10001	10111
−0011	−0011	+0011	+0011
0110	1011	10100	11010

FIGURE 8.3.2.   Addition of XS3 digits with correction.

corrected sum of the codes is three more than the proper binary sum and is hence the XS3 code of the sum.

Suppose that the sum of the two digits is ten or greater. The sum of the codes is sixteen or greater. In a four-bit system, X and $(X + 16)$ have the same code. Let us add A to B. The XS3 code for A and B respectively is A_3 and B_3 given by

$$A_3 = A + 3 \qquad (8.4.1)$$

$$B_3 = B + 3 \qquad (8.4.2)$$

Add these codes to get a sum C_6.

$$C_6 = A_3 + B_3 \qquad (8.4.3)$$

$$= A + B + 6 \qquad (8.4.4)$$

Assume also that there is a carry so that the proper sum digit, C, is

$$C = A + B - 10 \qquad (8.4.5)$$

$$C = (A + B + 6) - 6 - 10 \qquad (8.4.6)$$

$$= A_3 + B_3 - 16 \qquad (8.4.7)$$

But because of the property of the four-bit word that X is the same as $X + 16$,

$$C = A_3 + B_3 \qquad (8.4.8)$$

The excess three code for the sum digit is called C_3, and

$$C_3 = C + 3 \qquad (8.4.9)$$

so that

$$C_3 = A_3 + B_3 + 3 \qquad (8.4.10)$$

To add two digits coded in XS3 whose sum is greater than nine, the codes are added and a binary 3 (XS3 coded 0 or 0011) is added to the sum. This is demonstrated in the examples, Figures 8.3.2(c) and 8.3.2(d). The complete rule for XS3 addition may be stated as

> *Rule for Adding XS3 Coded Digits:* Add the XS3 codes using the rules of binary addition; if this generates a carry, add 0011 to the sum; otherwise subtract 0011 from the sum (or add 1101 and neglect the carry).

8.4.   OTHER FOUR-BIT BINARY CODES—WEIGHTING

There are innumerable four-bit codes which can be set up to represent decimal digits. The exact number of codes, in fact, is

$$16 \cdot 15 \cdots 7 = 16!/6! = 29{,}059{,}430{,}400$$

This is because any of the sixteen codes can be chosen to represent first decimal digit; any of the remaining fifteen codes can be used for the next decimal digit; any of the remaining fourteen codes can be used for the next decimal digit; and so fourth. Most of these codes do not have a simple rule of generation. Quite a few codes can be generated by a system of weights discussed below.

Consider a set of four weights, W_4, W_3, W_2, W_1, each of which is an integer. One of these weights is assigned to each of the four bits of the code. The decimal digit, D, is encoded as $d_4 d_3 d_2 d_1$, where each of the d's is either 1 or 0, so chosen as to satisfy the relationship below.

$$D = d_4 W_4 + d_3 W_3 + d_2 W_2 + d_1 W_1$$

6421 System

To demonstrate this principle let us take a system of weights, 6, 4, 2, 1. The digit 3 is then encoded as 0011 because this is the only set of bits which satisfies the relationship above. Thus,

$$3 = 0 \times 6 + 0 \times 4 + 1 \times 2 + 1 \times 1$$

Similarly, the decimal digit 8 will be encoded as 1010 because

$$8 = 1 \times 6 + 0 \times 4 + 1 \times 2 + 0 \times 1$$

However, a difficulty arises when the decimal digit 7 is to be encoded. It can be encoded with this system of weights as either 1001 or 0111. In order to have a *unique* coding for each of the decimal digits, it is necessary to have an *additional* rule or rules. Such a rule in this case might be: "If there is more than one acceptable coding for a digit, choose the coding for which $d_4 = 0$." This would yield a unique coding with 7 = 0111 and 6 = 0110. Using the code we have generated above, the number 347 translates into 0011 0100 0111 and 891 into 1010 1011 0001.

A weighted four-bit decimal binary code is described by giving the four weights and additional rules to make the code unique. The rules for addition of numbers in a weighted code must be derived for each weighted code. Note that the weights 8421 define the NBCD system.

8.5. FIVE-BIT CODES—DECIMAL BINARY WITH PARITY CHECK

The need for accuracy in handling all processing within the computer is paramount. A means is available for protection against the corruption of the code by the loss or pickup of a single bit. This method requires an extra bit called a **parity bit** to be used in the coding of each decimal digit. This bit is adjusted so that the total number of 1's in each binary decimal bit set for the code is even (odd). The parenthetical word indicates that either "odd" or "even" can be chosen, but once the selection is made it remains the same for all digits coded. Examine the sixteen possible four-bit combinations. There are exactly eight which contain an even (odd) number of 1's. Therefore, to obtain ten separate codes with an even (odd) number of 1's, it is necessary to use combinations of five bits each. One customary procedure is to use an existing four-bit code and augment it with a fifth bit to make the number of 1's in the code even (odd). To exemplify this, an odd-parity natural binary decimal code is shown in Table 8.5.1. The final four bits are NBCD; either a 1 or a 0 is inserted in the initial position to make the total number of 1's odd.

TABLE 8.5.1 ODD PARITY NATURAL BINARY DECIMAL CODE

Digit	P8421	Digit	P8421
0	10000	5	10101
1	00001	6	10110
2	00010	7	00111
3	10011	7	01000
4	00100	9	11001

Another code of importance is the odd-parity XS3 code of Table 8.5.2.

TABLE 8.5.2 ODD PARITY XS3 CODE

Digit	P8421	Digit	P8421
0	10011	9	11100
1	00100	8	01011
2	10101	7	11010
3	10110	6	11001
4	00111	5	01000

The listing in the table places 9's complements in the same row. Notice that the coding of 9's complements has complementary bits except for the parity bit, which is the same for both the digit and its complement.

Two-out-of-five Code

Another code which has an extremely good automatic check built into it, although it is less convenient for arithmetic, is called the two-out-of-five code. There are ten possible arrangements of the five bits each of which has exactly two 1's in it. These arrangements may be set up in a semi-weighted form as shown in Table 8.5.3. The sum of the weights

TABLE 8.5.3 TWO-OUT-OF-FIVE-CODE

Digit	Weight 74210
0	11000
1	00011
2	00101
3	00110
4	01001
5	01010
6	01100
7	10001
8	10010
9	10100

times codes is equal to the digit to be coded except for 0 (whose weights total eleven!).

8.6. BIQUINARY CODE

Biquinary code is a two-out-of-seven bit code. (There are exactly two 1's and five 0's in each digit code.) It is a weighted code. Since there are a constant number of 1's in the code, it is a self-checking code. By the same token, no character consists entirely of 0's.

TABLE 8.6 BIQUINARY CODE

Digit	50	/	43210	Digit	50	/	43210
0	01		00001	5	10		00001
1	01		00010	6	10		00010
2	01		00100	7	10		00100
3	01		01000	8	10		01000
4	01		10000	9	10		10000

The system of weights which defines the biquinary code, Table 8.6, is 5, 0/4, 3, 2, 1, 0. A 1 is found on each side of the slash. The left-hand 1 is called the **quinary bit**; the other 1 is the **binary bit**. Addition in the biquinary system is not too difficult, because the successor relationship discussed earlier in connection with addition is defined simply as a shifting to the left of the binary bit. Thus, in adding 1 to 0, the right-hand binary bit moves from the 0 position to the 1 position. In adding 1 to 1, the binary bit moves from the 1 position to the 2 position, and so forth. Adding 1 to 4 moves the binary bit from 4 to 0 and the quinary bit from 0 to 5. A similar condition applies in adding 1 to 9. The binary bit moves from the 4 to the 0 position; the quinary bit moves from the 5 to 0 position and a carry is created.

The **qui-binary** system is similar in principle to the biquinary system. The weights used are 8, 6, 4, 2, 0/1, 0.

8.7. ALPHABETICAL CODING

Computers that handle primarily arithmetic problems, such as the Univac® 1101 or 1103 or the IBM 704, do not have any need to handle letter-symbol information. In the business world, however, dealings are between people or organizations and concern goods. People, organizations, and goods all have names; hence they require the use of alphabetical symbols. A business computer is as concerned with operations upon alphabetical data—editing, translating, manipulating, and storing—as well as arithmetic; sometimes the business computer does little or no arithmetic.

When information may consist of both numbers and letters, it is sometimes called **alphanumeric** (or **alphameric**) information; business computers almost always handle alphanumeric information. How is it coded?

Double-Numeric Alphanumeric Coding

In a binary-coded decimal computer a simple approach to coding is to use two decimal digits to code letters. This system is used in the Datatron 205. Here the letter b is represented by the number 61, c is represented by 62, and so forth. When numbers are to be used, they too must be coded in this double digit system: 0 is coded as 40, 1 is coded as 41, and so forth.

The Datatron 205 uses the NBCD system. To code a letter into machine language we do a double conversion:

$$b = 61 = 01100001$$

If an odd-parity bit is included so that there are five bits per digit we have

$$b = 61 = 1011000001$$

The double-numeric coding is rather inefficient—ten bits offer 1024 combinations—of these, only 36 (26 letters and ten digits) or a few more (for \$, @, and so forth) are actually used. But the efficiency is traded for simplicity in logical design and conservation of parts. This may result in a somewhat cheaper machine with a longer operating time.

Multiple-Bit Alphanumeric Coding

To encode 36 symbols we find that six bits are a minimum. Five bits offer 32 combinations—not enough; six bits offer 64 combinations—more than adequate.

Figure 8.7 shows the Univac® code. The table is arranged according to a four-by-sixteen array. The "four" direction is a two-bit portion of the six-bit code called the *zone*: the other four bits follow the XS3 pattern. For the zone *00* the XS3 code yields the decimal digits, except in the cases of the forbidden codes. Thus

$$000110 = 0110(\text{XS3}) = 3$$

The alphabetical sequence of letters follows the number sequence in the XS3 code in the increasing zone combinations so that, in terms of binary representations,

$$0 < 1 < 2 < \ldots < A < B < \ldots < Y < Z$$

This follows since

$$000011 \ (0) \ < \ 000100 \ (2) \ < \ \ldots \ < \ 010100 \ (A) \ < \ 010101 \ (B) \ < \ \ldots \ <$$
$$111100 \ (Z)$$

This construction permits comparison of alphabetical information, necessary when alphabetical information is to be in order in listing (then CONWAY < COOK < COOLEY, and so on).

XS3 \ Zone	0000	0001	0010	0011	0100	0101	0110	0111	1000	1001	1010	1011	1100	1101	1110	1111
00	O Ignore	Space	—	0	1	2	3	4	5	6	7	8	9	'	&	(
01	Carriage return	,	•	;	A	B	C	D	E	F	G	H	I	#	¢	@
10	Tab	//	I	)	J	K	L	M	N	O	P	Q	R	/	*	?
11	Ɛ	⌐	:	+	/	S	T	U	V	W	X	Y	Ƶ	%	=	Delete

FIGURE 8.7. The six-bit Univac® code.

Multiple-Bit Coding with a Parity Bit

To adapt the six-bit code for error detection during data transversion, one extra bit is necessary. A seven-bit code is easily produced in which all (English) letters and numerals and many symbols ($, %, and so forth) are included and which has error-detection properties.

The Polyvac

But for this subsection, the observant reader would discover an apparent inconsistency in the Polyvac description. The Polyvac is said to use a four-bit parallel-bit serial-character code structure. Yet the programming code uses letters for the commands—how can this be?

We might allow this inconsistency in a machine existing solely to explain computer principles and programming. However, if we wish to remedy it we might change the Polyvac to a seven-bit code machine; or we might change the instruction code. Neither of these is appealing. But there is an approach that is consistent, and a practical possibility. The instruction code is really an illusory one—there are keys on the input equipment for the alphabet. However, these keys do not enter a letter code; they enter a digit equivalent. Thus the programmer codes the add order as ADD but when the operator enters this into the keyboard, the result is NBCD coded 144 or 000101000100. Similarly, subtract is entered as SUB, but this results in NBCD 132, or 000100110010, and so forth.

PROBLEMS

1. Write these numbers

$$3692581470, \quad 7418529630, \quad 0918273645$$

in the following codes:

(a) NBCD   (b) XS3   (c) 2421
(d) 742 −1   (e) two-out-of-five   (f) biquinary

2. Do this problem

$$
\begin{array}{r}
3989 \\
+22912 \\
\hline
\end{array}
$$

in these codes:

(a) NBCD   (b) XS3

3. How many are bits required in the natural binary code to represent numbers up to:

(a) 10^6 (b) $5 \cdot 10^7$ (c) 10^9

4. How many decimal numbers can be represented with

(a) 20 bits   (b) 36 bits   (c) 40 bits

5. Encode into NBCD, XS3, two-out-of-five, 2421, 742 −1, the following numbers:

(a) 95   (b) 371   (c) 4238   (d) 78137   (e) −1932

6. Find in NBCD and XS3

(a) $a + b$ (b) $a + c$ (c) $b + c$
(d) $a + d$ (e) $b + d$ (f) $c + d$

7. Develop the rules for addition in the 5421 code. This code is the modified biquinary code and digits five or greater contain a five bit.

8. Do Problem 6 for the 5421 code.

9. What is natural binary coded octal (NBCO)? Code $(371)_8$ in NBCO. Code $(1000)_{10}$, $(1381)_{10}$ and $(100101111)_2$, into NBCO.

10. Show that NBCO is identical with natural binary. Convert $(371)_8$ to $(\quad)_2$.

11. Show how subtraction is done by complementation and addition in the base 8. Do by this method:

$$
\begin{array}{r}
3271 \\
-2317 \\
\hline
\end{array}_8
$$

12. Put "Conway," "Cook," and "Cooley" into the Univac® code. How does this yield an alphabetical order?

N I N E

LOGIC

9.1. INTRODUCTION

The term *logic* as applied to the computer describes the interrelation among the primary building blocks of the computer. It also applies to the relationship among entities other than those used in a computer. Since the logic connecting the functional units of the computer is similar to the logic applying to other entities, it might be well to discuss logic more generally.

The aim we will keep in mind is an understanding of the interrelation of the elementary units for the performance of arithmetic, especially, as well as the editing and transportation of information.

Entities

Various statements may be made about reality as it exists in our environment. The relationship that exists among these statements and their similarity to reality is referred to in a philosophical sense as *logic*. The validation of propositions compounded from simple statements rests upon the words connecting the statements. These words are called **logical connectives.** One such logic connective is "and." The proposition resulting from the combination of two simple statements and the connective "and" is valid only when each of the original simple statements is valid.

123

A table of logical connectives and symbols used for them in both symbolic logic and its computer equivalent, Boolean algebra, appears as Table 9.1.1.

TABLE 9.1.1   LOGICAL TERMS AND SYMBOLS

Language term	Mathematical Logic Equivalent	Boolean
and	&,	· (dot)
or	V,	+
not	− (bar), ′ (prime)	− (bar)
neither	↓	
if ... then ...	⊃	
if and only if ... then	≡	

Take the two simple statements, "John is here," and, "Mary is here." The proposition obtained from combining these two statements and the logical connective "and" is, "John is here and Mary is here." This proposition is true only when both the statements "John is here" and "Mary is here" are true. That is, the statement is true only when both John and Mary are here. This first interpretation of logic deals with statements and logical connectives.

Letter Symbols

For each of the statements discussed above, we may substitute a **letter symbol.** We can also develop a vocabulary of symbols for the connectives. If A stands for "John is here," B stands for "Mary is here," and "&" stands for the logical connective "and," then the proposition compounded from these three is written simply as A & B. Since all compound propositions can be reduced by this method into symbolic propositions, this kind of logic is referred to as **symbolic logic.**

Truth Values

Propositions in symbolic form can be tested for validity by substituting truth values for statements. A statement has a **truth value** 1 when it is true and a truth value 0 when it is false. Many books have been written about the concept of truth. We will refrain from digressing on this topic and merely remind the reader that an intuitive interpretation of this word is satisfactory. Here a statement will be said to be true when it corresponds to reality (whatever that means).

A method or set of rules is devised for dealing with truth value of statements using 1's and 0's to represent these truth values. The set of rules applying to these statements and the manufacture of the statements themselves is covered by the study called **Boolean algebra.**

Boolean algebra contains rules for handling the truth values concerning the connective "and":

$$1 \,\&\, 1 = 1 \quad \text{or} \quad 1 \cdot 1 = 1 \qquad 0 \,\&\, 1 = 0 \quad \text{or} \quad 0 \cdot 1 = 0$$
$$1 \,\&\, 0 = 0 \quad \text{or} \quad 1 \cdot 0 = 0 \qquad 0 \,\&\, 0 = 0 \quad \text{or} \quad 0 \cdot 0 = 0$$

Notice the similarity between the "$\&$" and algebraic multiplication. The proponents of Boolean algebra prefer the use of algebraic symbols to logical symbols.

A summary of the three forms of connectives—language, symbolic, and Boolean—is contained in Table 9.1.1.

Truth Tables

Another way of specifying or defining the logical connectives is to construct a truth table. One column of the **truth table** is assigned to each of

TABLE 9.1.2 TRUTH TABLE FOR $\&$

A	B	$A \,\&\, B$
0	0	0
0	1	0
1	0	0
1	1	1

TABLE 9.1.3 TRUTH TABLE FOR $\vee$

A	B	$A \vee B$
0	0	0
0	1	1
1	0	1
1	1	1

the statements constituting the logical proposition, and the last column is assigned to the compounded proposition. A value, 1 or 0, is given to each statement and the resulting truth value of the proposition appears in the last column. Truth tables for three connectives appear as Tables 9.1.2, 9.1.3, and 9.1.4. The first entry in the "and" table shows that when A is false ($A = 0$) and B is false ($B = 0$), then the statement $A \,\&\, B$ is false ($A \,\&\, B = 0$).

TABLE 9.1.4 TRUTH TABLE FOR "NOT"

A	$\bar{A}$
0	1
1	0

Pulses √

Consider two electrical wires entering a box as in Figure 9.1.1. Let each of these wires have a voltage which is either below or above fixed level E. When the voltage on a wire is below the level E, it will be assigned the value 0; when it is above the level E, it will be assigned the value 1. The set of voltages on the input wires and the associated voltages on the output wire are then similar to the truth values discussed above.

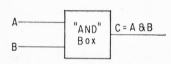

FIGURE 9.1.1. The "and" box.

If the output of the box is determined by one of the truth tables, Table 9.1.2, 9.1.3, or 9.1.4, then this box can be said to act in a manner similar to that logical connective.

Let us examine the "and" circuit box of Figure 9.1.1. Suppose the voltages on the incoming wires A and B are as shown in Figure 9.1.2. We are interested in the voltages on these lines at times t_1, t_2, t_3, and t_4. These are the bit times referred to in Chapter 2. At time t_1 both the A and B wires have pulses representing values of 1 on them. To conform to the truth table for the logical function "and" of Figure 9.1.2, the output line C must also have a 1 on it at time t_1 (for $C = A$ & B.) Note that the other three combinations of 1's and 0's for the presence or absence of pulses at A or B at the times t_2, t_3, and t_4 of Figure 9.1.2 correspond to the other

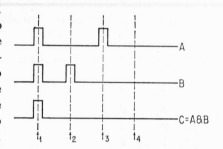

FIGURE 9.1.2. Voltages which might appear on the wires A, B, and C of Figure 9.1.1.

entries in the truth table for &; the result C is 0 in all three cases (for $C = A$ & B.)

The &-gate

The &-block can be used like a switch: one signal, called an "enabling voltage" or "gating voltage," is applied to the &-block to "throw the switch"; a pulse on the other line can pass through the block only if the enabling voltage is present, that is, if the switch is thrown; if a signal is absent at the gating input, no pulse at the other input can pass through the &-block.

The Mixer ✕

The V-block is a circuit that simulates the "or" function and duplicates the "or" truth table; for one or more inputs an output is produced. The V-block acts very much like a mixer except that it is digital. It produces a voltage on the output line corresponding to the largest input (presumably, they are only 0's or 1's).

Basic Logical Block Symbols

Other "boxes" can be constructed producing, for binary inputs (1 or 0), outputs that are a logical function of the input. And this function

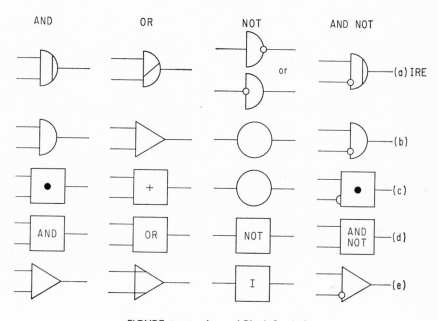

FIGURE 9.1.3. Logical Block Symbols.

corresponds exactly to the truth table of one of our logical connectives. Assemblies of these primary boxes or blocks can be made to manipulate voltages in such a fashion as to perform our editing and arithmetic. It is very useful to have a separate symbol for each basic logical function which can be realized in hardware. The symbol should be unique and immediately identifiable regardless of its orientation on a block diagram. It should also be possible to determine the function purely from the geometrical consideration rather than from information written in the block.

In addition, the shape of the block should convey which of the lines carries the input and which the output signals so that arrowheads can be eliminated.

The D symbols proposed by IRE Subcommittee 21.3 on Symbols fulfill the above qualifications. The proposed IRE symbols, which will be used throughout this book, are shown on line (a). Other sets of symbols which the reader may encounter elsewhere are found in Figure 9.1.3, lines (b) through (e). For the IRE D-symbols the lower limit of the ratio of the height—flat side or chord—to the width is 2 (a semicircle); there is no upper limit. The input lines are always indicated by lines entering the D normal to the flat side; the output is a line emerging opposite the flat side and approximately normal to it. The &-function is indicated by drawing a line parallel to the flat side about 2/3 the width away from the flat side. The $\lor$ function requires that a line oblique to the flat side be drawn within the D from the flat side to the side opposite. The "not" function is indicated by placing a little circle either at the intersection of the input line and the D or at the intersection of the output line and the D.

You see that there is plenty of room in the D to put numbering or identifying information. An &, $\lor$, or "not" block numbered 6 would be indicated in our discussions respectively by &6, $\lor$6, or $\bar{6}$.

9.2. FUNDAMENTAL POSTULATES

There are both theorems and postulates that may be used in manipulating logical entities. Some of them stem from the properties of the entities and the connectives; others are derived from these properties by simple steps.

Hereafter in this section the Boolean notation of "$A + B$" for "$A \lor B$" or "A or B," and "$A \cdot B$" or simply "AB" for "$A \& B$" or "A and B" will be used because of its prevalence in the computer field and its brevity in writing.

The first two identities to be noted are

$$A + A = A \tag{9.2.1}$$

and
$$AA = A \tag{9.2.2}$$

These identities are verified by examining the truth tables for $A + B$ and AB. "And" and "or" are defined by the truth tables and the properties (9.2.1) and (9.2.2) are fundamental to these definitions. Thus, $A + A$ is true when A is true, and $A + A$ is false when A is false, so that $A + A$ and A are identical; similarly, AA is true when A is true, and AA is false when A is false, so that AA is identical with A.

Commutativity

The meaning of "and" and "or" does not depend upon the sequence of the entities that they connect. This is stated as

$$A + B = B + A \tag{9.2.3}$$

and
$$A \cdot B = B \cdot A \text{ (or } AB = BA) \tag{9.2.4}$$

This relationship (9.2.3) can be shown to hold by examining the truth table for "or" in both cases under consideration. Notice that when the two entries A and B are interchanged, the truth table is unaffected. Similarly, the truth table—or (9.2.4)—for the "and" function is the same if the entries for A and B are reversed—the "and" function is true only when both statements connected by "and" are true regardless of which comes first.

Associativity

In relating several entities by using the same connective, it does not matter how they are grouped. Thus

$$(A + B) + C = A + (B + C) \tag{9.2.5}$$

$$(AB)C = A(BC) \tag{9.2.6}$$

This can be verified by making one truth table to represent the relationships found on each side of the two above equations. The *results*—final column of both truth tables—are identical.

Another way to look at it is that the "or" relationship is true when *one or more* of the statements connected by *or* are true. Thus, the "or" relationship is not affected by how the terms it connects are grouped together. Similarly, the "and" relationship is true only when *all* the statements connected by "*and*" are true, so that it too is not affected by the grouping of the terms.

Distributivity

When "and" and "or" are used together in the same proposition these two groupings are equivalent,

$$A(B + C) = AB + AC \tag{9.2.7}$$

$$A + BC = (A + B)(A + C) \tag{9.2.8}$$

These two identities may be demonstrated by constructing a truth table for each side of the " = " and determining that the last columns of these tables are the same. This was done for (9.2.7) in Table 9.2.1. As an exercise the reader should verify (9.2.8) in the same fashion.

TABLE 9.2.1 Verification of $A(B + C) = AB + AC$ using Truth Tables

A	B	C	$B + C$	$A(B + C)$	AB	AC	$AB + AC$
0	0	0	0	0	0	0	0
0	0	1	1	0	0	0	0
0	1	0	1	0	0	0	0
0	1	1	1	0	0	0	0
1	0	0	0	0	0	0	0
1	0	1	1	1	0	1	1
1	1	0	1	1	1	0	1
1	1	1	1	1	1	1	1

Same

"Null" and "All" Elements

It is handy to have a concept that stands for *all* definable propositions. This is the totality of all true propositions. I is the symbol for such a class and always has the truth value 1. It is equivalent to the "1" used by other authors for the *all* element. I is used here to avoid confusion with the truth value, 1. Two rules for the use of the *all* element I are

$$A + I = I \qquad (9.2.9)$$

which means, "A or *anything* is equivalent to *anything*,"

and
$$AI = A \qquad (9.2.10)$$

which means, "A and 'anything' is equivalent to just A."

Similarly the *null* class is one which contains no admissible or true elements and hence always has the truth value 0. Where some authors might use 0, the symbol $\wedge$ is used here to avoid confusion with the truth value 0. Two identities involving the null element are

$$A + \wedge = A \qquad (9.2.11)$$

which means, "A or *nothing* is the same as A,"

and
$$A \wedge = \wedge \qquad (9.2.12)$$

which means "A and *nothing* are true is the same as *nothing* is true."

"Not"

The truth table for the *not* function appears in Table 9.1.4. Three rules for its use are

$$A + \bar{A} = I \tag{9.2.13}$$

which says ,"either A or not A is always true." We may also say A and $\bar{A}$ are logical complements of each other. This is the assumption of Aristotle: logical propositions and their denial form mutually exclusive and exhaustive classes. This is undeniably true for computer logic although it does not satisfy the more sophisticated philosophers.

Also

$$A\bar{A} = \wedge \tag{9.2.14}$$

says "both A and not A at the same time are impossible."

$$\bar{\bar{A}} = A \tag{9.2.15}$$

says "not-not-A is the same as A."

Simplification of Logical Statements

To indicate how the above rules are used, consider the expression $(P + Q)(P + R)$. First let us use the distributivity relation of (9.2.7) with $P + Q$ for $B + C$ and $P + R$ for A. Then

$$(P + Q)(P + R) = P(P + R) + Q(P + R) \tag{9.2.16}$$

Applying (9.2.7) again to each of the terms of (9.2.16) we have

$$(P + Q)(P + R) = PP + PR + QP + QR \tag{9.2.17}$$

The first three terms of the right side of (9.2.17) are then grouped together. Apply (9.2.7) in reverse this time, and (9.2.17) yields

$$(P + Q)(P + R) = P(I + R + Q) + QR \tag{9.2.18}$$

Applying (9.2.9) to the first term of (9.2.18) we have

$$(I + R + Q) = I \tag{9.2.19}$$

and by (9.2.10),

$$PI + QR = P + QR \tag{9.2.20}$$

so that

$$(P + Q)(P + R) = P + QR \tag{9.2.21}$$

This procedure might be considered a derivation of the distributivity relation of (9.2.8).

9.3. LOGICAL PROPOSITIONS

It is the purpose of this section to find means for simplifying existing logical expressions and for constructing new expressions to fulfill given conditions. This is done by using pictorial representations such as the Venn diagram, tabular representations such as the Veitch diagram, and algebraic manipulations such as De Morgan's laws.

Venn Diagrams

Geometric means may be used to convey the principles of logic. A rectangle may be used to represent all the acceptable statements, I. The

FIGURE 9.3.1. Venn diagram for proposition A.

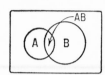

FIGURE 9.3.2. Venn diagram of proposition AB.

statements of a given kind, A, can be shown as a circular or other area. Statements which are not of the same type as A are what is left when the area A is removed from the rectangle. In Figure 9.3.1 the area inside the circle represents A and that outside represents $\bar{A}$.

Two statement types, A and B, are shown in Figure 9.3.2. The area which is in both the A circle and the B circle represents AB; the area within either the A or B circle represents $A + B$; the area outside both circles is $\overline{A + B}$. Now let us see an application of this simplification.

De Morgan's Laws

These laws are stated as

$$\overline{AB} = \bar{A} + \bar{B} \qquad (9.3.1)$$

and
$$\overline{A + B} = \bar{A}\bar{B} \qquad (9.3.2)$$

Reverting to our other notation for clarification, notice that $\overline{AB}$ means $\overline{(A \ \& \ B)}$ and that $\bar{A}\bar{B}$ means $\bar{A} \ \& \ \bar{B}$. Hence it should be remembered that the expressions $\overline{AB}$ and $\bar{A}\bar{B}$ are quite different.

De Morgan's laws may be derived with Boolean algebra from the earlier postulates, but we shall be content to demonstrate them using the Venn diagrams of the previous paragraphs.

Refer again to Figure 9.3.2 and notice the crescent area, all the area outside the crescent represents $\overline{AB}$. This is what is left when AB, the unsectioned area, is removed from the whole, I. In Figure 9.3.3 the vertically striped area is $\bar{A}$; in Figure 9.3.4 the horizontally striped area is $\bar{B}$. These

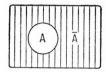

FIGURE 9.3.3. Venn diagram of proposition $\overline{A}$.

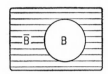

FIGURE 9.3.4. Venn diagram of proposition $\overline{B}$.

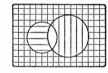

FIGURE 9.3.5. Venn diagram of proposition $\overline{A} + \overline{B}$.

are superimposed in Figure 9.3.5; the area which is striped either horizontally or vertically is $\bar{A} + \bar{B}$. This corresponds exactly to $\overline{AB}$ of Figure 9.3.2.

The demonstration of (9.3.2) by Venn diagrams is left to the reader as an exercise.

Let's take a simple example of this principle. Let I refer to the class of people; let A represent all those who are rich; let B represent all those who are males. AB then represents all the rich men; $A\bar{B}$ represents rich women; $\bar{A}B$ represents poor men; and $\bar{A}\bar{B}$ represents poor women.

$A + B$ then represents all those people who are either rich or male or both. Notice that $\overline{A + B}$ represents all those who are not (rich or male, or both); this is the same as $\bar{A}\bar{B}$ = poor women. In a similar vein $\overline{AB}$ represents all those who are not rich men; this is identical with $\bar{A} + \bar{B}$, all those who are either poor or are women or both.

9.4. BLOCKS AND HARDWARE

Compound Functions

Blocks symbols may be used to indicate compound functions similar to those discussed above if modifications are added to the notation.

INHIBIT. When an L touching the flat side is placed on an input line to the D figure, it indicates that a voltage on that line inhibits or blocks the performance indicated by the symbol. Figure 9.4(a) shows the inhibit added to an &-gate. The output of this block is $A \& B \& \bar{X}$. That is, there is an output only when both A and B are present and X is absent.

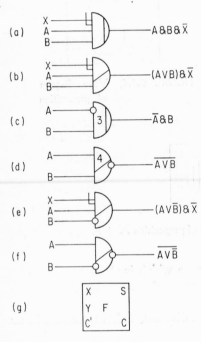

(a)

(b)

(c)

(d)

(e)

(f)

(g)

FIGURE 9.4. Compound logical symbols.

In Figure 9.4(b) the line labeled X inhibits the mixing function. The output from this block is $(A \lor B) \& \bar{X}$. There is an output from this block when either A or B or both are present but X is absent.

NOT COMBINATIONS. The circle can be added to the gate or mixer to invert an input or output. In Figure 9.4(c) the A input has a circle about it which inverts that input. The output of this block is therefore $\bar{A} \& B$. Since an input signal A prevents *any* output, it is often said that A is the inhibit input of $\&'3$. Similarly, in Figure 9.4(d) the circle around the output causes the output of the mixer to be inverted. The output of this mixer is then $\overline{A \lor B}$. The block in Figure 9.4(c) is referred to as $\&'3$ (as above) to indicate an &-circuit with which an inverter (or inhibit) is associated; the symbol in 9.4(d) is referred to as $\lor'4$ where, again, the prime indicates the presence of an inverter or inhibit.

BLOCKS WITH BOTH **inhibit** AND **not**. In Figures 9.4(e) and 9.4(f) are shown symbols which incorporate both the inhibit and not function or include two not functions. The reader can verify these diagrams.

Functional Symbols

Very often *combinations* of logical elements will recur. To facilitate description, these **functional units** will be given a unique symbol. This symbol is usually a *rectangle* into which a designation letter has been inserted. The symbol for the full adder, for instance, which is discussed in detail in the next chapter, is found in Figure 9.4(g). This is a rectangle with an F in it to show that it has the function of a full adder. The block has three inputs and two outputs which are unique to it, with which we will become familiar in the next chapter.

Hardware

It is necessary to construct **hardware,** the circuitry and components which carry out electronically the function represented by these pictorial

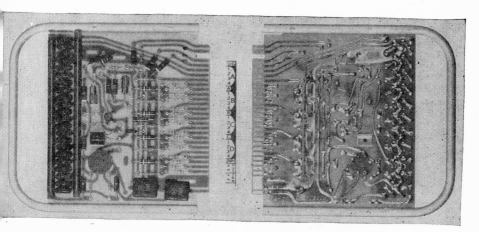

FIGURE 9.4.1.   Printed Circuit Package of four 4-input &'s mixed by a 4-input V.   Courtesy of Computer Control Company, Inc.

symbols. In doing this it is not possible to equate the quantity of hardware required for any single block symbol. The number of components for a given symbol increases with the number of inputs and the number of outputs. Also, in general, each *invert* and *inhibit* function adds to the components required to realize the given block.

A typical printed-circuit package consisting of four four-input &'s whose outputs are mixed in a four-input mixer is shown in Figure 9.4.1.

9.5.   LOGICAL SIMPLIFICATION

Definition

To **simplify** a logical configuration means to reduce its complexity or remove logical blocks without changing the intent or output of the configuration. But simplification really depends on the kind of logic employed and the design of each logical element. In general, reduction of the number of terms in a Boolean algebra equation or the number of blocks in a logical configuration amounts to simplification, although this is not always so.

Consider the equation $A = AI = A(B + \bar{B}) = AB + A\bar{B}$. Hence, A is logically equivalent to $AB + A\bar{B}$. Obviously in this case the single term is simpler than the expression $AB + A\bar{B}$. On the other hand, consider the equality resulting from De Morgan's law $A + B = \overline{\bar{A}\bar{B}}$. Depending on the logical system involved, either one of these may be viewed as simpler than the other.

Since simplification is a function of system design, our methodology will be to develop a means for converting from one logical expression to another, or alternately, to present a number of equivalent logical expressions. The decision as to which of these expressions is simpler can then be determined from the system concept. If there is no system criterion present, the expression requiring the least number of terms will be considered the simplest.

As an example of the flexibility demanded of the concept of simplicity, consider the design of a computer using printed-circuit component cards of a fixed design. Such a card might, for instance, contain 3 &'s of 3 inputs each and 3 V's of 6 inputs each. A logical simplification which replaced 3 2-input &'s (requiring 3 3-input &'s on the card) with 1 6-input V would obviously provide a substantial component saving in view of the existing card specification. This would not be apparent simply from an examination of the logical equations without regard to the engineering restraints.

Karnaugh Maps and Venn Diagrams

The Venn diagram is a means for simplifying logical expressions. An example for a single variable appears in Figure 9.5.1. The universe of possibilities I is divided into two sets by the line a. These two sets are labeled A and $\bar{A}$ and represent a partition according to a single variable or quality A.

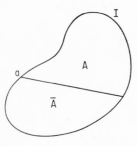

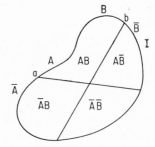

FIGURE 9.5.1. Single variable Venn diagram.

FIGURE 9.5.2. Two variable Venn diagram.

Consider now the case of two variables—the Venn diagram in Figure 9.5.2 shows a further partition of the diagram of Figure 9.5.1 by the line b. Thus b further divides the universe of possibilities I already partitioned by the line a. The area on one side of line a is now cut by the line b into two parts AB and $A\bar{B}$; similarly, the area on the other side of a has been divided by the line b into the two components $\bar{A}B$ and $\bar{A}\bar{B}$.

There is no reason why the area in the Venn diagram must be irregular. If a square is used for the area representing I, Figure 9.5.3 results. The lines a and b cut the square into four subsquares which correspond

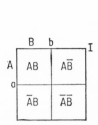

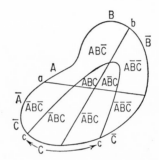

FIGURE 9.5.3. Two variable   FIGURE 9.5.4. Three variable
          Karnaugh map.   Venn diagram.

exactly to the areas delineated in Figure 9.5.2. These two diagrams are equivalent; in fact, the mathematician calls these two diagrams topologically equivalent.

Notice in either of the two diagrams that adjacent areas play an interesting role. Examine any two areas in one of these figures. Notice first that the expression for the combination of two simple areas is found by connecting their symbolic representation by $+$ ($\lor$, or). Thus, when the areas labeled $\bar{A}\bar{B}$ and $A\bar{B}$ of Figure 9.5.3 are added, the result is $\bar{A}\bar{B} + A\bar{B}$. Next, notice that a variable may be dropped or factored from the expression representing this combination of these two areas.

Take, for instance, the two areas in Figure 9.5.3 on the right-hand side of line b. The expression for the combination of these two areas is $A\bar{B} + \bar{A}\bar{B}$. This is obviously equivalent to simply $\bar{B}$. Well, of course this is true, because before the line a was inserted into the figure, the line b defined the area on the right side of b as $\bar{B}$.

Let us add another variable to the map. In Figure 9.5.4, line c divides the area defined by I into twice as many areas as there were previously. It is a little more difficult to represent the irregular area of Figure 9.5.4 in a systematic form.

The diagram of Figure 9.5.5 is topologically equivalent to that of Figure 9.5.4. A little imagination must be used to make this diagram useful. The line a in Figure 9.5.5 clearly cuts the area I in half. The line b passes vertically through the center of the figure, but this line must also be associated with the two outside vertical edges. To imagine this more clearly, line b has been continued as a dashed line in the figure so that it connects the lines on the outer vertical edges of the figure.

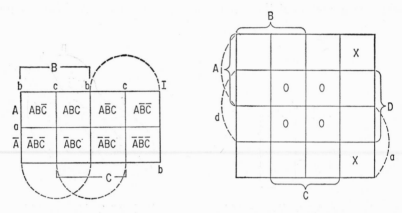

FIGURE 9.5.5. Three variable Karnaugh map.

FIGURE 9.5.6. Four variable Karnaugh map with two entries, $\overline{B}\overline{C}\overline{D}(X)$ and $CD(O)$.

Line c is similarly defined in the figure by a connecting dashed line. The reason that we must go to these lengths to define these boundaries is so that we may associate the proper squares together as being adjacent. It is immediately clear that the two squares on the left-hand side of the figure are adjacent to each other: they represent the expression $AB\bar{C} + \bar{A}B\bar{C}$, which is hence simplified to $B\bar{C}$. However, we should associate the boxes $AB\bar{C}$ and $A\bar{B}\bar{C}$ together. This is pictorially presented, since we have associated the left-hand side and the right-hand side of the areas with line b. Therefore, the two boxes $AB\bar{C}$ and $A\bar{B}\bar{C}$ lie on "opposite" sides of the line b. This is seen to be true because the expression $AB\bar{C} + A\bar{B}\bar{C}$ simplifies to $A\bar{C}$. Again notice in Figure 9.5.4 that the areas ABC and $A\bar{B}C$ are adjacent, confirming the legitimacy of our presentation.

To complicate matters further, let us consider a line d which cuts each of the eight boxes of Figure 9.5.5 as in Figure 9.5.6, forming a total of sixteen boxes. This transforms Figure 9.5.5 into the conventional Karnaugh diagram for four variables of Figure 9.5.6. Here again the bounding lines which are associated together are connected by dashed lines.

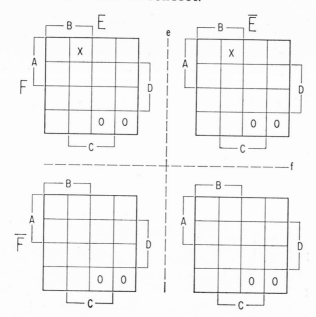

FIGURE 9.5.7.   Six variable Karnaugh map with two entries, ABCD̄F(X) and ĀB̄D(O).

The simple rule to remember is that any two boxes adjacent within the diagram are candidates for simplification, as are any two boxes at opposite extremes of the square. In Figure 9.5.6 the two boxes with X's in them represent the terms $A\bar{B}\bar{C}\bar{D}$ and $\bar{A}\bar{B}\bar{C}\bar{D}$. The area defined by these two boxes can hence be simplified to the expression $\bar{B}\bar{C}\bar{D}$. The four mutually adjacent boxes in the center of Figure 9.5.6, each of which has an O in it, can be double simplified to CD (check me!).

Functions of five, six, seven, and eight variables can be simplified by the use of multiple Karnaugh maps. In Figure 9.5.7 is shown a quadruple Karnaugh map for six variables. The concept of adjacency must be broadened here so that squares in corresponding positions in different maps are considered to be adjacent. Thus, the two boxes with X's in them in Figure 9.5.7 simplify to the term $ABC\bar{D}F$; the eight boxes with O's in them simplify to $\bar{A}\bar{B}\bar{D}$.

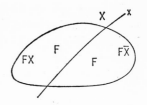

FIGURE 9.5.8. Illustrating simplification by adjacency for Karnaugh maps.

The principle of adjacency can be visualized by the simple diagram of Figure 9.5.8. The area F is cut by the line x. On one side of this line is found the area FX and on the other side $F\bar{X}$. Taken together these two pieces form $FX + F\bar{X} = F$. The two areas are adjacent now; before the line x was drawn, the area F was uncut. In combining the areas on either side of the line x, we reform the area F and cause the desired simplification.

How to Use the Karnaugh Map

Suppose that we have a function of three variables such as $AB + \bar{A}BC$. We will make a Karnaugh map of three variables using the layout of Figure 9.5.5. Before simplification can be done we must fill in areas corresponding to each term of our function. We consider the function term by term and expand it into the "sum" of terms, each term being the "product" of exactly three variables. Here "sum" and "product" mean "or" and "and." For instance, the first term of our example is AB. But AB contains only two variables. To expand AB into terms composed of exactly three variables connected by &'s we proceed as follows:

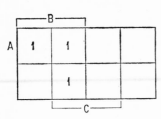

FIGURE 9.5.9. Using the Karnaugh map to simplify AB + $\overline{A}$BC.

$$AB = ABI = AB(C + \bar{C}) = ABC + AB\bar{C}$$

There are boxes in our Karnaugh map which represent both ABC and $AB\bar{C}$. We place a 1 in each of those boxes, as in Figure 9.5.9. Next we fill in a 1 in our Karnaugh map corresponding to the term $\bar{A}BC$. Our map is now complete for $AB + \bar{A}BC$.

To simplify we look for adjacencies. Note that there are two horizontal 1's which are adjacent and two vertical which are adjacent. The horizontal 1's have the line c passing through them and hence the reduced expression will not contain the variable C. These two boxes simplify to AB. The vertical boxes have the line a passing through them and so the variable A may be eliminated between them. These two boxes simplify to BC. (Note: lines are designated as per Figure 9.5.5.)

The whole map simplifies to $AB + BC$. The fact that one box, namely ABC, was combined into both terms is quite acceptable.

9.6. EXAMPLES

Symbolic Realization in Logical Elements

Let us again consider one of De Morgan's laws (9.3.1). The left side $\overline{AB}$ can be realized in blocks as Figure 9.6.1; the right side, $\bar{A} + \bar{B}$ is realized with the block composition of Figure 9.6.2. Suppose now we take a train of pulses as the inputs A and B and see what the outputs are from each construction. This was done in Figure 9.6.3. Notice that the two

FIGURE 9.6.1.   Logical block for $\overline{AB}$.   FIGURE 9.6.2.   Logical block for $\overline{A} + \overline{B}$.

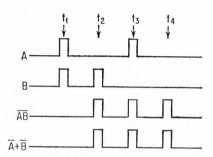

FIGURE 9.6.3.   Inputs and outputs for figures 9.6.1. and 9.6.2.

trains used for A and B exhaust the possibilities for combinations of inputs. The results for $\overline{AB}$ and $\bar{A} + \bar{B}$ are identical as they should be.

Boolean Algebra Reduction

There may be reasons for preferring one type of logical expression to another, such as a lower cost or more reliable operation for a given logical block. Hence it is necessary to show the equivalence of logical expressions. As an exercise of this nature, we shall show that

$$\overline{AB + BC + CA} = \bar{A}\bar{B} + \bar{B}\bar{C} + \bar{C}\bar{A}$$

First group the terms,

$$\overline{AB + BC + CA} = \overline{(AB + BC) + CA} \qquad (9.6.1)$$

Then by (9.3.2) $\qquad\qquad\qquad = \overline{AB + BC}\ \overline{CA} \qquad (9.6.2)$

where the overhead bar acts as parentheses. Next, using (9.3.2) again

$$\overline{AB + BC + CA} = \overline{AB}\ \overline{BC}\ \overline{CA} \qquad (9.6.3)$$

Now with (9.3.1) applied to each term, $\overline{AB}$, $\overline{BC}$, and $\overline{CA}$,

$$\overline{AB + BC + CA} = (\bar{A} + \bar{B})(\bar{B} + \bar{C})(\bar{C} + \bar{A}) \qquad (9.6.4)$$

and with distributivity (9.2.5), (9.2.6)

$$\overline{AB + BC + CA} = (\bar{A}\bar{B} + \bar{A}\bar{C} + \bar{B}\bar{B} + \bar{B}\bar{C})(\bar{C} + \bar{A}) \quad (9.6.5)$$

But since $\bar{B}\bar{B} = \bar{B} = \bar{B}I$, then

$$\bar{A}\bar{B} + \bar{A}\bar{C} + \bar{B}\bar{B} + \bar{B}\bar{C} = \bar{A}\bar{B} + \bar{A}\bar{C} + \bar{B}(I + \bar{C}) \quad (9.6.6)$$

$$= \bar{A}\bar{B} + \bar{A}\bar{C} + \bar{B} \quad (9.6.7)$$

$$= \bar{A}\bar{C} + \bar{B} + \bar{A}\bar{B} \quad (9.6.8)$$

$$= \bar{A}\bar{C} + \bar{B}(I + \bar{A})$$

$$= \bar{A}\bar{C} + \bar{B} \quad (9.6.9)$$

So that (9.6.5) becomes

$$\overline{AB + BC + CA} = (\bar{A}\bar{C} + \bar{B})(\bar{C} + \bar{A}) \quad (9.6.10)$$

and with distributivity

$$= \bar{A}(\bar{A}\bar{C} + \bar{B}) + \bar{C}(\bar{A}\bar{C} + \bar{B}) \quad (9.6.11)$$

$$= \bar{A}\bar{C} + \bar{A}\bar{B} + \bar{A}\bar{C} + \bar{C}\bar{B} \quad (9.6.12)$$

$$= \bar{A}\bar{C} + \bar{A}\bar{B} + \bar{C}\bar{B} \quad (9.6.13)$$

9.7. *Nor* LOGIC

In the past few years a logical element which has good possibilities of vying for the title of the universal element has gained popularity. The reason is that it has been realizable in a circuit proved to be reliable yet simple. This is the *nor* element. The logical symbol for *nor* is "$\downarrow$" and it is pronounced "pierce," since it was named after the philosopher, C. S. Pierce. The statement, "$A \downarrow B$" (A pierce B) is true only when *both* A and B are *false* as is shown by the truth table, Table 9.7.1. The

TABLE 9.7.1 TRUTH TABLE FOR THE PIERCE

A	B	$A \downarrow B$
0	0	1
0	1	0
1	0	0
1	1	0

unstandardized block symbol appears in Figure 9.7.1. The "not" function is formed, as shown in Figure 9.7.2, by

$$\bar{A} = A \downarrow A \quad (9.7.1)$$

The "or" function is formed as shown in Figure 9.5.3 by

$$A \vee B = \overline{A \downarrow B} = (A \downarrow B) \downarrow (A \downarrow B) \qquad (9.7.2)$$

The "and" function is formed as shown in Figure 9.5.4 by

$$A \And B = \bar{A} \downarrow \bar{B} = (A \downarrow A) \downarrow (B \downarrow B) \qquad (9.7.3)$$

Further use of the *nor* block in logical construction is found in Chapter 10.

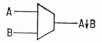

FIGURE 9.7.1. The pierce block symbol.

FIGURE 9.7.2. *Not* using the pierce.

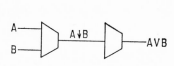

FIGURE 9.7.3. $\vee$ formed from the pierce.

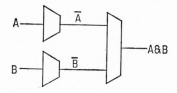

FIGURE 9.7.4. & formed from the pierce.

PROBLEMS

1. Simplify by Boolean algebra first:

(a) $X\bar{Y} + \bar{X}Y + Y\bar{Z} + \bar{Y}Z$

(b) $AB + AC + A\bar{B}C + \bar{A}B\bar{C}$

Then do the above with a Karnaugh map. Make D drawings for both unsimplified and simplified expressions.

2. Demonstrate with Venn diagrams that $\overline{A + B} = \bar{A}\bar{B}$

3. Simplify by algebra

(a) $(A + \bar{B}C)(\bar{A} + \bar{B} + C)$

(b) $\bar{P}(\bar{Q} + R) + P + QR$

(c) $U\bar{V} + (U + \bar{V})\bar{W} + W$

4. Prove the generalized De Morgan theorems

$$\overline{ABC \ldots N} = \bar{A} + \bar{B} + \ldots \bar{N} \quad \text{and}$$

$$\overline{A + B + C + \ldots + N} = \bar{A}\bar{B}\bar{C} \ldots \bar{N}$$

5. The logical function "if A then B" sometimes spoken "A implies B" is symbolized as $A \supset B$. The only case for which "$A \supset B$" is false is $A\bar{B}$.

This is reasonable and is justified in the literature on mathematical logic. Make a truth table for $A \supset B$ and for $A \subset B$. (This is the same as $B \supset A$.)

6. The function $A \equiv B$ is defined as $(A \supset B)(B \supset A)$. Make a truth table for this function.

7. Replace $A \equiv B$ and $A \supset B$ by combinations of $\vee$'s, &'s and $-$'s. Define $A \supset B$ and $A \equiv B$ using only $\downarrow$'s.

8. Show

    (a) $(A \supset B)(B \supset C) = A \supset C$

    (b) $(A \supset B) \supset A = A$

    (c) $(A \supset B)(B \supset C) \vee (C \supset A) = I$

    (d) $[A \supset (B \equiv C)] = [(A \supset B) \equiv (A \supset C)]$

    (e) $A \supset B \vee C = (A \supset B) \vee (A \supset C)$

    (f) $AB \supset C = (A \supset C) \vee (B \supset C)$

    (g) $(A \vee BC) \equiv (A \vee B)(A \vee C) = I$

9. Construct a Karnaugh map with W as the two left columns, X the two middle columns, Y the two top rows, and Z the two middle rows for:

$$\bar{W}\bar{X}YZ + \bar{W}\bar{X}YZ + \bar{W}X\bar{Y}Z + \bar{W}X\bar{Y}Z + \bar{W}XY\bar{Z} + W\bar{X}Y\bar{Z}$$
$$+ W\bar{X}YZ + WX\bar{Y}\bar{Z} + WX\bar{Y}Z + WXY\bar{Z}$$

and simplify.

10. As above, map

$$WY\bar{Z} + \bar{W}\bar{X}Z + W\bar{Y}Z + \bar{W}\bar{X}Y + \bar{W}X\bar{Z} + W\bar{X}Z + \bar{W}\bar{X}\bar{Y}$$

and simplify.

11. As above, map

$$\bar{X}Y\bar{Z} + \bar{W}\bar{X}\bar{Z} + \bar{W}XY + \bar{W}\bar{X}\bar{Y} + W\bar{X}\bar{Z}$$

and simplify.

12. As above, simplify by Karnaugh maps:

    (a) $WY\overline{WYZ\bar{X}} + \bar{W}Y\overline{WYZ\bar{X}} + W\bar{X}\bar{Z} + \bar{W}\bar{X}\bar{Z}$

    (b) $Z\overline{W}\bar{X}\bar{Z} + \bar{W}YZ$

    (c) $UXY + UX\bar{Y}Z + \bar{U}WYZ + \bar{U}\bar{W}\bar{X}\bar{Z} + \bar{U}W\bar{X}\bar{Y}\bar{Z} + \bar{U}\bar{W}XYZ$

Draw with D blocks before and after simplification.

13. Simplify with a Karnaugh map:

$$UV(X\bar{Y} + \bar{W}\bar{X}YZ + \bar{X}\bar{Y}Z) + U\bar{V}(\bar{X}YZ + X\bar{Y})$$
$$+ \bar{U}V(\bar{Y}\bar{Z}) + \bar{U}\bar{V}(X\bar{Y}Z + \bar{X}YZ)$$

14. Simplify with a Karnaugh map:

$$UV(\bar{W}Y\bar{Z} + \bar{W}\bar{Y}\bar{Z} + \bar{W}\bar{X}) + U\bar{V}(\bar{W}YZ + \bar{W}\bar{Y}Z)$$
$$+ \bar{U}V(\bar{X}\bar{Z} + \bar{W}YZ + \bar{W}\bar{Y}\bar{Z} + \bar{W}\bar{X}Z) + \bar{U}\bar{V}(\bar{X}\bar{Z} + \bar{W}X\bar{Z})$$

LOGICAL CONSTRUCTION

The rules developed in the previous chapter will be put to work to obtain combinations of functional units which will perform arithmetic and the editing chores which comprise processing. The first process to be composed will be that of binary addition. But before this, other functional units are introduced to facilitate this construction.

10.1. BIT STORAGE AND DELAYS

The Bit Storage

From the discussion of codes and number systems it is evident that the smallest unit of information to be dealt with is the *bit*. Bistable devices are capable of storing one bit of information because of their ability to maintain one of two possible states. Since it is this property that concerns us and not the magnetic or electrical specifications of these devices, we shall group them in one "logical" category, that of bit storage. The common name for the familiar form of this device is the *flip-flop*.

The true bistable or **bit storage** device has four possible connections and two possible states. For convenience and consistency, these states are referred to as 0 and 1. One input line is used to set the device to 0 and another input line sets it to 1. These lines are called the "to 0" and "to 1" lines, respectively. Two output lines (both of which may or may not be used or shown on a diagram) may be connected to the device to read its state. The "1 line" conveys the "1" state of the device and the "0 line" the 0 state of the device. The method used to "read" depends upon the circuitry and the convention of the designer. Thus it is arbitrary whether a high or a low voltage is read as "1." This should not concern us, since

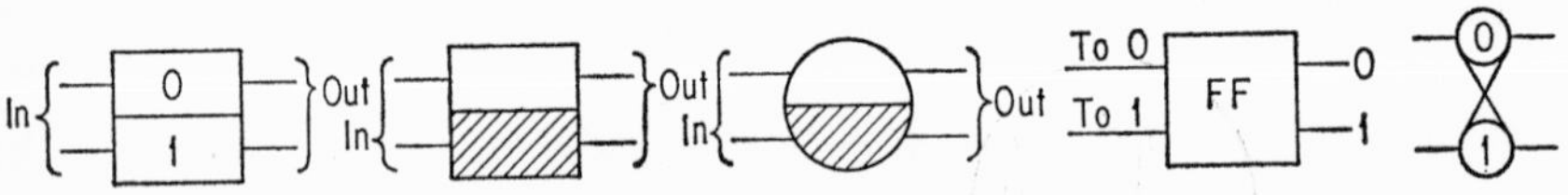

FIGURE 10.1.1.   Bit storage symbols.

we shall consider the rule of reading as integral with the storage device. We simply say some voltage appears on the "1" output line (without reference to direction or magnitude) if the device is set to 1; a detectably different voltage appears on the "0" line if the device is set to 1.

Logical symbols for bit storage are found in Figure 10.1.1. There is no standard symbol for them; the left-hand symbol will be used throughout this book. A single-bit storage is also called a **flip-flop,** a **bistable multivibrator** or just a **multi.** It is set by either a short pulse or a voltage on one of the input lines; it assumes the state corresponding to the input regardless of its previous state; it maintains this state until another input causes it to change.

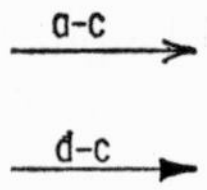

FIGURE 10.1.2.   Information flow arrowheads.

To clarify the form of information in logical diagrams, two kinds of arrowheads are sometimes used to terminate the flow of information, as shown in Figure 10.1.2. Pulse inputs, also called "a-c" because of their *comparatively short* duration, have open arrowheads; inputs emanating from bit storage devices, where information is maintained for *comparatively long* duration, have closed or filled-in arrowheads and are called "d-c." In general, this distinction is not necessary unless confusion might arise. *In this book* the direction of flow of information and its form is usually apparent from the diagrams and *no arrowheads are used;* hence arrowheads are omitted except where confusion may arise. They are necessary with other symbols where the direction of signal flow is not apparent.

The Trigger

A bit storage circuit can be so designed that it has a common input. This input acts to set the storage to the state opposite to that to which it is now set: if the bit storage is now set to 1, the input pulse sets it to 0; if it is now set to 0, the input pulse sets it to 1. Such a device is called a **trigger** and is symbolized as in Figure 10.1.3. This is simply a bit storage with the two inputs connected together. A bit storage can be used interchangeably as a trigger or a flip-flop by including two "or" circuits in the

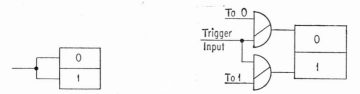

FIGURE 10.1.3. Bit storage connected as trigger only.   FIGURE 10.1.4. Bit storage doubling as a trigger.

connection as in Figure 10.1.4. When connected as a trigger, bit storage is especially useful in constructing a binary counter.

The Uni

There are circuits which hold information for a fixed time only. These are called **monostable multivibrators, univibrators,** or simply **uni's,** or **delay flops.** *Uni* is used in this book. The duration that information is stored in the uni is determined by its circuit elements and is fixed (within tolerances) over the range of operation of the equipment. The uni is normally in the 0 state; it is set to 1 by a pulse and remains so set for the storage period; it then resets itself to 0. If an attempt is made to set the uni to

FIGURE 10.1.5. Block symbol for the uni.   FIGURE 10.1.6. Block symbol for the astable multi.

1 again while it is at 1, it usually maintains the 1 setting for the storage period; but this period is timed from the *second* setting pulse, not the first. The symbol for the uni in Figure 10.1.5 contains one input or setting line and two read-out lines, 0 and 1. It is the same symbol used for bit storage but the " ✕ " replaces one of the inputs, indicating pictorially that the uni has only one input. Although it is arbitrary, we will indicate that *the input always sets the uni to 1.*

The Timing Generator or Clock

Figure 10.1.6 shows an astable multivibrator. It is not a storage device but is used to generate timing pulses at fixed intervals. The pulse rate depends on the timing constants of the multivibrator. Since this is a self-regulating device, it has no inputs and two outputs, 0 and 1. The two "✕'s" at the input sites convey the lack of inputs. Because of the circuit similarity between astable multivibrator and bit storage, similar symbols are used for each.

The Delay

A device whose output is identical to its input, except that the output occurs at some fixed period after the input, is aptly named a **delay.** This ideal specification is not usually met in practice, and the degradation of the output is often proportional to the duration of the delay required. The delay device is particularly pertinent here because its action on binary information can be reproduced using bit storage units as covered later in this section. The symbol for the delay proposed by the IRE Standards Committee 21.3 and used in this book is shown in Figure 10.1.7. The input to this rectangle is at the end with the two lines normal to its length. Information which is delayed travels from the end with lines to the end without lines; hence arrowheads are not necessary to indicate the direction of information passage.

FIGURE 10.1.7. Block symbol for the delay.   FIGURE 10.1.8. Block symbol for the shaper.

The Shaper

The **shaper,** for which we shall use *the diamond* of Figure 10.1.8 for want of a standard symbol, operates to convert the d-c output of a unit such as the multivibrator into a pulse or a-c output. The circuit is a simple resistor-capacitor differentiator and a diode clipper. The shaper produces an output pulse only when the bistable device to which it is connected changes states *to* the state corresponding to that to which the shaper is connected. When connected to the 1 output of a bit storage device, it emits a pulse when the multi changes from the 0 state to the

1 state, but no pulse when the multi changes from 1 to 0; when connected to the 0 output of a multi it emits a pulse when the multi changes from 1 to 0, but no pulse when the multi changes from 0 to 1. This is illustrated by the timing diagram of Figure 10.1.9 showing a typical shaper input and output waveform.

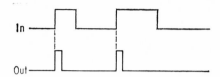

FIGURE 10.1.9.   Typical input and output waveforms for the shaper.

Using the shaper, strings of triggers can be coupled together to form a binary counter as in Figure 10.1.10. Counter logic is discussed in detail in Section 11.5.

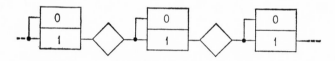

FIGURE 10.1.10.   Triggers and shapers combined to form a counter.

The Binary Delay

A **binary delay** mentioned above is constructed using only *uni's* and *shapers* as in Figure 10.1.11, and the waveforms associated with the inputs and outputs are shown in Figure 10.1.12. An information pulse is entered

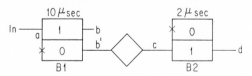

FIGURE 10.1.11.   A binary delay using two unis and a shaper.

into this logical circuit at 10.1.12(a). It sets the bit storage B1 to 1. B1 remains set to 1 for a time determined by the time constant of B1 (here 10 microseconds), as shown in Figure 10.1.12(b) and 10.1.12(b'). When the time constant of B1 expires, it resets itself to 0. The 0 output of B1 is the input to the shaper S2, which emits a pulse of short duration as B1 switches from the 1 to the 0 state. This pulse is applied to the 1 input of bit storage B3. It is set to 1. It resets itself 2 microseconds later. The purpose of B3 is to provide a neatly shaped, uniform output pulse. In cases where a time constant is associated with uni, it may be inserted in or next to the symbol of the uni as was done in Figure 10.1.11.

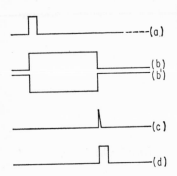

FIGURE 10.1.12. Waveforms at points in the binary delay, F i g u r e 10.1.11.

10.2. THE HALF ADDER

The first logical circuit we will tackle is the half adder. It adds two binary digits (bits) and produces a sum and a carry output. It is called a *half* adder because it does not provide for a carry from the previous set of digits added—it only does half the job needed for binary addition. The special symbol used for the logical circuit of the half adder appears in Figure 10.2.1. This symbol stands for the several logical units which when combined properly perform the logical function of the half adder. The H in the box indicates that it is a half adder; the two inputs, X and Y, are for the augend and the addend, respectively; since addition is commutative (which is added to what doesn't matter), it is really unimportant whether the addend or augend is entered into X (or Y); S is the sum output and C is the carry output.

FIGURE 10.2.1. Block symbol for the half adder.

The four possible combinations of augend and addend bits are shown in Table 10.2.1; their sum is found below the addition line. The sum and carry which occur in binary addition are presented in tabular form in Table 10.2.2. X and Y are used for the two inputs to distinguish between them in the discussion, although they are functionally interchangeable. From examination of the table it can be seen that the sum is 1 when either X or Y is 1, *but not both*. There is a carry *only* when *both* X and Y are 1. This is put in the form of a Boolean equation by "adding" (or) the terms for which the dependent variable (S or C) is 1, as follows:

$$S = \bar{X}Y + X\bar{Y} \qquad (10.2.1)$$

$$C = XY \qquad (10.2.2)$$

TABLE 10.2.1 BINARY ADDITION

Augend (X)	0	0	1	1
Addend (Y)	0	1	0	1
Sum	0	1	1	10

TABLE 10.2.2 TABLE OF BINARY ADDITION

X	Y	S	C
0	0	0	0
0	1	1	0
1	0	1	0
1	1	0	1

These two logical statements can be composed in hardware with basic logical units, as in Figure 10.2.2.

An alternate Boolean expression for the sums is composed by taking the expression "either X or Y" which is $X + Y$ and excluding the case where "both X and Y are 1" which is XY. This is stated as,

$$S = (X + Y)\overline{XY} \qquad (10.2.3)$$

Then (10.2.3) and (10.2.2) can be composed with basic logical units as in Figure 10.2.3.

One further combination can be made recalling from De Morgan's law that $\overline{XY} = \bar{X} + \bar{Y}$ so that (10.2.3) becomes

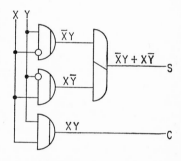

FIGURE 10.2.2. Half-adder logic.

$$S = (X + Y)(\bar{X} + \bar{Y}) \qquad (10.2.4)$$

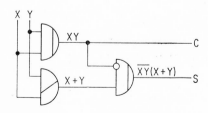

FIGURE 10.2.3. Another half-adder logic.

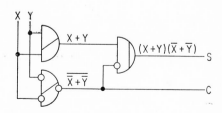

FIGURE 10.2.4. Still another half-adder logic.

and (10.2.1) is then

$$C = \overline{\overline{X} + \overline{Y}} \tag{10.2.5}$$

This is realized in basic logical elements as in Figure 10.2.4.

If the pulse inputs to the input terminals of the logic of Figures 10.2.2, 10.2.3, or 10.2.4 are those labeled X and Y of Figure 10.2.5, the S and C outputs of those figures will be the S and C of Figure 10.2.5. Hence the logic of Figures 10.2.2, 10.2.3, and 10.2.4 may be represented by the symbol of Figure 10.2.1. Note that this confirms that if X and Y are used to distinguish the two inputs, it is immaterial which input is used for the augend and which for the addend.

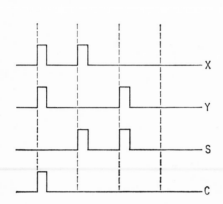

FIGURE 10.2.5. Pulse inputs and outputs of half-adder logics.

10.3. THE FULL ADDER

A full adder receives as input the augend bit and the addend bit and the carry bit produced by the addition of the preceding bits.

A sample problem of adding two binary numbers is illustrated in Table 10.3.1. What is done to find one of the sum digits, say the ith digit from the right, S_i? The ith addend digit from the right, X_i, is added to the ith augend digit from the right, Y_i, *and to this* the carry from the previous stage $[(i - 1)$th$]$, C_{i-1}, is added. Of course, C_{i-1} is 1 if there is a carry and 0 if there is no carry from the $(i - 1)$th digit addition.

TABLE 10.3.1 Adding two binary numbers

$$
\begin{array}{l}
01101100 \\
01011010 \\
\hline
11000110
\end{array}
$$

Thus, for each sum digit, *three* binary digits are added, X_i, Y_i, and C_{i-1}. Since this is the case independent of the digit position that we choose, we will simply call these input digits, X, Y, and C' respectively. A device which will produce the sum is a three-bit adder, then. First, two of the bits may be added, say X and Y; then C' is added to this partial sum to complete the addition of the three bits. The full sum is obtained from two half adders, H_1 and H_2, in "cascade" as shown in Figure 10.3.1, using this reasoning.

When does a carry *out* (*C*) occur for this "full addition"? A carry occurs if any *two* or more of the bits X, Y, or C' are 1's. Notice that if a

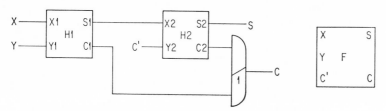

FIGURE 10.3.1. Full adder using two half adders.   FIGURE 10.3.2. Full-adder block symbol.

carry, C_1, occurs in H_1 which is adding X and Y (X and Y are both 1's), a carry is generated in full addition; also, if a carry, C_2, occurs in H_2 which adds S_1 and C', a carry is generated in the full adder [C' and one of (X or Y) are 1's]. The carry C for full addition results when C_1 or C_2 are 1; they cannot both be 1. This is obtained with the logical function $C_1 \lor C_2$ which is formed in Figure 10.3.1 by the "or" circuit, $\lor 1$. Thus, the full-adder sum and carry is realized by two half adders and a mixer as shown in Figure 10.3.1. The special symbol for the full adder is shown in Figure 10.3.2.

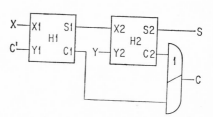

FIGURE 10.3.3. Another full adder using two half adders.

The reader should study the alternate arrangement for the full adder shown in Figure 10.3.3 to see why it is equivalent to that of Figure 10.3.1.

Theoretical Justification of the Full Adder Made from Two Half Adders

Before analyzing the full adder, a truth table is made up as in Table 10.3.2 giving the desired results of binary addition. In the first entry, 0's for addend, augend, and carry, result in 0 sum and carry output. If one, but only one, of X, Y, and C' is one, then S is 1 and C is 0, as in entries 2, 3, and 5; if any *two* of X, Y, and C' are 1, then S is 0 and C is 1—entries 4, 6, and 7. When X, Y, and C' are all 1, S is 1 and C is 1—entry 8.

The sum, S, is 1 for entries 2, 3, 5, and 8. Using " $+$ " to connect all these terms in a Boolean equation, we obtain the result:

$$S = X\bar{Y}\bar{C}' + \bar{X}Y\bar{C}' + \bar{X}\bar{Y}C' + XYC' \qquad (10.3.1)$$

Similarly, connecting forms 4, 6, 7, and 8 with the Boolean "or" we have

$$C = XY\bar{C}' + X\bar{Y}C' + \bar{X}YC' + XYC' \qquad (10.3.2)$$

To justify by Boolean algebra the composition of Figure 10.3.1 of the full adder with two half adders we shall determine the defining equations for that figure and compare them with (10.3.1) and (10.3.2).

TABLE 10.3.2 SUM (S) AND CARRY (C) TRUTH TABLE FOR FULL ADDER IN TERMS OF ADDEND (X), AUGEND (Y) AND THE CARRY FROM THE PREVIOUS DIGIT ADDITION (C')

Entry	Term	C'	Y	X	S	C
1	$\bar{C}'\bar{Y}\bar{X}$	0	0	0	0	0
2	$\bar{C}'\bar{Y}X$	0	0	1	1	0
3	$\bar{C}'Y\bar{X}$	0	1	0	1	0
4	$\bar{C}'YX$	0	1	1	0	1
5	$C'\bar{Y}\bar{X}$	1	0	0	1	0
6	$C'\bar{Y}X$	1	0	1	0	1
7	$C'Y\bar{X}$	1	1	0	0	1
8	$C'YX$	1	1	1	1	1

Call the output of the first half adder, S_1 and C_1, and of the second half adder, S_2 and C_2. S_1 and C_1 are defined by (10.2.1) and (10.2.2) for the inputs X and Y as

$$S_1 = \bar{X}Y + X\bar{Y} \qquad (10.3.3)$$

$$C_1 = XY \qquad (10.3.4)$$

The inputs to H2 are S_1 and C'. When these are entered into (10.2.1) we have

$$S_2 = \bar{C}'S_1 + C'\bar{S}_1 \qquad (10.3.5)$$

Substituting (10.3.3) into (10.3.5) we have

$$S_2 = \bar{C}'(\bar{X}Y + X\bar{Y}) + C'(\overline{\bar{X}Y + X\bar{Y}}) \qquad (10.3.6)$$

To simplify $\overline{\bar{X}Y + X\bar{Y}}$, recall that I is composed of all possibilities; for two variables X and Y then

$$I = (\bar{X}Y + X\bar{Y}) + (XY + \bar{X}\bar{Y}) \qquad (10.3.7)$$

The complement or denial of the variable is defined by

$$I = Z + \bar{Z} \qquad (10.3.8)$$

Hence it follows that

$$\overline{\bar{X}Y + X\bar{Y}} = XY + \bar{X}\bar{Y} \qquad (10.3.9)$$

Substituting (10.3.9) into (10.3.6) we have

$$S_2 = \bar{C}'(\bar{X}Y + X\bar{Y}) + C'(XY + \bar{X}\bar{Y}) \qquad (10.3.10)$$

Expand (10.3.10).

$$S_2 = \bar{C}'\bar{X}Y + \bar{C}'X\bar{Y} + C'XY + C'\bar{X}\bar{Y} \qquad (10.3.11)$$

Comparing term for term we find (10.3.11) and (10.3.1) equivalently define the full-adder sum output.

Similarly for C_1 we have

$$C_1 = XY \qquad (10.3.12)$$

Since H2 has S_1 and C' as inputs,

$$C_2 = C'S_1 \qquad (10.3.13)$$

or substituting (10.3.3) into (10.3.13) we have

$$C_2 = C'(\bar{X}Y + X\bar{Y}) \qquad (10.3.14)$$

The output C of F is defined as

$$C = C_1 + C_2 \qquad (10.3.15)$$

and substituting (10.3.12) and (10.3.14) into (10.3.15) and expanding, we have

$$C = XY + C'\bar{X}Y + C'X\bar{Y} \qquad (10.3.16)$$

But

$$XY = XYI = XY(C' + \bar{C}') \qquad (10.3.17)$$

so that

$$C = XYC' + XY\bar{C}' + C'\bar{X}Y + C'X\bar{Y} \qquad (10.3.18)$$

which is identical to (10.3.1).

Direct Realization of the Logic from the Boolean Equations

Let us suppose now that our line of reasoning started with the truth-table definition of the full adder, Table 10.3.2, and then we derived the defining Boolean equations (10.3.1) and (10.3.2). Can we now compose a logical design to realize these equations? Each of the terms of (10.3.1) and (10.3.2) (e.g., $X\bar{Y}C'$, $\bar{X}Y C'$, and so forth) can be composed with one three-input &-gate. These terms are then "added" together with a four-input V-mixer. The complete logical diagram of the adder then appears as in Figure 10.3.4.

Karnaugh Map Simplification

There should be a simpler construction (having fewer blocks). To investigate the possibilities we make one Karnaugh map each for S and C from (10.3.1) and (10.3.2) respectively, as in Figure 10.3.5. A 1 is put in the box corresponding to each term of the Boolean equations. The first term of (10.3.1) is entry 2 of Table 10.3.2. It corresponds to box 2 in Figure 10.3.5. The other boxes of that Figure for which 1's are

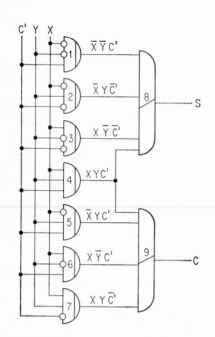

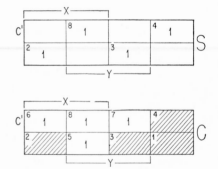

FIGURE 10.3.4. Full-adder logic derived directly from defining equations, (10.3.1) and (10.3.2).

FIGURE 10.3.5. Karnaugh map, sum (S) and carry (C) of the full adder.

entered are numbered as shown.

Let us start with the carry map, C, of Figure 10.3.5. In terms of the boxes numbered in that Figure, C is given by

$$C = B_6 + B_8 + B_7 + B_5 \qquad (10.3.19)$$

Now C' is given by

$$C' = B_6 + B_8 + B_7 + B_4 \qquad (10.3.20)$$

Then C can be formed by subtracting B_4 and adding B_5 to C' thus,

$$C = C' - B_4 + B_5 \qquad (10.3.21)$$

Now

$$B_4 = \bar{X}\bar{Y}C' \qquad (10.3.22)$$

and

$$B_5 = XY\bar{C}' \qquad (10.3.23)$$

However, if we intend to deny (subtract) B_4, we might just as well deny B_4 and B_1. That is, since B_1 does not appear in (10.3.20), the equation for C', denying it does not affect C'. Similarly, if we affirm (add) B_5, we might just as well affirm both B_5 and B_8. (B_8 being affirmed in this equation for C'.) Since these pairs of boxes are adjacent, one variable is eliminated as

$$B_4 + B_1 = \bar{X}\bar{Y}C' + \bar{X}\bar{Y}\bar{C}' = \bar{X}\bar{Y} \tag{10.3.24}$$

and

$$B_5 + B_8 = XY\bar{C}' + XYC' = XY \tag{10.3.25}$$

Then we have

$$C = C' - (B_4 + B_1) + (B_5 + B_8) \tag{10.3.26}$$

or

$$C = C'(\overline{\bar{X}\bar{Y}}) + XY \tag{10.3.27}$$

This is so, for to remove (subtract) an area B from an area A (to perform $A - B$) is equivalent to the logical function $A\bar{B}$, read "A and not B." Recalling De Morgan's law,

$$\overline{\bar{X}\bar{Y}} = \bar{\bar{X}} + \bar{\bar{Y}} = X + Y \tag{10.3.28}$$

Then

$$C = C'(X + Y) + XY \tag{10.3.29}$$

To realize (10.3.29), the logic of Figure 10.3.6 is used. $X + Y$ is formed by $\lor 1$; $\&2$ uses this input and C' to form $C'(X + Y)$; XY is formed with $\&3$; $\lor 4$ finally forms $C = C'(X + Y) + XY$.

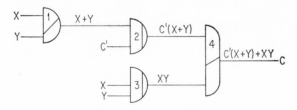

FIGURE 10.3.6.   Full-adder logic for carry from Karnaugh map simplification.

The Karnaugh for S in Figure 10.3.5 does not permit any simplification—no two of the four boxes are adjacent, so that the four terms they represent must be combined with "or's" to form S. There is no simple way to represent S.

However, if we are willing to use C as obtained in (10.3.29), a simplification may be made. The empty boxes of Figure 10.3.5 represent the map of C: the crosshatched boxes are then the map for $\bar{C}$. Notice that S

can be formed from $\bar{C}$ by adding box 8 and subtracting box 1, or

$$S = \bar{C} - B_1 + B_8 \tag{10.3.30}$$

and
$$S = \bar{C}(\overline{B_1}) + B_8 \tag{10.3.31}$$

or
$$S = \bar{C}\overline{\bar{C}'\bar{X}\bar{Y}} + C'XY \tag{10.3.32}$$

From De Morgan's law recall that

$$\overline{\bar{C}'\bar{X}\bar{Y}} = \bar{\bar{C}}' + \bar{\bar{X}} + \bar{\bar{Y}} = C' + X + Y \tag{10.3.33}$$

and
$$S = \bar{C}(C' + X + Y) + C'XY \tag{10.3.34}$$

Equation (10.3.34) can be realized as in Figure 10.3.7. $\vee 5$ forms $C' + X + Y$ which is one input to $\&'6$; the other input to $\&'6$ is C (from Figure 10.3.7) and its output is then $\bar{C}(C' + X + Y)$; $C'XY$ is formed by $\&7$ which $\vee 8$ "adds"—these two to yield S.

The logic of Figure 10.3.8 combines those of Figures 10.3.6 and 10.3.7 but uses only eight basic logical units of two inputs each. The numbers correspond from one figure to the next so that the reader may verify this.

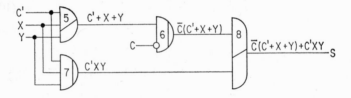

FIGURE 10.3.7.   Full-adder logic for sum from Karnaugh map simplification.

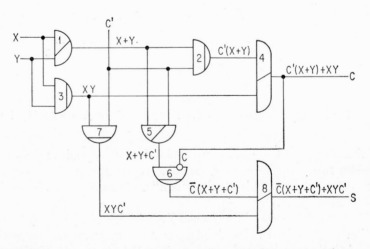

FIGURE 10.3.8.   Combined full-adder logic from Karnaugh map simplification.

10.4. *NOR* ELEMENTS AND ADDERS

In Chapter 9 the *nor* element was discussed and defined using the pierce, as follows:

$$A \downarrow B = \bar{A}\bar{B} \tag{10.4.1}$$

Several logical elements and blocks will now be composed from the *nor* element.

Inhibit (&')

The input X is said to inhibit the input A to a block if the output of the block is given as $A\bar{X}$. It is composed with *nors* if we recall that $A = \bar{\bar{A}}$ so that

$$A\bar{X} = \bar{\bar{A}}\bar{X} \tag{10.4.2}$$

From the definition (10.4.1)

$$\bar{\bar{A}}\bar{X} = \bar{A} \downarrow X = A\bar{X} \tag{10.4.3}$$

But
$$\bar{A} = A \downarrow A \tag{10.4.4}$$

so that
$$\bar{A} \downarrow X = (A \downarrow A) \downarrow X = A\bar{X} \tag{10.4.5}$$

as is shown in Figure 10.4.1.

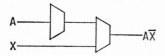

FIGURE 10.4.1. Inhibit logic from nors.

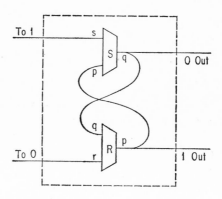

FIGURE 10.4.2. Bit storage using nors.

Bit Storage

A bit storage composed of *nors* is found in Figure 10.4.2. The inputs to each *nor* are a setting pulse and the output of the other *nor*: one input to S is the setting input s; the other input to S is the output of R called p; one input to R is the setting pulse r; the other input to R is the output of

S, called q. S has an output q if

$$q = s \downarrow p = \bar{s}\bar{p} \qquad (10.4.6)$$

Similarly R has an output P only if

$$p = r \downarrow q = \bar{r}\bar{q} \qquad (10.4.7)$$

The bit storage may be in one of two possible states; there may be an input pulse applied to either of the terminals. These four possibilities are now examined.

0 INPUT DURING 0 SETTING. Here $r = 1$ (0 setting pulse), $q = 1$. Since there is an input to R (there are two inputs, r and q, to R), there is no output, p; since there is *no* input to S, there *is* an output q. Thus the bit storage B reads 0.

1 INPUT DURING 0 SETTING. Here $s = 1$ (1 input), $q = 1$ (0 setting). When a pulse appears at s, by (10.4.6) the output at q must cease. For an instant both p and q are 0. At that point, there is no input to R; this causes an output to appear at p; since there is already an input at s (and even if it is later removed) S will remain with no signal output ($q = 0$). The bit storage now reads 1 (signal at p).

0 INPUT, 1 SETTING. Here $r = 1$ (0 input), $p = 1$ (1 setting). When the pulse appears at r, the output at p disappears. There are then no inputs to S so that a signal appears at q. This state is preserved after the input at r is removed so that the bit storage reads 0.

1 INPUT, 1 SETTING. Here $s = 1$ (1 input), $p = 1$ (1 setting). Another input to S does not affect either p or q.

Univibrator

Two *nors* and a delay element arranged as in Figure 10.4.3 form the uni element. Assume that there is a 0 output, q. An input on the *to 1* line, s, prevents an output from S ($q = 0$). There is then no input to R ($q = 0$ and $p' = 0$) so that there is an output from R ($p = 1$). After a time determined by the delay, the signal at p appears at p' which is an input to R. This prevents a further output from R so that $p = 0$. When this happens, there is no longer an input to S so that an output appears at q ($q = 1$)—the bit storage resets to 0.

Half Adder

Consider now how to build a half adder from *nors*. Formulas for sum, S, and carry, C, to be used are: [(10.2.1) and (10.2.2)]

$$S = X\bar{Y} + \bar{X}Y \qquad (10.4.8)$$

$$C = XY \qquad (10.4.9)$$

First (10.4.8) is revised thus:

$$I = \bar{X}Y + X\bar{Y} + XY + \bar{X}\bar{Y} \qquad (10.4.10)$$

$$\bar{X}Y + X\bar{Y} = I - (XY + \bar{X}\bar{Y}) \qquad (10.4.11)$$

$$S = \bar{X}Y + X\bar{Y} = \overline{XY + \bar{X}\bar{Y}} \qquad (10.4.12)$$

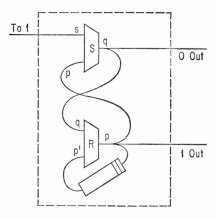

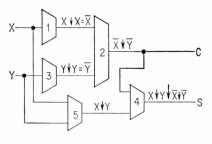

FIGURE 10.4.3.   Uni using nors.   FIGURE 10.4.4.   A half adder using nors.

To put this into *nor* notation that by De Morgan's law,

$$\overline{XY + \bar{X}\bar{Y}} = \overline{XY}\,\overline{\bar{X}\bar{Y}} \qquad (10.4.13)$$

but $\qquad (\overline{XY})(\overline{\bar{X}\bar{Y}}) = XY \downarrow \bar{X}\bar{Y} \qquad (10.4.14)$

so that $\qquad S = XY \downarrow \bar{X}\bar{Y} \qquad (10.4.15)$

Recall that

$$XY = \bar{X} \downarrow \bar{Y} \qquad (10.4.16)$$

and $\qquad \bar{X}\bar{Y} = X \downarrow Y \qquad (10.4.17)$

Combining (10.4.15), (10.4.16), and (10.4.17) we have

$$S = (\bar{X} \downarrow \bar{Y}) \downarrow (X \downarrow Y) \qquad (10.4.18)$$

Now $\bar{X}$ or $\bar{Y}$ can be written as

$$\bar{X} = X \downarrow X; \qquad \bar{Y} = Y \downarrow Y \qquad (10.4.19)$$

so that S can be written completely with $\downarrow$'s as

$$S = [(X \overset{1}{\downarrow} X) \overset{2}{\downarrow} (Y \overset{3}{\downarrow} Y)] \overset{4}{\downarrow} (X \overset{5}{\downarrow} Y) \qquad (10.4.20)$$

where the numbers over the $\downarrow$'s stand for numbers of the *nor* block in Figure 10.4.4.

From (10.4.16), the carry C is represented simply by

$$C = (X \overset{1}{\downarrow} X) \overset{2}{\downarrow} (Y \overset{3}{\downarrow} Y) \tag{10.4.21}$$

The complete *nor* logic for a half adder is found in Figure 10.4.4.

10.5. SHIFT REGISTERS

Registers are composed of many units of bit storage. The attribute of the register that interests us most is that the content of each bit position may be shifted simultaneously to the next bit position on command. The crucial factor here is the timing that allows the bits to be moved without interfering with each other.

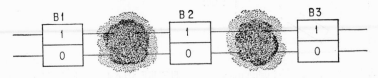

FIGURE 10.5.1.   Pictorial representation of bit storage.

Consider three bit-storage units, B1, B2, and B3, as in Figure 10.5.1, which are part of a larger shift register. The problem is to move the contents of B1 to B2 and of B2 to B3, and so on, *at the same time.* If the transfer is attempted sequentially, the transfer of information from B1 to B2 may set this bit in B2 before the information from B2 is sent to B3, and so forth down the line. Thus, if B1 is 1, B2 is 0, and B3 is 0, B2 could be set to 1 to record B1 before B2 is recorded in B3. Then when a transfer is made from B2 to B3, it will falsely be recorded as 1 (the content of B1).

To assure a simultaneous transfer from one bit storage to the next, temporary storage is used between each bit storage—an auxiliary device is used to hold information temporarily as it is passed along from one bit position to another. The procedure is to place each bit in an auxiliary device, clear the entire main register, and then move the bit from the auxiliary device to the *next* stage of the main register. There are four phases to this process then: store, clear, record, and reset the auxiliary device.

The auxiliary device may be another bit storage, a delay line, or a circuit element such as either a capacitor or indicator used as a delay component.

First Design

Figure 10.5.2 shows the connection between three bits, B1, B2, and B3, using delays and &-blocks. The shift pulse is transmitted by either

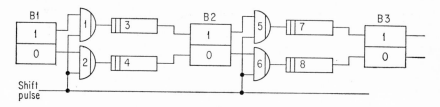

FIGURE 10.5.2. Shift register using two delays and two gates per bit.

&1 or &2 depending upon the setting of B1; it is then entered into either Δ3 or Δ4 accordingly. B2 is set either to 1 by Δ3 or to 0 by Δ4 after the delay period. Of course, if B2 is already in the state into which the setting pulse tries to place it, then nothing happens. Hence the recording operation also clears. At the same time, &5 and &6 allow B2 to be read out into Δ7 or Δ8.

Second Design

For an n-bit register, $n - 1$ delays may be saved by the logic of Figure 10.5.3. The shift pulse puts a pulse into Δ2 if B1 stores a 1; otherwise

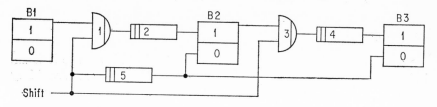

FIGURE 10.5.3. Shift register using approximately one delay and one gate per bit.

Δ2 remains empty; the shift pulse, delayed by Δ5, clears all the bits of the entire register to 0 (just B2 and B3 are cleared in the figure); for bits which are to be 0, there is no pulse in the delay at the "to 1" input of the bit storage so that the bit storage remains cleared to 0. The delay Δ5 must be smaller than all the other delays to assure that each bit storage is cleared before the set pulse passes through the delay.

Third Design

Another shift-register logic encountered in some designs appears in Figure 10.5.4. Here, if there is a 1 in bit storage B1, it is entered into an

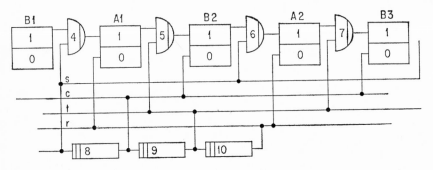

FIGURE 10.5.4.   Shift register using one auxiliary bit storage and one gate per bit.

auxiliary bit storage A1 through &4 by the shift pulse s; similarly, a 1 in B2 is entered into auxiliary bit storage A2 via &6, and so forth down the line. All main bit storages (the B's) are then cleared by the clear pulse, c (the shift pulse delayed by Δ8); the bits in the auxiliary storage are transferred to the next bit position by the transfer pulse, t (the shift pulse delayed by Δ8 and Δ9)—a 1 in A1 is entered into B2 through &5, a 1 in A2 is entered into B3 through &7, a 0 in A1 does not permit t to set B2 via &5, and so forth; all the auxiliary storages (the A's) are cleared by the reset pulse, r (the shift pulse delayed by Δ8, Δ9 and Δ10).

Another Design

Logic which acts similarly using unis instead of bit storage is found in Figure 10.5.5. Here the shift pulse sets (or fails to set) each auxiliary

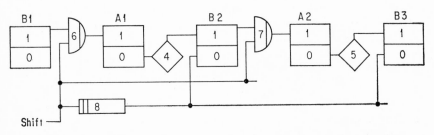

FIGURE 10.5.5.   Shift register using one uni, one shaper, and one gate per bit.

storage univibrator depending on whether the content of bit storage is 1 or 0. Bit storage is then cleared by a delayed shift pulse, c. When a univibrator resets itself (which can happen only *after* c), a shaper such as S4 emits a pulse which sets the next bit position to 1. When a 0 is in bit storage, the auxiliary storage uni is not set; after the next stage is cleared it remains so because no pulse is generated by auxiliary storage.

Built-in Storage for Shift Registers

The auxiliary storage may be built into the circuit. It is possible to design coupled flip-flops so that when each is reset to 0, a capacitor is charged if the flip-flop was previously set to 1; the capacitor is not charged if the flip-flop was set to 0. This capacitor is coupled to the next flip-flop, so that its discharge will cause that flip-flop to be set in correspondence to the previous stage when the clear pulse is removed.

In choosing a shift register logic the designer not only considers the cost and number of components but also the speed requirement. The logic of Figure 10.5.2 requires that bit storage be set, at most, once per shift cycle; the logics of Figures 10.5.3, 10.5.4, and 10.5.5 require that the bit storage be able to change states twice between each shift pulse.

Magnetic-Core Shift Register

A shift register may be constructed from *magnetic-core elements*. These elements consist of a toroid or doughnut of ceramic or plastic material around which is wound a strip of thin magnetic tape—the doughnut is "sugared" with a magnetic metallic film. Three or more coils are then wound around the toroid. The magnetizable tape has a very square hysteresis loop. This means that although it is possible for it to be magnetized to a greater or lesser degree, its threshhold is sharp. In operation, it can then be used so that it is always in one of the two extreme states of magnetization. When a current of the proper level and direction flows in the input or setting winding, it magnetizes the core in a direction which is arbitrarily called the 1 direction. A core previously set to 0 will remain in that state or be set to 1, according to whether a current does or does not flow in the input winding.

A register is composed using magnetic elements by connecting the input winding of one magnetic core to a second or output winding of the previous core. Supplementary components discussed below are also needed.

To shift the information from one core to the next, a shift pulse of sufficient magnitude and proper direction to set the core to the 0 state is applied to the third or shift winding of all the cores. If a core was in a 0 state before the shift current arrives, the shift current in the shift winding has very little effect on the magnetic flux surrounding the core; very little, if any, current is induced in the output winding of the core; no current can then appear on the input winding of the *next* core caused by *this* core. On the other hand, if the core was in the 1 state, the shift current will clear it to the 0 state; this causes a complete reversal of flux through the output winding, inducing a large current there.

Two-Core-Per-Bit Magnetic-Core Shift Registers

The simplest way to interconnect magnetic cores to form a shift register, and to solve the auxiliary storage problem, is to use two cores for each bit required. These are connected as in Figure 10.5.6. Previous to use,

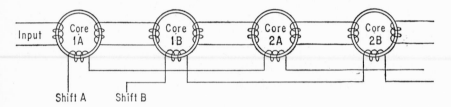

FIGURE 10.5.6.   Two-core-per-bit magnetic shift.

cores 1B and 2B have been cleared. The input to core 1A is the serial-bit information to be stored. The output winding of core 1A is connected through a diode (not shown for simplicity) to the input 1B; the output of 1B through a diode to the input of 2A; the output of 2A through a diode to the input of 2B; and so forth. The purpose of the diode is to allow current to flow from left to right in the figure and to prevent it from flowing from the output to the input but not from the input to the output, right to left in the figure. The third or shift windings of the A cores are connected to the A shift line; the shift windings of the B cores are connected to the B shift line.

Information (1 or 0) is entered into 1A; shortly thereafter, a pulse sets all A cores to 0. This induces a current on the 1A output line if a 1 was entered in core 1A previously and none if a 0 was entered previously; the 1 current is sufficient to set 1B to 1 if 1A was set to 1, but not otherwise. A little later the B shift pulse transfers the information from 1B to 2A by the same procedure. This is a full character cycle; the bit has been moved from 1A to 2A. A new bit may now be entered at 1A.

The timing for a two-core-per-bit register appears in Figure 10.5.7. The information pulse I_1 sets core 1A to 1; core 1A is set to 0 by the shift pulse A1; the time during which 1A is set to 1 is indicated in Figure 10.5.7 as 1A1. When 1A is set to 0, 1B is set to 1 because 1A *was* set to 1; 1B remains set to 1 until pulse B1 sets it to 0; in so doing, 2A is set to 1; 1B is set to 1 for the duration of 1B1. Core 2A remains set to 1 during 2A1.

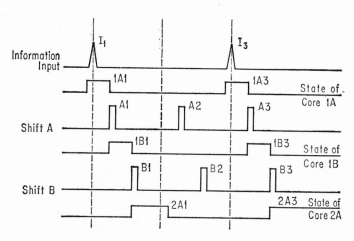

FIGURE 10.5.7. Timing for the two-core-per-bit magnetic register of Figure 10.5.6.

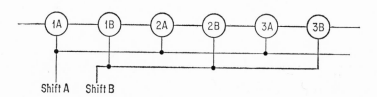

FIGURE 10.5.8. Symbolic notation for two-core-per-bit magnetic shift register.

No information is entered into core 1A during the second information cycle because there is no pulse I_2. Hence no information is shifted into core 1B by the A shift pulse or into core 2A by the B shift pulse.

The reader may follow the third cycle using the information-input pulse I_3. This cycle is almost identical to the first cycle.

A convenient symbolic notation for the core register discussed above is shown in Figure 10.5.8.

One-Core-Per-Bit Registers

A register using only one core element per bit may be constructed as in Figure 10.5.9. Only one shift input is used. Information shifted out of each core must be stored temporarily while the next core is being set to 0. An inductor-capacitor network of the proper time constant (the delay) is used for this. When the shift current is removed, the current stored in this circuit (if *this* core stored a 1) sets the *next* core.

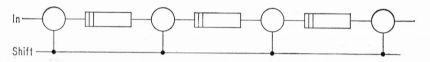

FIGURE 10.5.9.   One-core-per-bit magnetic shift register.

Each core element, with its windings and the inductor-capacitor storage circuit and a diode to prevent a current induced in the input winding of the *next* core from setting *this* core, is packaged as a single unit. Extra windings can be specified for special applications such as inhibiting and gating functions. Shift registers composed of such units are reliable, but often costly and limited in their information-flow capacity (the pulse-repetition frequency currently permissible is relatively low).

Static Shift Register Operation

No matter what kind of shift register is used, the operation using auxiliary storage is similar: set auxiliary storage from main storage; clear main storage; set next main storage stage from auxiliary storage; clear auxiliary storage. Thus the circuit details are unimportant—the register performs the function of storing and moving information.

The Dynamic Register

In a synchronous machine where a register is examined at specific intervals, it is possible to use a dynamic principle to construct the register.

The dynamic register is like a merry-go-round: the information is continually circulating; an observer will see the stored word repeatedly passing by a fixed point in the register. The register consists of a number of delays, one for each bit as in Figure 10.5.10. The end of the register is connected back to the input, so that once information is entered into the register it is continually fed back and circulates through the delays.

Information thus continually passing through delay circuits is subject to attenuation. It must be frequently regenerated by amplifiers in the circulation loop. This is *not* a logical function but rather a circuit necessity caused by the losses introduced by circuit elements, the delay. The logical designer, strictly speaking, is not concerned with this *non-logical* function. Amplifiers only mess up the already complicated, logical diagrams of many computers, and neither belong there nor aid in the comprehension of the machine and so are omitted here.

Figure 10.5.10 includes means for influencing the operation of the dynamic register. The gate &1 may have a voltage applied to it to read out the register (without affecting the word stored therein); to enter new serial information &'2 inhibits or eliminates the old information while &3

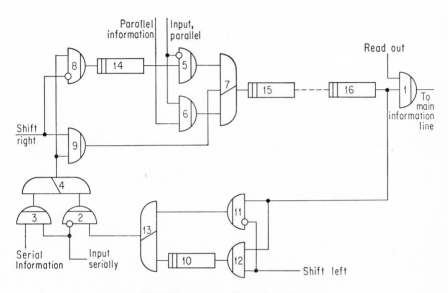

FIGURE 10.5.10. Dynamic register.

passes the new information; both old and new information must pass through ∨4 which receives information from either &'2 or &3. To enter information in parallel requires for each bit two gates and a mixer arranged as &'5, &6, and ∨7; to shift right one bit on each circulation, the information is shunted past the first bit delay Δ14 using &9 and ∨7 instead of the usual path, &'8, Δ14, &'5, and ∨7; to shift left an additional delay Δ10 is introduced with the aid of &'11, &12, and ∨13 (since the word is delayed an extra bit time for each circulation, this amounts to a single bit shift to the left).

The need for complete synchronization and a fixed word length is apparent from the discussion. Another practical but not logical limitation is the destruction of information in the register because of a power line failure (the circulating information is unable to pass through inoperative amplifiers).

Shift-Register Symbol

In the remainder of this book, the rectangular symbol in Figure 10.5.11 will be used to indicate the single-word shift register. The input and output may be serial-character serial-bit or serial-character parallel-bit or parallel-character parallel-bit or combinations of these. Only the facilities used are indicated in the symbol. The shift line is a long line entering at one side and continuing almost to the other end—with an arrowhead internal to the rectangle (*a*). A number of input lines (*b*) or output lines

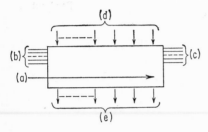

FIGURE 10.5.11. Generalized single-word shift-register symbol showing: (a) shift inputs; (b) serial-character input; (c) serial-character output; (d) parallel-character input; and (e) parallel-character output.

FIGURE 10.5.12. Shift register showing serial-character parallel-bit output (double line) returned to the most significant digit input to the register.

(*c*) or one double line emerging from or entering one end indicate serial-character parallel-bit operation. Inputs (*d*) and outputs (*e*) along the long side of the figure indicate parallel-character inputs and outputs. In Figure 10.5.12 the input line displaced somewhat from the beginning of the register shows that the influx of information circumvents the sign position leaving it stationary in the shifting process. The shift input (the line with the arrowhead within the box) in this figure carries a train of pulses which affects all the characters except the sign.

The register symbol is meant to convey a complete unit which contains delays or logic to obtain auxiliary pulses, such as clear or transfer pulses, for proper operation of the register.

10.6. MULTIPLE INPUT BLOCKS

To study functional blocks and logical diagrams which handle parallel-bit information, a symbolic convention is adopted that increases efficiency.

Parallel-bit information is indicated by a pipe—a double line—as the input or output of any *suitable* parallel-bit device. Thus the output of register A is connected to the register B in Figure 10.6.

A connecting junction such as the tee between register A and B is made so that one side of one *pipe* has a hole where the connection is made to the other *pipe*. A non-connecting junction is seen where the output of

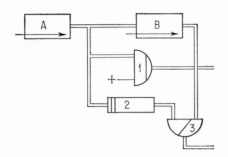

FIGURE 10.6. Parallel-bit logical diagram.

&1 crosses *under* the output of B—the sides of the *pipe* from B are not broken.

Multiple devices can be shown using this convention. Thus &1 is a set of gates, one for each bit-line of parallel-bit information, and all of which have a + input. Similarly Δ2 is a set of delays, each of identical characteristics and one in each of the parallel bit lines. Also V3 represents a number of mixers; there is one mixer for each pair of corresponding input leads. In this case the inputs must be commensurate and there must be a corresponding member in each *pipe;* there must be the same number of lines in each *pipe*.

PROBLEMS

1. A half subtractor is a device which determines the *difference* of two bits, without considering whether a *borrow* had occurred on the previous *subtraction*. Write a truth table for the difference D and the borrow output B (to the next bit to the left), in terms of the minuend Y and the subtrahend X. What are the Boolean expressions for D and B? Draw a logic using D-blocks for D and B. Can you find an alternate expression and representation?

2. The full subtractor is analogous to the full adder, but has the borrow input (from the previous bit) B', as well as the minuend Y and the subtrahend X. Write a truth table for D and B, Boolean expressions for D and B, and a logic using D-blocks. Are there alternate expressions and representations? Tell how you might use a full subtractor in a computer.

3. Construct a full subtractor using half subtractors.

4. Convert the equations of Problem 1 into *nor* notation. Develop a half subtractor using *nor* logic.

5. Convert the equations of Problem 2 into *nor* logic. Develop a full subtractor with *nor* logic.

6. Convert (10.3.29) and (10.3.33) into *nor* equations. Draw *nor* logic to realize the full adder.

7. Draw (on a large sheet of paper) a five-character, four-bit-per-character dynamic shift register of the type shown in Figure 10.5.10.

8. Draw a complete five-character, four-bit-per-character shift register of the type illustrated in Figure 10.5.4. Include gates and mixers for end around shift, shift out, and transfer in and out. Add logic for shifting, at will, all but the left-hand character.

E L E V E N

FUNCTIONAL UNITS

We shall now describe the blocks of logic that perform large pieces of arithmetic and editing. For each type only a few of the many possibilities for logical design at the computer engineer's disposal are explored, showing how the logical blocks are combined to form these functional units. Many variations exist. The designer must decide what aspects of each logical design are compatible with, and contribute favorably to, the over-all function of the given computer. His judgment is based on components already chosen, required speed, capacity, economy, reliability, and the environmental conditions which prevail. The blocks discussed now do a large fraction of a computer command. In the next chapter we will put these blocks together to make units which will do full orders.

11.1. ACCUMULATORS FOR NATURAL BINARY COMPUTERS

Accumulators in General

An **accumulator** is a device for adding multiple-digit numbers, not just single digits (this the adder does, the adder being a subunit of the accumulator). The mechanics of the accumulator depend on (1) the coding used in the computer and (2) the mode of operation—whether addition is done a digit at a time (serially) or all at once (in parallel).

A complete accumulator consists of a register which holds the augend (the accumulator register), a register to hold the addend (the addend register), a register to hold the sum (usually the accumulator register too), an adder with the logic to produce the sum, and control logic to guide the operation. A complete order procures the addend from memory, places it in the addend register, adds it through the adder to the augend, and places the result in the accumulator register.

The accumulator is so named because successive sums obtained by adding successive numbers together can be "accumulated" in its accumulator register. Most accumulators can be used interchangeably for subtraction, hence they can also accumulate differences.

The adder for the accumulator depends upon the computer language and upon whether the computer operates in a serial-character or parallel-character fashion.

Serial-Character Natural Binary Accumulator

In Figure 11.1.1 a schematic drawing of a serial-character natural binary accumulator is shown. The "accumulator register" is hereafter shortened to "accumulator" where no confusion results. The accumulator (so labeled in Figure 11.1.1) feeds the augend into the full adder F at input X (FX); the addend is moved from its register into the Y input of the adder (FY); the carry from the previous digit is stored in the delay $\Delta 1$, to be fed in now with *this* digit. The sum output of the adder (FS) is returned to the

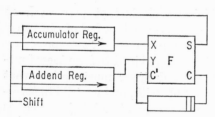

FIGURE 11.1.1.　Serial binary accumulator.

input of the accumulator. Sum digits as they are created are pushed down the accumulator until the full sum sits in the accumulator.

Parallel-Character Natural Binary Accumulator

Figure 11.1.2 shows a parallel-character natural binary accumulator. There is an adder (F) for each digit of the register word except the sign. This adder is designed somewhat differently from the full adder because a number of such adders must operate together and simultaneously. The structure of parallel natural binary adders is discussed in Section 11.3.

In Figure 11.1.2 the digits of the augend are entered into the X inputs of the corresponding adders; the addend bit is entered into the X input of corresponding adders (i.e., adder F_5 for digit #5); the carry output C from each adder is entered into the carry input, C', of the next adder to left;

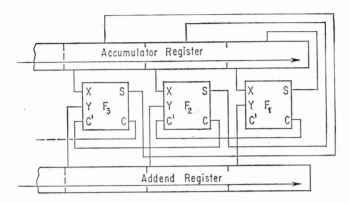

FIGURE 11.1.2.   Parallel binary accumulator.

the sum output of each adder is returned to the corresponding accumulator register input.

Serial-Character Parallel-Bit Accumulator

The binary coded-digit serial-character parallel-bit adder and accumulator is shown in Figure 11.1.3. This kind of logic is associated with computers using languages such as XS3 or NBCD. There is one input line,

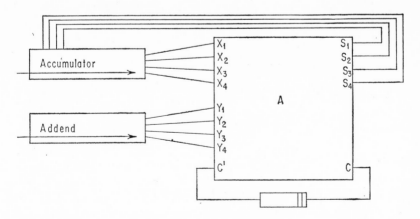

FIGURE 11.1.3.   Serial-character parallel-bit coded-digit accumulator.

X_1, X_2, and so on, for each parallel bit of the digit code as received from the accumulator register; there is one input per bit, Y_1, Y_2, and so on, to the adder from the addend register; there is one output per bit, S_1, S_2, and so on, from the adder—this is usually re-entered into the accumulator as is shown; there is only one carry *bit* output C from the adder which is usually returned through a delay to the adder carry input, C'. Coded decimal adders are discussed in Section 11.5 and 11.6.

Parallel-Character Parallel-Bit Accumulator

With a little imagination a number of coded-digit adders such as those used in Figure 11.1.3 can be assembled to resemble the logic of Figure 11.1.2. This would form a parallel-character parallel-bit coded-digit accumulator.

11.2. SERIAL-CHARACTER NATURAL
BINARY ACCUMULATOR

Little auxiliary equipment is needed to implement the serial natural binary accumulator shown in Figure 11.2.1. The first augend bit (binary

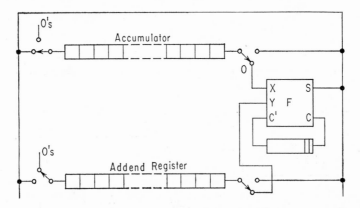

FIGURE 11.2.1. Serial binary accumulator.

digit) is entered from the accumulator register into the X input; the first addend bit is entered from the addend register into the Y input; there is no information at the C' input, since the delay was cleared in previous usage; the sum bit which is produced immediately appears on the main information line which enters it at the input to the accumulator register; the carry output bit, C, is entered into the delay.

The next step (or shift) enters the second accumulator bit into one of the adder inputs and the second addend bit into the other; the carry bit from the previous addition now appears at C'—it has been delayed exactly one bit time so that it will occur at the precise time the augend and addend bits enter the X and Y inputs of the adder; the second sum bit then emerges onto the main information line and appears at the input of the accumulator register; the carry bit is entered into the now-empty delay.

As each augend bit is shifted out of the right side of the accumulator register, a sum digit is entered into the left side; the first sum bit is entered on the first shift operation as the leftmost accumulator bit; as the process continues, this first sum bit is shifted to the right; on completion, it is at the rightmost position where it belongs. Zeros may be entered at the left of the addend register to clear it as addition proceeds, or the addend may be re-entered instead.

The reader may perceive two problems postponed for later solution: (1) a carry may occur on adding the most significant digits; (2) the sign of the sum must be determined from that of the augend and addend.

Carry Storage

It is important that the delay for the carry output of the adder is such that the carry input will coincide with the next digit input. If the bit frequency has any tendency to drift, trouble could arise. To circumvent this, the circuit of Figure 11.2.2 is used. The carry output bit has been stored in B1. The shift pulse which enters the augend and addend digits also reads the carry storage by means of &2. In T microseconds the carry storage B1 is reset; this is done by the shift pulse which is entered into Δ3, a delay of duration T. The carry output of F from FC is entered into Δ4; it is delayed by 2T microseconds so that it is recorded after B1 is reset to 0. As long as both delays Δ3 and Δ4 of Figure 11.4.2 are smaller than the bit time, no difficulty arises.

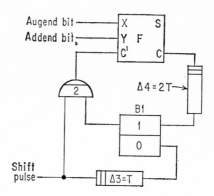

FIGURE 11.2.2. Serial binary accumulator carry circuit.

11.3. PARALLEL NATURAL BINARY ACCUMULATOR

This section discusses the principles of parallel binary accumulators and presents a detailed explanation of three kinds of logic typical to such creatures. Many variations have been devised, but this section is not exhaustive.

The procedure in the *parallel* binary accumulator is to add all the bits *simultaneously*. Of course, the difficulty discussed in Chapter 6 called the *carry ripple* plagues us here: as a carry is added from one digit to the next-higher-order sum digit, a further carry may be created by this addition; when this carry is added to the next digit, another carry may be generated; and so forth.

Parallel accumulators designed with a high-speed carry to circumvent the carry ripple do not use the full-adder logic of Chapter 10. Instead, the adding is done directly into the accumulator register which is set up as a trigger. The carry process is done as a separate operation.

The Question of Carry

In order to exploit all the possibilities for the high-speed carry, it is essential that we be aware of the alternatives. For a given stage of the parallel adder there are four possibilities:

1. There is a carry from the *previous stage and* there is a carry to the next stage—carry transmission.
2. There is *no* carry from the *previous stage, but* there is a carry created in *this stage*—carry generation.
3. There is *no* carry from the *previous stage nor* to the *next stage*.
4. There is a carry from the *previous stage and* a carry *generated in this stage*.

CARRY TRANSMISSION. A carry passes through this stage if either the addend digit X or the augend digit Y or both is 1.

CARRY GENERATION. A carry is generated in this stage only if the addend digit X and the augend digit Y are both 1.

CASE 4 is covered by the case of carry generation.

CARRY OMISSION accounts for the remainder of cases.

Multiple-Phase Addition System

The operation of parallel adders can usually be analyzed into four phases:

1. Form the sum of the accumulator and addend digit (before or after the carry is considered).
2. Check for carry generation and generate it if necessary.
3. Check for carry transmission and transmit it if necessary.
4. Record carry when present.

These steps may not follow in just that order but they must be done at one time or another.

Accumulator Bit-Storage Participation

It is customary to design the natural binary accumulator so that each bit storage of the accumulator register takes part in the addition process. Recall that in serial addition, as each sum digit is formed, it is pushed into the left-hand side of the accumulator register, the left-hand bit storage. It is later moved down the register to end at the proper place. We could use this principle in the parallel process: the accumulator digit could be read out into the corresponding adder of a set of adders; the sum would then be returned to the accumulator as it was formed.

It is more economical to incorporate each bit storage of the accumulator register into the adder logic. This is done as follows. The addition logic examines the accumulator and addend bit to determine if or how the register must be altered to obtain the sum digit; the accumulator bit storage is then operated as a trigger; if it is to be altered (a 1 made a 0 or a 0 made a 1), it is triggered once; if it is to remain as set (it should be 1 and is 1 or vice versa), it is either triggered twice or not at all, the latter being more economical, of course.

Primitive Parallel-Bit Adder

A primitive version of a parallel-bit adder is shown in Figure 11.3.1. Its action can be analyzed into four
successive steps:

(1) If the addend bit is a 1, trigger the accumulator bit storage.
(2) Check to see if the addend is 1 and the accumulator bit is 0; if so, the accumulator was 1 before step (1) and a carry should be generated to the *next* stage, which is then done.
(3) The carry pulse from the previous stage checks to see if there is carry transmission. *This* pulse becomes the transmitted carry pulse if and only if the accumulator is now 1.
(4) The carry-in pulse is now recorded—it is used to trigger the bit storage of the accumulator register.

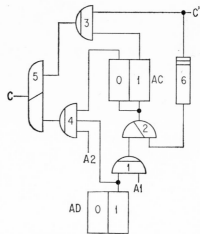

FIGURE 11.3.1.   First example of a parallel binary adder.

The first phase is performed by reading out the addend bit. The pulse on line A1 is called the add pulse because it is used to count the accumulator bit. It is applied to &1, and if the addend bit is 1, the accumulator bit storage is triggered via V2. The accumulator AC is reversed only if the addend bit is a 1; otherwise, it maintains status quo.

Next, carry generation is checked. A carry test pulse appears on the carry line, A2. A carry pulse is *generated* for *this stage only* if AD is 1 and AC is 0. This condition allows the carry pulse to pass through &4 into V5, the carry output from this stage.

For the third phase, carry *transmission*, the carry pulse from the *previous* stage enters *this stage* on line C'. The carry entering this stage will be transmitted to the next stage only if AC is now 1. This is checked and the pulse C' is transmitted when required through &3 via V5. Notice that it is conceivable that pulses appear at both &3 and &4, but since AC cannot be both 1 and 0 at the same time, an output *is not possible* from both &3 and &4. Thus, one accumulator stage may either generate or transmit a carry but not both.

The fourth phase records the carry. A carry either generated or transmitted by the previous stage enters this stage via the C' line. It is delayed by Δ6. This delay is necessary because the C' pulse both tests and counts AC. If it did both at once, the two would interfere with each other. The carry check done using &3 occurs before the recording, via V2 delayed by Δ6, so that the two do not interfere.

Second Design

Sometimes it is desirable to read out the addend only once during the first phase—so that it can be used or altered during the rest of the add cycle without messing up the addition. This requires an extra bit storage labeled CY for each bit of the accumulator. Figure 11.3.2 shows this logic, which follows the same steps as the primitive version.

The first phase pulse A1 tests the addend register AD at &7. A pulse appears at V2 if the addend digit is a 1; none appears if the addend digit

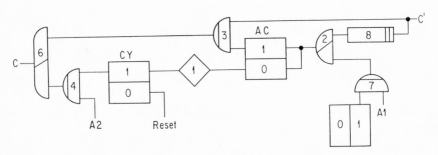

FIGURE 11.3.2.   Second example of a parallel binary adder.

is a 0. If there is an output from V2, it triggers AC; only if AC is now set to 0 does it cause a pulse to be generated via the shaper S1 (the diamond). When present, this pulse from S1 sets the carry storage CY to 1.

The carry-generate phase is activated by the carry phase pulse A2 which checks the carry bit storage CY via &4 and is passed to the next stage via V6.

The carry-in pulse C' checks the accumulator AC for a setting of 1 by &3 to determine if carry transmission should occur; if so, it leaves this stage via V6.

The carry must be delayed before it is recorded so that the testing of AC by the C' pulse via &3 is not interfered with by AC changing state prematurely. This is accomplished by interposing Δ8 in the path of C' before it reaches V2 to trigger AC.

Third Method

It is time-consuming to trigger the accumulator bit storage twice if it is going to remain in its present state. This third method provides only one pulse to the bit storage and that only when the derived result requires a single change in state. This method consists of three simultaneous decisions:

1. Trigger the accumulator register bit storage for a carry from the previous stage or a 1 in the addend bit, but not both.
2. Carry generation.
3. Carry transmission.

The logic for this method appears in Figure 11.3.3. The condition of either a carry-in (C') or a 1 in the addend bit storage (X) is constructed

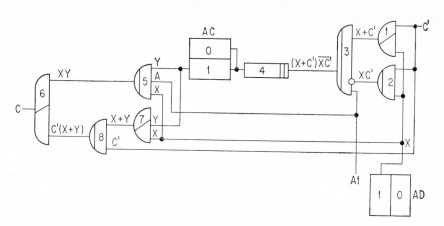

FIGURE 11.3.3. Third example of a parallel binary adder.

in $\vee 1$ as $X + C'$. The condition that there is both a carry-in (C') and a 1 in the addend (X) is formed in &2 as XC'. The condition for either carry or 1 in the addend bit *but not both* $(X + C')\overline{XC'}$ is composed by &'3. The add pulse A1 passes through &'3 only when AC is to be triggered. There is no hurry to trigger AC, so the triggering pulse is placed temporarily in the delay $\Delta 4$ until the carry function is performed.

There is a carry generation if both the accumulator register bit storage is now 1 (Y) and the addend bit storage is now 1 (X); in that case pulse A1 passes through &5 and $\vee 6$ to emerge as the carry pulse C into the next stage.

There is carry transmission if either the accumulator or addend bit is 1 $(X + Y)$ *and* if there is a carry C' from the previous stage. $X + Y$ formed in $\vee 7$ permits the pulse C' to pass through &8 as the condition $C'(X + Y)$ and then through $\vee 8$ as a carry-out C to the next storage.

After the carry has been tested for and propagated (transmitted or generated), the bit emerges from $\Delta 4$ and if it is a 1 it triggers the accumulator register bit storage.

Other Versions

There are many different logics which have been devised for parallel binary adders. The reader is referred elsewhere for other treatments (see references 8 and 29).

11.4. NATURAL BINARY CODED DECIMAL ADDITION

NBCD coding has been described extensively in chapter 8. It is a machine language in which each of the ten decimal digits has a unique four-bit code. It has six forbidden four-bit combinations—codes for which there is no corresponding decimal digit. We now wish to find some means for adding decimal digits so coded; the result we expect is another coded decimal digit and a carry *bit*. Notice we say "carry bit" because this is binary information—carry or no carry.

The inputs to our adder are the four bits of the addend $X1$, $X2$, $X3$, and $X4$, the four bits of the augend $Y1$, $Y2$, $Y3$, and $Y4$, each noted from least to most significant bits, and the carry in, C'; the outputs are the four sum bits $S1$, $S2$, $S3$, and $S4$ and the carry-out C.

We are first going to add the codes for the decimal digits as though the codes were binary numbers. If the result is the correct code, all well and good; otherwise, we correct this result.

We recall the rules developed in Section 8.2 for adding NBCD digits:

1. If the sum is 9 or less, the sum digit code is then correct.
2. If the sum is 10 to 15, the sum digit code is not correct and a carry

has not been generated as required. To correct this, a coded 6 is added to the sum-so-far producing the correct sum and the carry.
3. If the sum is 16 or more, there is a carry created but the sum is wrong. Again this is corrected by adding a coded 6.

To do the job, we shall require a set of four full adders to add the respective bits of each coded digit and the carries from previous bit additions. We shall need means for determining when the output of this set of full adders indicates that the decimal sum is greater than 9. And when it is, we need another set of adders (the correctors) which add a binary coded decimal 6 to the sum produced by the first set of adders.

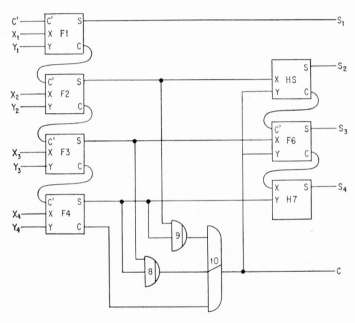

FIGURE 11.4.1.   Natural binary-coded decimal adder.

The logic of Figure 11.4.1 does the entire job. The full adders, F1, F2, F3, and F4 perform the first addition. The carry input F1C' is the carry resulting from the previous coded decimal digit addition. For the other carry bits, the carry output of one full adder is connected to the carry input of the next full adder, e.g., F2C is connected to F3C'.

To see how sums greater than nine may be detected, let us review the forbidden combinations which may arise. They are 1010, 1011, 1100, 1101, 1110, 1111. All of these combinations have a fourth bit which is 1; but so do the codes for 8 and 9 so that this is not a sufficiently distinguishing characteristic. Examining these forbidden codes again, we note that each contains either a second or third bit which is 1 which is not the case for 8(1000) or 9(1001). Together, these characteristics distinguish a forbidden code from a correct combination. A correction is also required when the sum code is an acceptable combination but there is a carry present. The conditions requiring correction of the first sum (the output of F1, F2, F3, and F4) and the detection of these conditions are now itemized:

1. Bits four and three of the first sum are both 1, detected by &8.
2. Bits four and two of the first sum are both 1, detected by &9.
3. A carry is produced by F4 for which a 1 is present at the carry output F4C.

For any one of these there is an output from V10. Note that this is also an indicator of a carry-out for the NBCD adder, so that the output of V10 is also labeled C.

Now when there is a carry-out, C, we wish to add coded six—0110—to the sum out of the first adder. We could use another set of four full adders, but with a few observations we can reduce our requirements:

1. The first bit may only have 0 added to it and is never affected—eliminate one full adder.
2. The second bit may have 1 added to it but there is never a carry from the first bit—use a half adder H5 for this.
3. The third bit requires a full adder, F6, since it has three inputs; the partial-sum bit, the coded-6 bit, and carry-out bit from H5.
4. The fourth bit may only have a 0 added to it but there may be a carry bit input from F6—a half adder, H7, will do.

The coded-6 input to the corrector (H5, F6, and H7) is the C output applied to H5Y and F6Y. The outputs from the natural binary coded decimal digit adder are the four partial sum bits, $S1$, $S2$, $S3$, and $S4$ and the carry C.

Use

The NBCD digit adder is used in serial-character parallel-bit accumulator as in Figure 11.4.2. The parallel-bit output of the accumulator is entered into the X inputs of the adder; the parallel-bit output of the addend register is entered into the Y inputs of the adder; the carry output C of the adder is returned through a single-digit-time delay to the adder carry input C'; the sum outputs of the adder are returned to the most significant digit inputs of the accumulator; both the addend and accumulator registers are shifted simultaneously.

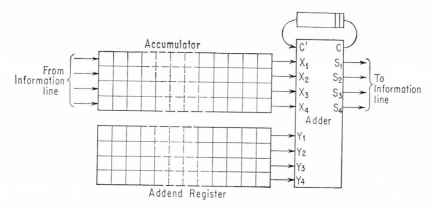

FIGURE 11.4.2.   Serial-digit parallel-bit accumulator.

11.5. THE XS3 ADDER

Addition in XS3 code was described in Section 8.3. One of two conditions arises in adding two XS3 coded digits:

1. If the decimal sum is 10 or more, the XS3 code produced does not correctly represent the sum, but the required carry is present. The partial sum is corrected by adding 0011 to it.
2. If the decimal sum is less than 10, again the XS3 code does not represent the sum, but the carry is absent as it should be. Correction is made by subtracting 0011 from the partial sum or by adding 1101 to the partial sum and neglecting the carry which is generated.

In either of these cases the sum obtained by adding the codes must be corrected. There are then three steps to be taken:

1. Add the codes using a set of four full adders.
2. Determine the kind of correction required.
3. Make the correction by adding the correction code to the initial sum in another set of adders.

The logic to do this is found in Figure 11.5. The nine input bits are those of the addend $X1$, $X2$, $X3$, and $X4$, those of the augend $Y1$, $Y2$, $Y3$, and $Y4$ and the carry in, C'; there are four sum output bits $S1$, $S2$, $S3$ and $S4$ and the carry out C. The four full adders, F1, F2, F3, and F4 are connected as in the last section to add the codes.

The two cases indicating the two kinds of correction are clearly delineated by the presence or absence of a carry F4C from the adder F4. In other words, add 0011 if there is a 1 at F4C; add 1101 if there is a 0 at F4C.

The first bit correction adder can be eliminated if we note that any correction requires the addition of a 1 to the first bit of the partial sum first. Hence we can obtain a corrected first bit by inverting the first bit of the initial sum F1S using $\bar{8}$. Three other full-correction adders are necessary.

The second bit of the initial sum F2S is entered at F5X. There is a correction input when there is a carry on the initial sum; F4C is connected

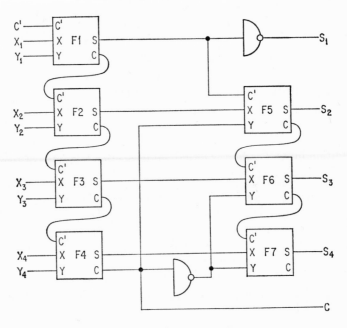

FIGURE 11.5.   XS3 adder logic.

to F5Y. There would be a carry from the first bit correction whenever the first bit of the initial sum is 1; hence F1S is connected to F5C'.

The third bit of the initial sum is entered into the third bit correction adder by connecting F3S to F6X. There is a correction for the *third* bit when there is no carry from the initial sum; $\overline{F4C}$ the output of $\bar{9}$ is connected to F6Y. The carry from the second bit correction is entered by connecting F5C to F6C'.

The fourth bit of the initial sum is entered into the fourth bit correction adder by connecting F4S to F7X. There is a correction for the fourth bit when there is no carry from the initial sum; $\overline{F4C}$ from $\bar{9}$ is connected to F7Y. The carry from the third bit correction is entered by connecting F6C to F7C'.

The carry-out for the entire XS3 adder is the same as for the initial sum, i.e., $C = F4C$.

Use

The XS3 adder is incorporated into an accumulator in the same fashion that the NBCD adder is. Hence Figure 11.4.2 is also applicable for an XS3 serial-digit parallel-bit accumulator.

11.6. COMPLEMENTERS

We've discussed the complement before. Regardless of the number system, a digit complement is one less than the difference between the base and the digit. When dealing with coded digits, we find that some codes are **self-complementary**: the code for the complement of a digit is the complement of the code for the digit. The XS3 code is self-complementing, so we may find an illustration of this principle by examining it. The XS3 code for 3 is 0110; the complement of 3 is 6 in the decimal system; the XS3 code for 6 is 1001; the complement of the XS3 code for 3 is 1001. It is seen by examining the XS3 codes for other decimal digits that it is truly a self-complementing code.

In this section we shall examine complementation of natural binary numbers, self-complementing codes, and non-self-complementing codes.

Self-Complementing Codes and Bit Complementers

For this kind of complementation it is merely necessary to change each 1 to a 0 and each 0 to a 1.

If the number to be complemented is in bit storage, it is a simple matter to read out its complement by reading the 0 state of the bistable device instead of the 1 state. When this is done the 1 reads as a 0 and the 0 as a 1.

Figure 11.6.1 shows logic for using a bit adder for serial-bit serial-character addition *and* subtraction for a self-complementing machine code. "ADD" indicates a

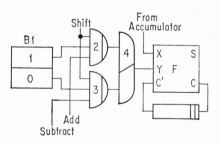

FIGURE 11.6.1. Bit adder and subtractor.

d-c signal present when addition is called for; "SUB" indicates a d-c signal present when subtraction is required. B1 is the least significant bit of the addend-subtrahend register. As the register is shifted through &2

during addition, the addend is transmitted properly through V 4 to the adder F. During subtraction, the complement of this register is passed through &3 and V 4 to F. Since a self-complementary code is used, F is supplied the minuend at X and the subtrahend complement at Y and produces the difference at S.

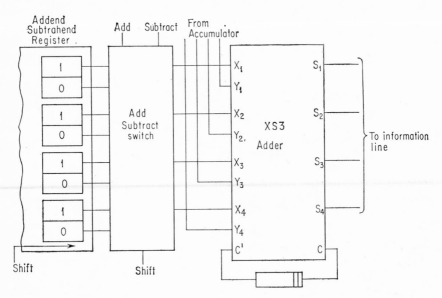

FIGURE 11.6.2. XS3 coded binary decimal parallel-bit serial-character adder and sub-tractor.

Figure 11.6.2 shows how an assembly of four such add-subtract switches (A-S) are used for XS3-coded serial-character parallel-bit addition and subtraction.

Non-Self-Complementing Codes

The procedure for deriving complementing logic for various codes is similar. The natural binary coded decimal is the most important of such codes and we will develop complementing logic for it as an illustration of the principles involved.

Natural Binary Coded Decimal Complementer

The table of codes for each decimal digit and its complement appears in Table 11.6.1. We assume that the bit and its inverse are both available,

TABLE 11.6.1 NBCD DIGIT CODES AND DIGIT COMPLEMENT CODES

Digit	NBCD code	NBCD complement	Digit complement
0	0000	1001	9
1	0001	1000	8
2	0010	0111	7
3	0011	0110	6
4	0100	0101	5
5	0101	0100	4
6	0110	0011	3
7	0111	0010	2
8	1000	0001	1
9	1001	0000	0

which is true if the digit is in bit storage. The Boolean equation for the complement is now obtained. The complement of the digit X which is coded using the bits X_4, X_3, X_2, X_1, is C coded using the bits C_4, C_3, C_2, C_1.

From the table we see the complement of an even digit is always odd and vice versa. Hence the first bit of the complement will always be inverted, which we write as

$$C_1 = \bar{X}_1 \qquad (11.6.1)$$

Again from the table we note that either both the number and its complement contain identical second bits which we write as

$$C_2 = X_2 \qquad (11.6.2)$$

The third complement bit (C_3) is 1 when the second bit is opposite from the third in the code, written as

$$C_3 = X_2\bar{X}_3 + \bar{X}_2X_3 \qquad (11.6.3)$$

The fourth bit of the complement is 1 only when there is a 0 in the second, third, and fourth position of the code, written as

$$C_4 = \bar{X}_4\bar{X}_3\bar{X}_2 \qquad (11.6.4)$$

The equations are realized by the logic of Figure 11.6.3.

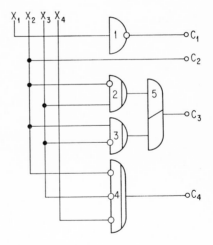

FIGURE 11.6.3. A natural binary-coded decimal complementer.

11.7. COMPARISON

The decision-making facility of the modern computer rests for the most part on its ability to compare two numbers and to choose among several courses of action according to the results of the comparison.

The simplest and first means devised for comparing numbers was to perform two subtractions and observe whether the result of either is less than zero. To compare X and Y, we find $X - Y$ and $Y - X$. We have these results:

(1) if $X - Y < 0$ then $X < Y$

(2) if $Y - X < 0$ then $Y > X$

(3) if $X - Y \not< 0$ and $Y - X \not< 0$ then $X = Y$

This sometimes requires two subtractions. It is possible to perform a comparison in one step using a special comparison logic.

One-Step Comparison Method

This method assumes that the most significant digit of the number is at the left, as is true with all the natural number systems we have used and with most of the codes.

When we compare two numbers such as $X = 3328$ and $Y = 3319$, we begin at the left and scan the digits, comparing corresponding digits. The left-hand 3's are equal, so we are uncertain; the next two 3's are equal, and we are still uncertain; next, the 2 in X and the 1 in Y are scanned; because the 2 in X is greater than the 1 in Y we reach the (correct) conclusion that $X > Y$; the fact that the unit's 9 in Y is larger than the unit's 8 in X has no bearing on our decision.

In comparing $X = 1031$ with $Y = 879$, we immediately note that X has more digits than Y. More precisely, this is equivalent to saying that there is no bundle for Y of size equal to or greater than the largest bundle in X.

Serial-Bit Comparitor

The most important application for a serial-bit comparitor is with natural binary numbers and binary coded numbers. As long as the digits are the coefficients of ascending powers of the base in one direction, we can compare the numbers easily.

Consider any pair of single bits, calling them X_i and Y_i. These bits are equal if they are both 1 or both 0; $X_i > Y_i$ if X_i is 1 and Y_i is 0; $X_i < Y_i$ if X_i is 0 and Y_i is 1.

Our comparison logic should do several things:

1. If $X_i = Y_i$, nothing happens—make further comparisons.
2. If $X_i > Y_i$, set a bit storage BG indicating this.
3. If $Y_i > X_i$, set a bit storage BL indicating this.
4. In the latter two cases, further comparisons must be prevented to preserve the present result.

The logic for this is found in Figure 11.7.1. The input lines X and Y feed in serially, bit by bit, the two numbers to be compared. Corresponding bits of each pass through &'1 and &'2. The output of &'3 is $X_i\bar{Y}_i$ and is present only if $X_i > Y_i$; the output of &'4 is $\bar{X}_iY_i$ and is there only when $X_i < Y_i$; BG or BL is set respectively if $X_i > Y_i$ or $X_i < Y_i$. When either BG or BL is set to 1, a voltage at V6 is applied slightly delayed by Δ7 to &'1 and &'2. This voltage prevents any further bits from passing through &'1 and &'2 which might set the unset bit storage of the pair.

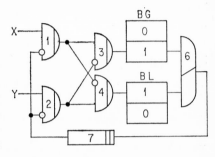

FIGURE 11.7.1.   Serial binary comparitor

Serial-Character Parallel-Bit Comparitor

It is possible to make parallel-bit comparison in two ways, making a simultaneous sum of all bits at once or serializing the information.

SERIALIZATION. The logic of Figure 11.7.2 enables us to perform serial-character parallel-bit comparison by comparing bits in sequence with four serial-bit comparitors. The serializing is done by inserting correspondingly longer delays in the lesser significant bits. The delays may be inserted either to delay comparison or to delay the recording of the results. The latter is illustrated in Figure 11.7.2. The four corresponding bits, one from each of the pair of numbers X_4 and Y_4, X_3 and Y_3, X_2 and Y_2, and X_1 and Y_1, are compared in CM4, CM3, CM2, and CM1 respectively. The result from CM4 (most significant bits) is recorded first without delay; for "greater" the pulse passes from CM4G through V7 and &'9 to set BG; for "less" the pulse passes from CM4L through V8 and &'10 to set BL. The result of the next bit comparison leaves as a pulse from CM3G (or CM3L), is delayed slightly by Δ1 (or Δ2), passes through V7 (or V8) and &'9 (or &'10) to set BG (or BL) *providing* that neither BG nor BL has been set earlier; if either BG or BL has been previously set, its output is applied through V11 and Δ12 to prevent passage of further results through &'9 or &'10. The result from CM2 is subjected to a longer delay by either Δ3 or Δ4; the results from CM1 are subjected to an even longer delay by Δ5 or Δ6. If this character-code comparison has not been

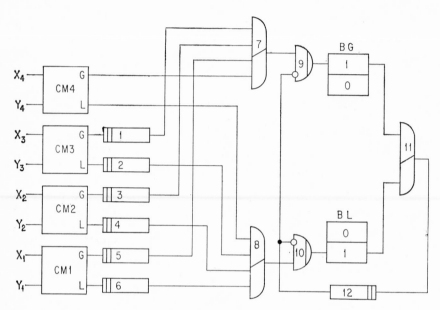

FIGURE 11.7.2.   Four-bit comparison logic for serial-character parallel-bit operation using serialization with Δ1 = Δ2 < Δ3 = Δ4 < Δ5 = Δ6; Δ12 < Δ1.

recorded in either BG or BL, the result of further character-code comparisons may be entered there; otherwise, further results will be inhibited by the voltage from V11 through Δ12 at both &'9 and &'10.

SIMULTANEOUS SCAN. The Boolean equations which determine from the two sets of four (or more or less) bits whether X is greater, less than, or equal to Y are not difficult either to set up or to implement, but they are rather too specialized to spend appreciable time on.

Parallel-Character Comparisons

The reader can see that the principles of either simultaneous scan or serialization can be used to formulate a parallel-*character* comparitor. It is left to him to apply these principles.

11.8. CODING, DECODING, ENCODING

Encoders

Coding and **encoding** are often used in the same sense, to mean the act of converting a baseless input into a binary code or number. "Baseless" is used as in Chapter 8 to indicate that there is a separate symbol or wire for each number capable of representation. Here only *one* input wire may carry a signal. The term *coding* is best reserved for setting a program into machine program language. An **encoder,** then, is a device which, for

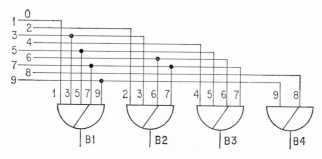

FIGURE 11.8.1. NBCD encoder.

a single pulse or d-c input, produces a multiple pulse or d-c output. This is done using as many multiple-input mixers as there are output bits. The baseless input is entered into each mixer for which a 1 output is required. Figure 11.8.1 shows a natural binary coded decimal encoder. Notice there is an input line in that figure for nine of the ten digits and that an output may appear on one or more of the four parallel output lines for one of these input signals. *0* has no *input* because there is no output for 0—it is coded as 0000 (a failing of NBDC).

A serial-character parallel-bit decimal-to-NBCD encoder might use the logic of Figure 11.8.1. In a time sequence one of the input lines to the encoder would have a pulse applied to it corresponding to the decimal number to be encoded. The four output lines would emit, at that pulse time, the set of signals corresponding to the NBCD code of the decimal digit currently being considered.

There is an easier form in which the encoder diagram may be drawn and presented. This is shown in Figure 11.8.2. One vertical line is assigned to each digit to be encoded; one horizontal line represents each bit of the coded output; any one or several of the output lines may have a signal on it, depending on the single signal input. The solid triangle at the junction of an input and output line indicates that this input signal causes a signal to appear on the output line. For instance, a signal on the 6-input line for the decimal-to-NBCD encoder of Figure 11.8.2 causes an output on lines B3 and B2 only, since the 6-line intersects the B3 and B2 lines at triangles in that figure.

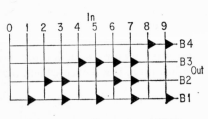

FIGURE 11.8.2. Decimal to NBCD encoder.

An N-character word, parallel-character parallel-bit encoder would require N such encoder units and a total of $10 \cdot N$ input lines and $4 \cdot N$ output lines. All the characters of the word would be encoded at once.

It is also possible to consider an encoder which translates a multi-digit decimal word into a binary word. Since there is no correspondence between the decimal digit and any set of bits of the binary number, such an encoder is not simply described. See Problem 13.

Decoders

Having several input lines, one or more of which carries a pulse or d-c signal, the **decoder** emits a single signal on one of a number of possible lines. This logic serves an opposite function to the encoder. Several of the input lines may carry signals but only one output signal occurs. Since it is a many-to-one device, it is constructed of &-blocks. A decoder to translate the single digit 6 from NBCD to a decimal is shown in Figure 11.8.3. Using only 2-input &-blocks, the logic of Figure 11.8.4 is a complete NBCD-to-decimal decoder.

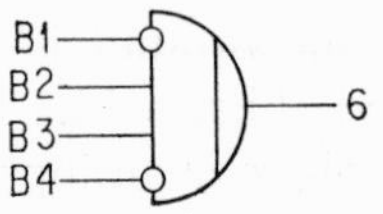

FIGURE 11.8.3. Decoder for base-less 6 output, NBCD-to-base-less.

Figure 11.8.5 shows a simpler representation of an NBCD decimal decoder. Note that for each bit there is a 1- and a 0-input line. The reason is that it is difficult to show an inverter input to a gate in this representation; it is much easier to use two lines per bit. There is an output line for each digit which may be decoded. There must be an input signal at *all* the intersections of input lines with the given output for which there is a semicircle—these are &-blocks. For instance, for a signal on the 9-output line there must be an input on $\overline{B4}$ (B4 = 0 line), B3, B2, and $\overline{B1}$. You see

B4 B2
B3 B1

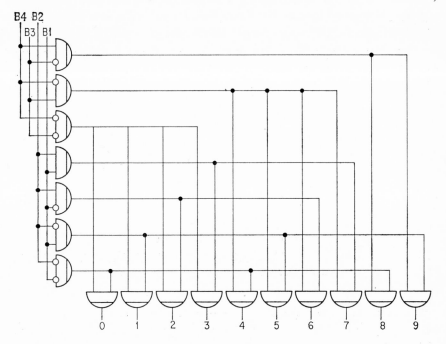

FIGURE 11.8.4. Full decoder, NBCD to decimal, using two-input &-blocks only.

that each output line has *exactly* four intersections with input lines; this is because NBCD is a four-bit code, and each bit must be accounted for as either a 0 or a 1.

A serial-character parallel-bit decoder functions as the name implies. A parallel-character decoder requires as many decoder units as there are characters. The binary-to-decimal decoder is found in Problem 14.

Character Detectors

It is often important to determine if a given symbol is stored in a register. Thus in multiplication it must be determined if the multiplier has been tallied down to 0. This detection is done with a decoder. The logic of Figure 11.8.3 serves as an NBCD "6" detector, for instance.

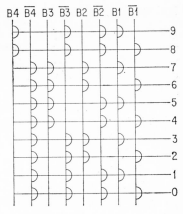

FIGURE 11.8.5. NBCD-to-decimal decoder.

Symbols

Character detectors and decoders are represented by a rectangle with a D in it as appears in Figure 11.8.6(a) and 11.8.6(b); there are several input lines for the binary coded digit input; the detector has a single output produced when the desired digit is detected, Figure 11.8.6(a); the

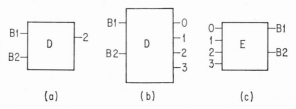

(a)   (b)   (c)

FIGURE 11.8.6.   (a) Detector block symbol.   (b) Decoder block symbol.   (c) Encoder block symbol.

decoder has an output for each digit represented in the code, Figure 11.8.6(b). The encoder symbol, a rectangle with an E in it, is shown in Figure 11.8.6(c).

11.9. COUNTERS

Counters are used to keep track of things—for internal bookkeeping. Many counters use bases other than two. However, modern high-speed computers mainly use binary counters and we will limit our discussion to their study.

The counter was mentioned in passing earlier in the book; the logic for one is illustrated in Figure 11.9.1. Before use, each bit storage of the counter is cleared (set to 0) by a pulse applied to the reset line. The state of each bit storage is shown on the first line under the figure. The first input pulse to be counted is applied to the 1 input *and* to the 0 input of B1 through V4. B1 is thus used as a trigger. B1 is set by this pulse to what it is not; since it was just reset, it is now 0 and hence it is set to 1 by the first pulse. As listed below each bit storage, the counter then reads 001. The second pulse sets B1 back to 0; in so doing the shaper circuit S5 emits a pulse; this pulse is applied to both the 1 input of B2 and the 0 input of B2 through V6. B2 is set to what it is not and hence is set to 1; the three bits now read 010. The next input pulse sets B1 to 1; the setting is then 011. The next input pulse sets B1 to 0; this enters a pulse into the next bit, setting it to 0; this in turn enters a pulse into the third bit setting it to 1; the setting is now 100. As you can see below the diagram, successive pulses cause the bit storage to assume states corresponding to successive natural binary numbers.

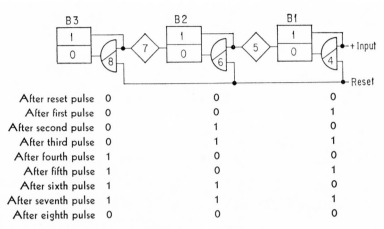

	B3	B2	B1
After reset pulse	0	0	0
After first pulse	0	0	1
After second pulse	0	1	0
After third pulse	0	1	1
After fourth pulse	1	0	0
After fifth pulse	1	0	1
After sixth pulse	1	1	0
After seventh pulse	1	1	1
After eighth pulse	0	0	0

FIGURE 11.9.1.   Counter logic.

The counter just described is called a scale-of-N counter. In the type of logic illustrated, N is always equal to 2^n where n is the number of stages. This scale-of-eight counter can store 0 as 000 or 7 in binary form as 111.

When registering 111, the next pulse sets all three stages to 0 so that the counter next reads 0 in binary as 000; the eighth pulse resets the counter. Thus the "eight" in "scale-of-eight" refers to the number of the pulse which resets the counter; it really cannot store an equivalent of 8.

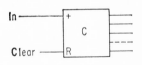

FIGURE 11.9.2.   Counter symbol.

The functional block symbol for a counter appears as Figure 11.9.2. Counting pulses are entered at + and the counter is reset to 0 by a pulse entered at R. Each of the N bits may be set to 0 or 1; there are $2n$ different possible outputs for a scale of 2^n.

Foreshortened Counters

A counter can be made to reset "before its time" as in Figure 11.9.3. Here the scale-of-eight counter becomes a scale of six. It counts normally until it reaches 6. At that time B1 is set to 0 and B2 and B3 are both set to 1. Only then does &6 have an output, since it performs a decoder func-

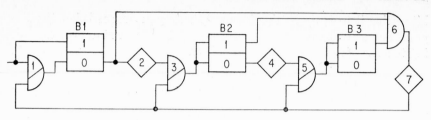

FIGURE 11.9.3.   Scale-of-six bit storage counter.

tion; this is shaped into a pulse by S7: this pulse is then applied to V1, V3, and V5, setting B1, B2, and B3 to 0. When the counter reaches 6, B1 should be set to 0 so V1 can be eliminated. The logic of Figure 11.9.3 is represented more succinctly by the two blocks of Figure 11.9.4.

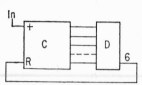

FIGURE 11.9.4.   Scale-of-six symbol.

Core Counters

Core elements may be assembled to make counters, too. In Figure 11.9.5 four cores are used to make a scale-of-four counter. The first core is preset (set to 1 before the counter is used). Each count moves this 1 to the right one core. A number of shift pulses equal to the number of cores causes the 1, preset into the first bit, to be shifted out from the last core. This bit may be re-entered into the first core to make ready (preset) for the next count of four; this is shown by the dotted line in the diagram.

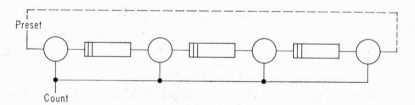

FIGURE 11.9.5.   Core counter.

If this is omitted, the counter must be externally preset for each count of four it is to make.

The core counter produces a pulse output (a-c) when the full scale count is reached. This is in contrast to the bit storage counter, for which the count information is available until the next count is entered.

Multistage Core Counters

To reduce the required number of cores from one per count for full scale count, several *sets of cores* (stages) may be used. To count to 12, seven cores are arranged as in Figure 11.9.6. Each *fourth* count from the first stage is used as a shift pulse for the second stage; three such 4-counts cause the second stage 1 to emerge at the right end of the second stage as

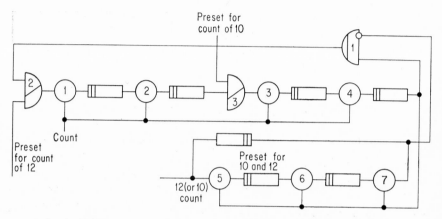

FIGURE 11.9.6. Two-stage count of 12 (or 10) using cores.

a *12-pulse*. Each first-stage-output pulse is re-entered into the first core of that stage. &1 and V2 will prevent this re-entry on the *12-count*, if this is desired.

Short Counts

To count to 10 with the multistage counter of Figure 11.9.6, a 1 is preset into the *third* core (remember in the previous subsection a 1 is preset into the *first* core to count to 12). The counter then acts as though a 1 were preset into the first core *and* two counts had already been made (this is before the first real count comes along). &1 and V2 are then *mandatory* to assure that the first core is not set to 1 on the last count.

A miscount could not be avoided if more than one 1 were stored in the cores of either stage. When the last count (10) is emitted from the output, it inhibits the re-entry of a 1 from the output of the first stage, back to the input of the first stage at &'1. This leaves the first stage empty. Hence the first stage *must be preset*. In the figure this preset 1 is entered at V3.

The Ring Counter

Bit storage can be combined in the same fashion as the cores to make a ring counter. Whether core or bit storage logic is used, the counter resulting is called a **ring counter** when the path of the 1 used for counting is *circular*. There is then one core or bit storage per stage and the 1 is shifted down the counter. Figure 11.9.7 is a ring counter using bit storage.

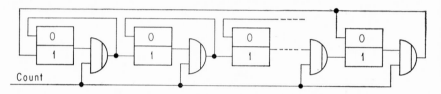

FIGURE 11.9.7.   Ring counter using bit storage.

The counting pulse tests all the gates; it passes only through the gate held open by the 1 stored in bit storage; the output *sets* the *next* bit storage and *clears this* bit storage. The last stage of the counter is returned to the first stage as it is cleared. Special logic is required so that there is always one, but only one 1, entered into the counter when the machine is turned on (or at some other time before use of the counter).

How counters are used to keep track of events and messages for internal bookkeeping is demonstrated in the next section which discusses a popular application of the counter.

FIGURE 11.10.1.   Pulse-train generator.

11.10.   PULSE-TRAIN GENERATORS

Often a train (time-sequential set) of pulses of a fixed number is required. This may be obtained by several logics, one of which is shown in Figure 11.10.1. A start pulse from another part of the equipment is used to signal the generator when a train of pulses is desired. This start pulse is also used to reset the counter in case any disturbance has modified its zero count.

As the operation begins, the start pulse resets the counter C4 to 0; it also goes through V1 and checks &'2 and &3. The count in the counter,

C4, is fed to the decoder D5 which produces an output when the counter stores a count of N; since the count is now 0, there is no decoder output. The start pulse passes through &'2 but not &3 and appears as the first pulse of the train. This first pulse is also entered into the delays Δ6 and Δ7 (where Δ6 < Δ7). The pulse emerges from Δ6 and sets the counter to a count of 1. Later the pulse emerging from Δ7 passes through V1 to test &'2 and &3. Since the counter is set at 1 for the second pulse, this pulse passes through &'2 and into Δ6 and Δ7. This continues, the counter containing a count less than N during the production of all pulses including the Nth pulse. As the Nth pulse emerges from &'2, the counter contains a count of $N - 1$; that pulse passes through &'2 and into Δ6 and Δ7. When this pulse leaves Δ6, it sets the counter to N. The decoder now produces an output

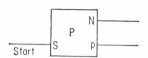

FIGURE 11.10.2. Pulse-train generator symbol.

signal which is applied to &'2 and &3. The pulse leaving Δ7 passes through V1 to test &'2 and &3. It cannot pass &'2 because the inhibiting signal from the decoder D5 is applied at the other input to &'2. It does pass through &3 to emerge as a post-train pulse. There is therefore no pulse entered into either Δ6 or Δ7 this time; the post-train pulse is the last pulse produced from the original pulse input. The rate at which pulses appear at the output &'2 is completely determined by Δ7.

A rectangle with a P in it is the functional block symbol for the pulse generator as in Figure 11.10.2; S is the start pulse input; N pulses are emitted from N; the post-train pulse emerges from p.

Asynchronous Pulse-Train Generator

The logic for another pulse generator is shown in Figure 11.10.3. This generator gates the proper number of pulses obtained from a pulse source.

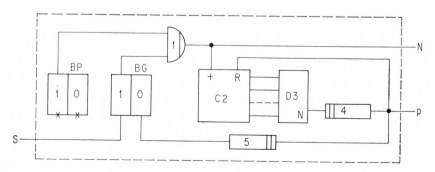

FIGURE 11.10.3. Pulse generator, asynchronous.

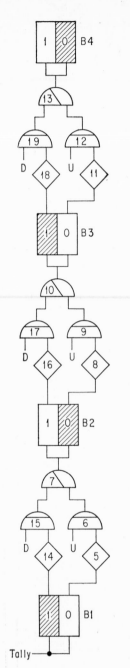

FIGURE 11.11.1. Tally up, down logic.

A counter determines when the proper number of pulses has been passed and a decoder operates the gates.

The astable multi BP is the constantly running source of pulse. The start pulse sets bit storage BG to 1. The pulse output of the astable multi is then applied to the output line N. The pulses can then pass through &8 which is "opened" by the 1 setting of BG. Each pulse which appears on the output line is counted by the counter C2. The decoder D3 emits a signal when the counter records the Nth pulse. This signal, after a short delay provided by $\Delta 4$, becomes the post-train pulse. The post-train pulse delayed by $\Delta 5$ is used to reset both the counter C2 and the "guard" bit storage BG (so called because it guards against pulses being donated by BP until called for by the start pulse). When the counter is reset, the decoder D3 no longer senses a count of N. There is hence no signal at D3N. The output on line p is thus a pulse which starts a fixed time ($\Delta 4$) after the count is reached and ends a short time ($\Delta 4$) later.

There are two objections to the output provided by this logic: since the astable multi is not synchronized with the incoming pulse, the time at which the first pulse of the train starts is unpredictable; the post-train pulse occurs closer to the last pulse than the next multi pulse would come, because it must arrive in time to inhibit further multi pulses. Neither of these objections militates against the use of this logic for most applications.

11.11. TALLIES, TALLY REGISTERS

Recall that during multiplication we wish to tally down the least significant digit of the multiplier. Also, during division, the least significant quotient digit is tallied up. One (or more) digits sitting in a register may be tallied up or down with appropriate logic. And with a little ingenuity we can devise logic which allows the *same* digit to be tallied either up or down.

Consider a single four-bit digit of a serial-character parallel-bit NBCD register, as in Figure 11.11.1, containing the digit 5 (coded as 0101) as indicated by the crosshatching. The tally digit bit storage is set up using two sets of gates so that it may be tallied up on the signal U or it may be tallied down on the signal D. In either case, the count pulse is entered into the least significant (right-hand) bit.

To tally up, the transition of any bit *from 1 to 0* is used to generate a pulse to the next stage up (more significant). The first count, which must change the count from 5 to 6, triggers B1 from 1 to 0; this generates a pulse out of S5 which passes through &6 and V7 to trigger B2 to 1; this is not a 1-to-0 transition, so that no pulse is generated by S8 to be transmitted up. The second count pulse triggers B1 to 1; no pulse is generated by S5. The third count triggers B1 to 0, which generates a pulse at S5 which passes through &6 and V7 to trigger B2 to 0. This generates a pulse at S8 which passes through &9 and V10 to set B3 to 0. This in turn generates a pulse at S11 which passes through &12 and V13 to set B4 to 1 so that finally the digit register is tallied from 7 to 8. The count continues in the same fashion.

To tally down, the transition *from 0 to 1* must generate a pulse which is applied to the next stage on a D signal. Returning to Figure 11.11.1, NBDC 5 (crosshatched) is tallied down when the first count pulse triggers B1 to 0; no pulse is generated by S14. The next count pulse triggers B1 to 1—this is a 0-to-1 transition and so S14 generates a pulse which passes through &15 and V7 to trigger B2 to 1. This is another 0-to-1 transition, so that S16 generates a pulse which passes through &17 and V10 to trigger B3 to 0. No pulse is generated by S18. The reader may continue the tally down as far as he chooses (but don't go past 0, i.e., 0000!).

In order to be useful, the tally principle must be capable of incorporation into the complete shift register design. Figure 11.11.2 shows how the right-hand digit of a register can be tallied either up or down and how a digit may be entered by shifting it in from the left.

The numbers of the blocks in Figure 11.11.1 correspond to those of Figure 11.11.2. Hence the tallying feature of the two figures is the same. The bits of the second-digit bit storage are labeled B21, B22, B23, and B24, respectively, from the least to most significant. To shift this digit to the right (into B4, B3, B2, and B1 respectively), the shift pulse SH is applied to &28, &27, &26, and &25; 1's are entered into Δ32, Δ31, Δ30, or Δ29 if the corresponding bit storages are so set 1. The pulse SH is also entered into Δ33. The output of Δ33 clears B4, B3, B2, and B1 before the

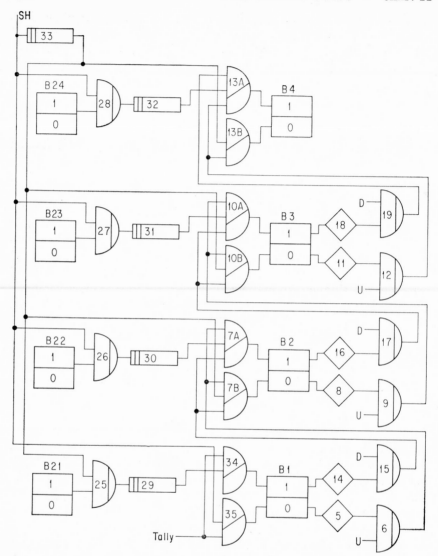

FIGURE 11.11.2. Register, last bit of which may be tallied up or down.

output of Δ32, Δ31, Δ30, or Δ29 enters the information from the previous digit stage.

If it is desired to tally more than one digit, it is necessary to incorporate recycling logic for the transition of the digit from 0 to 9 and 9 to 0 and the carry count from one digit to the next.

A register capable of being tallied is indicated by the conventional

register symbol with an extra tally input at the approximate digit position
of the register which is to be tallied and with appropriate labeling giving
the direction of tally. The multiplier register of Figure 12.5.2 (page 224)
is an example of this.

11.12. HOW FUNCTIONAL BLOCKS ARE
INCORPORATED INTO THE CONTROL UNIT

The functional blocks we have just discussed can be seen in action in
the control unit. An examination at this point of the large relationships

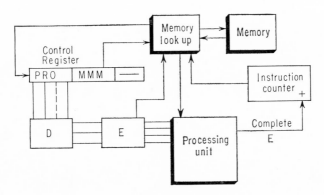

FIGURE 11.12.   Control unit organization.

which prevail in the control unit serves two purposes: it provides an
immediate application of some of the functional blocks we have just
studied, and it prepares us for a more thorough study of this important
section of the computer to which all of Chapter 14 is devoted. The discussion which follows serves to introduce the principles for integrating the
functional blocks into operational units.

The control unit supervises the procurement of a sequence of instructions. There is a special additional register used to contain the instruction
word as the computer performs the order. This control unit register is
called the **control register** or, in the case of the Polyvac, simply the C
register. Before the order is performed, it must be fetched from memory—
fetch is the computer term for obtaining an order from memory.

A typical control unit organization is shown in Figure 11.12. The
instruction word is stored in the C register, as shown. The instruction
part of the word at the left, PRO, is the input to the instruction decoder.
There is a separate output from the decoder for each order in the computer's repertoire; there is one more output from the decoder which indi-

cates when a forbidden (impossible) combination for an instruction is stored in the C register. The decoder outputs comprise the input to the encoder unit; its function is to set up the gates and subunits in the processing unit so that the order specified is performed. Since some of the gates and subunits are used for more than one order, the encoder is the means for causing several orders to activate the same gate or subunit.

Not all orders require that an operand be obtained from memory. Whether this is required is determined from the encoder output. The encoder directs a memory look-up which finds the operand datum at the address specified in the M portion of the C register. This is done before the processor gets to work to do its job.

After the operand is delivered to the processing unit, the information flow is directed within the paths set up by the encoder.

When processing is complete, the location of the next order must be determined. A counter is used to store the location of the *this* order. It is tallied up to become the location of the *next* order. Then memory look-up is initiated. When the instruction word is located, it is entered into the control register and another cycle begins.

In the next chapter, we shall examine some of the arithmetic commands, keeping in mind that when the command starts, the path of information flow has been determined and set up by the decoder and the encoder. All of Chapter 13 is devoted to the logic of memories; the discussion of the arithmetic cycle begins after the operand has been located, procured from the memory, and placed into a register.

PROBLEMS

1. Construct parallel binary subtractors analogous to the logic of Figures 11.3.1, 11.3.2, and 11.3.3 and explain each.
2. Draw a complementer for the $742-1$ code; for the 6321 code; for the two-out-of-five code.
3. Derive the equations for a simultaneous four-bit comparitor. Construct a complete logic for such a comparitor.
4. Construct a NBCD subtractor using full subtractors.
5. Construct an XS3 subtractor using full subtractors.
6. Construct, using full adders, a logic for $742-1$ BCD addition; for 2421 addition.
7. Show a logic, using full adders and D-blocks, for direct NBCD subtraction (without complement inputs for the NBCD digits).
8. Construct encoders for XS3, $742-1$, and 2421 codes; construct decoders for them also. Use the matrix (grid) notation.
9. Construct a two-stage scale-of-fifteen core counter. Show how it can be used to count to twelve.
10. Construct a pulse-train generator as in Figure 11.10.1, but use a ring counter

and no decoder. Also connect delays in series instead of the way $\Delta 6$ and $\Delta 7$ are connected. What conditions apply to the series delays?

11. Show in full detail the last three digits of a NBCD serial-character parallel-bit shift register of the type in Figure 10.5.3, the last *two* digits of which can be *tallied up*. Provide means for preventing forbidden combinations, for carry from the least significant digit, and for alarm when the register is tallied up beyond 99 in the last two digits.

12. Devise a parity check device for a four-bit binary code with an even number of 1's.

13. Design a decimal-to-binary encoder for the decimal numbers up to 29 (thirteen inputs, 10 units and 3 tens).

14. Design a decoder, binary-to-decimal to match that of Problem 13.

T W E L V E

THE LOGIC OF
ARITHMETIC

12.1. INTRODUCTION

In earlier chapters it was mentioned that arithmetic can be done either by referring to built-in tables or by incorporating within the computer the rules for finding the answer. The second method, discussed here, finds the answer directly by construction. Arithmetic consists of addition, subtraction, multiplication, and division. However, these processes as performed by the computer are all reduced by it to addition, complementation, and repetition. There are more complicated problems which a computer can do. These problems require that the programmer request the computer to perform a sequence of arithmetic operations. Repeating or iterating such operations enables the computer to take roots, to integrate, to differentiate, to develop transcendental functions, and so forth.

The functional units which were discussed in the previous chapter are now assembled, together with other logical elements, into an operational unit which does a complete arithmetic command. The logic for performing a given command is not unique; it can be obtained in many ways. For each arithmetic process we will discuss one or sometimes two logical designs of an operational unit in order to convey to the reader the general methodology.

208

Some blocks, such as pulse-train generators, may be common to several operational units; the same train generator may be used for many arithmetic commands and for transfers, too, but it is discussed as though it were a different generator in each application.

The discussion of each command begins after the operand has been procured from the memory and has been placed in the proper register. This is signalled by the appearance of an "ST" pulse emitted by the memory logic indicating that the operand has been procured (STart command pulse) on the line labeled "ST". When the command is finished, the command logic issues a pulse which appears on the line labeled "E" (End of order).

Address Systems

The way the computer does arithmetic also depends on the address system incorporated in the computer. The single-address system has one of the operands in one of its registers before an arithmetic order is given. The second operand is obtained from memory. After arithmetic is performed, the result is found in a specified register and must later be transferred to the memory, if that is where it belongs by a separate order. In the three-address system, each of the operands must be obtained from the memory and placed into a separate register. Before the arithmetic order is completed, the results must be transferred to a memory location. We can make our descriptions independent of the address system if we assume that the operands have been placed in registers beforehand and will be transferred later if necessary. The control circuitry emits a pulse labeled "ST" which is transmitted to the arithmetic unit. Our description starts at the time this pulse reaches the arithmetic unit. Similarly, when the result of arithmetic has been obtained, a pulse labeled "E" emitted by the arithmetic section of the computer is returned to the control circuitry.

Serial-Character Arithmetic

The descriptions in this chapter apply to serial-character arithmetic. This means that arithmetic is done by examining the digits of each operand consecutively and not simultaneously. This is the method currently used in most slow and medium-speed computers and many high-speed computers. Although parallel-character arithmetic increases the speed of the machine, it also increases the cost correspondingly. Since current machines are usually limited by the input/output equipment, often such a speed advantage cannot be used efficiently. To reiterate, serial-character arithmetic is studied here mainly because it is typical, straightforward to explain, and presents a consistent picture of the computer.

Asynchronous Decentralized Computation

When the control of a process is delegated to a subordinate but temporarily autonomous control unit used only for a few commands, the operation is said to be **decentralized**; if the time allotted for the processing is not fixed but rather depends on the size of the operands, the operation is said to be **asynchronous.**

The description of the asynchronous decentralized computer is tutorially simpler. To understand the operation of a synchronous computer requires that the reader be familiar with a generalized arithmetic cycle. On the other hand, the asynchronous computer can use many steps for the long process of division or a few steps for a simple addition, and both of these can be combined in a consistent machine. Each substep in one arithmetic process is hence independent of any other arithmetic process. This makes the presentation easier to understand and visualize.

Logical Design

It would be nice to have an encyclopedia of the various logical designs of arithmetic units of the many computers now in use. We shall only attempt to present one of the myriad of conceivable designs. The purpose of examining such a logical design is to understand how one arithmetic unit might work and possibly inspire the reader to look into other current designs. The logical circuits discussed typify the operating principles but do not illustrate any one particular computer.

12.2. ADDITION

First Look

As we start our description we find the operands are in two registers. The augend is in the accumulator and the addend is in another register assigned to it. The registers are serial by character and parallel by bit. The number of bits per character need not be specified at this point. The logic we are discussing would apply equally well if the machine language were natural binary, excess-three coded decimal, or natural binary coded decimal.

The main work of addition is done by an adder. For natural binary numbers the adder is the full adder discussed in Chapter 10; for excess-three or natural binary coded decimal, a suitable coded decimal adder is used. There is one input per bit into the adder provided for each bit of both the augend and addend; there is one output per bit for the sum;

there is a single output for the carry and a single carry input to the adder. In the logical diagrams that follow, multiple-bit parallel-bit information is indicated by a double line. Of course the natural binary language has only one bit per character but it is included as one of the languages to which the logic applies.

The principle by which we add numbers was sketched briefly in Figure 11.1.1 and described in Section 11.1. To review briefly, the augend and addend are each simultaneously "pushed" into the adder; the result is "pushed" out the other end of the adder. The carry produced by the adder is returned through a delay and re-entered with the next successive digit.

A Little Closer Look

The operands are stored in registers which can be shifted by applying pulses to their shift lines. If we apply shift pulses simultaneously to both registers, we shift out successive digits simultaneously, the bits of each character emerging simultaneously in parallel. We start by entering the right-hand digits, the least significant characters, into the adder. A sum digit is produced and possibly a carry. The carry bit is entered into a delay for temporary storage. We might enter this sum digit into a third register. However, we can improve the efficiency of operation and conserve registers by entering this sum digit into the *opposite* (left-hand) end of the accumulator register. That is, the sum digit replaces the left-hand digit or most significant character which has just been shifted down one position. In our registers we use the extreme left-hand place for the sign. It is not shifted during the addition process. The sum digit produced in the adder is entered into the position just to the right of the sign position—the most significant digit place in the number.

The second digit of both operands is now in the right-hand position of both registers. The next shift pulse moves the second digit from each register into the adder. If there was a carry stored from the previous digit addition, it too is now entered into the adder. The first sum digit which was just placed in the left-hand end of the accumulator is now also moved one position to the right. The *second* sum digit is produced and it is entered into the most significant position which has just been vacated by the first sum digit. This procedure continues until all the digits of both numbers have been added. At that time the first sum digit originally entered into the left-hand end of the accumulator has now been "pushed" all the way to the right and rests in the least significant position where it belongs.

The addend register may work in one of two ways: either the addend may be re-entered into the register as addition is being performed or zeros may be entered into the addend register so that it will be cleared at the end of the addition process.

Implementation

The logical diagram for an adder appears in Figure 12.2. The augend is stored in the accumulator register AC; the addend is stored in the register labeled AD. The adder is labeled A9 and its associated delay is labeled Δ4. Each of the registers in an actual computer has innumerable gates

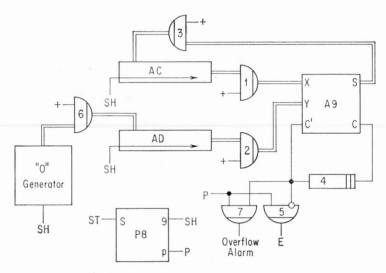

FIGURE 12.2.   Addition logic, serial character.

for switching its input and output. Only the gates necessary to the explanation are shown in this and in the following figures. A pulse generator P8 is used to generate pulses for shifting the registers. A zero generator is used to fill the register AD so that it will be cleared by the end of addition.

The shift generator, P8 of Figure 12.2, is started by the start pulse, ST. It emits a number of pulses corresponding to the number of numerical digits in the word—nine for the Polyvac. The figure indicates nine shift pulses emitted on the line labeled "9" from P8. These pulses are applied to shift the accumulator, AC, and the addend register, AD. Both of these registers have a number of gates at their input and output, only one set of which is shown for the registers in the figure. A d-c signal, labeled +, corresponding to the add order, is applied to the output gates of the accumulator, &1, and the output gates for AD, &2; these gates lead into the adder A9. The signal which appears on the three lines labeled + is the output of the command encoder from signals supplied to it by the decoder which, in turn, acts upon the instruction code for the add order stored in the C register as "ADD" for the Polyvac.

Each digit of the augend is entered through &1 into the X input of the adder A and each digit of the addend is entered through &2 into the Y input of the adder A by the nine shift pulses, SH.

The sum output of the adder is entered into the main information line; this signal A9S appears at an input gate of each register; it is entered only into the accumulator register, AC, through &3 because these input gates to the accumulator are the only gates connected to the main information line which have an enabling signal applied to them. The addend register input gates, &6, from the zero character generator have a + signal applied to them, thus allowing 0's to be entered as the addend is shifted out.

The carry bit produced on each addition at A9C is entered into Δ4. It appears one digit time later as the input to A9C'. As addition starts, Δ4 is empty of course, so that there is no input to A9C'.

Each shift pulse simultaneously causes: (1) one accumulator and addend digit to pass into the adder, (2) the sum digit to pass into the opposite end of the accumulator, (3) a carry bit to be stored in the single-bit-time delay Δ4, and (4) a 0 to enter the left end of the addend register. After nine such shifts, addition is complete; the post-train pulse appears at gates &'5 and &7. An **overflow** is defined as a carry which occurs on the addition of the last (most significant) digits. If there is no overflow, the post-train pulse P passes through &'5 into the E line to herald the end of addition; when an overflow occurs, the post-train pulse cannot pass &'5 but does pass through &7 to sound the alarm. In this case since there is no E pulse, the computer stops in its tracks to await further orders.

12.3. UNSIGNED SERIAL-DIGIT SUBTRACTION

Orientation

We are going to discuss subtraction of positive integers (natural numbers). That is, no sign is associated with either the minuend or the subtrahend. Still, subtraction is not as straightforward as addition, which was just discussed. If the subtrahend is smaller than the minuend, subtraction is done by complementing the subtrahend and adding it to the minuend. On the other hand, if the subtrahend is larger than the minuend, we must complement the minuend and add it to the subtrahend. This happens when we must do something like subtract 5 from 3. The difference is a negative number, and some indication must be made to show that the result is negative.

Offhand the approach might seem to be to determine which is larger, the minuend or the subtrahend, but this task involves as much effort as performing subtraction. There is another way, however. What we do is assume that the minuend is larger than the subtrahend. We then take the complement of the subtrahend and add it to the minuend. Call this first result D_1. If our assumption is correct, in generating D_1 an overflow should occur. This was discussed in Section 6.3. Then if an overflow occurs, our answer is correct and subtraction is complete.

On the other hand, if no overflow occurs, the answer D_1 is not correct—our assumption was wrong—the subtrahend is larger than the minuend. It is now a simple matter to correct the intermediate result, D_1. The proper result is the complement of D_1. The next step is then to complement D_1 and indicate in some way that our result is a negative number.

As an example, consider that we wish to find $17 - 11$. Then to 17 we add the complement of 11, which is 88 and 1 more. Then $D_1 = 1/06$ where the 1 to the left of the slash indicates the overflow. This tells us the difference is 6.

On the other hand, to find $11 - 17$ we add 82 (the complement of 17) to 11 and add 1 more. The result, D_1, is 0/94. The 0 indicates no overflow so that D_1 must be complemented and a minus sign inserted. To 0 is added 05 (the complement of 94) and 1 more. D is hence -06.

Method

Our method consists of three possible steps:

1. Add the complement of the subtrahend to the minuend.
2. Check to see if there is an overflow:
    (a) if there is an overflow, the present result is correct and subtraction is complete;
    (b) otherwise do step 3.
3. Complement the result obtained above, record a negative sign, and subtraction is now complete.

Implementation

The logic for unsigned subtraction appears in Figure 12.3. The accumulator AC contains the minuend; the register SD contains the subtrahend. A14 is an appropriate adder. Δ5 is the carry delay—there are intervening gates and mixers between the carry output and the carry input in order to check for an overflow. A bit storage BC is used to determine which phase of subtraction is under way: the phase designated by $\bar{C}$ corresponds to step 1 above; the phase C applies to step 3 where the result of subtraction is complemented. Two pulse generators are indicated, one for the $\bar{C}$ phase and the other for the C phase of the subtraction.

The start pulse ST sets the storage-phase bit BC to 0, starts the first pulse generator, P12, and enters a pulse into the C' input of the adder A through V4. This latter step is the end-around carry which is entered now to save time later on. The minuend digits are entered from AC

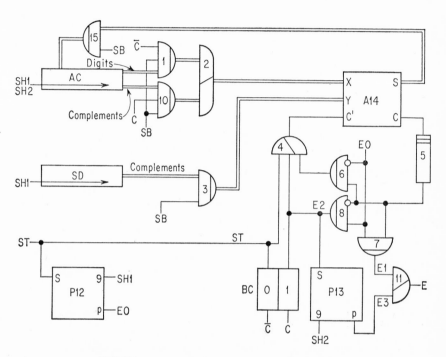

FIGURE 12.3.   Unsigned serial character subtraction.

through &1 and V2 into the X input of A14; the complemented subtrahend digits pass through &3 into the Y input; the difference passes out of the sum output A14S into the left side of AC; the carry bit is entered into Δ5. For all but the last digit, the carry bit passes through Δ5, &'6, and V4 and is entered into A14 at C' one digit time later because there is no E0 pulse present to inhibit &'6.

After the minuend and the subtrahend complement have been added and the result is placed into AC, the post-train pulse, E0, emitted by P12, tests for an overflow. E0 inhibits an overflow pulse from Δ5 from passing through &'6. E0 allows an overflow pulse from Δ5 to leave &7 as E1, which passes through V11 as an end-of-order pulse E, since subtraction is correctly completed if an overflow occurs. If no overflow is present, E0, otherwise inhibited by the overflow from passing through &'8, now passes through as pulse E2 and starts the second phase of subtraction.

The second phase complements the result when $M \leqslant S$. A second pulse-train generator, P13, is started by E2; E2 also sets bit storage C to 1. The 9's complement of the number now in AC is fed into the adder at the X input through &10 (C being set to 1) and V2 by shifting AC with pulses SH2. Nothing is entered into the Y input because no SH2 pulses are applied to SD.

To produce the complement of D_1, we must form $W - D_1 + 1$. Entering the pulse E2 through V4 into A14C' on the first digit addition adds 1 to $W - D_1$ now instead of waiting for an end-around carry to produce the complement of D_1, which is the desired difference D. When this complementing step is complete, P13 issues a post-train pulse, E3, which passes through V11 to indicate the end of the order.

12.4. SIGNED ADDITION AND SUBTRACTION

Introduction

In practice, the computer deals with addition and subtraction in almost the same manner. Sections 12.2 and 12.3 are purely of introductory and academic interest because the practical computer deals entirely with signed natural numbers—the integers. Whether the computer is asked to add or subtract, it winds up doing addition—sometimes directly and other times using complements.

To determine whether to add or subtract we must now consider whether:

1. The computer is asked to add or subtract.
2. The sign of the first operand—the number in the accumulator—is positive or negative.
3. The sign of the second operand is positive or negative.

Examining the sets of conditions which might prevail, you will note that there are eight possibilities—two alternatives in the first case × two alternatives in the second case × two alternatives in the third case. The alternatives appear in Table 12.4.1. For instance, if both numbers have the same sign and the process specified is addition, the process performed is addition: if the operands are opposite in sign and the process specified is addition, the process performed will be subtraction and the result will have the sign of the larger number.

The first task of our logical system is to determine from the signs of the operands and the process specified what process should be performed by the computer to arrive at the correct result. From examination of Table 12.4.1, it is apparent that this table corresponds to the truth table for the full adder discussed in Section 10.3 if 1 is substituted for + and 0 for −. Then a full adder can be used to determine the process to be performed by the arithmetic section: two of its inputs correspond to the

TABLE 12.4.1 PROCESS PERFORMED, IN TERMS OF THE PROCESS SPECIFIED AND THE SIGNS OF THE OPERANDS

Process specified	Augend or minuend	Addend or subtrahend	Process performed	Sign of result
+	+	+	+	+
+	+	−	−	?
+	−	+	−	?
+	−	−	+	−
−	+	+	−	?
−	+	−	+	+
−	−	+	+	−
−	−	−	−	?
C	X	Y	S	

signs of each operand; the third input is the sign of the process specified; the sum output corresponds to the process the computer should perform.

Results

We know how to produce the results of addition or subtraction but have not yet ascertained its proper sign. From Table 12.4.1, when the process performed is addition, the sign of the operand in the accumulator is also the sign of the result. This holds except when addition causes an overflow because the sum is greater than the word size, W. In that case the quantity obtained will be incorrect anyhow.

When subtraction is performed, the occurrence of an overflow indicates that the subtrahend is smaller than the minuend. The result of the subtraction is therefore correct and the sign of the result should hence be the sign of the minuend—the quantity originally in the accumulator.

If subtraction is performed without an overflow, then this indicates that the subtrahend is larger than the minuend. The result must be complemented. It must be given a sign opposite to that of the operand originally in the accumulator. These four cases appear in terms of an overflow Ω in Table 12.4.2, which the reader should study.

TABLE 12.4.2 SIGN AND VALUES OF PHASE 1 RESULT IN TERMS OF THE PROCESS
PERFORMED AND OVERFLOW

Process performed	Overflow (Ω)	Indication	Remarks
1	0	$|X| + |Y| \leqslant W$	Sign of result correct
1	1	$|X| + |Y| > W$	Result wrong
0	1	$|X| \geqslant |Y|$	Sign of result correct
0	0	$|X| < |Y|$	Sign of result reversed and the result must be complemented

A Plan of Action

A block diagram of the approach which we take to perform addition
and subtraction is found in Figure 12.4.1. In box 1, the operands are
entered into their respective registers. In box 2a the signs of the operands
and the process specified are noted. A decision is made in box 2b whether
addition or subtraction should be performed. For addition, box 3a adds

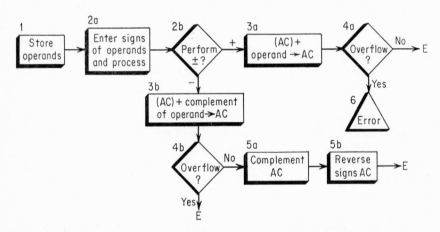

FIGURE 12.4.1. Plan of action, signed serial addition and subtraction.

the second operand to the accumulator, placing the result in the accumulator. We check to see if an overflow has occurred in box 4a. If not, our
result is correct, the sign of the result is correct, and the E pulse is produced. If an overflow occurs in box 4a, an error has occurred—the sum
numbers of the added is larger than the capacity of the register. The
computer stops and the operator is informed of the occurrence of an addition error.

For subtraction, the content of the accumulator and the complement of the second operand are added and the result placed in the accumulator. Box 4b checks to determine whether an overflow has occurred. If it has, our result and the sign are correct and an E pulse is issued. If no overflow has occurred, the result must be complemented in box 5a and the sign of the accumulator must be reversed in box 5b. Then the process is complete and an E signal is emitted.

Implementation

The logic for performing addition and subtraction of signed serial-character numbers appears in Figure 12.4.2. Still only two registers are required, one for each operand. As before, the result is returned to the accumulator. A number of entry and exit gates are required. The full adder A23 is used to determine the process to be performed from the sign of the operands and the process desired. The output A23S sets the bit storage BA' according to the process to be performed. A6 is an adder appropriate to the computer language. The pulse generator P4 operates during the noncomplementing phase, and the pulse generator P20 during the complementing phase. Bit storage BC stores the information as to what phase is currently being performed. There are also more gates performing functions such as checking for overflow and determining if the complementing phase is necessary.

Operation

The start pulse ST sets BA' and BC to 0 and after a short delay, Δ21, it is used to check the process-to-be-performed circuitry.

PROCESS PERFORMED. The delayed start pulse from Δ21 is applied to the three gates &1, &2, and &3. These serve as inputs to the full adder A23. The output A23S sets BA' to 1 only when addition is to be *performed* (regardless of the process requested).

NONCOMPLEMENTING PHASE. The start pulse delayed by Δ21 also starts the pulse generator P4, which issues nine shift pulses labeled SH1. These cause the accumulator and the second operand register to be shifted. The digits from the accumulator pass out directly through &6 and through V7 into the X input of the adder A6. The digits pass through &6 since it is held open by $\bar{C}$ (BC was set to 0 by ST) and A or S (addition or subtraction are called for). When addition is to be performed (A'), the output of the second register is fed directly through &8 and V9 into A6Y. For subtraction ($\bar{A}'$) the complement of the content of the second register passes through &10 and V9 into A6Y. The result always passes from A6S

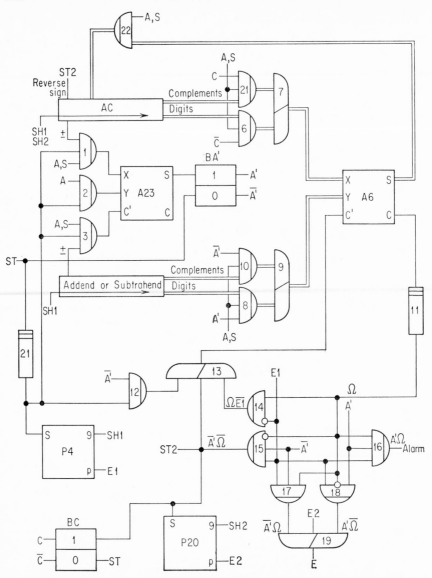

FIGURE 12.4.2. Addition and subtraction of signed serial character numbers, logic.

and is returned to the input of the accumulator. The carry bit is entered into Δ11. During addition, when there is no E1 signal present, the carry bit leaving Δ11 can only pass through &'14 (not &'15, &16, &17, or &'18) to be re-entered through ∨13 into A6C'. At the end of the noncomplementing phase, the pulse E1 is produced. It is applied to &'14, &'15, &16,

&17, and &'18. Other signals, either A′ or Ā′, appear at these gates. If an overflow, Ω, is produced during *addition* (A′), it passes out through &16 as an alarm pulse and the computer hangs up; if no overflow occurs when addition is performed, the pulse E1 passes out of &'18 through V19 as an E pulse. If an overflow occurs during subtraction (Ā′), the pulse E1 passes through &17, through V19, and emerges as an E pulse. If no overflow occurs during subtraction, the pulse E1 passes out of &'15 to start the complementing phase.

COMPLEMENTING PHASE. The pulse from &'15, Ā′Ω, will now be called ST2. It sets BC to 1, which designates the complementing phase of the process. It is also entered through V13 into A6C′ to provide the extra 1 required in complementing. ST2 also starts the complementing phase pulse generator P20. This pulse generator emits nine shift pulses SH2 which are applied only to the accumulator. The complemented accumulator output passes through &21 and V7 into A6X; there is no input into A6Y. The fully complemented output passes from A6S through &22 to be returned to the accumulator. It does not matter whether there is an overflow, for there will be no pulse E1 to test for it. When the complementation is completed, the pulse E2 is emitted from P20 and it passes through V19 to emerge as an E pulse, indicating that the process is complete.

12.5. MULTIPLICATION

The method the computer uses for multiplication was discussed in Section 6.4. It consists of performing repeated additions.

Introduction

Multiplication of two computer words can result in a product larger than either. It is possible for this product to occupy two words. Provision must be made for this full two-word product. Our register requirements are, then, one register for the multiplicand, a second register for the multiplier, and a double register for the product.

It is advantageous when programming to be able to add the product of two numbers to the number stored in the accumulator. The accumulator can still be used for storing a part of the product.

Although our apparent requirements are for four single-word registers, we can double up on one of them so that only three are actually used. As each multiplier digit is used up one product digit can be entered into the multiplier register, pushing out the used-up multiplier digit.

To start, the accumulator stores some number which is the result of previous processing. The multiplicand is in the multiplicand register, and the multiplier is in the multiplier register. The multiplicand is added to the accumulator a number of times equivalent to the least significant digit of the multiplier. This multiplier digit is no longer of use and can be destroyed. The accumulator containing a partial product is now shifted one digit to the right. Its least significant digit is entered into the multiplier register and the next multiplier digit is pushed to the right. The multiplicand is added to the accumulator a number of times equivalent

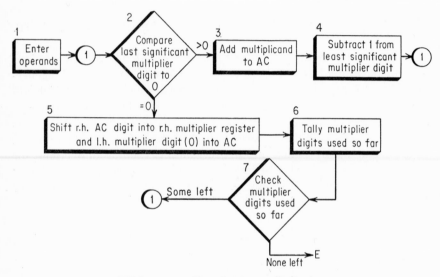

FIGURE 12.5.1.   Plan of action, multiplication.

to the next multiplier digit. This process continues until the multiplication is complete. Since multiplication only occurs for nine digits, the product digits are never used as multiplier digits.

Plan of Action

The plan of action is set forth in Figure 12.5.1. Box 1 indicates that the operands are first entered into the appropriate registers. In box 2 the least significant digit in the multiplier register is compared to zero. If it is greater than zero, the multiplicand is added to the accumulator, box 3. One is subtracted from the least significant multiplier digit in box 4 and we then return to box 2. Again the least significant multiplier digit is compared to zero. Since it is continually being reduced by one, eventually it is reduced to zero. At that time we enter box 5. The right end, or least significant digit, of the accumulator is entered into the left-end position of the multiplier register; the right-hand multiplier digit, which is now equal to zero as per the test which occurred in box 2, is moved around and entered into the left-hand digit position of the accumulator. A count is kept of the number of multiplier digits so far examined. This count is tallied in box 6. The count is examined in box 7 to determine if all the multiplier digits have been used. If some digits are still left, we return to box 2 to examine the next one; if all the multiplier digits have been used, multiplication is complete and the E pulse is returned to the control unit.

Hardware

The logical circuit for multiplication is shown in Figure 12.5.2. Of course the first thing we notice is the three registers just discussed. Next we note the adder A7, *appropriate to the machine language of the computer.* The pulse generator P5 is used to shift the contents of the registers through the adder. The decoder D4 is used to examine the least significant digit of the multiplier to determine when it has been tallied down to zero. This is tested by &'2 and &3. The bit storage BM stores the information as to which of the two phases of the process is going on, the multiple addition which adds the multiplicand to the accumulator, or the shifting of the accumulator and multiplier when the multiplier digit has reached zero. The digit counter C10 counts the number of multiplier digits we have used and the decoder D11 decodes this information.

Operation

With the quantities in their assigned registers as discussed above, the start pulse ST passes through V1 to check the gates &'2 and &3. These gates will pass this pulse according to whether the least significant digit of the multiplier is or is not zero.

Suppose that the aforementioned digit is not zero; the start pulse passes through &'2 to start the pulse generator P5. The nine shift pulses SH1 from P5 shift both the accumulator and the multiplicand registers. The bit storage BM is a univibrator, so we can be confident that it is now in its zero state, $\overline{M}$. The content of the accumulator is entered into the adder through A7X; the content of the multiplicand register is entered directly into A7Y and also re-entered into the multiplicand register; the sum digits as they are created are moved out of A7S through &15 and V14 and back into the accumulator. This completes a single addition of the multiplicand to the accumulator.

The post-train pulse, p, from P5 is sent to the least significant digit of the multiplier and tallies down this digit. The pulse P5p delayed by Δ8 passes through V1 to test &'2 and &3. If the multiplier digit is still

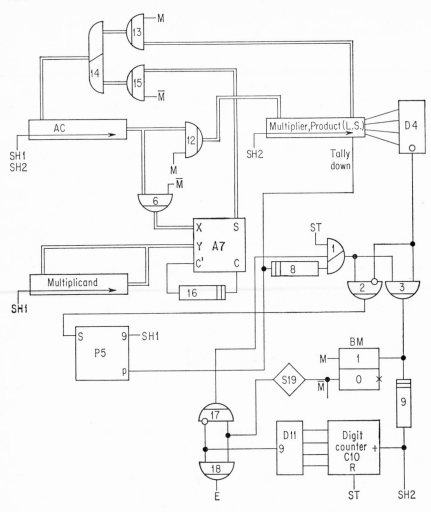

FIGURE 12.5.2.   Serial character multiplication.

greater than zero, the pulse passes through &′2 and starts another cycle of addition by the means just described.

When the multiplier digit becomes zero, there is an output from D4. This prevents the passage of a pulse through &′2; it permits the pulse from V1 to pass through &3. This sets bit storage BM to 1 (M) to signal the start of a shifting cycle. The pulse from &3 slightly delayed by Δ9 counts up the digit counter C10. It also shifts the accumulator into the multiplier register one digit to the right, an end-around shift. The digit passes from AC through &12 into the multiplier register; the zero in the multiplier register is passed through &13 and V14 to be entered into the left-hand side of AC.

The time constant of BM is such that it resets to zero after the end around shift has been completed. When it returns to zero, the shaper S19 issues a pulse. This pulse tests &'17 and &18: if all the multiplier digits have been examined, this pulse passes through &18 and emerges as an E pulse; otherwise, it passes through &17, entering V1 to start a new series of additions.

The signs associated with the multiplier, multiplicand, and product are discussed in Section 12.7.

12.6. DIVISION

Introduction

If division of any two numbers were permissible, we might ask the computer to divide W by 1. This would require more than W operations with most methods. For a machine requiring ten microseconds per subtraction and with a word length of nine coded decimal characters, this division ($W/1$) would take about 1000 seconds! Those who have used a hand calculator may recall that the same problem arises. When the machine is asked to do a division like the one above, it just keeps grinding on indefinitely unless stopped by the operator. In our computer we incorporate a rule which the programmer must observe in programming the computer and which is tested for by the computer, causing the machine to halt if disobeyed.

The rule for division which the programmer must observe is that the divisor must be larger than the dividend. Otherwise, a misalignment error will stop the machine.

Division is performed by the following steps:

1. The divisor is subtracted from the dividend.
2. The quotient is tallied up for each successful subtraction.
3. A *successful* subtraction is said to occur as long as the difference remains greater than zero.
4. When the partial remainder goes negative, it is restored by adding back the divisor.
5. The tally up of the quotient is inhibited when an unsuccessful subtraction of the divisor from the partial remainder occurs.
6. The quotient and partial remainders are shifted left after the restoration following an unsuccessful subtraction.
7. The number of quotient digits produced is checked.
8. When sufficient quotient digits have been produced, division is terminated; otherwise, the quotient digit count is tallied up.

Plan of Action

The plan of action is pictorially presented in Figure 12.6.1. First, box 1, the operands are entered. Next, box 2, the divisor is subtracted from the dividend. The result is compared with zero in box 3. If it is greater than zero, the divisor is smaller than the dividend, the programmer has broken his contract and the machine stops. Otherwise, the divisor is

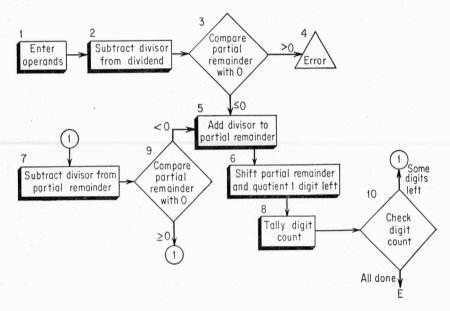

FIGURE 12.6.1. Plan of action, division.

added to restore the dividend, box 5. Next, the partial remainder (this time around, the dividend) and the quotient are each shifted one digit to the left. The number of times this shift process is performed is kept track of in box 8. This digit count is checked in box 10. If division has produced a sufficient number of quotient digits, division is complete and the E pulse is generated. Otherwise, we pass via circle 1 to box 7. Here the divisor is subtracted from the partial remainder. The partial remainder is compared with zero in box 9. If it is still greater than zero, we return via circle 1 to box 7 for another subtraction. If the partial remainder has become less than zero, it must be restored. We pass from box 9 to box 5 to repeat a restoration, shift, tally, and digit count check.

Hardware

Three registers are required, one each for the dividend, divisor, and quotient, as shown in Figure 12.6.2, the logical diagram for division. The adder A5 appropriate to the machine language performs the subtraction. Three modes of operation are used: subtraction, restoration, and shift left. Two bit storage units labeled BD1 and BD2 store the information as to which phase is being performed. Bit storage BL stores the information that alignment is correct. Corresponding to each phase, and in the order mentioned above, are three pulse generators, P3, P16, and P22. There is also a quotient digit counter C21 and a quotient digit decoder D20.

Operation

Let's discuss the operation of the logic diagrammed in Figure 12.6.2.

START OF DIVISION. Once the operands are stored and the quotient register cleared, the start pulse ST sets bit storage BL to 0 and through V1 sets BD1 to 1 and BD2 to 0. The start pulse through V1 and V2 starts the pulse generator P3. The start pulse is also entered through V1, V2, and V4 into A5C′, as the extra carry pulse required for subtraction.

SUBTRACTION CYCLE. The pulse generator P3 delivers nine shift pulses SH1. These pulses cause the accumulator digits to be entered via &7 and V8 into A5Y. The partial remainder created at A5S is moved through &9 and V10, to be returned to the accumulator.

CARRY. The carry bit from A5C is entered into Δ11. One digit-time later (determined by Δ11) it is applied to &′12, &′13, and &14. During the time P3 is producing pulses SH1, P3p is absent so that the delayed carry can only pass through &′12. The delay carry pulse leaving &′12 passes through V4 and into A5C′ to be added with the next digits.

OVERFLOW. The carry bit produced on the *ninth* digit addition is also entered into Δ11. One digit-time later it appears at &′12, &′13, and &14. But now the post-train pulse P3p is also present at the input to these gates. It cannot pass through &′12 since it is inhibited; it passes through &14 or &′13, according to whether it is a 1 (overflow) or not, respectively.

ALIGNMENT CHECK. If no overflow occurs on the very first subtraction, we are safe—the divisor was larger than the dividend. But if an overflow pulse appears at &14, it passes through &15 to issue a misalignment alarm. For correct alignment, the pulse P3p passes through &′13 to start P16

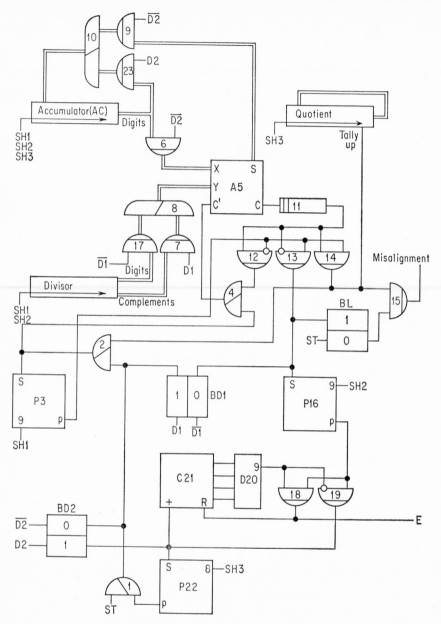

FIGURE 12.6.2.   Serial character division.

for a restoration cycle. Also, the first time around it sets the alignment storage BL to 1 so that there is no chance that a misalignment signal will be issued at a later time.

RESTORATION CYCLE. The restoration-cycle start pulse from &'13 sets the bit storage BD1 to zero. It also starts the restoration-cycle pulse generator P16. The restore-cycle pulse generator P16 issues nine pulses labeled SH2. These pulses shift the accumulator digits through &6 into A5X; they shift the divisor digits directly through &17 and V8 into A5Y to perform *addition*. The sum digits appear at A5S and pass through &9 and V10 into the accumulator.

DIGIT COUNT CHECK. When restoration is complete, the pulse P16p tests &18 and &'19 to check how many quotient digits have been produced. If division is complete, the pulse passes through &18 to emerge as an E pulse; if further quotient digits are to be generated, a pulse passes from &'19 to tally up C21, set BD2 to 1, and start a shift-left cycle.

SHIFT LEFT. The shift-left cycle pulse generator P22 issues *eight* pulses SH3. These pulses are applied to the accumulator and quotient register. Remember that nine shift pulses would shift the contents of a nine-digit register completely around to where they started; hence, eight shift pulses shift both registers eight positions to the right, which is equivalent to one digit to the left. The accumulator digits are shifted out through &23 and V10, from which they return into the accumulator. When the shift is complete, pulse P22p passes through V1 to start another subtraction cycle.

QUOTIENT TALLY. During division proper, after each subtraction cycle, the pulse P3p tests &'13 and &14. If subtraction is successful, an overflow pulse is produced from Δ11 simultaneous with the pulse P3p so that there is an output from &14. This output tallies up the quotient register; it also passes through V2 to start another round of subtraction. When subtraction is unsuccessful there is no pulse from Δ11. The pulse P3p cannot pass through &14 so that the quotient register is not tallied up after an unsuccessful subtraction. The pulse P3p does pass through &'13 to start a restoration cycle described earlier.

12.7. SIGNED MULTIPLICATION AND DIVISION

Multiplication and division of signed numbers is much simpler than the problem of signed addition and subtraction. The rule for multiplication is: *the sign of the product or quotient of like-signed numbers is positive; the sign of the product or quotient of unlike-signed numbers is always negative.* At any time during multiplication or division the sign of the two operands may be examined and the sign of the result set. The testing to determine the signs is done by means of & and V logical elements.

PROBLEMS

1. Alter Figure 12.3 by adding D-blocks so that one pulse generator can serve to replace P12 and P13.
2. Replace P4 and P20 with one pulse generator and D-blocks in Figure 12.4.2.
3. In Figure 12.5.2, replace BM by a multi; what other changes are then necessary? Show the detailed logic of D4, C10 and D11.
4. Combine Figures 12.5.2 and 12.4.2 into one, three-register, add-subtract-multiply logic with only one pulse generator.
5. In Figure 12.6.2 show how to replace P3, P16, and P22 by one pulse generator. Is there some way to replace BD1, BD2, and BD3 with a simpler set of bit storages?
6. Combine Figures 12.6.2 and 12.5.2 into *one* logic with *one* pulse generator and *three* shift registers.
7. Draw a complete logical block diagram for division using the *second* method described in Section 6.5.
8. Simplify the division logic of the above example by using just one pulse generator.
9. Show a three-register arithmetic logic which can add, subtract, multiply, and divide for parallel-bit serial-character operation.
10. Show logic for parallel-character multiplication, both binary and coded decimal.
11. Devise a logic for multiplication using the method described in Problem 4 of Chapter 6.

THIRTEEN

MEMORY DEVICES AND

THEIR LOGIC

13.1. INTRODUCTION

The purpose of storage is to provide a place to keep information for future use. By now we should be resigned to using information in binary form. This chapter discusses the operation of devices used primarily to store binary information and the logic required to make possible the access to this storage.

Earlier we discussed short-term storage—the bit-storage device used to store a single bit and the register, a fast-access device which stores a single word. These devices are necessary to, and integrated with, the working logic of the computer. The memory and buffer, which store large segments of information, perform supplementary functions, for it is conceivable to construct a computer without them. Computers have been built that process information only as it is supplied from the outside; others have been built which directly process data from an intermediate external storage medium such as magnetic tape, punch cards, or punched paper tape. Because of the very high speeds of modern computers and the push for even higher speeds, it is inconvenient, to say the least, to be tied down by the time that is needed to get data to and from one of these external sources. The internal memory, with the help of buffers, enables big chunks of data to be transferred and stored so that each datum is easily and rapidly accessible to the computer proper. Internal memory has a significantly lower access time than external storage and hence makes for more efficient operation. It is safe to say that any *recent* computer or any computer now on the drawing board includes an internal memory of fair size.

Although this book emphasizes logic in contrast to circuitry or components, we will pause here a moment to discuss the properties of the components used to build memories. This is necessary because the properties of the components determine how they are used to memorize and remember. The logic required to communicate with the memory is, in turn, dictated by the properties of the components.

Dynamic Versus Static Storage

Information can be stored in two ways. (1) Using **dynamic storage,** an electrical waveform, bearing information by virtue of its shape, may be preserved in toto by entering it into a delay of some sort. This delay emits the original waveform some time later without any significant change other than attenuation and tolerable distortion. (2) Using **static storage,** digital information in the form of one of a multiplicity of choices of states may be stored in a multistable device by setting such a device to one of its alternate states. Thus a four-position switch may store one-out-of-four or quaternary information by the way it is set.

Notice that the intent of dynamic storage is to maintain the information in its original form. The information-bearing wave phenomenon is made to persist by interposing a transmission path which hinders its transit. It is the nature of such a device to cause degradation of the waveform so that it must be repeatedly amplified and reshaped to resemble its original form.

Static storage is a mapping of the information into a number of devices which have as many possible states as there are possibilities for each "piece" of information. Hence, for binary information, bistable devices are appropriate.

Sections 2 and 3 discuss the logic of dynamic and static memories. Logic for specific memories is discussed in Sections 13.4, 13.5, 13.6, and 13.7.

13.2. DYNAMIC MEMORIES

From Section 13.1 it can be gathered that dynamic devices are merely delays with associated amplification or rejuvenation circuitry. The storage capacity of such a medium depends upon the speed of propagation of the wave phenomenon through the medium and the length of the transmission path. Electromagnetic waves are but slightly retarded by common transmission lines; for this reason only information being handled at high pulse repetition rates (up in the kilomegacycle region) can be stored (delayed) in the form of electromagnetic energy. Mechanical ultrasonic vibrations have been used in several computers as the wave phenomenon to be stored in physical materials. This is discussed below under the specific title headings.

Right now we will consider the logical principles relating to memorizing and remembering in delay memories in general.

Logical Principles

The strategy used with dynamic memories is similar to that used with dynamic registers. Data is entered into the delay and it is caused to circulate in the delay by connecting the output (after shaping and amplification) back to the input. The difference is only in the length of the delay used; it must be long enough to store many data words.

Consider the computer with a bit time, t_β with b bits per character, and c characters per word. A delay of length $T = wcbt_\beta$ can store serially w words. To make this data accessible, there must be some means for referencing the beginning of the information. Locating a specific word is then a question of either timing or counting.

The means for locating a word depends on whether the reference signal contains supplementary timing information or the timing is done independently of the stored waveform. When independent timing is used, the accuracy of the delay time T and of the external timing signals determines the accuracy with which information may be located. Because of the small tolerances involved in this kind of system, it would be extremely expensive to develop circuitry with timing which remains superstable over any reasonable period of time.

The external timing and synchronization problem can be surmounted by a single expedient—retime the information after *each* circulation. This is called **forced external synchronization** and is discussed below. The method using supplementary reference information is described in the next subsection thereafter.

Forced External Synchronization

Forced synchronization "retimes" the circulating information by sampling it after each trip through the delay, using a time reference independent of the delay line. The regenerated information is then returned to the delay line.

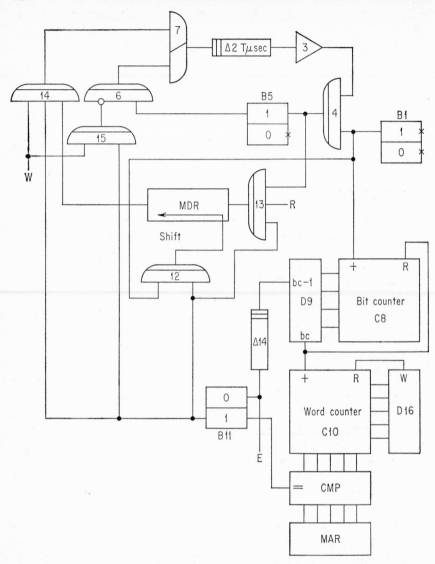

FIGURE 13.2.1. Logic, using forced external synchronization, for a delay-line memory.

The logic of Figure 13.2.1 requires a generator B1 whose fixed frequency is maintained accurately. The frequency of this generator corresponds to the pulse repetition rate of the input information and is a fraction of the delay time T. These intervals are held as closely as possible to their specified value: the bit time of the computer, the bit time for the memory delay logic (the time constant of B1), and the delay time T.

Since perfect synchronization is impossible, a sampling scheme is used. The information in the delay, $\Delta 2$, is amplified and shaped by A3. It is the characteristic of the delay to lengthen the pulses and increase the rise time of the leading and trailing edges. On the other hand, the pulses generated by B1 should be sharp and narrow. These timing pulses from B1 are used to sample the information by allowing a signal to pass through &4 only during the pulse times of B1. Thin pulses come out of &4 only when the timing pulse and the information coincide; there is no output from &4 for 0 information pulses. The uni, B5, broadens the 1's so that they can be sampled the next time around.

During a non-read-write cycle, information passes out of $\Delta 2$ and is regenerated by A3, &4, and B5; since no inhibiting signal is present at &'6, the information passes through &'6 and V7 to re-enter $\Delta 2$.

READING. Reading can be done only when the desired information word is passing out of the delay. The time at which this happens is determined by referring to the address previously sent to the Memory Address Register (MAR) by the computer control. The address is the number of the desired word counting from an arbitrary word circulating in the delay. The number of bit times counted from the start of the arbitrary reference bit in a reference word is entered into the bit counter, C8. This counter was initially set to read 0 at time $t = 0$, the start of the reference word (or $t = kT$ for integral values of k); it counts up the pulses from B1; when the total reaches the number of bits, bc, in a word, there is an output from the decoder D9. This output from D9 marks the beginning of each word time. It is used to reset the bit counter and also to count into the word counter, C10. The word counter keeps track of the number of the words which have passed since the reference word has passed by; when the count reaches the word number of the desired word (whose address is stored in the MAR), the comparator CMP emits a signal. This is an indication of the equality of the addresses of the currently-passing and the desired words. The signal from CMP sets B11 to 1. The 1 output of B11 is applied to &12 and &13. The desired word is about to pass out of $\Delta 2$ and through A3, &4, and &13, (&13 is held open by both B11 and the read signal), and into the memory data register MDR. Pulses from B1 pass through &12 to shift the information into the MDR. When the last bit time of the word being read occurs, this is detected by D9 which produces an output at the point labeled $bc - 1$. After a slight pause supplied by $\Delta 14$ to be sure that the last bit passes through &13, the signal from the $bc - 1$ output of D9 delayed by $\Delta 14$ sets B11 to 0. The function of $\Delta 14$ is to make sure that B11 resets *after* the last bit of the desired word but *before* the first bit of the next word. The return pulse, E, to the computer control signalling the end of the remember process is also the $(bc - 1)$ pulse delayed by $\Delta 14$.

WRITING. Writing requires that a specific word be removed from the delay line "merry-go-round" and replaced by a different word. The identification of the proper word location is the same as for reading. The comparison box CMP issues an equal signal when the word count agrees with the content of the Memory Address Register. This signal from CMP sets B11 to 1. No information enters the MDR because there is no read signal, R; but the word previously placed in the MDR by the computer control to be stored in the memory is now shifted out by pulses from B1 which pass through &12. This message passes through &14 now enabled by the write signal W and by B11 and through V7 into the delay; the old message in storage is destroyed because it cannot pass &'6 which is inhibited by &15, since W and the 1 output of B11 are both present at the input to &15.

Addressing Using Supplementary Reference Information

Where it is possible to depend on reference signals *internally correlated* with the information, then the external timing, with its consequent synchronization problems, may be dispensed with. Since the delay line is essentially an analog device, it can handle several levels of signals. The timing reference signals can occupy a separate level of the delayed waveform. For instance, negative pulses could be used for timing and positive pulses for 1 information.

Such a system does not find favor among designers, because information theory indicates that the full capacity of the delay for binary information is not efficiently used. The maximum useful bit capacity of a delay is a compromise between resolution (rise time), timing, and the structure (and cost) of the delay; requiring three-level information instead of two-level to be stored uses this capacity inefficiently and reduces the number of information words which may be stored.

The logic of Figure 13.2.2 can be used with a self-synchronizing three-level system. Information in the storage delay Δ4 is amplified and reshaped by A5. The extract circuit, block 6, regenerates both the timing and information pulses. The rejuvenated information passes through &'2 and V3 on non-read-write cycles and is re-entered into Δ4.

READING. A second-level reference pulse is present in our system, Figure 13.2.2, *between* each word stored in the delay and serves to distinguish the words. The extract block numbered 6 recognizes this pulse and applies it to the word counter, C7. When the word counter contains a count equal to the address preset by the computer control into the Memory Address Register, MAR, the compare circuit emits an "equal" signal. This starts the pulse generator, P8. It issues N pulses to shift the Memory Data

Register, MDR. The information following the reference pulse is entered into MDR through &9 which is enabled by the read signal and the "equal" signal. The next reference pulse adds 1 to the word counter. This prevents contamination of the MDR from the following word by shutting the gate, &9. The post-train pulse from P8 tells the computer control unit to take over by issuing an E pulse.

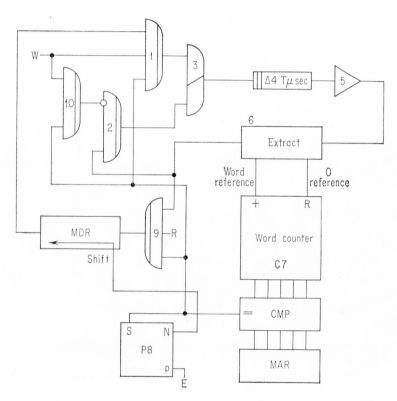

FIGURE 13.2.2. Logic using supplementary reference pulses for a delay-line memory.

WRITING. Addressing is the same for writing as for reading. However, information from the MDR must be written into the delay Δ4. P8 again issues shift pulse to the MDR. Because there is no read signal R at &9, no information enters the MDR; information passes from the MDR through &1 which has an enabling W signal and an equal signal from CMP applied to it and into Δ4 via V3. The old message cannot pass through &'2 because the combined write and equal signal produces an output at &10 which inhibits &'2.

Parallel Storage

The methods just described are for serial storage, since a single delay line at a given instant can furnish only one bit of information. However, it is possible to store information in parallel in a number of delay lines as shown in Figure 13.2.3, a totally parallel system.

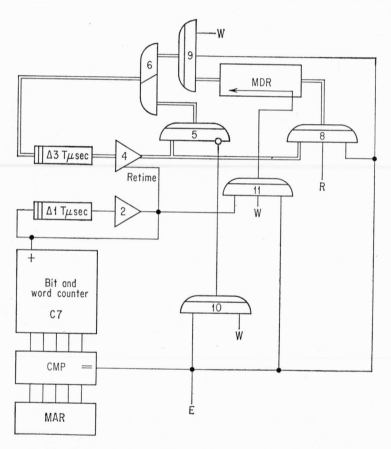

FIGURE 13.2.3.   Delay memory logic parallel storage.

$\Delta1$ is a timing delay with a set of timing pulses circulating in it. These pulses are shaped and amplified by A2. $\Delta3$ is really a number of identical parallel delays with a set of amplifiers labelled A4. Each of the components associated with these delays is symbolized by a single gate, mixer, and so forth, which represents a *set* of such blocks; the double information line feeding these sets of components indicates that parallel information is being manipulated.

Parallel information in Δ3 is resynchronized by A4 by some method similar to that of Figure 13.2.2, using the timing pulses emanating from A2. The non-read-write path is through &'5 and V6. The timing pulses are used to tally the word counter C7; the comparison block emits a pulse when the counter and the Memory Address Register concur. For reading, the parallel bit datum is entered through &8 into the MDR, since &8 is enabled by R and the CMP equal signal. For writing, the old datum is blocked at &'5 and the new datum moved from the MDR through &9 and V8 into Δ3 by the timing pulses from A2 which pass through &11 enabled by W and the CMP equal signal.

Combinations of delays may be used to construct a serial-parallel storage system. The control logic for such combinations is left to the reader as an exercise.

Kinds of Delay Lines

This subsection enumerates the kinds of delays which might be used and their pertinent properties.

MERCURY LINES. For low pulse repetition rates, the information may be transformed into supersonic mechanical vibrations by a quartz-crystal transducer. A path of mechanically conductive material is interposed between this transmitter and the corresponding receiving device at the other end of the path, which reconverts the mechanical vibrations to electrical impulses. Mercury has a transmission rate of about 57 inches per millisecond. Mercury is most suitable because of the mechanical impedance match looking into and out of the transducers, which makes for a high energy transfer. A tank of mercury may be set up with several transmitters and receivers so that several noninterfering delay paths exist through it.

QUARTZ CRYSTALS. The mechanical vibrations in the mercury line follow a straight line until intercepted by the walls of the container where they are detected. The vibrations in the crystal delay line also follow a free path, but when they hit an intercepting internal crystal surface they rebound. The total path may consist of several subsequent internal reflecting surfaces; the wave is finally detected by a transducer on the last surface. Reflections from each wall obey the principle that the angles of incidence and reflection are equal. By having the mechanical vibrations transmitted through a crystal polygon rebound from say, 15 or more sides, the path of the vibrations may be made many times the diameter of the figure, so that a long delay may be packaged in a small volume. The conversion and reconversion of energy here, too, results from the piezo-electric effect.

LUMPED CONSTANT LINES. By using a number of inductors and capacitors connected together, a transmission line with a low propagation velocity may be made. The need for a large number of different small components stems again from the resolution problem and the need to provide for the possibility of a number of different voltage levels along the line. These lumped constant delays have inherent losses which prevent the assembly of very long delays unless amplifiers are used.

MAGNETOSTRICTIVE LINES. Some materials deform when a magnetic field is applied; such a material under strain in a magnetic field distorts the field. This pair of principles is used to obtain a delay element. A magnetostrictive wire is held firmly between two damping elements (to prevent reflections). A "transmitting" coil encircles one end. When a voltage is applied and current flows in the coil, a field is produced which mechanically deforms the wire. This deformation travels down the wire as a strain wave. A transducing coil at the other end converts the strain wave into an electric pulse; thus pulses are stored in the wire in the form of strain waves.

MAGNETIC DRUM. A channel on a revolving magnetic drum can be used like a delay. The write head is used as the input; the read head is the output; information read by the read head is then constantly rewritten on the drum. Only if the information is constantly regenerated can the drum be considered to be a delay line; otherwise, it behaves like a static storage element.

MICROWAVE. Experimental computers are being designed which use fractions of a millimicrosecond for bit times. A delay of a few microseconds can then store much information. X-band hardware is appropriate and distributed parameter wave guides make acceptable storage devices.

13.3. STATIC STORAGE

This discussion is confined to the storage of binary information. Static storage requires one bistable element for each bit to be stored. Other qualities which distinguish static storage elements are now covered.

Volatility

Some elements have a tendency over a period of time to lose the information stored in them. This property is called **volatility.** The Williams tube, an electrostatic storage device, leaks the charge indicating a 1 from one spot (storage element) to another in a matter of fractions of a second. Frequent regeneration cycles are required to maintain the information without loss. Historically this was the first high-speed storage device to find use in automatic computers. Because of its volatility it is no longer popular as a memory device, since nonvolatile devices are now available.

Devices whose elements are not subject to deterioration in the discrimination between two states over long periods of time—days, months or years—are called **nonvolatile** storage elements.

Destructive Read-out

If scanning the elements to retrieve the information causes the information to be removed from the elements, they are said to have destructive read-out. Core memories, for instance, require that each core be set to 0 to be read out. Destructive read-out elements can be used to construct a nondestructive-remembering memory; in that case the remember cycle includes a read and a rewrite phase (see Section 13.4 on core memories).

Addressing

The means for scanning the storage elements to insert or retrieve information is called addressing. It should be fast, simple, and require as little equipment as feasible. Although it is possible to use a separate wire to address each element, such a system is almost obsolete.

Logic

Because a static memory depends upon the three properties of elements discussed above—volatility, destructability, and addressability—it is difficult to discuss their logic in a completely general manner.

A Few Static Elements

Core and drum memory logic is discussed in separate sections; other static memories are currently less popular and are not discussed in detail. Some of these static elements are described briefly below.

ELECTROSTATIC STORAGE. A number of ingenious schemes have been developed for storing a charge on devices closely resembling cathode ray tubes. These charges are detected by such means as secondary emission. Devices such as the Williams tube, the barrier grid tube, and the Selectron—each used in earlier machines—are discussed elsewhere (Ref. 10).

CAPACITOR STORAGE. A bank of capacitors, together with supplementary diodes, can adequately store moderate quantities of information (a thousand or so bits) for short periods (a few seconds). A capacitor is charged to store a 1; discharged for 0. It is read by discharging the capacitor; if a current flows, 1 was stored there; if none flows, a 0 was stored there.

FERROELECTRIC STORAGE. The polarization of a dielectric is affected by the polarity of the charge to which it has been previously subjected; it is polarized differently according to the direction of the voltage applied across it. Bits can be stored on ferroelectric dielectrics by the direction in which the dielectric is polarized.

THYRATRONS. Once a thyratron is fired, it remains so until its plate voltage is cut off. Information may be stored in a (rather expensive) bank of thyratrons with one gas tube for each bit. It can be readily scanned for remembering with no possibility of destroying the data. Memorizing is done by momentarily opening the plate circuit of the addressed bits to set them to 0 and then setting to 1 the required bits by firing the associated thyratrons.

13.4. PROPERTIES OF MAGNETIC-CORE MEMORIES

Magnetic cores for use as memory components are extremely small in size. Thousands of words of information may be stored in a few cubic feet. Because of their properties they may be addressed rapidly. Information may be memorized or remembered typically in six microseconds. Although much electronic equipment is required to properly insert (or withdraw) information into (or from) core memories, they are popular for most large computers; they are also used for buffers in medium- and large-size computers. They produce the fastest arbitrary-access memories available; and core memories are nonvolatile—there is no necessity to rejuvenate information between references.

A common size for units of memory is about four thousand words of between ten and forty bits per word. Prefabricated complete units of this size can be purchased for less than $100,000.

Often computers have expandable memories enabling the user to add units (of about four to five thousand words) so that the increased use of the computer will not be impeded. This expandable feature makes for versatility in custom tailoring the computer to the consumer's needs.

The magnetic core used for memories is normally of a ceramic type. A powdered mixture of iron salts and clays is pressed into the form of a toroid (a doughnut) whose outer diameter might be only a twentieth of an inch. The toroids are fired into this permanent shape. For this reason they are called *ferrite* cores. They should be distinguished from bobbin-wound cores used principally for shift registers.

If a wire is wound about the core and a current passed through the wire, a magnetic field is set up surrounding the wire and the core. Part of this field will pass through the core which, being of low reluctance (offering little opposition to the magnetic lines of force), will take a circular path within the core as in Figure 13.4.1. This field presents a magnetomotive force which tends to magnetize the core to one of two possible states. The core is designed so that it retains most of the magnetic energy

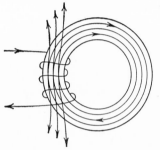

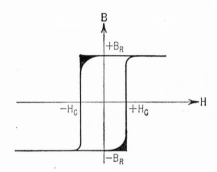

FIGURE 13.4.1. Magnetic field about a ferrite core.

FIGURE 13.4.2. Core hysteresis loop.

contained in the field after the field is removed. **Remanence** is the term which describes the ability to store the magnetic energy obtained from the temporary field; ideal cores are said to have high remanence.

The most important property of the core material is best presented graphically using the characteristic **hysteresis loop**. A typical loop appears in Figure 13.4.2. Here H is the magnetomotive force applied to the toroidal core by passing current through the coil wound about it; B is the remanence, the magnetic flux remaining when the magnetomotive force (mmf) is removed. The desired shape for this loop is called "square" because, unless a minimum mmf is applied, the magnetic state of the core does not change appreciably; when this minimum mmf (or more) is applied, the core suddenly switches to its opposite state. The core thus has a bistable property. The mmf required to switch the core from one state to the other, and for which an increase in mmf does not increase the magnetic flux through the core, is called the **coercive force** and labeled H_c; the magnetic flux remaining after H_c is applied is called the remanence and labeled B_R.

A core stores a 0 when the residual flux in the core is $-B_R$; this designation is arbitrary. The remanence $-B_R$ results, of course, from an mmf of $-H_c$ or less. If the mmf, H, applied to the core is increased, the core is not affected until it reaches the value $+H_c$; at this point the core remanence switches from $-B_R$ to $+B_R$. The residual flux when $+H_c$ is removed is then $+B_R$ so that the core then stores a 1.

In practice, it is impossible to obtain a *perfectly square* hysteresis loop. This is manifest by the top or bottom of the loop not being parallel to the H axis or by the rounding of the corners of the loop. Hence if the mmf is increased from 0 to some intermediate point, say $+H_c/k$ with $0 < k < 1$, there will be some change in flux in the core as shown in Figure 13.4.2 by the black wedges near $+B_R$ and $-B_R$. The merit of a core is judged by the squareness of its hysteresis loop; the core with the squarest loop has least variability in its residual magnetism; this describes the quality of its performance as a bistable device.

Writing

It is apparent that a bit of information may be stored in a core by applying to a winding of the core a current of sufficient magnitude and in the assigned direction. This causes the core to have a remanence corresponding to a 1 or a 0 as desired.

Reading

There is no simple way to determine the information stored in a simple toroidal (one hole) core without destroying (at least temporarily) the information. This is therefore termed **destructive read-out.** If an mmf $-H_c$ is applied to one winding of the core, there are two alternative possibilities: if the core is set to 1, B will be changed from $+B_R$ to $-B_R$; if the core is set to 0, B will remain at $-B_R$. This reading pulse, $-H_c$, will set the core to 0 regardless of its former state. Another winding on the core can sense whether there has been a change in the state of the core: a positive voltage will be induced in such a winding only if the core was previously set to 1 and the flux changes from $+B_R$ to $-B_R$; otherwise, if it was set to 0, no voltage will be induced in the winding.

Restoring Information

Because of the destructive nature of core readout, magnetic cores are not immediately satisfactory for a computer memory system. To remedy this, it is possible to replace the information withdrawn from the core at some short time later. This is done by applying the delayed and amplified readout signal to the core in such a manner as to set to 1 those cores which were so set previously and no others.

The Structure of the Memory

The memory stores a quantity of information which runs into many thousands, sometimes millions of bits. Some systematic means must be used to catalog the information so it is easy to find. Information is manipulated in words; the bits in these words may be examined totally in series,

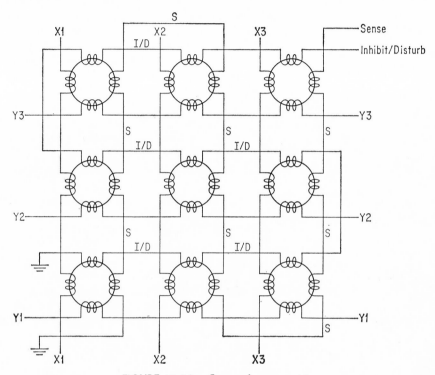

FIGURE 13.4.3. Corner of a core matrix.

all in parallel, or in serial-parallel fashion. An integral multiple of words, usually one, is stored at a given address.

The arrangement of information in the memory must then be such that any set of bits is immediately available by the memory control logic; the location and relation of the set of cores representing the set of bits depends on the word structure.

The method for addressing a single core or a set of cores is the same: $-H_c$ is applied to a single core or to a set of cores, and it sets the core(s) to the 0 state. In parallel, the set is read out on the *sense* winding(s). Let us speak generally of a set, since a set may have one or more members. At this point then it requires a separate line to address each set of cores—

for one thousand words, one thousand separate drive lines are required. Since a good fraction of an ampere is required on each line to drive the cores, an amplifier is normally needed for each drive line.

To improve the efficiency of the memory (in terms of the equipment required) the square property of the hysteresis loop is now invoked. If two addressing windings are supplied to each core, the core will set to 0 only when the *total* mmf is $-H_c$. Imagine sets of cores, each representing a computer word, arranged in a square matrix, 32×32, say. A small corner of such a matrix is found in Figure 13.4.3; each core in the figure

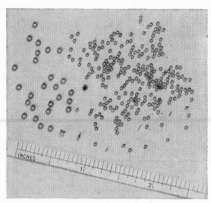 

FIGURE 13.4.4. Assorted cores. Courtesy of General Ceramics.   FIGURE 13.4.5. A Wired core plane. Courtesy of General Ceramics.

could represent a *set* of cores. Passing through each core, there is one row and one column winding, numbered and distinguished respectively by the prefix Y and X. There are no *two* sets of cores which lie in the *same* row and column; therefore, choosing a *pair* of *coordinates* (for this is a coordinate system, you see) uniquely determines a set of cores.

Now, to choose a set without affecting the other sets, a current such as to provide an mmf of $-H_c/2$ is applied to the selected row and column; in the figure, X2 carries current to produce $-H_c/2$ in the cores along its length; Y3 also carries current to produce $-H_c/2$ in the cores it passes through. This current (equivalent to $-H_c/2$) is not sufficient to affect any core storing either 0 or 1 in the selected row or column except the core through which both X2 and Y3 pass; this set of cores is subjected to an mmf of $-H_c$ and will be set 0 to be read out on the sense winding of each matrix of the set.

The same method is used to *write* 1's into the cores. The lines labeled

FIGURE 13.4.6.   A core memory stack.   Courtesy of General Ceramics.

X2 and Y3 are each driven with sufficient current to obtain $+H_c/2$ in order to *write* into the core(s) at X2Y3.

We have used a two-dimensional system (row and column); it is easy to carry this principle to higher dimensions. Consider a three-coordinate system, X, Y, Z. To read a core set, apply a current to produce $-H_c/3$ to one each of the X, Y, and Z lines. Note that some core sets have $-H_c/3$

applied, some have $-2H_c/3$ applied, but only one core set has an mmf of $-H_c$ applied to it. Addressing one thousand words in a three-dimensional system could be done with a $10 \times 10 \times 10$ word array.

Systems of more than three dimensions may be constructed, of course. The limitation is that each core set for n dimensions must set to 0 for an mmf of $-H_c$ but must not be set to 0 for $-(n-1)H_c/n$. This must be true of each of the hundreds of thousands of cores required for a memory of respectable size. The practical limitation to number of dimensions in which a core memory can be constructed is imposed by the tolerances to which the cores can be made and the squareness of the hysteresis loop of the materials used. If, out of many thousands of cores previously set to 1, all will set to 0 for $-H_c$ and none for $-(n-1)H_c/n$, then an n-dimensional memory can be constructed.

Appearance

Cores of assorted sizes are shown in Figure 13.4.4. When wired into a plane, they appear as in Figure 13.4.5. A stack of planes as might be found in a small memory is shown in Figure 13.4.6.

13.5. STRUCTURE OF THE CORE MEMORY

The word structure in the memory may correspond exactly to the word structure in the computer—both may be serial, parallel, and so forth. Or, they may differ and a temporary storage register may be used to convert from, say, serial to parallel and so forth. We will concern ourselves here with the memory word structure and not the later conversion, when it is necessary.

Serial-Bit Memories

This means reading and writing occur bit by bit, so that each core must be scanned sequentially.

ADDRESSING. There is only a philosophical difference between addressing the memory bit by bit or selecting the word and then examining the bits in order. In a three-dimensional array, for instance, it is customary for the word address to fix two coordinates of the cube: this selects one straight line along which the information bits lie. A 1024-word memory of 40-bit words would consist of forty frames, each a 32×32 core matrix. 32 X wires and 32 Y wires pass through *each* frame. For each frame we can make up a pair, choosing one X and one Y wire. A word is chosen by fixing the number of the X and of the Y wire of this pair. Current is then applied to the chosen pair of X and Y wires in each frame of the forty frames successively. The sequence in which the frame is addressed (current applied to the pair) is the sequence in which the bits of the word are read out.

READING. All the sense windings (the computer label for the read windings) for the cores are connected in series, observing the proper polarities. The *bit* to be read out is addressed so that an mmf of $-H_c$ appears at the core, setting it to 0. If it was set to 1, a voltage appears on the sense line; otherwise none appears there.

WRITING. There are four cases which may arise in writing into a core. These are due to the two possible previous states of the cores and the two possible desired states. A positive system would write the desired 0 or 1 into the core regardless of the previous state. A second method would require reading—setting all the bits of the word to 0—before writing; then write 1's only where required. Both of these methods are difficult to implement. The most common system performs writing in three steps:

1. Read all cores of the selected word (set to 0) by applying $-H_c$ to all of the word bits, either in sequence or all at once.
2. Address with write current (such as to produce $+H_c$) all cores which comprise the selected word.
3. Apply simultaneously with the second step an inhibit current, $-H_c/2$, through an inhibit winding to all cores (bits) of the word for which 0 is to be written.

A core thus has an mmf of $+H_c$ owing to the addressing current alone when a 1 is to be written; it has an mmf of $+H_c$ owing to the addressing current and $-H_c/2$ due to the inhibit current applied to it when a 0 is to be written, so that it remains unaffected (only $+H_c/2$ is applied). The same principle works for higher-dimensional arrays, as the reader may verify.

The core with windings is represented as in Figure 13.5.1. Because the cores are so small in size, the ampere-turns necessary to produce

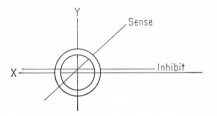

FIGURE 13.5.1. Core and windings.

H_c are small, too; in practice each winding is simply formed by a wire passing through the core, so that Figure 13.5.1 is a fairly accurate representation of the core and windings.

Parallel-Bit Memories

A full word is memorized or remembered all at once in a parallel-bit memory.

ADDRESSING. The 1024 × 40 bit memory discussed earlier is again realized with 40 arrays, each 32 × 32. But now a given X winding passes not only through all the wires in one column of one frame; it is also connected to the same column in all the frames. Corresponding X and Y windings of all frames are connected together; the corresponding bits in each frame array are simultaneously addressed. Thus to address the word at X2 Y3, a current to produce $-H_c/2$ (to read) is sent through the X2 windings on all 40 frames and also to the Y3 windings on all 40 frames.

READING. One output wire passes through all the cores in a single frame; there is one output wire for each bit to be read. In our example there is one sense wire threading all 1024 cores of each of the 40 frames—40 sense wires. When the cores are addressed for reading, each of the 40 sense wires, one from each frame, carries the 1 and 0 message stored in the memory to one of the bits of a temporary Memory Data Register.

WRITING. The X and Y windings for the word to be written are driven with current to supply $+H_c/2$ to each core on each frame which they thread. The bits of the chosen word then have $+H_c$ supplied. The word to be stored must be simultaneously entered in complement form into the inhibit windings; there should be current to supply $-H_c/2$ in the inhibit windings corresponding to the 0 bits and no current in the inhibit windings for the wires in which 1's are to be written.

Serial-Parallel

To return to the 1024-word memory, suppose that each word contains, as in the Polyvac, ten characters, each of four bits. The principles just discussed may be combined to make up a serial-parallel memory. Each *word* is addressed separately by choosing one each of two sets, X and Y, of 32 windings; the characters are addressed sequentially using a third set of windings. Each of these ten character windings passes through all the cores on each of four frames. The four-bit read-out lines pass through ten frames each: on each bit line appear ten information bits sequentially. Similarly to write-in, we activate the character lines sequentially and in synchronism with the four inhibit lines for each character.

The Disturb Current

Of course, it is not possible to get cores with perfectly square hysteresis loops. That is why cores that have been just written have somewhat different properties from "old" cores. When a core is subjected to half-read and half-write cycles (an mmf of $-H_c/2$ or $+H_c/2$) it recovers to a somewhat different residual magnetism after each cycle.

Figure 13.5.2 shows a highly exaggerated portion of a hysteresis loop. A core that has just been set to 1 has a remanence indicated by point A. A half-read cycle consists of applying and removing $-H_c/2$ to the core. The remanence follows the path AFD. This results in a change of remanence indicated by AD. Such a change in flux induces a voltage in the sense winding. When this happens for a number of cores, a considerable background noise may appear on the sense line when reading is

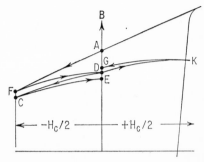

FIGURE 13.5.2. Portion of exaggerated hysteresis loop to show effect of disturb current.

performed. Notice, however, that after the first cycle (AFD) succeeding cycles such as DCE or DKG produce only a small change in remanence and hence little, if any, noise.

If it were possible to subject a core to a pseudo-half-read cycle before use, the remanence of the core would be at point D and further half-read or half-write cycles would have little effect. This is just what is often done in practice. Immediately after writing but before actual reading, a false read cycle is performed. To distinguish this cycle, it is called a **disturb** cycle for it disturbs the fresh writing just done. After the disturb cycle all cores storing 1's have about the same remanence.

13.6. CORE MEMORY LOGIC

To facilitate our study we shall investigate a typical memory system first and discuss some possible variations later. The core memory which might be used in the Polyvac has 1000 words of 40 bits each. It consists of 40 arrays each 50 × 20. Each word is referred to in parallel—all 40 bits at once.

Previously it has been stated that cores have a destructive readout.

Most applications require that information in memory remain there *after* remembering has been done. Remembering is accomplished by following each reference to the memory by a cycle that rewrites the datum erased by readout. This is typical of modern core memories. Recall that in order to write information the word storage must be previously cleared by reading. Hence both memorizing and remembering in our design have a cycle calling for reading followed by writing.

This discussion is divided into several parts. A description of the timing cycle for both remembering and memorizing includes a list of things to be done and their sequence. The control logic section describes the functional units to generate the proper timing. The system layout is then described. A final section discusses variations.

Remember Cycle

A command requiring remembering is decoded and then encoded by the computer control. One of the encoder outputs is a read signal. Any command involving reading *begins* with such a process.

START READ PULSE. A gated start pulse enters the read circuitry as a start read pulse.

CLEAR THE MEMORY DATA REGISTER (MDR). The MDR is a register which will hold the information when it is read from memory and from which information will later be distributed to its destination in the computer. The MDR must be cleared to hold the new word.

ADDRESSING. The address from which the datum is to be read is stored in the Memory Address Register (MAR). This address must be decoded into a double baseless system, 50×20; this addressing signal must be maintained for the duration of the reading.

PROBE. Because of the variability of the waveforms from the cores, especially at the beginning and end of the reading, a "cleaner" output is obtained by sampling the waveform from each sense line at some time close to the middle of the reading period. Each sense-line output, properly amplified and shaped, and a probe pulse are both applied to an &-block. This cleaned-up bit is then the input to the Memory Data Register.

IDLE PERIOD. To avoid undesirable transients signals on the read windings between reading and writing, and to let the cores settle down to point A in Figure 13.5.2, the cores are rested between addressing and rewrite.

REWRITE. The location just read from is addressed again, but this time the current is in the opposite direction to that used for reading, and it produces $+H_c$ in the cores of this word.

INHIBIT. For each core from which a 0 was read, an inhibit pulse is sent to the inhibit winding of that array. The inhibit pulse must overlap the write pulse at both ends so that these cores cannot possibly be set to 1.

DISTURB. Any core which was not inhibited has a 1 written in it. These cores should be disturbed after writing. This is done by the disturb pulse which applies $-H_c/2$ to all addressed cores shortly after writing is complete.

READY. It is no longer necessary for the memory to communicate with the Memory Data Register. The datum in the MDR may now be transferred to its destination in the computer.

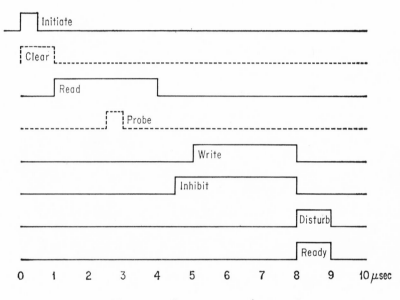

FIGURE 13.6.1. Core memory read-write timing.

The juxtaposition of the timing pulses is illustrated in the timing diagram, Figure 13.6.1.

Memorize Cycle

The Polyvac commands which call for writing are only the transfer orders, such as XAM, and so forth. The transfer order, after being decoded and encoded, calls first for the transmission of the datum to the Memory Data Register.

START WRITE PULSE. This pulse is received by the memory control logic after the datum is placed in the MDR. It would defeat our purposes to clear the MDR at this point.

READ ADDRESS. It is necessary to set to 0 each core to be written by supplying it with an mmf of $-H_c$. During this clearing operation the sense windings are *not* connected to the Memory Data Register, for then this would contaminate the datum stored there to be written.

PROBE. No probe is needed.

IDLE PERIOD. This serves the same function as in the read cycle.

WRITE. Now writing can be done from the Memory Data Register into the cores via the X and Y lines which are addressed with a current producing $+H_c/2$.

INHIBIT. The 0's to be written require an inhibit current to produce $-H_c/2$ in each such core.

DISTURB. For the 1's which are written, a short disturb pulse producing $-H_c/2$ is passed through the inhibit winding.

WRITE COMPLETE. When writing is finished, the transfer command is also complete and an E pulse may be returned to the control unit to start the next command.

Timing Chart

Figure 13.6.1 shows the temporal relation of the timing pulses for a typical memory. The time scale begins at 0 and is in units of 1 microsecond per division. The pulses required for remembering only are represented by dotted lines; solid lines represent the pulses used both for memorizing and remembering.

Core Memory Logic

Figure 13.6.2 shows the timing logic. The initiate pulse sets bit storage B1 to 1; it remains so set for 2 microseconds. This pulse, serving also as the clear pulse C, is applied to the two delays Δ2 and Δ3 and sets the multi B4 to 1. The output of Δ3 occurring 6 microseconds later sets B4 to 0. The 1 output of B4 which lasts for six microseconds is the read pulse R. It starts at the same time as C but lasts longer. The delayed clear pulse P is the probe pulse; Δ2 is adjustable so that P occurs at an optimum time. Δ3 is connected to Δ5 and Δ6. The former determines the period between read and write; the latter, which is adjustable, determines the start of the inhibit pulse, I. The multi B7 is started by the output of

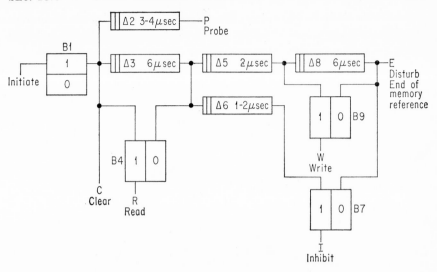

FIGURE 13.6.2. Core memory timing logic.

Δ6 and maintains a 1 output until the end of writing, as determined by the output of Δ8; the 1 output of B7 is the inhibit pulse I, which can be adjusted so as to completely overlap the write pulse. The inhibit pulse for each frame is gated separately for each frame by the 0-bit information in the Memory Data Register. Thus, each frame where 0 is to be written receives current in its inhibit winding; each frame where 1 is to be written receives no current in its inhibit winding. The write pulse is the 1 output of B9. It is set to 1 by the Δ5 pulse and reset to 0, 6 microseconds later by Δ8. The output of Δ8 is a 2-microsecond pulse, starting when writing stops. This is the disturb pulse D and also indicates the end of reference to the memory, which accounts for its being secondarily designated as E.

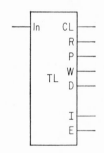

FIGURE 13.6.3. Block symbol, core memory timing logic.

The block symbol TL of Figure 13.6.3 is used to indicate the timing logic.

System Layout

The system layout of the core memory is shown in Figure 13.6.4. The cube in the center is the core array assembly which comprises the memory proper. The timing and control unit just discussed receives two of three possible signals from the computer, memorize or remember and start ("Now!" in the figure). The datum address is stored beforehand in the Memory Address Register for both read and write. For memorization, the

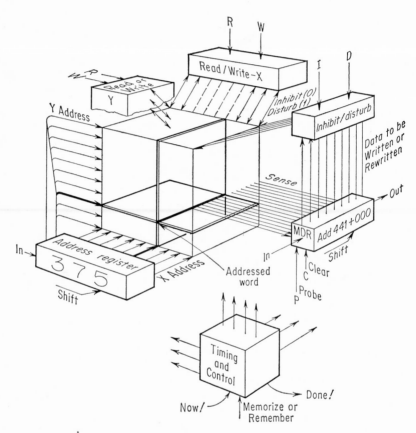

FIGURE 13.6.4.　Logic for the core memory system.

datum to be stored has been placed in the Memory Data Register before the start signal reaches the timing center. The MDR is cleared for remember by the C pulse from the timing center. Current in the proper direction is sent from the address register amplifiers through the read/write switch under the control of the timing center. For read, the sense information is entered in parallel to the MDR. The MDR gates are probed by the timing center probe pulse P.

During the write operation, the datum in the MDR is passed through the inhibit/disturb switch. Inhibit current is applied to the inhibit winding, for which 0's are to be written, and disturb current to the windings for which 1's are written, also through the inhibit windings. Both of these occur at the intervals specified by the timing diagram, Figure 13.6.3.

When the full cycle is complete, the memory timing center issues a "Done!" (E) pulse; the computer control then takes over. The computer control unit may then shift out the datum when needed.

13.7. SOME ADDITIONAL REMARKS ON CORE-TYPE MEMORIES

This section discusses three other aspects of cores. *Core matrix switches* are a *nonstorage* use for cores. *Apertured core planes* are assemblies of core-like devices. *Deposited core plates* are assemblies of cores which can be fabricated in mass production for use in multiple core memories.

Matrix Switches

Decoders discussed earlier use &-blocks to obtain an *output* on *one* of many lines for an *input* on *several* lines. There is one &-block required for each output line.

The core is used like a *nor* block to function as a decoder. Recall the &-block decoder of Section 11.4. It is presented here as Figure 13.7.1.

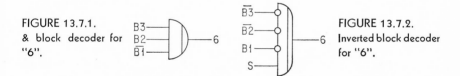

FIGURE 13.7.1. & block decoder for "6".

B3 — B2 — B̄1 — 6

B̄3 — B̄2 — B1 — S — 6

FIGURE 13.7.2. Inverted block decoder for "6".

The same results are obtained if the complementary bit is used at each input and the input inverted as in Figure 13.7.2. This is so because Ā̄ = A. The input S to the gate may be called a *sampling input*. Figures 13.7.1 and 13.7.2 operate equivalently.

The core functions as a *nor* block when the three current inputs are made $-I_c$ (when present, of course), where $-I_c$ is the saturation current required for the core to assume a 0 state. The S input is $+I_c$. Prior to its use as a decoder, the core is set to 0. Then, if *all* the input signals are *absent*, the S input will take effect and set the core to 1; if any one input is present the core will tend to remain as set—to be set to 0; since it is already set 0, no change occurs. The core switches to 1 only when all signals except S are absent.

The schematic representation of a core decoder is found in Figure

13.7.3. The preset winding is required to set all cores to 0; the three signal inputs are the complements of the code desired; the sample input carries $+I_c$ at the sample time; the sense line is the output. There will be a current at the sense line only when the core switches from 0 to 1—when it detects the code. The sequence for a full array of these matrix switches is as follows:

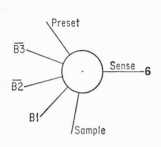

FIGURE 13.7.3. Core decoder for "6".

1. Set all cores to 0.
2. Enter the set of signals to be decoded to all cores; signals are absent only on the core corresponding to the code being entered.
3. Try to set all cores to 1; only the core corresponding to the input core sets to 1.
4. The sense winding of only the selected core produces a read-out current.

The matrix switch does offer tangible advantages over the coincident-current method as a means for addressing core memories. Take a small 16×16 memory as an example. If it is fed by 256 separate addressing wires, the problem of half-select voltages and low signal-to-noise ratio is completely licked; one word is positively selected by current in a single lead and the 255 other leads carry no current.

The coincident-current matrix switch converts a 16×16 input into a 256-lead output or an $n \times n$ input into an n^2-lead output. The partial array of Figure 13.7.4 shows how the bias line is used both to preset and sample the array. First a bias current of $-I_c$ is applied to set all the cores to 0; then code lines of the code complementary to the desired code are energized; if the input is X3 and Y2 there will be *no* current on these lines only; on at least one line of each of other sets there is $-I_c$. Next $+I_c$ is applied to the bias line—only X3Y2 switches to 1. There is hence an output on the sense winding of X3Y2, which is sufficient to read out the 16×16 array to which it is connected.

Here's the picture, then. To address this 256-word memory, we have:

1. Two sets of bit storage of four bits per set, four input lines per set, and eight output lines per set.
2. Two &-block decoders, binary to 16 ways.
3. Two sets of 16 drivers each.
4. A matrix core switch with two sets of 16 inputs each and 256 output lines.
5. The memory itself, $16 \times 16 \times 40$ (say).

Note that if the bias current is reversed again after read-out to $-I_c$, only the selected core set is reset to 0. This causes a current of the opposite direction to flow in the sense winding of the core just selected. With additional inhibit logic, this can be used to rewrite the information read during remember order.

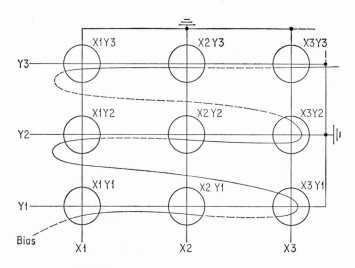

FIGURE 13.7.4. Part of a core matrix switch.

Other ingenious arrangements have been devised for using core matrix switches for addressing core memories.

Ferrite Apertured Plates

A solid slab of ferrite material can be designed to act like an array of cores. Holes are drilled at appropriately placed sites. Data are stored *around* the hole in the form of the remanent state of the material which is left there. The material is set by the current flowing in a wire passing through the hole. The magnetizing force within the material is inversely proportional to its distance from the center of the wire. For a fixed value of current, a critical radius is determined within which the magnetizing force is everywhere greater than the coercive force, and outside of which it is everywhere less than the coercive force. If this maximum current is always observed as a limit, the material surrounding the aperture can be considered to comprise a *core*, as it can be switched and yet its state does not affect the data stored in the surrounding cores.

Since ferrite material is essentially nonconductive, it is possible to *print* a conductive winding upon the plate as in Figure 13.7.5. Examine the apertured plate shown there and notice the pattern of ridges. On one side of the plate ridges such as R1, R2, R3, and R4 bound sets of two holes such as H1 and H2. This area has a metallic plating on it. Consider the sectioned holes H3 and H4; they are bounded on the top side by R1, R4, R2, and R7 (not shown) and these are ridges which are not conductive. It is quickly seen that a conductive path exists along the arrows: path *a* from the underside through hole H3 to the top; path *b* along the top; path *c* or *c'* through hole H4; along the underside, path *d*; up through

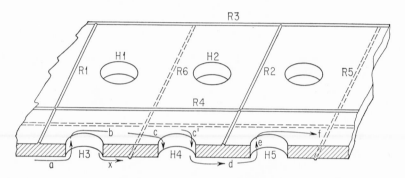

FIGURE 13.7.5.   Ferrite apertured plate.

hole H5, path *e*; along the top, path *f*, and so forth. Observe that path *x* ends at the nonconductive ridge, R6. By using such a pattern the entire sense winding can be *plated* onto the apertured plate.

The plate is made by spraying a conductive coating on a ferrite form which has ridges molded into it. The tops of ridges are then ground so that the conductive coating is removed and the ridges are no longer conductive. The conductive portions of the plate form a path so laid out that it weaves up the inside of one hole on the plate and down the inside of the next. This serves as the double-purpose sense/inhibit winding. For reading, if the addressed aperture stores a 1, it produces a current in this winding; for writing, inhibit current to produce $H_c/2$ passes through this winding when 0 is to be written in this frame, to cancel part of the $+H_c$ produced by the addressing currents.

Because the read winding threads all the holes in the same sense, the signal-to-noise ratio is worse than that in core-array systems. For this reason, the apertured plates are invariably addressed by a matrix switch such as that discussed in the last subsection. This switch is made from apertured plates too, so that only one kind of major component is necessary for this kind of memory and addressing system.

Deposited-Film Memory Plates

A memory has been constructed by depositing a thin magnetic material in the form of circular areas on a glass sheet. The circles are about 4 millimeters in diameter and spaced in a square array with 8 mm between centers. The elements are evaporated in vacuum onto a glass sheet 30 mils thick. Then upon this plate is deposited a layer of insulation, then a layer of copper. The copper is etched away, so as to leave a grid of wires lying on top of the matrix of cores; this is one set of windings. The other windings are deposited in the same fashion in layers on top of each other. These deposited-core planes seem to have good potential for future use.

13.8. DRUM MEMORIES

A rotating drum coated with magnetic material can be used to store information. Binary information is written onto the drum at very small areas on the drum; these areas may be magnetized in either of two directions as the areas pass beneath a writing head.

A simplified view of the drum appears as part of Figure 13.8.1. Heads which can either read or write are disposed longitudinally along the drum. The periphery of the drum which passes beneath one of these heads is called a **track.** Each track contains a large number of **cells.** Each cell is a small area where one bit of information is recorded. One hundred cells per linear inch is a common figure. Thirty or more tracks can be packed along one inch of the drum parallel to its axis. A speed of rotation of the drum of 17,500 rpm is being used by one recently released computer. The pulse repetition rate for the drum is determined by the rotational speed and the number of cells per peripheral inch; common bit rates range from 50 kc to 300 kc.

The cylinder is a developable surface, so let us take a drum and slit it longitudinally, calling the line along which we cut it the 0 reference line. When it is flattened out, the surface appears as in Figure 13.8.2. The letters indicate the tracks; the numbers indicate the cell on a given track. Each cell stores one bit; the track stores a series of bits. Information may be stored on the drum in a serial-bit serial-character fashion as the twelve-bit word is stored in track A; a twelve-bit word may be stored in parallel-bit parallel-character fashion as the word using the first cell of E through P; it may be stored in serial-character parallel-bit fashion using tracks B, C, and D, and cells 1 through 4. Of course, a drum stores information in *one* of these fashions only. Usually the data structure of the memory is the same as that used in the rest of the computer. The tracks required to store a datum are called here a **channel**. Thus in our example the all-serial method has but one track per channel in Figure 13.8.2; the all-parallel system uses twelve (or the number of bits per word) tracks per channel; the serial-character parallel-bit method shown uses three tracks per chan-

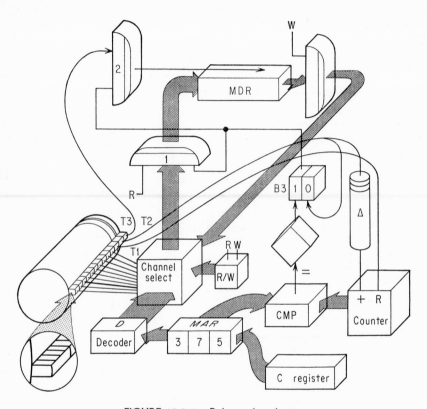

FIGURE 13.8.1. Polyvac drum logic.

nel; the Polyvac uses a four-bit code and so would have four tracks per channel in serial-character parallel-bit application to the drum.

Regardless of whether a serial, parallel, or serial-parallel storage system is used, the position which one word occupies within its channel is called a **sector**. At any given instant there is one word in each channel which might be read (or written); these words are on the same sector. A sector is a wedge-shaped portion of the drum.

For drum storage the address for the word to be memorized or remembered specifies two variables: the proper channel and the proper sector (ensemble of cells) in the channel. The set of heads which is specified is *arbitrary;* the selection (physical or electronic energization of the reading or writing head for the channel) may take place as soon as the data word is chosen (i.e., when the control circuitry is "notified" of what channel should be communicated with). The position of *words* is serial regardless of whether the bits or characters within the words (or channels) are serial or parallel; the word location in the channel in relation to the reading head is a function of the angle of rotation of the drum. If the beginning of the desired word is not now beneath the reading head, reading must be

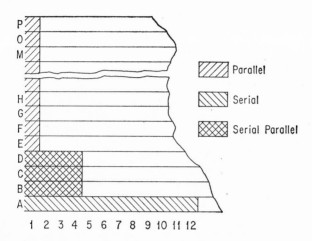

FIGURE 13.8.2. Drum track layout—serial, parallel, and serial parallel information.

postponed until it gets there. Reading cannot start until the word is in the proper position; then it *must* start.

In procuring a word from memory there are five steps:

1. Store temporarily the address of the desired word.
2. Translate the address into a form which can control the search.
3. Select the channel to read from (write into).
4. Determine when the proper sector on the drum starts to pass beneath the selected head.
5. Guide the word being read to the register intended for it.

Writing requires the same steps, except that the last step is to move the word *from* the register containing it and concurrently to write it *onto* the proper sector of drum.

Drum memories have nondestructive read-out and are nonvolatile. At the present state of the art, they are cheaper per bit than other memories. The access time depends upon the speed of rotation, which is limited by mechanical factors. For this reason—speed—cores are preferred if their price can be met.

The Polyvac Drum

Let us return to our demonstration machine. Because of its size (small-medium) it falls in a lower price range and would probably use a drum. We must store 1000 words on the drum. The drum has ten channels each containing 100 words. This arrangement permits us to use the first (binary-coded) decimal digit of the operand address to indicate the channel. The two other digits, then, indicate the sector where the word is found.

Memorizing and remembering for the drum are the same except for the function that the magnetic heads perform, i.e., writing and reading respectively. Both require that the proper address be found first.

The Memory Address Register

The first step is to store the address of the desired word. This address is transferred from the C register to the Memory Address Register, MAR in Figure 13.8.1. The register is constructed so that its first digit is accessible to the address decoder to effect channel selection. For memorization the datum to be stored must also be temporarily placed in the Memory Data Register.

Address Translation

The first digit of the address portion of the MAR is connected to a decoder D, Figure 13.8.1: the decoder produces a voltage on one of the ten channel-selection lines. The other two digits in the memory address register are applied to a coincidence circuit which determines when the proper sector is reached.

Channel Selection

Each of the ten sets of heads is fed into the channel-selection unit. The ten first-digit decoder output lines are also entered in the channel-select unit. The channel heads corresponding to the first digit of the address are connected to the output lines.

When computers were first conceived, channel selection could be done at leisure and relays were used. Relay selection takes from one to ten or more milliseconds. A few hundred thousand selections using relays would make a considerable dent in the available time for such a computer. Electronic selection may be made using biased tubes, transistors, or core arrays. Since the circuitry does not concern us here, suffice it to say that the selector connects the proper set of heads to the read/write switch (R/W).

The R/W switch connects the heads through the read amplifiers to the Memory Data Register to enter a datum there for READ; the R/W switch connects the Memory Data Register through the write amplifiers to the heads to enter a datum onto the drum for WRITE.

Sector Selection

A counter is used to determine which sector of the drum is approaching the reading heads. Notice it is the sector of the drum *approaching* the heads which interests us, for the control circuitry must be alerted *before* drum read-out starts.

Referring again to Figure 13.8.1 consider two timing tracks on the drum: the first, T1, contains a pulse in the last character position of each word for parallel-bit serial-character operation; the second track T2 contains a single pulse at the last character position of the last word. This single pulse is used to set to 0 the sector counter. The other pulses are used to tally up the counter.

Now, just before entering the sector numbered 75, the guard multi, B3, is set to 0 by the pulse in track T2 corresponding to the last character of the word sector numbered 74. The counter will be tallied up from 74 to 75 by the same pulse which has been delayed by Δ. If we desire to read out the word stored in sector 75, then the last two digits in the Memory Address Register, MAR, will be 75. These two digits comprise one input to the coincidence detector CMP; the other input is the output of the sector counter C; there is an output from CMP only when the proper sector is found (really, about to be found). This sets the guard bit storage B3 to 1 to permit the next phase.

Transfer from Memory

The output of the selector is one set of inputs to the set of gates, &1; the output of B3 and the READ order, R, are the other inputs to these gates. The information is thus read into the Memory Data Register at the proper time in the READ cycle.

The Memory Data Register must be shifted in synchronism with the information leaving the drum. This may be done with an accurate pulse generator. A recommended method for obtaining synchronized shift pulses is to take pulses from a third timing track T3. Since these pulses are generated at the same time that the information bits are being read, the timing pulses cannot fail to be in synchronism with the information pulses. The timing pulses from T3 are gated through &2 by the 1 setting of B3.

As the last character of the desired word is entered into the Memory Data Register, a pulse appears on the timing track, T1. It sets B3 to 0 which, in turn, prevents further information from being entered into the Memory Data Register which might obliterate what was just entered there.

The counter is reset after a complete drum revolution by the pulse in timing track T2. This pulse identifies the first sector, number 00.

Writing onto the Polyvac Drum

Here again, the number stored in the Memory Address Register is translated; a channel selection is made; the proper sector is looked for; when the correct sector is found, a coincidence pulse is emitted and the guard flip-flop, B3, set to 1. The WRITE order together with the 1 setting of B3 provides the proper information flow: the output of the Memory Data Register is connected to the channel selection unit; this line is connected through the write amplifiers to the proper set of heads to write onto the drum. The proper channel has been selected by decoding the first digit stored in the Memory Address Register. The T3 timing-track pulses are fed through &2 to the Memory Data Register to shift it, in perfect synchronism, into the writing circuits which write the information onto the drum. *Both 0's and 1's* are written onto the drum and all previous information at that address is entirely obliterated (replaced).

The writing order is completed when the pulse read from the timing track T2, appearing just after the last character of the word is written, resets the guard bit B3. This prevents further shifting of information for this command.

Other Sector-Selection Logic

There are methods of determining the proper timing, some using more than three timing tracks and some as few as one timing track.

COUNTER TRACKS. One track might be used for each bit of the sector-identification digits. For Polyvac this would require eight tracks (two binary-coded decimal digits of four bits each). These tracks have a code, corresponding to binary decimal code for the sector being entered, permanently written on them so as to indicate the end of *this* sector and the start of the *next*. This code is in machine language, and the number in the identification channel is the number of the sector which is about to be read or written. The output of these tracks (properly shaped) is one set of inputs to the decoder of Figure 13.8.3; the other set of inputs comes from the sector designation stored in the Memory Address Register. When these inputs correspond, the proper sector is coming up; at that time the decoder emits a pulse to set the guard bit to 1, and reading or writing then proceeds similarly to the logic of Figure 13.8.1.

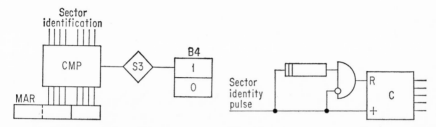

FIGURE 13.8.3. Logic for setting bit storage when sector identifi-
cation corresponds to the
memory address register.

FIGURE 13.8.4. Logic to reset counter
for missing sector pulse.

ONE-TRACK SECTOR IDENTIFICATION. A method of counting pulses can be used for finding the desired sector. The sector is identified by counting the pulses in a special track containing one sector-identification pulse per sector. If the pulse preceding a sector is missing, this identifies it as the initial sector, numbered 00. To detect the *missing* pulse and cause it to reset the sector-identification counter, the logic of Figure 13.8.4 may be used. Each sector pulse tallies the counter and is also entered into the one-word-time delay. The *previous* pulse emerges from the delay and enters &1 at the same time that *this* sector pulse appears, so that there is usually no output from &1. However, at sector 00 there is no sector pulse; the delayed pulse is not inhibited at &'1 and hence passes through to reset the counter.

Other Sector-Channel Combinations

If the 1000 addresses were laid out, because of some limitation in the drum design, so as to require 20 channels each of 50 sectors, the scheme for identifying each location would be more complex. A compound decoder with inputs consisting of all three digits (12 bits) of the address in the Memory Address Register would be required. It would select the

FIGURE 13.8.5. A magnetic drum memory assembly. Courtesy of Bryant Computer
Products Division.

channel and also furnish information to the coincidence detector to select
the required sector.

Appearance

A magnetic drum memory without addressing logic is shown in Figure
13.8.5.

13.9. BUFFERS AND REVOLVERS

Often core and drum memories are used for specialized purposes and therefore require specialized logic. The case where they are used as the main component for buffer storage is now treated briefly.

Core Buffers

Core storage has two properties which make it especially effective as a buffer: (1) it has fast access; (2) it is asynchronous, i.e., it may be made available to several units, each with different timing cycles, and with proper control logic it will adjust itself to the timing of each. A typical core buffer appears as Figure 13.9.

FIGURE 13.9.   A core buffer memory for 144 characters of 8 bits each.   Courtesy of Telemeter Magnetics, Inc.

INPUT/OUTPUT CORE BUFFERS. An input buffer receives information from a unit such as a punched paper tape reader or magnetic tape reader. The buffer stores data in consecutive word positions under the control of, and with the timing of, the input unit. Words are read out consecutively by the computer and are placed into the main memory as directed by the computer control. Memorizing and remembering for buffers is called **loading** and **unloading,** respectively.

Since consecutive words are referred to in a fixed sequence, the addressing logic may be simplified somewhat. The X and Y amplifiers are fed from X and Y ring counters. The X counter is advanced once as each word is loaded or unloaded by the control logic until the end of the load/unload cycle; when the last X word position is referred to, the X counter resets itself to its first position and advances the Y counter one position. When the last input word is entered, the X and Y counters both reset and signal the computer control that the buffer is loaded. The X and Y counters are connected as multistage counters discussed in Section 11.5. No memory address register or X and Y decoder is needed, as this function is performed automatically by the X and Y counters.

The unloading cycle is the same as the load cycle. Each word is unloaded into the computer memory when unloading is called for by the computer control unit. The X count is advanced after each word is unloaded.

In many computers, the loading of the input buffer may be completely delegated to the input and buffer logic. While the computer is doing calculations the computer control unit signals the buffer logic to load the buffer. From time to time the computer control unit may check the buffer to see if it is loaded. When the buffer is loaded, it can be unloaded at the convenience of the computer control.

Output buffers function in the same fashion as do input buffers. This extrapolation is left to the reader as an exercise.

MEMORY CORE BUFFERS. Buffers can be used in conjunction with essentially slower memories such as the drum or delay line. Data in a memory buffer is then much more rapidly available to the central computer. The buffer can also be used to transfer big blocks of data in a single operation instead of the many operations required using registers.

Usually the loading of a memory buffer is on a consecutive word basis. Data from memory are loaded into consecutive positions in the buffer; each buffer word, however, must be addressable in an arbitrary manner. Unloading, at the discretion of the program, may be either arbitrary or consecutive. In the latter case, the data in the buffer are transferred as a block into the main memory.

When the buffer combines both consecutive and arbitrary access, it must contain logic both for decoding a specific word address and for multistage counters for sequential addressing.

Drum Buffers

Channels on the drum can be used for the two functions, faster access and input/output buffering.

FAST-ACCESS BANDS. Each normal channel on the drum has but one set of heads. To procure a particular word, one might have to wait a full revolution; on the average, half a revolution is necessary. By placing additional sets of heads around the drum, the waiting time can be appreciably reduced. A channel with ten sets of heads will have an average (and maximum) access time of one-tenth as long as for a normal drum channel with only one set of heads.

Extra logic is required to determine which set of heads the desired word will pass under next. Consider how this would work for the Polyvac. Call the words in the fast-access ring F00 to F99. Suppose F37 is desired; suppose word F63 is passing under the 0 reference set of heads. Then F73 is passing the 1 reference set, F53 is passing the 9 reference set, and F33 is passing below the 7 reference set. This is the set which could be addressed in a little more than three word times. With a counter which contains the word number of the datum passing beneath the 0 reference head, the proper set of heads to use (here the 7 set) can be determined with simple logic.

OUTPUT BUFFER BAND. Information destined for a slow-output unit such as a paper punch can be placed in the buffer channel of the drum. The output logic reads the first digit from this channel and writes it into the output medium. A counter keeps track of the digits on the drum which have been written out. This counter is counted up once for each digit. When the output unit has finished punching a digit, the output buffer logic is alerted; when the next digit of the word called for appears at the buffer set of channel heads, it is transmitted to the output unit and so on, until punching is complete. The control unit is then alerted that the buffer can be filled again with output data. During the time required to punch one character the drum usually can make more than one revolution. An input buffer on the drum functions in the same manner.

PROBLEMS

1. What are some of the differences between magnetic cores used for shift registers and those used for memories?
2. What is half-read and half-write current?
3. Why is a square hysteresis loop so important for core memories?
4. How is remembering done so as not to erase the recalled information?
5. Examine four 10 × 10 core arrays. Draw and describe schemes for storing and reading out the following: 40 ten-bit parallel-bit words; 40 ten-bit serial-bit words; ten ten-character four-bit words in serial-parallel fashion.
6. What is the purpose of the disturb current?
7. Show a complete logic for a 100-word (10 × 10) ten-character (×10) parallel binary memory. Show the eight-bit MAR (using NBCD addressing), the double decoder (X and Y), the timing logic and MDR.

8. Show a complete logic for a ten-word ten-character four-bit (four frames, 10×10) serial-character parallel-bit core logic. Show the four-bit MAR (NBCD) and its decoder, the character counter and its decoder, the timing logic and the MDR (shift register).

9. Show a full 4×4 (16 output) matrix core decoder.

10. Consider a 100,000-bit drum memory with the drum making 7200 rpm and with 100 read/write heads. Find, for (a) 25-bit/word parallel operation, (b) 40-bit/word serial operation and (c) ten-character word, four-bit/character serial-parallel operation, the following: (1) tracks per channel, (2) channels per drum, (3) words per channel, (4) maximum, minimum, and average access time.

11. How many tracks has the Polyvac? How many bits can it store? How many bits per channel, words per channel, bits per track, sectors?

12. Make a two-dimensional drawing of the Polyvac drum-memory logic, filling in all appropriate boxes except the Channel Select.

13. Indicate fully the logic required for the fast-access bands of Section 13.9.

14. Describe how information from memory channels of the Polyvac could get to the output buffer band.

15. Restate the difference between dynamic and static memories.

16. Redraw Figure 13.2.1 to show how a four-bit-per-character parallel-bit memory would work. Do the same for Figure 13.2.2.

17. Show the complete control logic for a ten-word, ten-character-per-word, four-bit-per-character automatic load and unload serial-parallel input core buffer. It is controlled over three lines: start (pulse), load and unload (both d-c).

18. Do Problem 17 for a memory buffer with selective load/unload cycle (one to ten words).

19. Show the logic for a memory core buffer as per Problem 17 that may be loaded/unloaded as a block or may be addressed arbitrarily after block loadings.

FOURTEEN

THE CONTROL UNIT

14.1. INTRODUCTION

The virtues of the control unit have been extolled in preceding sections to the extent that the reader may feel it is some magical being that watches over the computer and manages its affairs. If that were the case, we would expect it to be made of some special *stuff* such as *flogistum*. On the contrary, it is of the same *stuff* as the rest of the computer, *logical building blocks*.

I like to think of the computer control as somewhat parallel to human control. Contrary to common belief, the human control system is decentralized. All information is not monitored at a single center; reflex information travels a different path from observation information. We are hardly aware that we are walking, sitting, or pronouncing words, because each process requires only the attention of decentralized automatic centers; the creative and communicative thought processes get our full conscious attention except in emergencies.

Just as the control of many of our automatic activities is decentralized, so the control of the decentralized computer takes place throughout its territory; each of the large functional blocks may become autonomous for part of the operating cycle. The directing aspect of the block can then be considered to be part of the control function of the computer. Of course, it is possible to control the computer from a physically central location,

273

but then all "stimulus," "response" and "control" messages must be transmitted to and from this location. Because it makes for simple explanation, the decentralized control unit is discussed in the first sections of this chapter. It should be remembered that in this kind of set-up, it is possible to share a functional block with two or more control functions, although the block appears each time in the discussions as a separate unit with a different label or designation. Thus the same pulse generator may be used for both addition and multiplication.

The job of the control unit was outlined previously; it selects the source and destination of the datum to be processed; it determines and controls whether a full or partial datum is to be processed; it determines at what address the next instruction will be found.

Centralized and Decentralized Control

In the **centralized control unit,** all selection and control functions are performed by the control unit. The **decentralized computer** to which we shall now confine ourselves consists of a main control unit and a number of autonomous secondary outposts. The main control unit determines which secondary control unit will conduct and supervise the operation presently called for and then surrenders autonomy to the secondary control unit. The outpost takes over until the job is done. It then surrenders its authority; the outpost can turn over its authority only to the main control, not to any other outpost.

MAIN CONTROL'S JOB. The main control unit in a decentralized control system does the full dispatching job.

1. It determines the process to be performed and turns over control to the secondary unit at the proper time.
2. It determines the source and destination of information to be processed, sets up the proper information flow lines.
3. It determines the quantity of information to be processed.
4. It coordinates the activities of the auxiliary control units, e.g., memory access control and process control, may be required on the same command.
5. It keeps track of the memory location from which each command was withdrawn and, from this and other knowledge, determines the location from which the next command should be taken.

AUXILIARY CONTROL'S JOB. The auxiliary control units are built to control one or a few functions. They start when ordered by the main control and surrender control to the main unit when their job is done. The auxiliary control unit does these tests:

1. It accepts control upon command from the main control unit unless it is otherwise occupied.
2. It determines when information is transmitted and processed in its control cycle.
3. It sets up previously arranged paths of information flow.
4. It determines the timing for each suboperation.
5. It indicates the completion of its obligation by informing the central control unit and surrenders control to the latter.

Communication between the Main Control and the Outposts

The main control unit transmits two different kinds of signals to the auxiliary control units of the computer. It transmits switching signals which last for the duration of the order and delineate the path of information flow. It also sends short, pulse-type signals to the decentralized control units in order to start them and initiate the decentralized processing.

Upon the completion of the order, main control receives a pulse signal from the auxiliary control unit concerned. Main control must then procure another instruction from the memory and act upon it.

Switching

At key points along possible flow lines of information, switching mechanisms must be posted. These mechanisms are set up to determine the arrival, routing, and departure of information. Since these routes must be set up very rapidly, mechanical switches which were quite popular in early relay computers are inconceivable for use in modern high-speed computers. The solution is to use &-gates. These gates are opened by enabling or switching signals

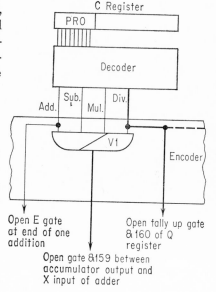

FIGURE 14.1.   Typical decoder-encoder function in control unit.

emanating from the control unit. *One* gate may be called for on several orders but, on the other hand, *many* gates are usually called for on any one given order. The method for giving the order to close a circuit is demonstrated in Figure 14.1. Here we see the decoder in the main control unit examining the process portion of the control register to determine what processing order is stored therein. The output of the decoder appears as a voltage on one of the many possible order lines. Since only one order can be requested at any one step, only one of these lines will be activated.

It is the encoder that selects the gates which must be activated during the order. The mixer $\vee 1$ in this figure is used to energize &159 (for example); &159 connects the output of the A register to the X input of the adder, for division. The path of division order signals is indicated by the heavy line in the figure. Since the outpost of the accumulator must be connected to the X input of the adder for the addition, subtraction, multiplication, and division orders, the decoder outputs for all these commands are inputs to the mixer $\vee 1$ which energizes the gate (&159) which makes this connection to the adder. Since the division order requires the input of information from the A register to the X input of the adder, there is a heavy line emanating from $\vee 1$. Many other functions are called for in division, among which, for instance, is the activating of the tally-up input of the Q register—and another heavy line in the figure indicates this.

For each gate which is activated by more than one order in one of the functional units of the computer, there must be a corresponding mixer to synthesize an enabling input to this gate.

Whereas the decoder consists entirely of &-gates, the encoder consists entirely of $\vee$-mixers—see Section 11.8.

Timing

The auxiliary control unit for any given process usually consists of one or more pulse generators. One of these pulse generators is started by an initiate pulse from the central control unit. The ensuing pulses from the local pulse generator actually *cause* the movement of information from one part of the processing unit to another. In transfer or arithmetic operations these pulses *are* the shift pulses which are applied to the source and destination registers to cause information to pass out of one register and into another. The paths have been set up by the switching voltages discussed previously.

Often several pulse generators are required for a given order, as was demonstrated in Chapter 12 on arithmetic. After one portion of a process is completed, a pulse is emitted which starts another pulse generator to do another portion of the job. When the full order is completed, the post-train pulse of the last generator used is transmitted to the central control unit to announce completion of the task.

Main Control Unit Operation

The general plan of action of the central control unit, discussed in detail in the next section, is divided into two phases. The first phase is to set up the flow of information within the functional units and to start the process going; this is called the *execute* phase. When the order is completed, the control unit then supervises the procurement of the next instruction; this is the *fetch* phase.

14.2. PLAN OF ACTION

An internal flow chart is found in Figure 14.2; this chart should not be confused with the programming flow chart discussed in Chapter 4. The purpose of this chart is to present visually to the reader the steps and decisions needed to control the information processing. Since it will be referred to throughout the chapter, the reader should study it well.

Fetch or Execute

Two separate control cycles are distinguishable. The **fetch cycle** procures the next instruction from the memory. The **execute cycle** performs what is indicated in the instruction just procured. Each activity of the computer is part of either a fetch or execute cycle.

Fetch Cycle

Upon determining that *this* is a fetch cycle in box 1, we leave by the arrow labeled F (for Fetch). The *next* cycle is set up as an execute cycle, box 2. The address of the next order which is stored in the Instruction Counter is transferred to the Memory Address Register, and in box 3 the memory is requested to remember the instruction word. This instruction word is placed by the memory control into the Memory Data Register, box 4. The instruction word is transferred to the C register, box 5, adding the content of the cycle register if required (recall the cycle index register function discussed in Chapter 5). Return is made to the first box via circle 1.

Execute

Check whether this is a fetch or an execute cycle, in box 1; it is an execute cycle so we leave box 1 along the arrow labeled X (for eXecute).

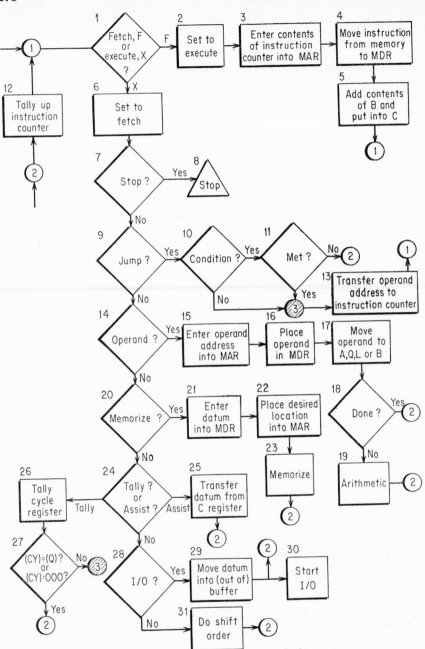

FIGURE 14.2. Plan of action for computer control.

Set the next cycle to be a fetch cycle, box 6. Is this a stop order, box 7? If so, stop, box 8, and notify the operator. Otherwise, is this a jump order, box 9? If so, is there a condition, box 10? If so, is it met, box 11? If there is a condition (such as "less than" on a previous comparison) but it is not met, we pass through circle 2 to box 12. In box 12 the instruction counter is advanced by 1 and then the fetch-execute test box entered. For an unconditional jump (box 10, "No") or a conditional jump for which the condition is met (box 11, "Yes"), box 13 is entered. The address of the *next* order in such cases is M, the operand address of *this* order, which is now in the C register. Hence the new instruction address must be transferred from its present position in the C register to replace the present contents of the Address Counter. After so doing, we return via circle 1 to box 1 for another fetch-execute test.

For non-jump orders we leave box 9 on the "No" line. Now does this order require an operand, box 14? If so, the operand address is sent to the Memory Address Register, box 15. The operand is delivered when procured by the memory to the Memory Data Register, box 16, and then transferred to the destination register, A, B, Q, or L, box 17. Is that all, box 18? If not, arithmetic is the only alternative. It is done in box 19. In either case, return is made via circle 2 to box 12 where the Instruction Counter is advanced.

If no operand is required, we leave box 14 on the "No" line. Then is this a memorize order, box 20? If so, we leave box 20 on the "Yes" line. The information to be stored is transferred from the source register to the Memory Data Register, box 21. The destination is transferred to the Memory Address Register in box 22 and the datum memorized, box 23. We return via circle 2 to box 12.

We leave box 20 on the "No" line if this is not a memorize order and check for a transfer from or to the C register as required for cycle register assist instructions, box 24 and, if required, perform it, box 25.

The cycle register is tallied, when required, in box 26. The cycle register content is compared with either (Q) or 000 as requested by the command, in box 27. If they are unequal, go via circle 3 to box 13 to do a jump; if equal, go via circle 2 to box 12 to tally the Instruction Counter.

Check for input/output operation, box 28, and transfer input (output) data from (to) the buffer, box 29. Return is made via circle 2 to box 12 and the input/output unit is started, box 30, simultaneously.

If no input/output operation is called for, we leave box 28 by the "No" line. Only a shift operation could now be required; this is done in box 31 if this exhausts the repertoire of orders.

Return via circle 2 to advance the Instruction Counter, box 12, and then do the next fetch operation.

14.3. FETCH LOGIC

Start Phase

This corresponds to boxes 1, 2, 3, 4, and 6 of Figure 14.2. A test pulse, T, enters circle 1 to make the first control test (fetch or execute?) in Figure 14.3.1. The T pulse tests &4 and &5 enabled respectively by the

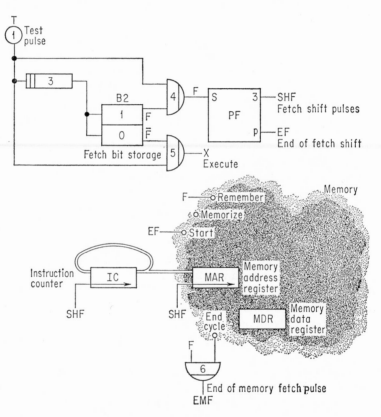

FIGURE 14.3.1. Start of the fetch cycle.

1 (fetch) and 0 (execute) states of B2. Delayed by Δ3, the test pulse then triggers B2 to a state opposite to its previous state.

For the fetch cycle, B2 was set to 1 and the pulse passes &4 to start the pulse generator, PF. It generates three shift pulses on the line SHF. These are applied to the Instruction Counter register IC which contains the address of the next command, to enter it into the Memory Address

Register, MAR. The postshift pulse, EF, starts the memory cycle. The 1 output of B2, (F), is applied to the remember input of the memory. The instruction is delivered by the memory as directed by the memory control to the Memory Data Register, MDR. The end-of-memory cycle pulse passes out of &6 as the end-of-memory-fetch pulse, EMF, which serves to start the fetch add cycle register phase.

Add Cycle Register Phase

Remember that before an instruction is executed, the content of a cycle register may be added to the operand address if there is a nonzero cycle register digit in the proper position of the instruction word. This task is now done. The operation is described only for cycle register #1, but operation of the other cycle registers is similar. This cycle register phase uses the logic of Figure 14.3.2 and illustrates box 5 of Figure 14.2.

The strategy is to pass the entire instruction word now in the MDR through an adder into the control register. If a cycle register addition is called for, its content is added, but only to the operand digits (M) of the instruction. All instruction words pass through the adder. The cycle index digit of each must be checked; if it is 0, nothing is added; for a nonzero digit, the corresponding cycle index must be added. All this is done "on the run," so to speak, as the word is being shifted *from* the MDR *through* the adder and *to* the control register.

The end-of-memory-fetch pulse EMF starts the pulse generator PC10. The ten shift pulses SHC shift both the Memory Data Register MDR and the control register. The first three digits of the instruction word pass right through the adder A12, since nothing is being entered during that time at A13Y or A13C'. These three digits go in the X input and out the S output, without any change. The pulses from PC10 are counted by the counter C1. When C1 holds a count of exactly 3, the decoder D2 issues a checking voltage CH. Three shifts have caused the cycle register specification digit (the fourth digit) of the instruction word to enter the right-hand position of MDR. For any digit which appears there the decoder D3 will emit a voltage on the corresponding line. Only when cycle register #1 is specified will the 1 output of D3 be present. It is applied to &4 to allow the CH pulse to pass through &4 and to enter Δ13, which provides a delay of a single digit time. By then, the fifth digit of the instruction word is in the right-hand position of the MDR. It is the fifth, sixth, and seventh digit of the instruction word to which the cycle register content is to be added.

Before the fifth digit of the instruction word is moved from the MDR, the pulse from Δ13 emerges to set BC1 to 1. The 1 state of BC1 is simply called BC. This signal BC is applied to &6, &7, and &8. &6 allows three

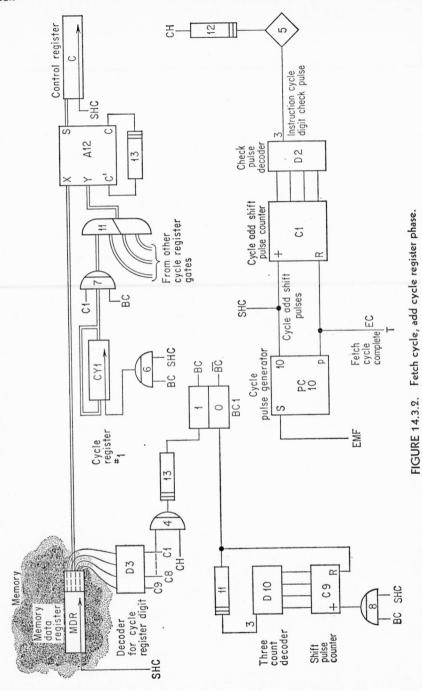

FIGURE 14.3.2.   Fetch cycle, add cycle register phase.

shift pulses SHC to shift CY1 completely around, also entering its content into &7; &7 passes the content of CY1 through V11 into the Y input of the adder A; shift pulses SHC are also entered through &8 to tally the counter C9. The detector D10 determines when three pulses, starting from now, have been used. It issues a pulse which is entered into Δ11. The purpose of Δ11 is to make certain the "third" shift pulse finishes its job. The output of Δ11 sets BC1 to 0 and resets the counter C9.

During the time when the fifth, sixth, and seventh instruction-word digits are entered into the X input of the adder, the content of the cycle register is being entered into the Y input of the adder. The modified instruction passes out of the S output of the adder into the control register. During the eighth, ninth, and tenth pulses from PC, BC1 is set to 0 so that the cycle register is not affected.

The instruction in the MDR has been moved to the C register, having had only the operand address altered by the quantity in the cycle register. The cycle register itself is unchanged.

The post-train pulse EC from PC signals the completion of box 5, Figure 14.2. The next operation is found at box 1 of that figure; it is to see if the next cycle is fetch or execute. The pulse EC is actually returned to the logic of Figure 14.3.1 as the test pulse T to start this check.

14.4. JUMP ORDERS

We now discuss boxes 7 through 13 of Figure 14.2. A jump order directs the computer to do no processing of data but rather to look for another instruction. Sometimes this instruction will be found at the next instruction location $(I + 1)$; at other times the new instruction will be found at a totally different location. In Figure 14.4 the output of the process decoder D13 for use in jump and stop orders is applied directly to a number of gates.

For non-jump and non-stop orders, the decoder feeds the gate encoder E14. The outputs of E14 open the gates required to set up the information flow for the given order. Also, a number of "start" gates indicated in the insert send signals to "start the specified command" to locations in the processing unit concerned with the command. These gates perform the functions illustrated by boxes 14, 20, 24, and 26 of Figure 14.2.

The job performed by the logic of Figure 14.4 consists largely of a series of tests to determine if the next instruction is found at M or $(I + 1)$.

After the fetch-execute logic has determined that this is an execute cycle, it issues an X (for eXecute) pulse. This pulse tests the series of gates on the left side of Figure 14.4. &1 corresponds to box 7 of Figure 14.2; it has as inputs the X pulse and a possible stop signal from the decoder. For a stop order, the X pulse passes through &1 and causes an

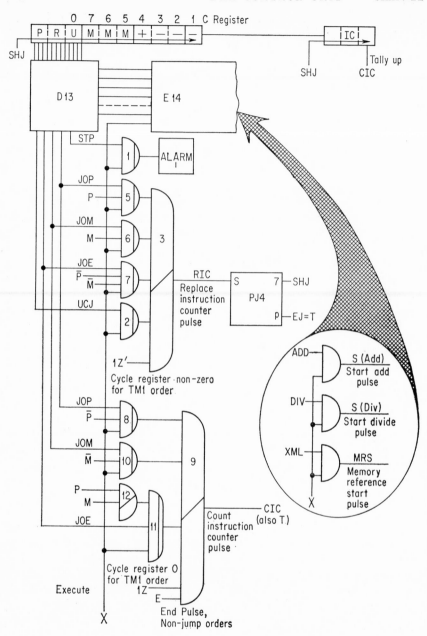

FIGURE 14.4.   Control unit operation for the jump orders.

alarm to arouse the attendant, if possible, box 8, Figure 14.2. Since there is no other destination of the output of &1, the computer, as it were, falls asleep—nothing further happens until the attendant intervenes.

The tests of boxes 8, 10, and 11, Figure 14.2, are all done at about the same time. Let's see how. In Figure 14.4 the X pulse tests &2, whose other input is the decoder output for an unconditional jump (UCJ). This pulse passes through V3 and emerges as a RIC pulse. This pulse initiates the Replacement of the content of the Instruction Counter by the operand location found in the control register. In other words, the location of the next instruction is now in the operand portion of the control register. To direct the memory to look up the instruction at that location it is necessary first to transfer that number into the instruction counter.

To do this, the RIC pulse starts the pulse generator, PJ4. This generator emits seven pulses. These pulses cause information to be shifted from the control register into the Instruction Counter (IC). This counter is a three-character register. No matter how many characters are entered into it, only the last three can possibly remain there; all the rest go into the "wastebasket." The operand portion of the instruction is located in the fifth, sixth, and seventh positions of the instruction word. Seven shift pulses will then place this portion of the instruction word in the Instruction Counter. Since a new instruction word is about to be procured, it is not important that the C register is out of kilter—that the information has been moved around to an abnormal position.

The post-train pulse labeled EJ from the pulse generator PJ4 will now be used to make another fetch-execute test; hence it is also designated as a T pulse as it enters the logic of Figure 14.3.1.

Recall that the comparison box is set to M (less than), E (equal to), or P (greater than) as the results of a previous comparison order. The box has four outputs: M, $\overline{\text{M}}$, P, $\overline{\text{P}}$. The equal condition E is indicated by $\overline{\text{M}}$ & $\overline{\text{P}}$.

The decoder output for a jump-on-plus (JOP) order is applied to &5. The plus (P) output of the comparison box, only the outputs of which are shown, is also applied to &5. The execute pulse, when it tests &5, will cause an output only for the JOP order *and* when the comparison box indicates the corresponding P (plus) information. The pulse from &5 passes through and out of V3 as an RIC pulse and starts the Replacement of the content of the Instruction Counter, so that the next order location appears there, as described earlier.

A similar situation exists for the jump-on-minus order (JOM). The line for this order is applied to &6 together with the minus condition (M) of the comparison box. The X pulse passes through &6 only for this conditional jump (JOM) when the minus condition is met (M is present at

&6). In that case the X pulse passes from &6 through V3 and emerges as an RIC pulse.

The jump-on-equal order (JOE) requires a gate with four inputs. This is because the comparison box consists of two bistable devices and the equal state is indicated by the zero output of both of them. The equal condition is thus indicated by $\overline{P}$ and $\overline{M}$ from the comparison box. The four inputs to &7 are hence: JOE, $\overline{P}$, $\overline{M}$, and X. If the equal condition exists when the jump-on-equal order is called for, the X pulse passes through &7 and V3 and emerges as an RIC pulse which starts the replacement of the instruction counter. There is one more kind of input to V3. This arises from the tally orders TMI and TPI. For TM1 when the cycle index register stores a number greater than zero, it is desired to jump to the memory location specified in the tally-down instruction. This is discussed in Section 14.7 describing the tally-down order. Should the result of inspection of the cycle index register show that it does not store zero on this order, we start an RIC cycle. This is indicated for cycle register #1 on Figure 14.4 by the line labeled 1Z' which enters V3 directly.

The next instruction will be procured from the location stored in the instruction counter after it has been tallied up if the conditional jump conditions have not been met *or* if this is a non-jump order.

For the jump-on-plus order, &8 determines when the condition is not met, for then the line labelled $\overline{P}$ is energized. The X pulse passes through &8 and V9 and emerges a CIC pulse. This pulse Counts the Instruction Counter. It is applied to the tally input of the instruction counter and adds 1 to its content. The instruction counter then holds the correct address of the next instruction. The CIC pulse is also a T pulse. Remember that the T pulse tests the fetch-execute logic to determine which cycle is next. When it determines that the fetch cycle is next, it will use the proper address which is now in the instruction counter to find the new instruction.

The X pulse tests &10 and will emerge from it only when a jump-on-minus condition is called for but not met. The output of &10 passes through V9 as a CIC pulse.

The jump-on-equal condition is denied when either line P or line M is energized. These alternatives are determined by V12 whose output is applied to &11. A pulse emerges from &11 when the equal condition is called for but not met. It passes through V9 and emerges as a CIC pulse.

When the cycle index test order is called for, as described in Section 14.7, and the cycle index register contains 000, a pulse is returned to V9 to cause a CIC operation as shown in Figure 14.4.

The pulse E emitted on the completion of a non-jump order also passes through V9 to emerge as a CIC pulse. For then it is also necessary to tally up the instruction counter and use its content to find the next instruction. The 1Z line entering V9 arises from the tally orders and is discussed in that section.

14.5. MEMORY REFERENCE ORDERS

All orders requiring reference to the memory including the arithmetic orders come under this classification. This discussion covers the boxes numbered 14 through 18 of the flow chart, Figure 14.2; arithmetic, box 19, was covered in Chapter 12.

All memory reference orders start when the control unit determines that the order to be performed requires memory reference and a pulse is used from the encoder start gates called a Memory Reference Start pulse (MRS) (see the insert of Figure 14.4).

Strategy

The strategy is now outlined below:

1. Enter the operand address M into the Memory Address Register without affecting the arrangement of information in the C register.
2. Start the memory look-up.
3. When the look-up is complete, transfer the datum from the Memory Data Register to its destination.
4. Send an end-of-distribution pulse ED to the central control.

Logic

The MRS pulse entering Figure 14.5 starts the memory reference pulse generator PR. The purpose of this pulse generator is to produce pulses to transfer the operand location in the control register to the memory address register, replacing the content of the instruction register in order. PR issues a set of ten pulses, SHR, which are applied to the control register and shift its content around completely. After being shifted, the instruction word will then appear as before. In so doing, the operand location, a three-digit number, is transferred to the Memory Address Register. It is all right if the right-hand digits of the instruction word pass through the memory address register and out the other side, as long as the digits after the operand address are not entered into MAR. This operation is controlled by a counter and decoder. The counter C2 counts the shift pulses. The decoder D3 issues a signal L as long as the count in C2 is less than but not equal to seven. The signal L which is applied to &1 therefore

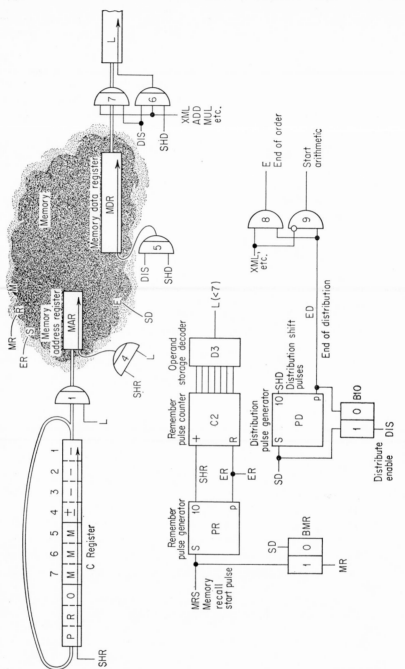

FIGURE 14.5. Memory reference orders, control.

allows only the first seven characters to enter MAR. The shift pulses SHR are gated by &4 to which the signal L is applied. Only seven shift pulses pass through &4 to MAR so that after the proper address is entered there, it will not be moved out.

The memory search is started by the post-train pulse from PR labeled ER. This pulse is applied to the S input of the memory. The memory knows that it is to recall information because the voltage MR is applied to the Remember input R of the memory. MR is the 1 setting of bit storage $\overline{B}MR$ which is set to 1 at the beginning of the remember cycle and reset to 0 by pulse SM which is issued when the desired datum is stored in MDR.

When the search is completed and the datum found, the memory stores it temporarily in the memory data register MDR. The memory logic also emits, from the E output, the pulse SD indicating that the search is complete. This pulse is labeled SD because it $\underline{S}$tarts the $\underline{D}$ata transfer from the memory to its destination; it starts a second pulse generator labeled PD. The purpose of this generator is to $\underline{D}$istribute the information from the memory to its destination. The pulse SD also sets B10 to 1, which applies a voltage DIS to all the gates which must be open while the information is DIStributed.

In the case of orders such as XML, ADD, MUL, the information is to go to the L register. We shall examine this situation. Shift pulses SHD from PD are applied to MDR through &5; they are applied to the L register via &6 on the DIS part of the cycle and when XML, ADD, MUL, and other orders requiring the operand in the L register are called for. The path between MDR and the L register is set up by &7 on the DIS cycle and L register operand orders. The ten pulses, SHD, can now maneuver the information into the L register.

After a simple remember order where a datum is transferred from the memory to the L register only (such as XML), the memory reference order is completed. Therefore, the post-train pulse ED of pulse generator PD passes through &8 and emerges as an E pulse, indicating the end of this order. In the case of arithmetic orders, the pulse ED passes through &'9 to start the arithmetic process called for. Since this is an inhibiting gate, the pulse will not pass to start arithmetic on an order such as XML.

14.6. MEMORIZATION AND TRANSFER ORDERS

Both memorization and transfer orders are in the same form: the operand portion of the instruction word contains the desired destination. Since the registers are addressable, register destinations must be sifted from the memory destinations to prevent an incorrect look-up in the memory—there is no memory location corresponding to a register address. This description covers boxes numbered 20 to 23 in Figure 14.2.

In Figure 14.6 decoder D1 detects a register destination address. Its

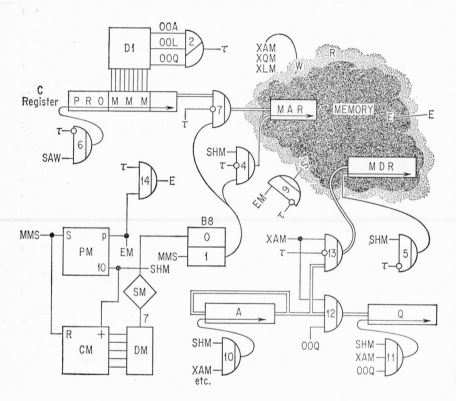

FIGURE 14.6.   Control for memorize and transfer orders.

output is used to inhibit memorization and enable register transfer operation.

Strategy

The strategy required for these types of order is outlined:

1. Determine whether this is a memorization or transfer order.
2. For memorization enter the operand address from the control register to the memory address register ending with the order in the control register in its original form.
3. For transfer orders, set up the route to the destination register.

4. Transfer one word from the source to the destination—in the case of memorization, the destination is the memory data register.
5. Request memorization of the datum in the MDR at the address in the MAR.
6. The transfer orders end with step 4 and the memorization with step 5.

The start of both types of order in Figure 14.6 is signalled by an MMS pulse; for both, it starts the pulse generator PM. The decision for the type of order, transfer or memorization, is made by D1; it examines MMM in Figure 14.6 and it energizes one of the lines 00A, 00L, or 00Q for a transfer. These lines are mixed by $\vee$2, which then produces an output on the line labeled τ for any transfer order.

Memorization

The plan here is to enter MMM into the Memory Address Register and to enter the datum to be stored from the source register into the memory data register. When this is complete, we may start memory memorizing.

On both types of orders the source register, (A, Q, or L) is shifted by the ten pulses, SHM; the ten shift pulses SHM also pass through &'5 to shift the datum into the memory data register when tau is absent.

The control register is shifted completely around by the ten pulses SHM, which pass through &'6, but only seven characters pass through &'7. Bit storage B8 is set to 1 at the beginning of the order by the MMS pulse; it remains so set for the first seven SHM pulses. The counter CM counts the shift pulses SHM; the decoder DM produces an output on the seventh pulse which is shaped by SM and resets B8 to 0. This removes the enabling signal from &'4 and &'7, which prevents the last three characters of the control register from entering the MAR. Remember that the memory address register is a three-digit register so that only MMM ends up in MAR.

Everything is now set for memorization; the memory is notified by the post-train pulse EW from PW which passes through &'9 that it is to start its job. The write signal is applied to the memory at the Write input W by the decoded command which is either XAM, XLM, or XQM.

The end pulse from the memory is also the end pulse for the memorization orders.

Transfer

The operation of the transfer logic when operating with the order XAM00Q can be followed in Figure 14.6.

The pulse MMS starts PM. Notice that &'4, &'5, &'6, and &'7 are all inhibited by the presence of the tau pulse so that the memory is in no way affected by this order. Shift pulses SHM are applied to the A and Q registers through &10 and &11. The word passes from the A register to the Q register via &12 held open by 00Q; for memorization it would otherwise pass from A through &'13. The datum from the A register is also re-entered into the A register.

This is all there is to the transfer process. Therefore, the post-train pulse EM from PM is the end-of-order pulse for transfer orders. It passes through &14 for those orders only when tau is present.

14.7. TALLY ORDERS

This section discusses three orders which affect the tally register and index cycling in general. These are the tally-up and tally-down orders, representing boxes 26 and 27 of Figure 14.2, and the order to transfer information from the program to the tally register, box 25 of Figure 14.2. The use of these orders has been described in Chapter 5.

Tally-Down Orders

We shall discuss as representative of TMI, the order TM1. This order requires that the content of CY1 be reduced by 1; then the content of CY1 is compared to 0; for (CY1) > 0 we jump to the address M; for (CY1) = 0 we go to I + 1 for the next order. Only CY1 (not CY2, and so on) is examined here.

The pulse STD indicating the start of the tally-down order TD1 is applied to the tally-down input of the register CY1 in Figure 14.7.1. The content of the register CY1 is thus reduced by 1. All the digits of register CY1 are decoded simultaneously in parallel by the decoder D1. It issues a constant voltage output on the 0 line only when the content of CY1 is 000. The pulse STD is also applied to the delay Δ2. This delayed pulse STD is applied to &3 and &'4; these gates contribute pulse outputs 1Z and 1Z' which respectively indicate that cycle register 1 (CY1) contains zero or does not contain zero. Only one of these pulses appears: the 1Z pulse becomes the count instruction counter pulse, CIC, of Figure 14.4 after it passes through V9 on that diagram; the 1Z' pulse becomes a reset instruction counter pulse, RIC, after it passes through V3 of Figure 14.4.

Tally-Up Order

Only the operation of CY1 is examined on order TP1. If a tally-up order is called for, a pulse appears on line STU in Figure 14.7.1. This is applied to the tally-up input of the register CY1. It is thus used to add 1 to the content of register CY1. The comparison circuit CM5 is constantly comparing the least significant three digits contained in the Q register with the content of register CY1. If they are equal, a voltage appears on the equal line emerging from CM5. This voltage is applied to &6 and &7'. The tally-up pulse STU is also applied to the delay Δ8. After register

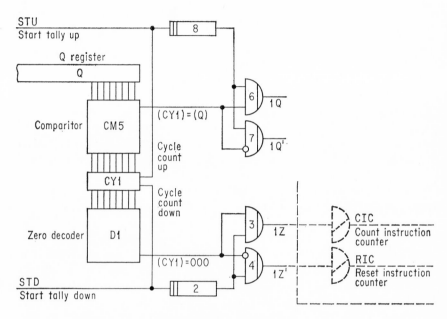

FIGURE 14.7.1.   Logic for the tally-up and tally-down orders.

CY1 has had a chance to be tallied, this pulse tests &6 and &7' to determine whether the content of register CY1 is equal to the content (three least significant digits) of the Q register. For equality, the pulse 1Q is emitted by &6; for inequality, the pulse 1Q' is emitted by &'7. These pulses are equivalent to the 1Z and 1Z' pulses and perform exactly the same action as the latter in Figure 14.4.

Transfer-From-Program Orders

A number which is written in the program by the programmer can be transferred into cycle register 1 by means of the XP1 order; similar orders are used for the other cycle registers. Of course, the number entered into the cycle index register does not come directly from the program; rather, it comes from the instruction information after it has been stored in the control register. This is a simple transfer operation from the control register, but instead of inserting the operand address into the memory address register, it is transferred to the cycle register called for.

The start of a program-to-cycle-register transfer is signalled by a pulse labeled SPC in Figure 14.7.2. It starts the pulse generator labeled PP, which issues seven shift pulses labeled SHP. These shift pulses shift both the control register and the cycle register. The gate &1 in Figure 14.7.2 allows information to pass from the control register to the cycle register. The cycle register only holds three characters; the characters MMM of the instruction word are the characters in positions five, six, and seven in the C register. Hence it is possible to shift seven characters from the C register into the indicated cycle register and then have the desired characters MMM stored there.

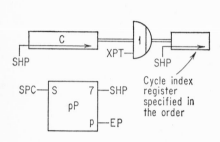

FIGURE 14.7.2.   Logic for transfer-from-program orders.

Since the content of the C register will no longer be used, it is permissible to leave the C register in a condition where the characters are not in their original position. The post-train pulse EP emerging from the pulse generator PP indicates the end of this type of order. It is the test pulse T which causes a new order to be fetched and placed in the control register.

14.8. THE SHIFT ORDER

The input/output orders represented by boxes 28, 29, and 30 of Figure 14.2 are omitted in this chapter because all of Chapter 15 is devoted to them. The shift orders, box 31 of Figure 14.2, are now analyzed.

Figure 14.8 illustrates a number of shift orders. The reader should recall that the shift orders do not change data but merely alter the position of a datum relative to the register which contains it, as discussed in Chapter 5.

For All Shifts

The pulse generator PS of Figure 14.8 is started by the shift start pulse SS. It issues nine shift pulses, not all of which may be required for a given shift command. These shift pulses are applied to shift pulse gates of all registers but are only entered into the register within which a shift is required. The number of pulses used so far is counted by the counter C1. These pulses are delayed slightly by the delay $\Delta2$ which is required to be certain that the shift pulse being counted has already done its work. The output of the counter C1 is compared with the operand location of the C register by the *two* comparison circuits included in CM3.

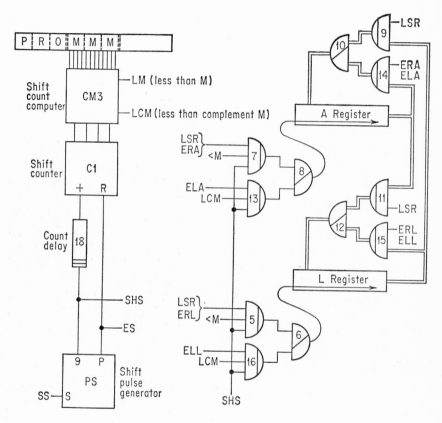

FIGURE 14.8. Control of the shift orders.

Right Shift

Let us see what happens on a typical right shift order such as ERL003. This order requires the shifting of the L register three places to the right and re-entering the digits on the left of the L register.

The order begins when the pulse generator PS is started by the Start Shift pulse. PS issues shift pulses SHS which go to gate &5. They pass through this gate, for it also has an ERL signal and a less-than-M (LM) signal. This LM signal is produced by CM3 as long as the count in C1 is less than MMM. The pulses SHS pass from &5 through V6 and shift the L register. Information passes out of the L register through &15 held open by the ERL signal, through V12 and back into the left side of the L register. After each shift, 1 is added to the counter C1 by shift pulse SHS slightly delayed by Δ18. When the count stored within C1 is no longer smaller than the number stored in the operand location of the control register, the voltage LM (less than M) is no longer produced. In our example, after three pulses have shifted the L register there will no longer be a voltage on this line labeled LM. Further pulses can therefore no longer pass through &5 and V6, and hence can have no effect on the L register. After nine shift pulses are produced by the pulse generator PS, it produces a post-train pulse signalling the end of this order.

Long Shift Right

This order requires that information be shifted out of the L register and into the A register, and at the same time the information from the A register is transferred to the beginning of the L register. Here the shift pulses SHS from the pulse generator PS are applied through &5 and V6 to the L register and also through &7 and V8 to the A register. Information from the L register passes through &9 and V10 into the beginning of the A register; information also passes out of the A register through &11 and V12 into the beginning of the L register. A count is kept by C1 as before and only sufficient shift pulses are supplied to both registers as are specified by the content of the operand location of the C register.

Shift Left

A shift to the left (ELA or ELL) is performed in this machine by shifting to the right a number of times equal to the complement of the desired number of shifts. The complement is taken in terms of the number of characters exclusive of sign which can be stored in the register—in our case this is 9.

To perform the order ELA005, the shift pulses are fed into &13, which is enabled by the shift-left order and the complement output of CM3, LCM. This comparator compares the content of the operand location of the control register with the counter C1 and issues a voltage as long as C1 contains a count less than the *complement of M*—as long as there is a voltage present on the line labeled LCM. The shift pulses therefore pass through &13 and V8 only until the A register has been shifted left the proper number of times. In our example, to shift the A register left five times, we shift the A register right four times because four is the complement of five with respect to nine, the number of characters exclusive of sign stored in our register.

The information in the A register for the ELA005 order passes through &14 held open by the ELA signal and then through V10 to return to the left side of the A register.

Shift-Out Orders

It is left to the reader to determine the logic required for the shift-out orders such as SRA, and so forth.

14.9. CENTRALIZED CONTROL

Some computers control the operation of individual functional units from a central location. In a decentralized computer, switching voltages come from a central point but timing pulses come from a pulse generator at the site of the functional unit. For a centralized computer, timing pulses are sent to all functional units. These pulses are controlled by switching voltages which also emanate from the central unit.

For this discussion two kinds of timing pulses will be circulated to all units: character pulses labeled π delineate the beginning of nine character times; there are ten character times in each word, and the last character time is issued on a line labeled ω. There is only one ω pulse per word so that it may be thought of as a word pulse. The voltage pulses issued by the central computer may last for varying periods during the operation of a given command in the computer.

Order Subdivision

An asynchronous centralized computer can be aided to a great extent by an asynchronous substep generator. It is appropriate to call the time division of a step a **substep.** This substep generator divides each instruction into periods whose duration may vary from one command to the next and from one substep to the next.

The substep generator might consist of a counter CS and a decoder DS, as shown in Figure 14.9.1. The counter tallies the number of substeps so far performed; the decoder issues a voltage on one of its several lines, the line corresponding to the number of the substep now being performed. The decoder output is maintained on the appropriate line for the entire duration of the substep. The counter is advanced at the end of the i'th substep by a pulse Ei returning from the functional unit involved and indicating that it has performed its subfunction. One command may con-

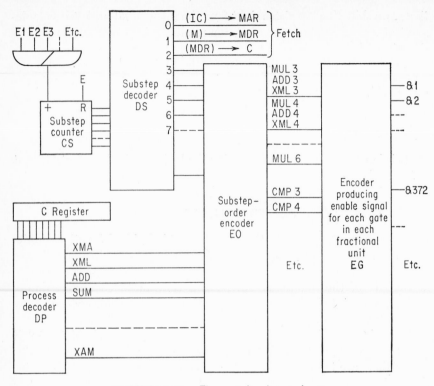

FIGURE 14.9.1.   The centralized control unit.

sist of more or less substeps than another. This is implemented by the ability of any functional unit to reset the substep counter instead of tallying it. After the substep counter is reset, it begins next time with the initial substep which is numbered 0.

Typical Substep Sequence

A typical sequence of substeps for a centralized computer control will now be discussed. The first three are common to all instructions, for they are used in the fetch activity.

SUBSTEP 0. The instruction counter stores the address of the next instruction. The content of the instruction counter is transferred to the memory address register during this substep.

SUBSTEP 1. During this period the memory takes over and performs a function of obtaining the datum stored at the location listed in the memory address register. It places this datum in the memory data register.

SUBSTEP 2. The datum, which is the new instruction, is transferred from the memory data register to the control register.

Since the substeps which follow are different for different instructions, let us examine what happens in the multiplication process. Substeps 3, 4, and 5 are used for memory reference.

SUBSTEP 3. The operand location is transferred from the control register to the memory address register to start the memory reference process.

SUBSTEP 4. The memory control logic is directed to place the operand in the memory data register.

SUBSTEP 5. The operand is transferred from the memory data register to the L register where it will be used.

SUBSTEP 6. Multiplication begins.

Control System

Figure 14.9.1 shows some of the features of a centralized control system. The counter CS is the substep counter. It is tallied by inputs from V1 which occur at the end of a substep, as determined by the particular function that it involves. The counter CS is connected to the decoder DS, the substep decoder. Notice that the first three substep lines specify the first three suboperations of the fetch cycle common to all orders. The process portion of the C register is connected to the process decoder DP. There is one line emanating from DP for each possible process which the computer can perform. The substep order encoder EO has numerous inputs. One set of these inputs is all the possible process-line outputs of the decoder DP; the other set of inputs comes from the substep decoder DS. The output of the encoder might be broken down in terms of both substeps and processes—for instance, one line bears the labels MUL3, ADD3, XML3, and so forth. The suboperation corresponding to this line is common to the multiplication order, the addition order, the transfer order, and so forth, on the third substep. Another line is labeled MUL4, ADD4, XML4, because this suboperation is common to all these orders on the fourth substep. Notice that the line labeled MUL6 does not have any other labels attached to it. This is because what is done for the multiplication order on substep 6 does not coincide with that done for any other order.

Another encoder EG is required to take the output of these suboperation lines and compose them into the control voltages for the individual gates within each functional unit of the computer. Thus, the gate &372 may be called for by MUL6, DIV7, XML4, and so forth. This additional encoder performs the function of mixing these signals as required by the individual gates of the centrally controlled computer.

Centrally Controlled Multiplication

Before discussing centrally controlled multiplication specifically, let us review what the multiplication process should achieve. Starting from the right-hand multiplier digit, we examine each multiplier digit successively. The multiplicand is added to the content of the accumulator register a number of times indicated by the multiplier digit under consideration. After each addition the multiplier digit is tallied down. When the multiplier digit becomes zero, the proper number of additions has been performed. The multiplier and the multiplicand are each shifted and the next multiplier digit examined.

The number of multiplier digits which have been examined is kept track of and when this number is equal to the length of the multiplier, multiplication is complete.

We shall now examine what happens on suboperation MUL6 for the centrally controlled computer which is illustrated in Figure 14.9.2. The description of Figure 14.9.2 starts when the last word pulse ω of the previous step passes through &1, which is enabled by the signal MUL5, the multiplication suboperation which precedes this one. This ω pulse coming out of &1 passes through V2 and sets bit storage B25 to 1. The 1 state of B25 and the multiplication substep signal MUL6 are combined in &3, whose output is μ; MUL6 and the 0 state of B25 are combined in &4 to yield the signal $\bar{\mu}$. The ω pulse on substep 5 also resets the multiplier digit counter C22 to a count of 0.

The first task of multiplication is to test the least significant digit of the multiplier; this digit is examined by the decoder D5. The decoder issues a signal only when this multiplier digit is zero. In that case no additions are to be performed until a shift of the multiplier and the accumulator has been made. On substep 6 the first word pulse ω tests &6 and &'7. For a non-zero digit this pulse passes through &'7 and sets B25 to 0. The output $\bar{\mu}$ then exists at all the appropriate gates. The case where the multiplier digit is 0 and the first ω pulse passes through &6 and does not pass through &'7 is discussed in a later paragraph.

The succeeding character pulses π which come along pass through &8 (upper right hand corner), since the $\bar{\mu}$ signal is present there. They go through V26 to shift the accumulator register through &9 into the X input of the adder A10. The character pulses π also pass through &11 to shift the multiplicand register through &12 into the Y input of the adder A10. The multiplicand is also re-entered into its register. The sum output S of the adder A10 passes through &13 since $\bar{\mu}$ is present there, and

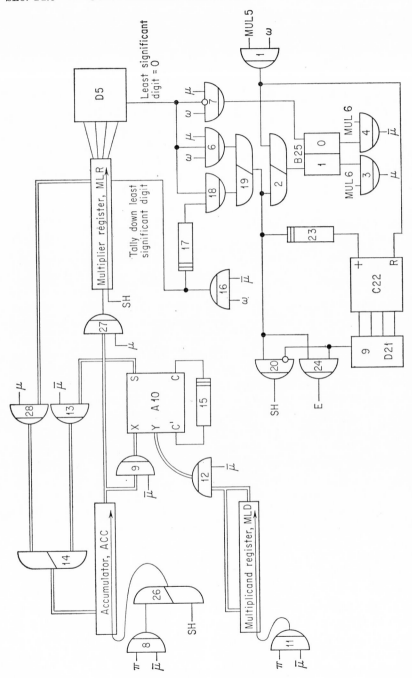

FIGURE 14.9.2. Multiplication in a centrally controlled computer.

through V14 and is entered into the accumulator ACC. The single-character delay line Δ15 is inserted between the output A10C of the adder and the input A10C'. Overflow detection has been omitted from the diagram for simplicity.

The next ω pulse, which comes directly after the nine character pulses π, passes through &16, enabled by $\bar{\mu}$, to tally down the multiplier register. The least significant digit of the multiplier must then be checked. In order to allow the register to quiet down after it has been tallied down, a small delay is supplied by Δ17. The ω pulse delayed by Δ17 is then applied to &18 to check the least significant multiplier digit.

If the ω pulse does not pass through &18—if the multiplier digit is not zero—nothing happens at this pulse time. The next set of character pulses coming in on the line labeled π cause another addition of the multiplicand to the partial product to take place by passing through &8 and V26 to shift ACC. The π pulses also pass through &11 to shift MLD. The next ω pulse tallies down the multiplier register again through &16 and then checks the multiplier digit through Δ17 and &18.

When the omega pulse finally passes through &18—when the multiplier digit has been tallied down to 0—the omega pulse continues on through V19 and V2 to set the bit storage B25 to 1. This causes a μ voltage on all the appropriate μ lines. This same ω pulse going through &16, Δ17, &18, and V19 is also passed through &'20 as a single shift pulse SH if all the multiplier digits have not been used for multiplication. Whether all the multiplier digits have been used is determined by the decoder D21 which examines the counter C22, continuously, to see if it stores a count of 9. If multiplication is not complete, the pulse from V19, delayed by a small delay Δ23 inserted to be sure that the full pulse has passed from &'20, is applied to the counter C22 to record the fact that another digit of multiplication is being performed.

The single shift pulse SH is applied to the accumulator through V26 and to the multiplier register directly. This brings the latest product digit from the accumulator into the left-hand side of the multiplier register through &27, since a μ signal exists at &27; it also shifts the *next* multiplier digit into the right-hand side of the multiplier register; the last multiplier digit which has just been tallied down to 0 is entered through &28 and V14 into the left-hand side of the accumulator. Nothing further happens during the ensuing character times. The next word pulse ω checks &6 and &'7 to determine whether or not the new multiplier digit is 0. If it is not zero, a new cycle of additions is initiated when the ω pulse passes through &'7 and sets B25 to zero.

If the new multiplier digit is zero, the ω passes through &6, V19, and checks the gates &'20 and &24 to determine if all the multiplier digits have been used and, if not, to issue a SH pulse to perform a one-digit shift.

This may happen at the beginning of multiplication too; if the least significant digit of the original multiplier is 0, the first ω pulse will cause a shift by passing through &6, V19, and &'20.

When the decoder D21 registers the fact that the count in C22 is 9 (all the multiplier digits are used), the ω pulse which is testing &'20 and &24 will then emerge from &24 to indicate that multiplication is complete. It is therefore labeled an E pulse.

PROBLEMS

1. Examine the Polyvac orders in Figure 5.7 and determine which (if any) were not covered in the figure and explain how they might be included in the Plan, Figure 14.2.

2. Review the two-address order system. Remake Figure 14.2 for that system, explaining the changes.

3. Review the three-address system. Make a chart of three-address orders arranged as in Figure 5.7. Determine combination compare-and-jump orders such as

$$\text{JOE} \quad (M_1) : (M_2); \quad (M_1) = (M_2) \Rightarrow M_3$$
$$(M_1) \neq (M_2) \Rightarrow I + 1$$

where M_1, M_2, and M_3 are the operand addresses in the order. Redo Figure 14.2 for this three-address system.

4. Expand the logic of Figure 14.3.2 to include three cycle registers instead of one.

5. How might the cycle registers be used in a three-address machine?

6. Redraw Figure 14.3.2 for a three-address system where all three operand addresses are similarly augmented by the content of the same cycle register. Illustrate for CY1 only.

7. Draw a *complete* logical diagram for the comparison order for a one-address system using functional blocks and D-blocks. Use the accumulator register and one other register for the comparands.

8. For a three-address system show the complete logic for implementation of compare-and-jump orders.

9. Discuss jump orders in the two address system.

10. Redraw Figure 14.2 for a two-address system.

11. Consider the addition to the Polyvac of a memory buffer which can hold ten (or more) words. Propose additional orders for block transfer of information from (to) the main memory to (from) the buffer and for reference to the buffer by the computer. Propose a buffer block symbol (which would include timing logic). Considering the buffer as a functional block, draw a complete logic for implementing the block transfer and buffer reference orders.

12. The memory reference order description (Section 14.5) omits the eventuality of using an addressable register as the operand. Redraw Figure 14.5 providing for this possibility.

13. Redraw Figure 14.6 to include the A, Q, and L registers and the adder, and show how the memorization and add orders are integrated. Use gates liberally.

14. Add two more cycle registers to Figure 14.7.1 and show common connections.

15. Using π (character) and ω (word) pulses show detailed centralized logic like that in Figure 14.9.2 for

    (a) the shift orders
    (b) memorization orders
    (c) memory per reference orders
    (d) jump orders
    (e) the tally orders

16. For a centralized computer show logic for parallel-bit serial-character

    (a) addition, unsigned
    (b) subtraction, unsigned
    (c) signed addition and subtraction
    (d) division

17. Draw a complete arithmetic unit for XS3 numbers using Polyvac specifications and centralized control.

FIFTEEN

INPUT AND OUTPUT

EQUIPMENT

15.1. INTRODUCTION

I have always had great admiration for the veterinarian who must diagnose the ailments of his patient without any discussion with him (or it). Similarly, I have great respect for my wife's work in the field of psychotherapy. Here the communication is present but is for the most part unilateral—the patient talks but the therapist, if he sticks to the rules, does not advise. Maybe this is why I am always somewhat surprised when I see the operator communicating with the computer. This is almost bilateral communication. At least the questions are usually answered politely by the computer. Still, the operator is obligated in determining the difference between a "well" answer and a "sick" answer. We shall now briefly study first the principles of communication with the computer and then the detailed procedure.

Communication between the Human and the Computer

The human can communicate directly or indirectly with the computer. Indirect communication involves an intermediate medium such as magnetic tape or punched cards and requires additional equipment to translate to and from this intermediate medium.

DIRECT COMMUNICATION. Information can flow between the computer and the human by means of the operator's console. Information is entered into the computer by means of switches on the console or by using the inquiry typewriter. Information is received from the computer in the form of visual displays or audible alarms. An intermediate human-language document may intervene; that is, one human may have written a document which a second human transcribes directly to the computer. This is still considered direct communication. Similarly, when the computer writes out information into the inquiry typewriter which the human can then read, this is also direct communication.

INDIRECT COMMUNICATION. Because of the great mismatch in speed between human input and computer consumption, an intermediate storage medium is often desirable. There are many places where information can be distorted in this type of operation. Consider the following steps which might occur: a human document is prepared which takes the form of a sales slip or inventory record; the human document is read by a human operator; the operator transcribes the document into key strokes in the transcribing unit; an intermediate machine document is prepared by the transcribing device; at a later date the machine document is transcribed by an input device; the information is thus submitted to the computer. Each of these steps is subject to error. A similar chain exists in indirect output communication from the computer to the human consumer.

One means of eliminating a number of these steps and the consequent errors is found in proposed systems of character recognition. By this means the chain described above might be reduced to the following: the human prepares a human document, using machine-recognizable characters in a special transcribing mechanism—the human document is hence also the machine document; it is inserted into document-reading equipment and the information is conveyed to the computer.

Instrument or Process Communication

When the computer is used to control a process or an instrument, it must collect data on which to base its calculations. Sometimes these data can be collected directly. Information thus supplied must be in a digital form: the temperature limit is either exceeded or not; an item is at one of several points or is in one of several areas.

Purpose of Communication

Two kinds of information are exchanged in the communication process: (1) data and (2) control information. Obviously, data to be processed must be entered into the computer and the results, to be useful, must be produced by the computer. Information *to* the computer for directing the processing of the data can be classified into two kinds: the program information consists of a set of long-term operational directions; short-term control information is entered directly from the operator's control panel. There is but one kind of information *from* the computer. Long-term control information is not *produced* by the computer. Short-term control information is produced by the computer and arises only as the result of exceptional operating conditions. Examples of exceptional conditions which are reported directly by the computer are interruptions, distortions in information or directions, data for which special handling has been detected, and inconsistencies among the data.

Intermediate Media

The media discussed here are the most popular ones, punched paper tape, punched cards, and magnetic tape. Some of the properties of the media and reasons for preferring one medium over another are now advanced.

ACCESS INTO AND OUT OF THE COMPUTER. Punched paper tape can be read by scanning the information as it is moved over some interpretive device. The speed at which information on the tape can be scanned restricts its use as an input medium. Transfer of information into paper tape requires that the information be punched mechanically into the tape and that the tape be moved and then stopped at the next character position. This severely restricts the rate at which information may be entered into paper tape. For punched cards, information can be entered and retrieved in much larger blocks. This increases the speed of communication via this medium. Magnetic tape may be communicated with most rapidly using currently available equipment. Here no mechanical operation is performed upon the tape for either writing or reading other than the moving of the tape; the physical state of the tape is affected, or sensed, using electromagnetic fields so that there is no speed limitation from that quarter.

PERMANENCE. Information stored on any of these media is permanent as long as the medium remains intact. Magnetic tape has the great advantage that it may be reused (erased).

COST. This refers to both the media and the equipment. The paper tape equipment and paper tape are by far the cheapest means of intermediate storage. Punched cards are next in cost. The price of magnetic recording equipment and tape is much higher and the reusability of this medium compensates in only a small measure for its increased cost.

SEQUENCE-ABILITY. The punched card has a definite advantage where it is necessary to put records into sequence before they are read by the computer. Sometimes this sequence-ability is an advantage on the output, too. In the inventory example discussed earlier, punched cards are produced in order of item number corresponding to the item which is in short supply. It is later desirable to sequence them in terms of the vendor so that only one purchase order need be issued to each vendor.

Specific equipment requirements will be discussed in the sections that follow.

15.2. DIRECT COMMUNICATION

Direct communication in the modern high-speed computer is restricted to "conversations" between the operator and the computer which occur during the course of computer operation. This need arises in several kinds of situations which are outlined in Table 15.2. It would be well to refer to this table often during the description. The reader might also get a preview by examining Figures 15.2.1 and 15.2.2, where drawings of operator panels of two current machines are shown.

Machine Stop

When the machine grinds to a halt, the operator must determine why and must remedy the situation if it is not due to some component failure. The latter is the worst case, because if the machine has really broken down it is probably in no condition to tell us so; the operator must determine this by a process of elimination. Usually the machine's cessation for causes other than component failure will be made highly evident by buzzes, bells, alarms, or flashing lights which hopefully will arouse the operator. It is also customary for the computer to display the reason for its sudden stoppage without being asked. One of a number of lamps corresponding to various conditions becomes lit. The cause might quite reasonably be the completion of the computer's task—a programmed stop. It might also be a **breakpoint** stop. This is a program device which enables the programmer to cause the machine to stop after it has completed an appropriate portion of its calculations. This allows the operator to check the program and results before restarting it.

TABLE 15.2 CLASSIFICATION OF DIRECT COMMUNICATION WITH THE COMPUTER

Information	From computer (F)		To computer (T)		Auxiliary (A)
	Form	Type	Form	Type	
1. Start-Stop	Display Alarm	Programmed stop Breakpoint Data error Arithmetic error I/O failure Accumulator overflow	Button or switch Button or switch Button or switch Button or switch Button or switch Button or switch	Halt! Start! Continue! Reset! Clear! Stop!	Breakpoint switch Skip switch Continuous/step operation switch
2. Data in registers	Display	1's & 0's in each register	Entry button Clear button Special typewriter	Enter 1! Enter 0's! Enter all 0's! Enter character!	Register choice switch
3. Operation	Display Alarm	Fetch or execute Step in program Operation in progress Substep	Button or switch	Fetch! Execute! Initiate! Substep	
4. I/O	Display Alarm	Choice of unit Unit operating Failure and its cause	Button Button Button	Start! Stop! Advance!	Suppress character Format control Choose unit Single advance/continuous operation
5. Power	Display	Meter readings On-off lights	Buttons Switches	Start Stand by a-c d-c	Filaments Time switches
6. Test	Display	Test progress	Buttons Switches	Test on Start test	Marginal voltage

The equipment may stop because of an error in transferring data. A parity check of the kind discussed earlier might reveal a distortion of the data. An arithmetic error determined by a programmed check also causes the machine to stop. A common type of I/O (abbreviation for input/output) equipment stoppage arises when the paper runs out in the printing equipment, or the reel of input or output tape expires. This simply requires the attention of the operator to remedy the situation. One more kind of stoppage occurs when the numbers manipulated are too large or too small for the registers causing an overflow condition.

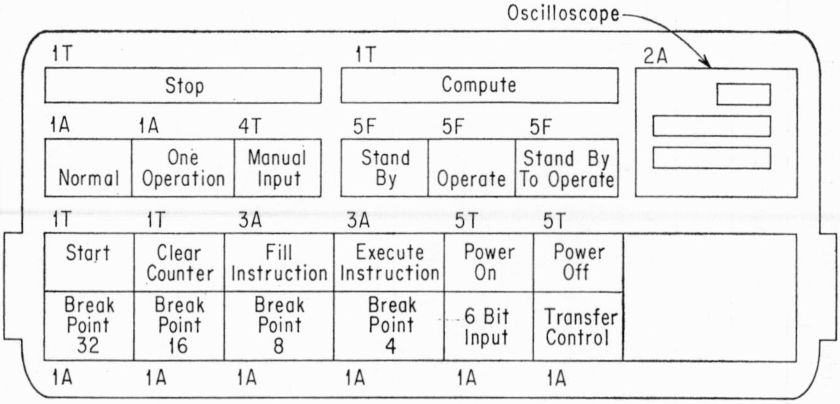

FIGURE 15.2.1.   Central console panel of LGP30.   Courtesy of The Royal McBee Corporation.

One indication of a component failure is the presence of *none* of the normal indications for stopping. Often a component failure will cause a computer to continue to run indefinitely instead of stopping—another reason why such failures are hard to detect.

In Table 15.2 direct communication is outlined. The kind of information communicated appears in the first column; in the second and third columns (labeled F) the form and type of information emanating *from* the computer is detailed; in the fourth and fifth columns (labeled T) the form and type of information which may pass *to* the computer is detailed; in the sixth column (labeled A) auxiliary controls for aiding the flow of information are listed. In the first row, start-stop information is analyzed. The kinds of displays or alarms are itemized in the third column of row 1, and these correspond to what was described in the preceding paragraph. The kinds of stops that the machine displays for the operator are programmed stops, breakpoints, data errors, and so forth. In the figures which follow,

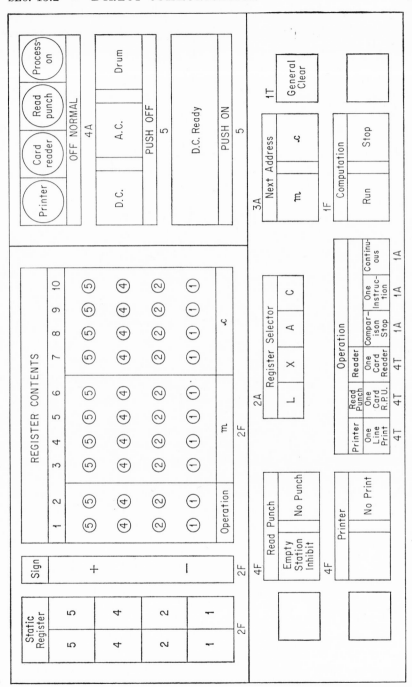

FIGURE 15.2.2. Control panel, Univac® Solid State Computer. Courtesy of Remington Rand Division, Sperry Rand Corp.

typical control panels are illustrated. Each type of button or display has a symbol next to it. This symbol corresponds to the listing in Table 15.2.

The reader will notice that the entries in this table completely classify all the buttons, controls, lights, and so on which appear—at least those appearing on the operator's panels presented in Figures 15.2.1 and 15.2.2. These Figures should be referred to as examples of the descriptions which follow.

Start-Stop

The operator can communicate start-stop information to the computer by means of push buttons. These commands are listed in the fifth column of Table 15.2. They instruct the computer to "Start," "Continue," "Reset," "Clear," or "Stop."

The auxiliary control for the start-stop operation is listed in the sixth column. A breakpoint switch may be used to stop the computer at a corresponding step in the program. The continuous/step operation switch allows the operator to choose between continuous or normal operation and single-step operation, the latter being very useful in checking out programs initially.

Data in Registers

During normal operation, data are being shifted about within the computer at an extremely fast rate. Since the eye is capable of responding only to changes which last a sixteenth of a second or more, it is impossible for the operator or observer to follow these rapid changes taking place within the computer as they are displayed on the control panel. However, if the computer stops for one reason or another, the information in each register is then static and the display can be examined without difficulty. The display usually corresponds exactly to the binary coding used within the machine. Thus, in an XS3 machine the presentation consists of four lamps for each character, one for each bit. Each bit is usually displayed on an individual neon lamp which, with a little squinting, is clearly visible. When a parity bit is used in the machine language of the computer, it is usually omitted from the display. A parity error when detected is displayed in the start-stop display.

Sometimes it is desirable to enter information into a register directly from the operator's panel. Different computers do this in different manners. The Burroughs 205, for instance, has a separate button for 1 and 0 for each bit of each register; the operator may change the state of any bit in any register simply by pressing one button. The Remington Rand File Computer has an inquiry typewriter whereby the operator may type information into the desired register. Other machines require that a register be cleared and information entered a character at a time from an auxiliary numerical keyboard. Still others have means whereby 1's or 0's may be entered, a bit at a time, into the register.

To conserve area, it is often possible to use the same display lights for several registers. A register selector switch, as in the Remington Rand Solid State Computer, determines the register being displayed.

Operation

Lights on the panel may indicate what operation is in progress at the moment—whether the fetch or execute phase of the operation is under way, what step in the program is being worked on by the computer, and what substep in the process is under way. This information is changing rather rapidly and so it is primarily useful when the computer stops. It then indicates where the computer has halted and enables the operator to evaluate the possibility of reprocessing some of the data, going ahead from here, or starting the whole problem from the very beginning.

Buttons or switches may be used to initiate a fetch or execute phase of the operation or to initiate any given substep.

Input/Output Unit

The operator's panel provides a central location where the operation of each of the many possible input/output units may be monitored. The units available to the computer may be shown there, as well as the time when each is actually processing data. Failure or stoppage of an I/O unit and the cause can also be indicated.

Buttons or switches may be used to start, stop, or make available to the computer, each I/O device and to bring the equipment to the proper portion of the data.

By means of auxiliary switches, the particular I/O units for a program may be chosen; characters to be suppressed on input or output may be chosen; the format for input or output may be selected; operation on a single-step or continuous-running basis may be selected.

Power

During start-up and shut-down of the computer, various switches must be turned on or off. Often voltages must be applied in a sequence. This too can be indicated on the operator's panel. The presence and absence of proper voltages can be indicated on this panel. Meters or lamps indicate proper voltage levels. Some of the terms which apply here are:

a-c Voltages, On and Off,
d-c Voltages, On and Off,
Filament Voltages, On and Off,
Standby Condition,
Operating Condition.

Test

Preventive maintenance is the key to successful functioning of most computers. At some time outside its operating period, the computer is put to work under test conditions. These test conditions may consist of lowered operating voltages or may be special test programs. In any case, they require indications and controls which would not normally be used under operation conditions. These test controls vary widely from computer to computer.

15.3.   INDIRECT COMMUNICATION TO AND FROM THE COMPUTER

Communication between the computer and I/O equipment is called *indirect* when the information is stored in an intermediate medium before entry into or after removal from the computer. For input the human enters information into an intermediate medium such as punched paper tape. This is later read by the input equipment and passed on to the computer; similarly, the computer via output equipment punches paper tape which is later interpreted by means of a tape-reading typewriter.

We shall now examine the means by which information passes between the intermediate information-carrying medium and the computer. The general scheme of things is recorded in Figure 15.3.

Let us examine the generalized flow of information from the input medium to the computer. The flow is similar in the output direction, but it simplifies the explanation to consider only the input flow.

The Input Mechanism Unit

Information is obtained from the input medium by the **input mechanism.** This may be a mechanical, optical, magnetic, or other transducing mechanism. It almost always involves some kind of mechanical motion imparted to the input medium. Information that is derived from the input medium is stored temporarily in the **input mechanism register.** This register is often restricted to one character. The **input mechanism control** oversees the operation of taking one character of information from the input medium and storing it in the input mechanism register. This requires the control and synchronization of the mechanical motion of the input medium with the information retrieval and transfer. These three items—the input mechanism, the input mechanism register, and the input mechanism control—are incorporated in one unit called the **input mechanism unit.** This is the kind of unit which is sold in a single package by a manufacturer of I/O equipment. This much equipment is the minimum

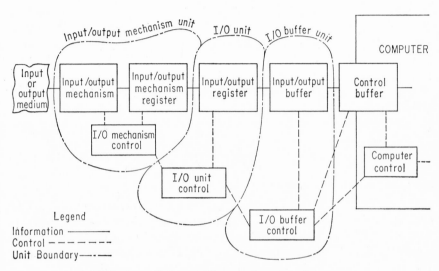

FIGURE 15.3. Relation of the input/output to the computer.

that the computer design engineer deals with when incorporating the purchased item into the computer.

The Input Unit

More and more buffering equipment is required as the difference in speed between the input/output equipment and the computer becomes more disparate. The amount of buffering is set forth by the designer. In Figure 15.3 we shall look at the situation in which the greatest disparity exists and the maximum buffering is needed.

The next unit includes an *input register* and an *input unit control* to form what is called an **input unit.** Physically, the package consists of the input mechanism and electronics which are housed in a single cabinet. On signal, the input unit control causes the input mechanism control unit to fill the single-character register with one character. Then the input unit control transfers this character to the input register. The input unit control then sends another signal to the input mechanism to fill its single-character register, thence taking that character and entering it into the input register. This continues until the input register is completely loaded, as determined by the input unit control. The input register is a single word in length.

The Input Buffer Unit

The next superstructure is the **input buffer unit.** When the input register has been filled, the *input buffer control* causes each word to be taken from the input register and loaded into the *input buffer*. When the buffer is full, the buffer control unit will have fulfilled its task and will emit a signal to the computer control to indicate this.

Let's look down the line, from the computer's view this time, to see what happens. The computer control issues a signal to the input buffer to reload. The input buffer directs the input unit to put a data word into its register. The input unit directs the input mechanism to put a character into the input mechanism register. The input unit control then puts this character into the input register. Input unit control continues to call for input characters until the input register is loaded. It then returns a signal to the buffer control, indicating that the input register is full. The buffer control takes over and loads a word from the input register into the buffer. If the buffer is not yet full, another signal is sent to the input unit control which, in turn, calls upon the input mechanism control. When the buffer is completely loaded, the computer is informed.

The Control Buffer

Still another buffer may exist, this one in the computer. It is called a **control buffer.** It is controlled by both the *computer* and the *input buffer control*. When the input buffer has been completely loaded by the procedure outlined, it then places the information into the control buffer. This buffer is then accessible to the computer at the rate of information usage that the computer is accustomed to.

As stated before, this is a general outline. For a small computer most of these intermediate steps are omitted. A small computer, for instance, might have the input mechanism unit under direct supervision of the computer control. Thus, once the input mechanism register is loaded with but one character, the computer control directs the transfer of information from the mechanism register into the computer. You can see that in general this is a highly inefficient practice, especially if the computer is fast. Any time taken away from its computing tasks detracts from the accomplishment of its most useful job.

How this is put into practice will best be seen in the next section on the punched paper tape input.

15.4. PUNCHED PAPER TAPE INPUT EQUIPMENT

General

Before examining the details of the tape reader mechanism unit, let us see how the paper tape reading situation fits into the over-all plan outlined in the previous section. A piece of punched paper tape is shown in a tape reader in Figure 15.4.1. As you can see, information appears on

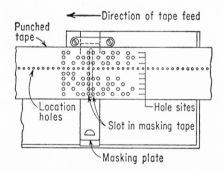

FIGURE 15.4.1. Reading of punched paper tape. Courtesy of Ferranti Ltd.

this tape at the **hole sites** where holes may or may not have been punched into the tape. A character consists of a crosswise row of hole sites. *Hole sites* are spoken of to indicate that this is where a hole may exist if the particular bit is to be a one, or where paper will not be removed if this bit is to be a zero. The characters are placed along the length of the tape. To read information from the tape, the character rows must be scanned sequentially. Notice in the figure that each character row has a small hole punched in it. Called a **location hole,** this hole serves to indicate the presence of a significant character and also as a mechanical means for grasping and moving the paper tape.

The tape is moved through the reading station of the paper tape reader, and all of the hole sites for a given character are examined simultaneously to determine where a hole exists. Then the information, which is read either mechanically or photoelectrically, is entered into the single-character register. This register consists of a set of bit storage elements. The general scheme can be followed on Figure 15.4.2. Unit control then causes this character to be dumped into the word register in the paper tape reader unit. When it has been placed there, the unit control issues a signal to the reader control. The reader control in turn initiates the movement of the paper tape so that the next character row to be read is under the reading station. This continues until the one-word register is filled. Then the paper tape reader unit control issues a signal to the punched-paper-tape-reader buffer control to indicate that a word of information is ready to be transferred. Buffer control takes over to move the

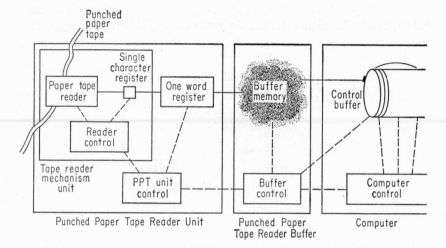

FIGURE 15.4.2. A typical arrangement for reading punched paper tape.

datum from the register into the buffer memory. When the buffer memory is loaded under the supervision of the buffer control by a series of the processes described above, it is entered into the control buffer. In the case in Figure 15.4.2, the control buffer is a channel of a magnetic drum within the computer. After the information from the buffer memory has been loaded into this channel, the buffer control issues a signal to the computer to indicate that information is now stored in the magnetic drum memory, accessible to the computer at its leisure.

The computer can put out a request for information and then go ahead and do useful processing while new input data are being gathered. At some later time the computer will find input information ready to be processed in the control. As it starts processing this information it can put in a request for more input data, thus making the best use of available time.

Description of a Typical Paper Tape Reader—the Ferranti Type TR5

A complete tape reader mechanism consists of a tape feed, an optical projection system, reading and location photocells, and a character storage device. A photograph of the complete unit appears as Figure 15.4.3.

FIGURE 15.4.3. The Ferranti Type TR5 Paper Tape Reader. Courtesy of Ferranti Ltd.

TAPE FEED MECHANISM. The motor power for the tape reader unit is derived from an electric motor geared to a differential gear. The two output shafts of the differential gear are called the *clutch shaft* and *tape drive shaft* (or simply *drive shaft*). These are concentric and appear respectively on the left and right of Figure 15.4.4. The drive shaft is the prime mover for the paper tape and by contact friction causes the tape to go past the reading station. Situated so as to inhibit the motion of each of these shafts is one brake mechanism for each shaft. The brake mechanisms are actuated by a bistable device so that either one of the brakes is energized, but not both. Now, if the left-hand brake, the clutch brake, is energized, the clutch shaft cannot rotate. The drive shaft receives the full energy supplied by the drive motor. The drive shaft moves in friction contact with the tape, causing the tape to move past the reading station. At a moment's notice, simultaneously, the drive brake may be energized and the clutch brake de-energized. This does not affect the rotation of the input shaft, but it does immediately stop the drive shaft; the motion is transferred to the clutch shaft.

The tape, which is being read at 300 characters per second, is stopped

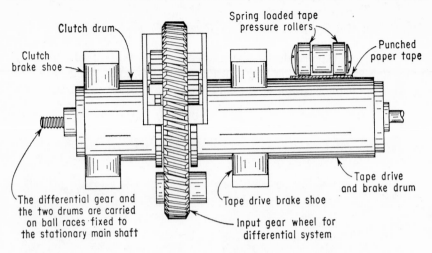

FIGURE 15.4.4.   Tape feed mechanism, paper tape reader.   Courtesy Ferranti Ltd.

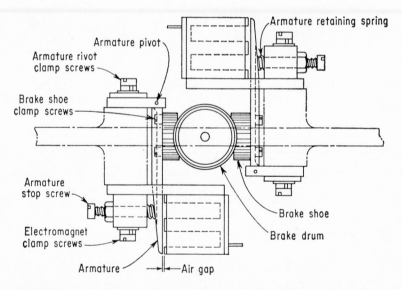

FIGURE 15.4.5.   Brake mechanism, paper tape reader.   Courtesy Ferranti Ltd.

in the space of one character by the arrangement illustrated in Figure 15.4.5. The adjusting screws indicated in the figure permit braking in minimum time.

OPTICAL READING SYSTEM. The optical system is disposed on either side of the reading station. Above the tape is a small electric lamp which is

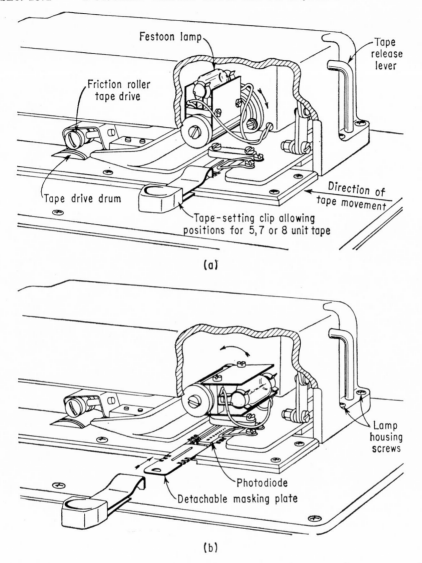

FIGURE 15.4.6.   Cut-away views of TR5 tape reader, (a) with lamp in reading position and (b) with lamp assembly moved up.   Courtesy Ferranti Ltd.

focused by a cylindrical lens. Light passes through a slot in the masking plate as shown in Figure 15.4.1. The size of the slot determines that only one row of information at a time is read from the tape. On the other side of the tape a number of small photocells are placed. These cells receive light only if there is hole at the hole site corresponding to that photocell.

The relation of the reading station to the rest of the I/O equipment is best seen in Figure 15.4.6.

THE TAPE MECHANISM CONTROL. The information from the first photocell PC1 is applied to the 1 input of the first bit storage element B1; the other photocells read into their bit storage units. This is shown in Figure 15.4.7. Photocell PC0 is the one which reads the location hole. It sets bit storage B0 to 1 for every character scanned. When B0 is set to 1, the shaper S8

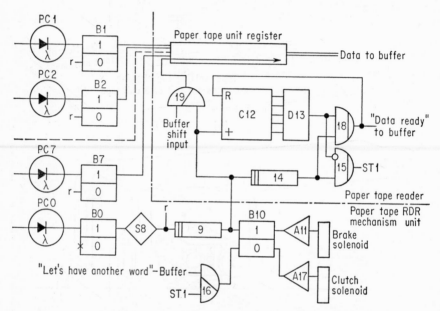

FIGURE 15.4.7.   Logic for the paper tape reader.

issues a pulse, r. The pulse r tries to reset all the bit storage elements, B1 through B7. If information is coming from the photocells, the corresponding bit storage will not be reset and will remain in the bit storage after the reset pulse r has lapsed; if the photocells are not receiving information, the bit storage elements will remain reset to 0 after the reset pulse disappears. Erroneous transients are thus erased.

The reset pulse is also entered into the delay Δ9. This delay sets the bit storage element B10 to 1. This state of B10 is amplified by the current amplifier A11 which applies current to the brake solenoid and tends to stop the tape.

Now the tape unit control circuitry takes over. The reset pulse, delayed by Δ9, tallies the counter C12 which is connected to the decoder D13. The tally pulse delayed by Δ14 is used to check the decoder. This is the way it determines whether the tape unit register has been filled. If further characters are to be added to the register, the pulse from Δ14 passes through &'15 and V16 as a new start pulse, ST1, which immediately resets B10 to 0. This removes the current from the brake solenoid. The 0 state of B10 is amplified by A17 which applies current to the clutch solenoid. This action happens so fast that the motion of the paper tape is not interfered with; if consecutive characters on the tape are to be read, the tape moves continuously.

The pulse from Δ9 through V19 has been used to shift the character information from B1 through B7 into the tape unit register.

When the tape unit register is completely loaded, the test pulse emitted from Δ14 passes through &18 instead of &'15. This pulse resets the counter C12 and also is returned to the computer or to the intermediate buffer stage to indicate that the tape unit register now contains a full word and may be emptied. B10 remains set to 1 so that the brake solenoid remains energized, stopping the movement of the paper tape.

The half-broken line in Figure 15.4.7 indicates the boundaries between the paper tape reader mechanism and the paper tape reader unit.

FIGURE 15.4.8. The Ferranti TR7 High Speed Paper Tape Reader. Courtesy of Ferranti Ltd.

The buffer control logic takes over when a word is loaded in the paper tape unit register. It then receives the "datum ready" pulse. It sends shift pulses to V12 of the paper tape unit register and empties it over the output line. It directs the datum to the proper place in buffer storage. If more words are needed for the buffer, the buffer control determines this and sends a "Let's have another word" pulse to V16 of Figure 15.4.7. This sets B10 to 0 and starts things going again in the paper tape reader mechanism unit.

Of course, there may be no paper tape buffer in some systems! In that case, the computer takes over when a pulse is emitted from &18. In this kind of set-up it may then be desirable that the register hold several words, rather than one.

The mechanical principles described apply to tape readers with speeds up to about 300 characters per second. Readers have been produced which read 1000 characters per second based on paper tape transport mechanisms quite similar to those used for reading magnetic tape, such as those discussed in Section 15.7. The Ferranti TR7 shown in Figure 15.4.8 is a high-speed (1000 CPS) paper tape reading mechanism. The logic described applies to all speeds.

15.5. THE PAPER TAPE PUNCH

Mechanisms to punch holes into paper tape are of two kinds. The synchronous mechanism has a motor which is constantly rotating but

FIGURE   15.5.1. High Speed Punch. Copyright 1952, 1954, & 1955 by Teletype Corp. Reprinted by permission of Teletype Corp.

FIGURE   15.5.2. High Speed Punch. Courtesy of the Soroban Corporation.

which can be actuated only during one portion of the cycle; an asynchronous device can be actuated at any time in the machine cycle. The difference between these mechanisms is not very great, but it should be mentioned that the machine we shall discuss is synchronous. Photos of typical units appear as Figures 15.5.1 and 15.5.2.

Two tasks are required of the paper tape punch: it must punch the proper information into the tape; it must move the tape one character width after each punch cycle. These are discussed in order.

Punching

A hole is punched at a given hole site only if the corresponding selector magnet is actuated in the mechanism illustrated in Figure 15.5.3. The

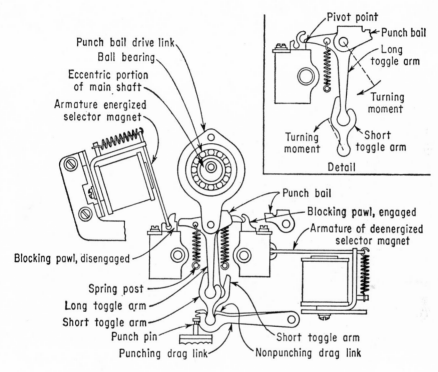

FIGURE 15.5.3. A typical mechanism for punching paper tape.

hole or no-hole condition is referred to in teletype parlance as a **mark** or **space** condition. These mechanisms originally arose from applications in the telegraphy field and this terminology has persisted.

In Figure 15.5.3 two selector magnets are shown. The one on the left-hand side of the page is energized; that on the right is de-energized. The energized selector magnet moves the blocking pawl to the left. The eccentric portion of the main shaft is continuously rotating and causes the punch bail to move up and down in synchronism with it. The blocking pawl is moved out of the way by the selector magnet when the punch bail drive link is at the top of its travel. As the link moves downward, the long arm toggle passes by the blocking pawl, since it is withdrawn. The short toggle arm which is riding on the pivot of the long toggle arm is pushed down with the long toggle arm. It, in turn, pushes down the punching drag link. The end of the punching drag link pushes the punch pin with great force into the paper at the point where a hole is desired.

For a space the selector magnet is not energized, as in the right-hand side of the illustration. The blocking pawl remains in a forward position. As the punch bail drive link is pushed down, its motion is intercepted by the engaged blocking pawl. This causes the long toggle arm to pivot about the engaged blocking pawl. The long toggle arm and short toggle arm move together and, you might say, break at the joint. The short toggle arm does not push down the drag link; hence the punch pin does not enter the paper tape.

The detail of Figure 15.5.3 shows the long toggle braced by the short toggle. The punch bail applies full force through the long toggle to the short toggle, the three acting as if they were one rigid member. When the pawl is interposed, it acts as a pivot point for the long toggle arm. The punch bail then conveys a turning moment to the long toggle arm, which pushes sideways upon the short toggle arm support, causing the short toggle arm to rotate. Motion is not conveyed downward because the three members—punch bail, and long and short toggle arm—now act independently.

In the teletype high-speed punch mechanism shown in Figure 15.5.1 discussed here, punching (or non-punching) occurs at the rate of 60 characters per second.

Tape Feed

The tape feed operation is illustrated in Figure 15.5.4. The tape feed out magnet must be energized at the proper time in the cycle. This time comes a fraction of a revolution after the punch selector magnets have been energized. When a tape feed is required, the feed magnet moves the blocking pawl out of the way of the long toggle arm. The pivot between the long and short toggle arms therefore remains straight. The toggle arm pushes down on the feed pawl adjustable link. This causes the feed pawl to be moved up; the feed pawl engages the ratchet on the feed wheel, causing it to turn. The detent arm roller assures the movement of the tape for only one character position. The feed wheel has sprockets (not shown) which positively engage the feed holes in the tape which have been punched previously, thus advancing the paper tape.

When the feed out magnet is not energized, the blocking pawl remains in a blocking position causing the long and short toggle arm to break at the pivot point. This prevents any motion of the feed pawl adjustable link so that the paper tape is not advanced.

Punching speeds higher than 60 characters per second have been attained by the ingenious design of the Soroban Engineering Corporation, shown in Figure 15.5.2. This equipment can punch paper tape at 300

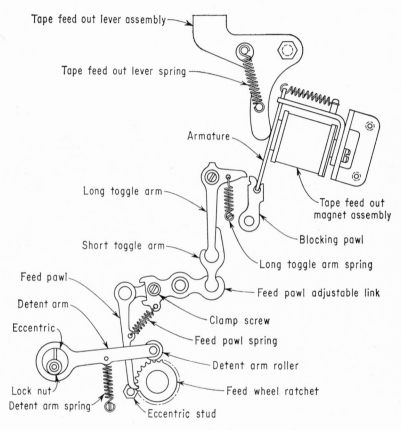

FIGURE 15.5.4. Tape feed mechanism of the paper tape punch.

characters per second. This is so fast that the quantity of *chad* (the name for the paper removed from the holes in the tape) produced must be removed by a vacuum feed so as not to clog the mechanism.

Control

The character to be punched is entered in binary form into the bit storage B1 through B7 in the logic of the paper tape punch mechanism shown in Figure 15.5.5. A cam-controlled switch SWB on the punch unit emits a pulse at the proper time during the punch cycle. This pulse is applied through &11, &12, ... &17 to the corresponding punch magnets. If there is information stored in any one of the bits B1 to B7, there is both an input and an output from V9. For a request of one or more holes to

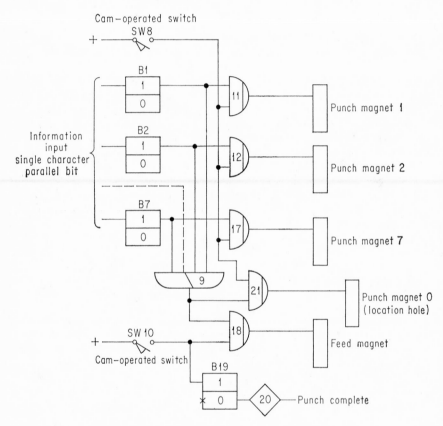

FIGURE 15.5.5.　Logic for paper tape punch mechanism.

be punched, there is an output from &21 which energizes punch magnet 0 to punch a location hole. At the proper time in the cycle for the punching of the location hole another cam-operated switch, SW10, on the punch mechanism issues a pulse. This passes through &18 to operate the feed magnet as long as there is an output from V9—a request for punch of *any* hole. It also sets the uni B19 to 1. When punching is complete, SW10 is opened by the cam and later B19 resets to 0. This causes a pulse to be issued from the shaper S20. This pulse is returned to the computer or

SEC. 15.5 ■ THE PAPER TAPE PUNCH 329

intermediate control unit to indicate that the punching of this character is complete.

15.6. PUNCH CARDS

The punched card, or simply punch card, is a medium similar in intent to punched paper tape. Information appears at a hole site in the form of

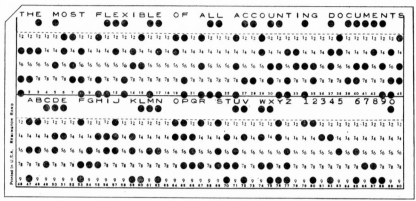

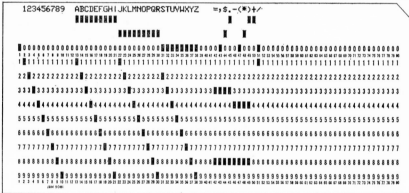

FIGURE 15.6. Punch cards. 90 column (top) and 80 column (bottom). Courtesy, respectively, of Remington Rand Division of the Sperry Rand Corp. and the International Business Machines Corp.

a punched hole or lack of a hole. There are two types of cards popular in this country—the 80- and 90-column cards used with equipment produced by IBM and Remington Rand, respectively. Sample cards appear as illustrated in Figure 15.6.

The 80-column card contains one coded character per column, each column occupying the full width of the card and containing 12 hole sites. There are 80 columns within the length of the card. The holes are rectangular in shape, the long dimension lying along the width of the card.

The 90-column card really consists of 45 columns, each divided into two parts, an upper and a lower, and each of which records one character. There are 12 circular hole sites in each column and 45 columns the length of the card.

Punching

Information may be entered into punch cards by means of keyboard equipment. This equipment may consist of a full alphabetical and numerical keyboard, although for some purposes only a numerical keyboard is required. The 80-column key punch works on a column-by-column basis; each column is punched as it is entered into the keyboard. All the information to be punched into the 90-column card is entered into the keyboard and set up mechanically in the punching guide before the card is affected. At the end of the entry part of the cycle, the card is punched in a single operation; this is called **block punching.**

There are many problems in designing a block punch, and these have not been satisfactorily solved for 80-column cards.

Another way to enter information into the card is to reproduce it from another card. Equipment aptly called a **reproducer** performs this function and can relocate groups of columns from the source card into new positions on the new card.

Single Record Processing

The punch card offers a great convenience because it carries a complete record on a single separable document. This allows operations to be performed upon stacks of punch cards which could be performed on a paper tape record file or a magnetic tape record file only by repeatedly reading and reproducing the file with multiple equipment units. Here are some of these operations.

Sorting. If the cards are examined with a particular group of columns in mind, called a **key,** they may be put in order with respect to this key by means of a sorting operation. Equipment called a **card sorter** is used to separate punched cards into piles with respect to the character punched into a designated column on the card. By performing successive sorts— one, or at most two sorts for each digit of the key—the cards can be placed in alphabetical or numerical order.

SELECTION. Specific cards may be chosen from a stack of cards by means of equipment called a **collator**. One input to the collator is the stack from which the cards are to be selected. The other input is a set of cards containing a key identical to that on the desired cards. The output of the collator is three stacks, one for the unselected cards, the second for the selected cards, and the third for the selector or key cards—the ones bearing the key identification.

MERGING. The collator may be used to return the selected cards to the original stack. The unselected and selected cards, both in proper sequence, are the inputs to the collator and the result at the output is a fully merged stack of cards in sequence.

COLLATION. Other activities may be performed with the collator. These include placing a blank card behind each card in the stack, or withdrawing duplicates from a stack of cards.

These card manipulations may facilitate the computer operation; they save the computer the time of looking up information in extensive files and also provide a method to hold files in order outside of the computer; hence they avoid tying up large and costly computer memory space and time.

Reading

To retrieve the information from the punch card, the array of hole sites must be examined. This may be done in one of three sequences: the card may be examined all at once, one row at a time, or one column at a time.

The method chosen for any given computer depends on the buffer storage and internal storage of the computer. Column-by-column reading is the slowest but it requires the least amount of auxiliary storage; conversely, reading the complete card is fastest, but all the information must be temporarily stored before it is placed in the internal memory of the computer. Row-by-row reading is a compromise adopted in many current computers.

Scanning of the information from the card may be done either mechanically or photoelectrically. The latter, of course, is the faster but requires more expensive equipment. Mechanical reading can use mechanical storage to hold the information; conversion into electrical impulses can then be done easily by means of a mechanical switch.

15.7. MAGNETIC TAPE

Magnetic tape offers a means for storing a larger amount of information than any of the media discussed previously. Information can be entered into or retrieved from magnetic tape faster than any other external storage medium—but it is also the most expensive.

Information is registered on magnetic tape in much the same fashion as upon punched paper tape. Along the tape, and perpendicular to its length, are character rows; situated in each row are sites. Each of the sites may be magnetized in one of two possible directions. An arbitrary assignment of a "0" direction and a "1" direction makes it possible to store information on tape.

Magnetic tape is superior to paper tape because the information, when no longer of use, may be erased and new information stored upon the old reel of tape. It is also possible to take a record stored on the tape, alter it within the computer, and rewrite it in its updated form where the original record previously appeared on the tape.

The number of magnetic sites per character is determined by the choice of input/output language and whether a parity check is incorporated within the code.

Oversimplified Tape System

Figure 15.7.1 shows the simplest possible representation of magnetic tape storage. Tape is stored on reel A. It is unwound from this reel over a reading head and back onto reel B. The tape is moved by power supplied to reel B. As the tape passes over the reading head, information is retrieved from the tape and is passed along to its destination. Information is entered into the tape in the same fashion.

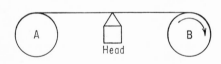

FIGURE 15.7.1.   Oversimplified tape system.

There are several difficulties with this simple system. The inertia of the tape reels makes it difficult to get the tape up to speed rapidly. When the take-up reel is full and the play-off reel empty, the take-up reel must rotate more slowly than the play-off reel. When the play-off reel is full and the take-up reel empty, the play-off reel must move more slowly than the take-up reel. A system which takes account of these problems follows.

Mechanical System Outline

The more sophisticated requirements for providing motion to control the tape are implemented by the mechanism shown in Figure 15.7.2. The first additional requirement is that since information might be sought from either direction, it must be possible to both read and write with the tape being moved in either direction. The second requirement is the ability to start the tape very quickly and to keep it in motion at a high but uniform speed. A third requirement is to stop the tape on a dime without harming the tape.

The path of the tape on the diagram is now traced out. It leaves reel A and enters tape reservoir A. Passing out of the tape reservoir, it goes

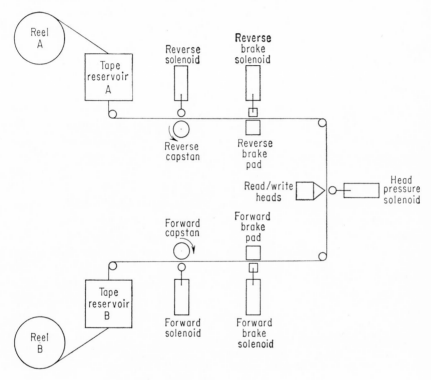

FIGURE 15.7.2.   Magnetic tape drive system.

through the reverse capstan station, the reverse braking station, the head reading and writing station, the forward brake station, the forward capstan station, and into tape reservoir B. From tape reservoir B, it is spooled onto reel B.

In the oversimplified version it was possible to move the tape by rotating reel B; because of the fast-start requirement, the inertia of the system cannot be overcome by rotating reel B without injuring or breaking the tape. The intervening **tape reservoirs** isolate the inertia of the supply and take-up reels from the tape reading system. Motion is supplied to the tape reading part of the system by the capstans. These **capstans** are continuously rotating shafts of accurate diameter, and with a large mass attached which provides high inertia to the capstan shaft, so that it moves at a uniform speed despite moderate loading. Movement is applied to the tape by energizing the capstan solenoid. The **capstan solenoid,** when energized, moves the capstan solenoid roller toward the capstan until the roller makes contact with the tape and presses the tape against the capstan. The motion of the capstan is then imparted to the tape, which is free to move against the capstan solenoid roller. Because of the high inertia of the capstan and the low inertia of the tape at the read section of the unit, it is possible to bring the tape up to the speed of the capstan in a very short time. The tape reservoirs serve to furnish tape on demand; they are places to dump tape after it is read and before the take-up reel gets up to speed.

Once the tape is in motion, the take-up and supply reels are started rotating. They take a substantial time to get up to the speed of the tape in the reading section of the system. The tape reservoir makes up for this time lag and either supplies or accepts tape to keep the system in equilibrium.

To stop the tape, the capstan solenoid is de-energized and the corresponding **brake solenoid** is energized. The brake solenoid applies pressure between the **brake pads** to the tape and causes it to come to a stop in a very short time. The tape reservoirs facilitate the stopping of the tape, again isolating the inertia of the take-up and supply reels from the tape in the reading section.

During reading and writing it is desirable that the tape be kept in close contact with the read/write head. A **head pressure roller** maintains the tape and head in contact during either reading or writing, but not during fast spooling (described later).

Let us examine a read forward operation of the magnetic tape unit as diagrammed in Figure 15.7.2. To start, the forward capstan solenoid is energized and the forward brake is released; these two work in opposition —at no time can both be energized. The tape is immediately set in motion; it is pulled from tape reservoir A through the reverse capstan and brake stations and past the reading head. The tape is kept in contact with the reading head by the head pressure roller. It passes through the forward brake station and into the forward capstan which is causing its movement. It then enters tape reservoir B. Some time after the tape has been set into motion, spools A and B are getting up to speed. Before tape reservoir A is exhausted, supply spool A will be supplying tape faster than it is leaving the reservoir. Similarly, take-up reel B will be removing tape from tape reservoir B faster than it is entering. Operation will continue until an equilibrium is reached and the reservoirs are filled to normal capacity. This requires that the speed of each reel be independently adjustable.

Tape Reservoirs

There are two kinds of tape reservoirs in common use. They are more commonly referred to as **magnetic tape servo control systems.** The first is a mechanical supply and the second, often called a **vacuum servo control,** is a low-pressure system. The mechanical system will be described first.

Mechanical Servo Control System

A block diagram of the mechanical servo control system is seen in Figure 15.7.3. The actual reservoir is indicated diagrammatically in Figure 15.7.4. The reservoir consists of a number of pegs around which the tape is wrapped. Some of the pegs are on a movable arm and others are fixed to the tape deck. As tape is played out of the reservoir toward the drive, the arm moves toward the fixed pegs; as tape is supplied to the reservoir from the supply reel, the arm is moved away from the fixed pegs by the tape tensioning spring. An indication of the fullness of the reservoir is the angular rotation of the supply loop and sensing arm. This is the means for actuating the supply reel. When tape has been pulled out of the reservoir by the capstan drive, the sensing arm is moved counterclockwise, causing the lower section of the control contactor detailed in Figure 15.7.5 to close a circuit to the supply reel. This causes the torque motor on the supply wheel to rotate as rapidly as possible. As soon as tape is entering the supply loop faster than it is leaving the supply loop, the sensing arm starts to turn clockwise. As it turns clockwise, the control contactor goes through two steps. The first step is to supply low power to the torque motor, and the second step is to supply no power to the torque motor. If the supply reel is still supplying tape faster than the capstan drive, the sensing arm continues to turn clockwise and at some point begins to supply power to the torque motor to take up tape. In this

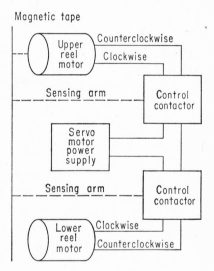

FIGURE 15.7.3.   Block diagram of servo control for magnetic tape system.

fashion the torque motor is made to follow the fluctuations of the tape reservoir.

Vacuum System

A vacuum servo system is shown in Figure 15.7.6, picturing only the system for one reel. The tape from reel A goes into the glass bin. A pump removes the air through a vent in the bottom of the bin. There is reduced

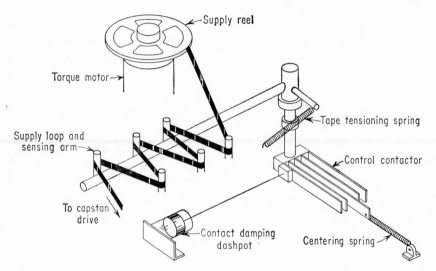

FIGURE 15.7.4.   Servo mechanism tape reservoir for magnetic tape system.   Courtesy of Ampex Corp.

pressure on one side of the tape and atmospheric pressure on the top of the tape, causing it to be pushed down towards the bottom of the bin. Without moving reel A, the tape can be pulled out of the bin when the capstan solenoid roller engages the capstan, applying a longitudinal force to the tape.

On one side of the bin are two spaced lamps; on the other side, directly opposite, are two photocells. A light path exists between each lamp and its photocell through the glass bin except when tape intervenes. The output of each photocell after amplification is applied to a relay. Energization of the relay causes a voltage to be applied to the reel motor. Thus, when the capstan has pulled too much tape out of the bin, both lamps energize both photocells; relays K1 and K2 are both energized; relay contact K1 is closed and relay contact K2 is opened; the reel motor therefore rotates clockwise, causing the bin to fill up. Similarly, when the tape bin

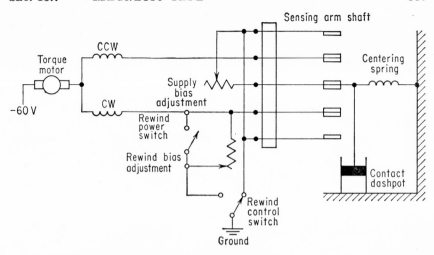

FIGURE 15.7.5. Simplified electrical control for the servo tape reservoir of the magnetic
tape system.   Courtesy of Ampex Corp.

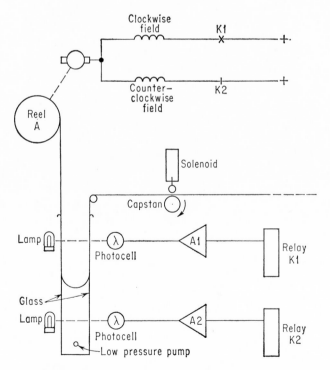

FIGURE 15.7.6.   Vacuum servo for a magnetic tape system.

is full, neither relay is energized; contact K1 is opened and K2 is closed; the reel motor revolves counterclockwise and removes tape from the bin.

Other means, such as pressure transducers, may be used to control the filling of such a reservoir.

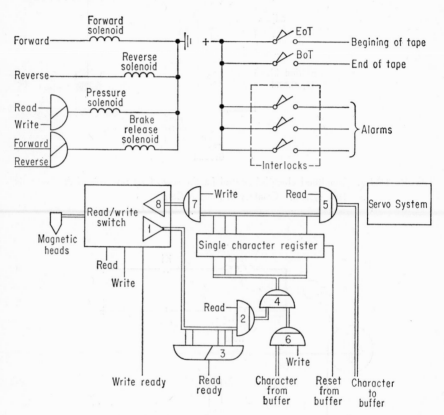

FIGURE 15.7.7.   Magnetic tape mechanism unit logic.

Magnetic Tape Mechanism Unit Logic

The logic for controlling the magnetic tape mechanism and the single-character buffer, usually a part of the tape mechanism unit, is seen in Figure 15.7.7.

In the upper left-hand corner the control solenoids are noted. The forward solenoid is energized on a forward signal, either manual or automatic; the reverse solenoid is energized on a reverse signal; the magnetic tape head pressure solenoid is energized for either a read or write signal (for either forward or reverse)—it is not energized for fast spooling of the tape; the brake release solenoid is energized on both forward and reverse signals.

The interlocks required in the magnetic tape system are shown in the upper right-hand corner of the figure. Plastic magnetic tape usually has a metal leader at either end of the tape. When this leader passes through a special contact, it closes a circuit indicating the end or the beginning of the tape. This information is communicated to the computer which uses it or transmits it to the operator. There are other interlocks in the system which determine emergency situations such as when the tape breaks or comes loose from the tape-winding mechanism. The function of any of these interlocks is to communicate to the computer the existence of the emergency situation.

The servo system, one of the types previously described, is indicated on the right-hand side of the figure merely as a box.

INFORMATION-HANDLING LOGIC. Information appears at the magnetic reading heads and is transmitted to the read/write switch. This switch is energized by a read or write signal appearing at its terminals. For reading, the signal is amplified by A1 and sent to &2 and V3. &2 is gated by the read signal. The information passes through &2 and V4 and into the single-character register. V3 detects the presence of a signal on any one of the read lines and produces a read-ready signal which is sent to the buffer. The information in the single-character register is accessible to the buffer through &5 during the read operation. The buffer makes use of the information and sends back a reset signal via the reset line which clears the single-character register. The buffer must function to accept information and clear the register alternately during the read operation and in synchronism with the reading of the tape.

To write, information is entered from the buffer through &6 and V4 and set into the single-character register. The buffer controls the timing of writing onto the magnetic tape. At the write-ready signal from the buffer, information passes from the single-character register through &7 and A8 and is written by the switched read/write amplifiers through the magnetic heads onto the reading tape.

The operation described above uses a single character register to accumulate information. In a slow system, communication may be made directly between the register and the computer. However, this is no longer a common practice.

The Magnetic Tape Buffer Logic

In Figure 15.7.8 the logic of a fairly typical buffer is displayed. In the upper left-hand corner is seen the information flow and control. The com-

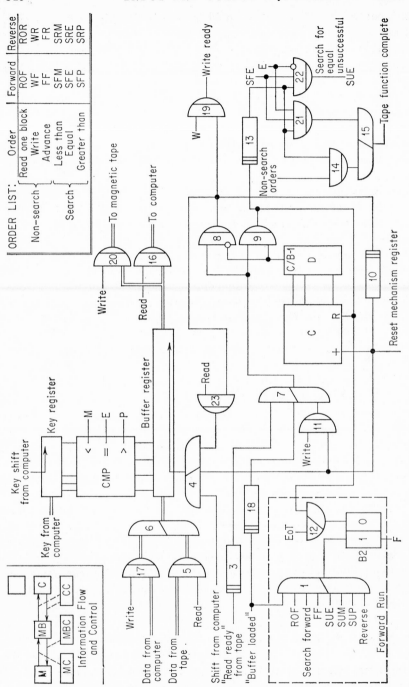

FIGURE 15.7.8.　Logic of the magnetic tape buffer.

puter control (CC) directs the flow of information to and from the computer (C); the magnetic tape unit control (MC) determines the timing of information emanating from the tape (M); the buffer control (MBC) determines the timing of information that is written from the buffer (MB) onto the magnetic tape (M).

A list of the orders commonly associated with magnetic tape units is found in the upper right-hand corner of the figure. The reverse orders use almost exactly the same logic; only the forward orders are discussed here.

READ ONE BLOCK. The *read one block forward* order signal ROF is applied through V1 to set bit storage B2 to 1. This applies a forward signal (F) to the tape unit which starts the tape moving forward. Blocks of information are laid out on the magnetic tape so that a space exists between each block of information. While the tape unit is getting up to speed, the read/write heads are over this **interblock space** and no information is being read. When the first character code appears under the magnetic reading heads, it is entered into the single-character register discussed previously and the read-ready signal is transmitted from the tape mechanism unit logic. The character is entered from the tape character register into the buffer register through &5 and V6. After a short delay provided by Δ3, the read-ready pulse (see Figure 15.7.2) appears at the input of V7. The delayed read-ready pulse passes through V7 and tests &'8 and &9. The number of characters which have been entered into the buffer register, as described subsequently, was recorded in the counter C and decoded by the decoder D. If the buffer register has not yet been filled with information from the magnetic tape, a pulse will emerge from &'8. This passes through &23 and V4 to shift the buffer register in preparation for the next character. It also enters the delay Δ10. From Δ10 it resets the tape mechanism register in preparation for it to receive the next character. It also tallies the counter C. It tries to pass through &11 but cannot, since this is a read cycle.

Subsequent characters are entered through &5 and V6 into the buffer register and shifted by the read-ready pulse which passes through Δ3, V7, &'8, &23, and V4. When the buffer register is full, the testing pulse at &'8 and &9 can no longer pass through &'8. It emerges from &9 and passes through V12 to set B2 to 0. The tape unit no longer gets a forward signal so that the brake release solenoid is de-energized and the tape is immediately stopped. Since this is a read one block order, a non-search order, the pulse from &9, slightly delayed by Δ13, also passes through &14 and V15, to return to the computer as a tape-function-complete pulse. The computer then takes over and empties the tape buffer. It does this by sending shift pulses through V4. Information then emerges from the buffer register through &16 to be entered into the computer.

WRITE FORWARD. Information to be written is sent by the computer through &17 and V6 into the buffer register. When the buffer register is full, a "buffer-loaded" signal from the computer appears at V1. This sets B2 to 1. The magnetic tape begins to move forward. Δ18 provides a delay sufficient for the magnetic tape to come up to speed. When this has happened, the delayed pulse passes through V7 to test &'8 and &9. Since none of the characters has yet been written, it passes out &'8 and emerges from &19 as a write-ready signal. One character of information is now read from the buffer register through &20 and entered into the single-character register of the tape mechanism. When the write-ready signal appears, the character is written onto the tape. The pulse from &'8 passes through delay Δ10 and is returned to the tape mechanism to reset the single-character register. The pulse from Δ10, besides tallying the counter, passes into the buffer register via V4 to present the next character to be written at the buffer output. It also passes through &11 and V7 to check &'8 and &9 again. When the information in the buffer is completely written, the pulse from V7 passes through &9. It resets the counter and passes through V12 to set B2 to 0. This stops the forward motion of the tape. The pulse from &9, delayed by Δ13, passes through &14 and V15 to communicate to the computer that the tape function is now complete.

ADVANCE. An advance function does not require the exchange of information. Its purpose is to wind or rewind the entire reel. The advance order passes through V1 and sets B2 to 1. This causes the tape mechanism to advance the tape. The tape continues to be reeled until an end-of-tape (EoT) signal is produced by the interlock switch. This signal passes through V12 and sets B2 to 0, which stops the tape.

SEARCH FORWARD EQUAL. There are six kinds of search orders, all of which are similar but only one of which is now described. To search for a given block of information, its key is entered by the previous order into the key register of this tape buffer. A block of information is entered into the buffer register as described in the paragraph entitled "Read one block." The comparison circuit compares the key of the block in the buffer with the information in the key register. It emits one of the signals, M, E or P, corresponding to a key which is respectively less than, equal to, or greater than the key in the buffer register. The equal signal, E, is either present on or absent from the line labeled E entering &21 and &'22. For the *search forward equal* order, the pulse from Δ13 will emerge from &'22 if the proper word has not yet been found. This pulse labeled SUE is entered into V1 and sets B2 to 1 again; B2 was reset to 0 by the pulse from &9. The time during which B2 was set to 0 and back to 1 again is so short that the tape unit does not even slow down; after reading through the interblock space, the next block is read and entered into the buffer register. If the search is completed, and the desired key found, the pulse from Δ13 passes through &21 and V15 and returns to the computer to indicate that the search is complete and the proper block is now in the buffer register. The pulse from &9, passing through V12, has set B2 to 0 and turned off the tape unit. Notice that if the proper block is not on the tape, the tape is stopped by an end-of-tape signal passing through V12 to set B2 to 0.

Appearance of Tape Units

The photograph in Figure 15.7.9 shows the external appearance of a tape unit with a mechanical servo tape reservoir as made by Ampex; the

FIGURE 15.7.9. Magnetic Tape Unit. Courtesy of the Ampex Corp.

FIGURE 15.7.10. Magnetic Tape Unit. Courtesy of the Potter Co.

details of a similar unit made by Potter are seen in Figure 15.7.10; a Remington Rand Univac® II surrounded by Uniservos® with a "vacuum" reservoirs appears in Figure 15.7.11.

FIGURE 15.7.11.   Console of the Univac® II surrounded by magnetic tape units, each having vacuum reservoirs.   Courtesy of Remington Rand Division, Sperry Rand Corp.

15.8. THE HIGH-SPEED PRINTER

The purpose of the high-speed printer is to take information from the computer at a rapid rate and produce a printed document giving the result of the computations or a journal of activities. High-speed printers can print about 120 characters per line. Printers which can produce 600 lines per minute have been out since the middle of the 1950's. Speeds of over 1500 lines per minute are now attainable.

The general idea of the operation of such a printer is shown in Figure 15.8.1. The message, "Here is a printer," is stored within the computer memory. Under the control of the computer it is entered into the buffer of the high-speed printer. The printwheel of the printer is constantly rotating. At the instant illustrated, the letter "e" appears on all of the 120 printwheels underneath the print hammers. The logic of the high-speed printer examines all the characters of the message to see which is an "e." While the "e's" of the printwheel are under the hammers, those hammers corresponding to the "e's" in the message are energized. Between the hammers and the printwheel is interposed the output document and a carbon ribbon. The hammer hits the paper against the ribbon and an impression is made of the printwheel character upon the paper through the carbon on the document and at the proper place. Although the printwheel is in motion, the actuation of the hammer is so rapid that the impression of the character is clear and without blur.

The printwheel continues to rotate and soon "f's" appear beneath the hammers. The message to be printed is again scanned completely. Hammers for which there are "f's" in the message (none in our example) are

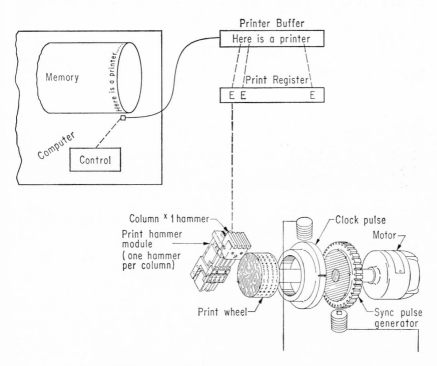

FIGURE 15.8.1.   High-speed printer, general idea.

energized. This cycle of rotate, scan, and print is repeated until the print wheel has made a full revolution. The message should then be all printed.

High-Speed Printer Flow Diagram

Let us discuss what happens within the high-speed printer logic. This is best illustrated by the flow diagram of Figure 15.8.2. Counters bearing the label i and j keep track, respectively, of the buffer address being examined and the number of print positions examined so far. Before starting, i is set to 1 and j to 0 as per the label. In box 1 the first step is to fill the printer buffer with information from the computer.

Attached to the printwheel is a small magnetic drum which rotates in synchronism with it. By some means information is taken from this drum, indicating the character on the set of printwheels now underneath the hammers. This information is in the same code used for the characters in the computer and in the printer buffer. The code of the character now under the print hammer is entered into the character code register, box 2. The number of print positions examined so far is then increased by 1 in

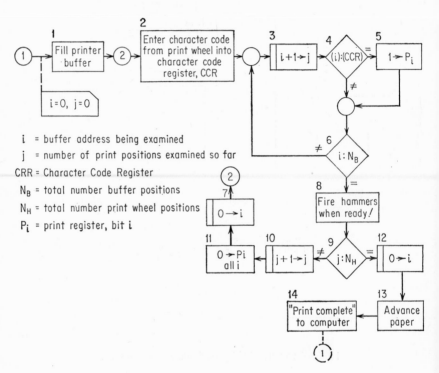

FIGURE 15.8.2.   Flow diagram, high-speed printer.

box 3. Since this number was originally 0, the print position counter *now* contains a count of 1, indicating that the first print position for this message is about to be examined. This could be any position on the printwheel. The first character in the buffer is compared with the code in the character code register in box 4. If they are not the same, nothing happens; if the printwheel character corresponds to the characters stored in this position in the buffer, a 1 is entered into the first bit portion of the print register. The print register holds as many bits as there are characters on the printwheels—in this case, 120. For a character to be printed at *this* print position, a 1 must be present for *this* hammer within the print register.

In box 6 the number of characters in the buffer register examined so far is examined. This is done by comparing the count in the buffer address counter with the total number of buffer positions—in this case, 120. If they are not equal, the next message character should be examined. The index i is increased by 1 in box 3 to indicate the next message position is to be scanned. We continue to box 3 where the code of the next message character is compared with that corresponding to the printwheel which is now stored in the character code register.

This process continues until all the characters in the message register have been examined. At that time i is equal to the number of buffer positions, and the equal arrow out of box 6 in the flow diagram is followed. And by now 1's have been stored in the print register for each character position in the message which is the same as the character on the printwheel now under the print hammers.

When the printwheel is in the exact position for good printing, a pulse is emitted from the firing section of the printwheel drum. This pulse fires the selected thyratrons which, in turn, send current through the print hammer electromagnets and cause the proper characters to be printed onto the document. After this, in box 9, the number of characters examined so far is compared with the total number of characters on the printwheel. A common figure for this is 51. If all 51 characters have not been printed message must be examined for the next print position. In box 10 the count in the print position counter is increased by 1. Before examining the message again for the new character coming up, the print register must be cleared to 0 for all bit positions, box 11 and the counter i reset to 0. Return is then made via circle 2 to box 2, and the next character code is read from the printwheel drum.

When all the printwheel character positions have been reviewed, both the buffer address counter and the print position counter are reset to their original values in box 12. The paper is advanced to receive a new line, box 13. A pulse is returned to the computer to indicate that the printing of this message is now complete, box 14, and a new message may be entered into the printer buffer.

Printer Logic.

Figure 15.8.3 shows one possible arrangement of logic to implement the high-speed printer just described. It assumes that the read-out from the computer is serial by character, parallel by bit.

LOADING. When the computer receives word that the printer is ready to start on a new message, it sends the first data character into the data

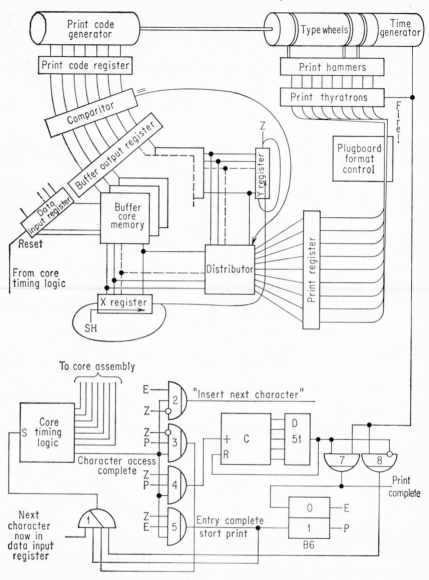

FIGURE 15.8.3. High-speed printer.

input register; it also sends a pulse to ∨1, indicating that the first character is ready. The output of ∨1 starts the core-timing logic. The message to be printed is now stored in the buffer core memory. This core memory together with its associated logic is similar to that described in Chapter 14. The core-timing logic block which appears on Figure 15.8.3

was described in that chapter. The X and Y registers hold the address where the next character is to be stored. In this instance, the X register consists of 12 cores and the Y register of 10 cores for a 12 × 10 character core memory. As each character is entered, the X register, a ring counter, is shifted once, which amounts to increasing its count by 1. After the X register has counted to 12, its output pulse is re-entered into the X register and also used to shift the Y register. In this fashion each of the 120 characters of the message is entered in sequence into buffer core memory. Each character from the computer first appears at the data input register and then is entered into the buffer core memory. After this, the X register is counted to advance to the next buffer address. Before this cycle is started by the computer, B6 was set to 0, indicating an entry cycle follows. After each character is stored, the "character access complete" pulse from the core-timing logic is applied to &'2, &'3, &4, and &5. During entry of the message from the computer, B6 is set for "E" and this pulse passes through &'2 and returns to the computer to request "Insert the next character," indicating that the previous character is now entered into the buffer memory.

After the last character is entered into the buffer core memory, a pulse labeled "Z" is emitted from the Y register. This guides the character-access-complete pulse through &5 to set B6 to 1, indicating the print cycle follows.

PRINT CYCLE. The high-speed printer is now on its own. Timing internal to the printer now takes over and the computer cannot communicate with the printer until the message has been placed in full on the document.

Having entered the last character into the core memory, the X and Y registers have automatically been advanced to the first buffer character position.

The pulse from &5 which has set B6 to 1 passes through V1 and starts the core-timing logic again. The core buffer is sent through a complete set of read cycles. The code for each character in sequence is entered into the buffer output register. The print code for the character now under the hammers was entered earlier into the print code register. The comparator compares the content of the print code register with each buffer register character, and emits a signal only when the two are identical. The identity signal is returned to the distributor. The distributor enters a 1 into the corresponding column position of the print register. The position at which the 1 is entered is determined by decoding the X and Y register counts, the address of the character under examination.

Through this procedure the entire content of the buffer core memory is examined and 1's are entered into the print register where the message contains the character now under the print hammers.

Each time a new character of the message is examined, a character-access-complete pulse is emitted by the core-timing logic. This passes through &'3 and starts the core-timing logic again. After the complete buffer has been examined, a Z pulse is emitted from the Y register, causing the character-access-complete pulse to pass through &4 instead of &'3. This tallies the print cycle counter C by 1. The decoder D emits a signal

FIGURE 15.8.4. High-speed printer. Courtesy of the Analex Corp. FIGURE 15.8.5. The Magnityper—a high-speed printer. Courtesy of the Potter Co.

only when the counter C contains the number equivalent to the number of characters around the typewheel.

After each complete examination of the core buffer, the timing generator emits a pulse to the print thyratrons which energizes the print hammer and causes characters to be printed at the proper position on the paper. This pulse also checks &7 and &'8. If each of the characters on the printwheel has not had a chance to be printed, the timing pulse passes through &'8 and starts the core-timing logic again. Each of the 51 character positions on the typewheels is thus examined in order, starting randomly from any given character. When all of the characters have been reviewed, the pulse from the timing generator passes through &7 instead of &'8, since a "51" decoder output is present, and is returned to the computer as a print-complete pulse to indicate that this line has now been inscribed upon the output document.

In Figure 15.8.4 appears a photo of a high-speed printer made by the Analex Corporation incorporating these principles, and another made by the Potter Company appears as Figure 15.8.5.

15.9. TYPEWRITERS

Typewriters can do three tasks. (1) They produce a printed copy, called **hard copy**, of the information that was entered into the keyboard. (2) They simultaneously produce coded impulses which may be entered directly into the computer: these same impulses may be entered into a punch unit and produce a punched paper tape. (3) They also may be used as output devices.

The Typewriter for Input

The means by which a typewriter produces its hard copy is obvious.

To produce a coded signal, each key when depressed actuates a multipole switch. There are as many poles to the switch as there are bits per character. One side of each contact is connected to a voltage source; the other side is connected to one of the information lines. Each of these switches hence operates as one input to a V-mixer of an encoder. This is the function which the typewriter performs during input—it is an encoder.

Mechanical Translation

Direct electrical translation requires one multipole switch for each key on the keyboard. Such switches are bulky and expensive and increase the size of the equipment. A more convenient means for translating the key motion into electrical form uses a mechanical translator.

Such a translator is constructed by the Flexowriter Division of the Friden Co. in a form which is easily installed on the bottom of a conventional electric typewriter. The frame of this device is shown in Figure 15.9.1. Sitting in the frame are a number of slides—one for each key of the typewriter. The depression of a key pushes a corresponding slide and causes the slide to move to the left as in Figure 15.9.2. In so doing, the cam surfaces along the slide, upon which the bails (cross pieces or bars) lie cause some of the bails to move upward. Each slide is different and causes a different set of bails to be moved upward. These bails correspond to the bits in the code for the character for which the key is depressed.

Returning to Figure 15.9.1, as the slide is pushed forward, bail #1 is pushed upward. The left-hand end of the bail sits in the contact shaft fork. The upward movement of the bail causes the contact shaft to rotate clockwise as indicated. As the contact shaft rotates clockwise, it pushes the code #1 contacts together, causing the generation of an electrical pulse. Only one bail is shown in the diagram. For each bit in the code there is one mechanical set consisting of a bail, a contact shaft fork, a contact escapement, and a contact.

There is one such complete set which is actuated by all keys. This is the set which generates pulses corresponding to the feed holes in the tape.

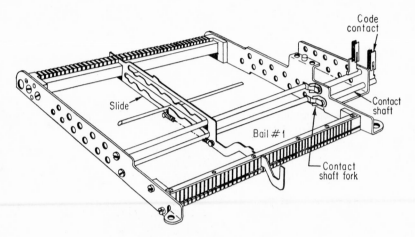

FIGURE 15.9.1. Contactor selector construction for the electric typewriter used as an encoder.

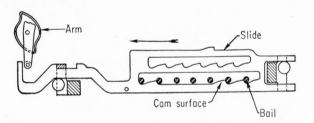

FIGURE 15.9.2. Slides for mechanical translation in the electric typewriter.

There is usually a paper tape punch associated with the typewriter and code generator. One contact is connected to each of the punch magnets, and the feed contact is connected to the paper tape feed clutch mechanism and location hole punch magnet.

The Typewriter for Output

The typewriter is limited in its ability to follow information that is entered into it. It is severely taxed to go at any greater than ten to twelve key strokes per second, or approximately 120 words per minute. It is therefore uneconomical to use it as the direct output of a computer. The computer can produce a punched paper tape much more rapidly; one or more typewriters can then transcribe the paper tape into hard copy.

MECHANICAL DECODING. The decoding of the electrical input to the typewriter could be done electrically. This would require one actuator for each key on the keyboard. A more economical way to perform the decoding is

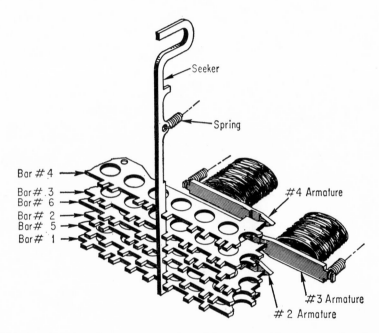

FIGURE 15.9.3.   A seeker in its operated condition as caused by the typewriter decoder. Courtesy of Friden, Inc.

to do it mechanically. Figure 15.9.3 shows a number of bars. Each position along the length of each bar corresponds to one of the keys on the keyboard. Each of the bars corresponds to one of the bits of each character. The code which is received by the typewriter mechanism is converted into mechanical motion of the corresponding bars. There are notches in the bars which are aligned only when the code corresponds to the character whose key should be depressed.

Figure 15.9.3 shows a seeker bar for which the notches on the permutation bars are aligned. Because the notches are lined up, the spring is able to pull the seeker bar toward the rear.

There is one magnet and permutation bar assembly for each bit to be read from the paper tape. This assembly is shown in Figure 15.9.4. In that figure the permutation bar is shown latched. The holding projection of the bar is caught and held by the armature. When the magnet is energized, the armature is attracted towards the magnet. This releases the permutation bar, which is pushed to the right by the plunger spring, the bar's motion being limited by a stop on its right-hand side (not shown). The notches in the full set of permutation bars of Figure 15.9.3 align for one and only one seeker.

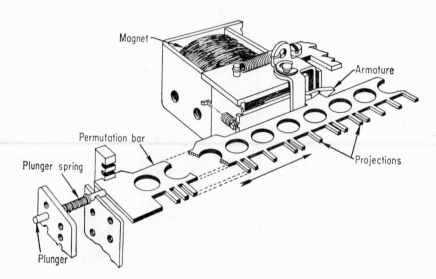

FIGURE 15.9.4. Permutation bar and magnet assembly in the latched position. Courtesy of Friden, Inc.

KEY SELECTION. At the normal position, with no magnets energized, the permutation bar assemblies appear as in Figure 15.9.5. One of the seekers is shown and you will notice that it is held forward by the projections on several of the permutation bars.

While one (and only one) seeker is being selected by the method discussed above, the feed-hole pulse actuates a clutch assembly attached to the typewriter motor. This clutch assembly functions quite similarly to the clutch assembly in the paper tape punch unit. When it is energized, it causes the output shaft to rotate for just one revolution. It is this motion which is now used to actuate the proper key. There are a number of cams attached to the clutch output shaft and these actuate various mechanisms which will now be discussed.

Figure 15.9.6 shows the seeker restoring bail mechanism. In normal

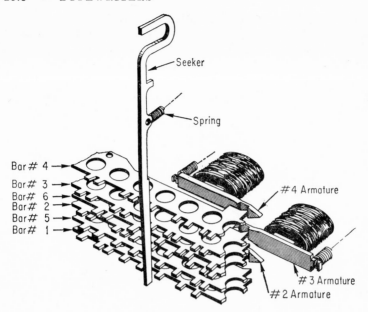

FIGURE 15.9.5.   A seeker in unoperated position held forward by projections on some of the permutation bars.   Courtesy of Friden, Inc.

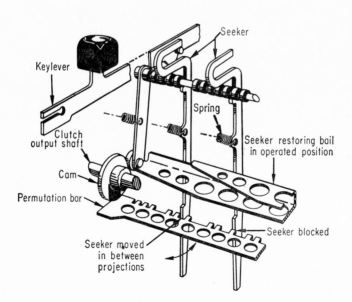

FIGURE 15.9.6.   The seeker restoring bail mechanism.   Courtesy of Friden, Inc.

position, when the clutch output shaft is not rotating, the seeker restoring bail cam holds the seeker restoring bail in a forward position. This prevents the seekers from falling into the slot which is produced by alignment of the permutation bars on actuation of the permutation bar magnets. Thus, when a character is called for and properly decoded by the permutation bails, nothing will happen unless the clutch mechanism causes the

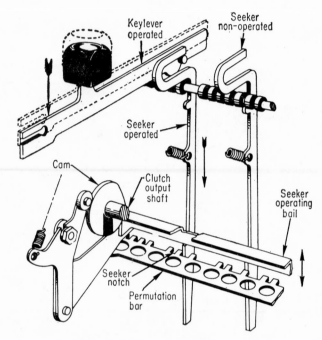

FIGURE 15.9.7.   The seeker operating bail operating the key lever.   Courtesy of Friden, Inc.

clutch output shaft to rotate. As soon as the shaft begins to rotate, the seeker-restoring bail cam allows the bail to move away from the seekers and allows the chosen seeker to fall into the permutation bail slot.

The seeker operating bail mechanism is shown in Figure 15.9.7. Shortly after the seeker has been released and allowed to fall against the permutation bar, the seeker operating bail is pushed downward. The only seeker that it contacts will be the one which was chosen by the permutation bar alignment. It will push this seeker downward because of a notch in the seeker which it encounters.

Each seeker is hooked about a projection on a corresponding keylever. The downward movement of the chosen seeker therefore operates the chosen keylever. Operation of the keylever causes the chosen key to be moved forward against the paper and the chosen character to appear printed on the paper.

The bar restoring bail is shown in Figure 15.9.8. It is the function of this bail to restore to normal position the permutation bars which were chosen to print this character. As each permutation bar is restored, it is

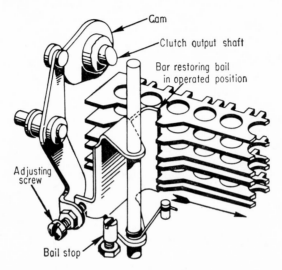

FIGURE 15.9.8. The bar restoring bail resetting the permutation bars. Courtesy of Friden, Inc.

latched by the now-released armature of the magnet assembly, Figure 15.9.4. As the clutch output shaft completes its revolution, it causes the seeker-restoring bar of Figure 15.9.6 to push all the seekers away from the permutation bars. The decoding mechanism is now completely restored and is ready to receive the next character code.

SUMMARY. To summarize, the typewriter decoding mechanism performs the following operations in sequence:

1. The proper magnets are actuated from the paper tape reader.
2. The corresponding permutation bars are unlatched.
3. The clutch mechanism is energized.
4. The seeker-restoring bail releases the seekers, and the chosen seeker falls into the notch formed by the permutation bars.
5. The operating bail causes the chosen key to be depressed.
6. The bar-restoring bail restores all the permutation bars and relatches them.
7. The seeker-restoring bail resets the seekers, pushing all of them away from the permutation bars.

The Full Typewriter Assembly

The usual typewriter assembly furnished for a computer installation consists of a typewriter, a mechanical encoder connected to a paper tape punch, and a paper tape reader connected to a mechanical decoder which

FIGURE 15.9.9.   The Automatic Electric Typewriter, trademarked Flexowriter.   Courtesy of Friden, Inc.

automatically operates the electric typewriter. A photograph of such equipment as manufactured by Flexowriter is found in Figure 15.9.9.

15.10. OFF-LINE OPERATION

Equipment is said to operate **off-line** when its operation does not in any way tie up the computer. Since use of auxiliary equipment is less expensive than the computer, it is advantageous to have such equipment operate by itself or together with other auxiliary equipment and not tie up the computer. Examples of off-line operation are now discussed.

Punched Cards and Punched Paper Tape

Both punched cards and punched paper tape are prepared on a keyboard device which obviates direct keyboard input to the computer. Information from the source document is transcribed in the keyboard device to the intermediate media. A high-speed mechanism can be used to get the information from the intermediate media into the computer. Information is entered by the computer into similar intermediate media. The punched paper tape can be transcribed into a document by means of the typewriter discussed in the previous section. Punched cards can be read on an automatic tabulator. These are off-line operations and do not tie up the computer.

Magnetic Tape

The magnetic tape unit is more equally matched in speed with the computer. Even so, the very fast computers can keep a large number of magnetic tape units rolling at high speed. It is possible to enter information into magnetic tape directly by keyboard equipment, such as the Unityper® made by Remington Rand. Since magnetic recording equipment is more costly than either card entry or punched tape entry equipment, this is still a moderately expensive process. It is often advisable to use two intermediate media. Information is punched into cards or paper tape by a keyboard device, and then a translating device takes the information from the cards or paper tape and produces a recorded magnetic tape. Two step-ups in speed result: paper tape and cards can be read much faster than keyboard entry; magnetic tape can be read much faster than paper tape or cards.

The same methodology prevails for output devices. Here the computer writes onto magnetic tape which is later converted into paper tape or cards. These, in turn, are used on slower output devices.

Off-Line Processing

The job of the computer can be shortened if information can be organized beforehand. In the section on punched cards, methods were described for arranging unit records before entry into the computer and after production by the computer. Analogous methods are available for handling records stored on magnetic tape. Off-line equipment called a **tape sorter** can be used to arrange information on magnetic tape. An off-line sorter is associated with the File Computer made by Remington Rand and with the Elecom 120 formerly produced by Underwood. The sorter has four tape units associated with it, and by shuffling information back and forth can produce an output which is in the proper sequence according to the key contained in each record.

Verification

Methods have been discussed earlier for recognizing errors committed by the computer in its calculations or in transporting data from one section or piece of equipment to another. Remember, complementary arithmetic was mentioned and so were the parity check and error-correcting codes. However, the greatest source of error arises from the human operator. We have no control over the key punch operator who misreads or inverts a number in transcribing a document. Because this kind of error can ruin a calculation, some means must be used to control it. For this reason, card and tape verifiers are used.

The card verifier produced by IBM works as follows. A card originally punched by another operator is inserted into the verifier. The verifier operator has a copy of the information which should appear on the card. She enters this information into the keyboard. When a discrepancy exists between the character on the card and that punched by the operator, the machine hangs up. An alarm lamp lights and the operator determines the reason for discrepancy. If she incorrectly inserted data, she can override the machine and continue to check the card; otherwise if the error was previously punched into the card she must duplicate the card up to that point, enter the correct character where the fault was found, and duplicate the rest of the card.

The Remington Rand system requires that the card be punched twice, the second time by a different operator. The verifying key punch is set to enter the duplicate information but slightly offsets the holes. The punched and repunched cards are inserted into the verifier. This machine examines all of the holes punched in the card. Any non-offset hole is an indication that the same information has not been entered by both operators. This card is offset from the pack; a new card may be made up to replace it.

The first system described has been found to be superior because it does not require a re-examination of the deck. Such a re-examination may create problems, especially if the deck must be kept in order. In the first system, errors are corrected when they are found.

PROBLEMS

1. In Figure 15.11 and 15.12 and the text with each, starting on page 362 show and describe the control console of the IBM 650 and IBM 1401

respectively. These were extracted from the operator's manual. For each machine indicate the function of each knob and light using Table 15.2 as a guide as was done for Figures 15.2.1 and 15.2.2.

2. Characterize direct and indirect communication. List the forms that input and output to the computer may take.

3. Make a chart contrasting speed, capacity, cost (per bit or per word), erasability, etc. for all the I/O media you can think of.

4. The computer stops with $+000014835$ in the A register. For an XS3 machine how does this appear on the control panel register display, where ○ means 1 (on) and ● means 0 (off)?

5. Draw the paper tape punch output system in a diagram similar to Figure 15.4.2.

6. For each punch card type appearing in Figure 15.6, show how *17RS59PZ* and *your name* would be entered into the card.

7. Describe the operation of the magnetic type buffer, Figure 15.7.8, for the following orders: (a) SFM (b) SFP. Add logic, if needed.

8. Add logic to Figure 15.7.8 for reverse operation including reverse advance (rewind). Describe the operation for the orders:

    (a) FR   (b) ROR   (c) SRE   (d) SRP

9. Devise a logic for reading 80-column cards. Show both the card reader and mechanism and the reader unit.

10. Do the same for a card punch.

11. Assuming six bits per character, show in logical detail the guts of the high-speed printer, Figure 15.8.3. This should include details on the

    (a) data input register
    (b) print code register
    (c) buffer output register
    (d) comparitor
    (e) X and Y registers
    (f) distributor
    (g) print register

12. Draw a timing diagram for the high-speed printer Figure 15.8.3 showing the outputs of the elements important to the cycle during:

    (a) a full print cycle
    (b) a buffer read-out cycle for a single print wheel revolution
    (c) a single print wheel character read-out

13. Describe how the high-speed printer is used on line with the computer and off line with a magnetic type unit.

14. Show in full what comprises the core-timing logic for the high-speed printer, Figure 15.8.3.

15. Some means must be used to synchronize the HSP print cycle with print wheel rotation. Make suggestions. Incorporate one into the logic of Problem 14.

16. Design a plug board for format control for the high-speed printer. Assume a 120-character printer and a 90-character buffer.

17. Design an "electronic" typewriter encoder with "baseless" input (one for each key—exclude shift control) and Univac® code output. (See Figure 8.7.) Design a decoder for Univac®-to-baseless operation.

IBM 650 CONTROL PANEL DESCRIPTION

Operating Lights

These lights indicate the operating status of the system. They can be very helpful in determining the reason for unscheduled machine stops.

Data Address. With program execution stopped, this light indicates that the next half-cycle will be an execute cycle.

Instruction Address. With program execution stopped, this light indicates that the next half-cycle will be a fetch cycle. This light will come on as a result of pressing either the computer reset or program reset key with the control switch set to RUN or ADDRESS STOP.

Program. This light is on only if program execution is stopped:

1. manually
2. by a programmed stop
3. by an address stop.

However, it does not come on if a manual stop takes place during the fetch cycle of an input-output command.

Accumulator. This light is on whenever the accumulator is in use.

Input-Output. This light is on during the execute cycle of any input-output instruction. It stays on until the interlock is removed. If program execution is stopped with this light on, it may indicate one of the following conditions:

1. No cards in one of the feed hoppers
2. A feed failure
3. Cards have not been run into one of the feeds
4. The stop key on one of the input-output units has been pressed
5. A read parity error or punch parity error has occurred. This is further signified by the storage selection light and a valid address showing in the address lights.
6. Using an input-output code for a unit that is not attached
7. Trying to execute an output code on a unit that has an error

Overflow. This light comes on if an overflow condition occurs. An overflow condition can be caused by one of the following:

1. An excessive accumulation
2. Trying to develop a quotient of more than ten digits
3. Trying to exceed the number of shifts called for in a shift-and-count operation

Checking Lights

These lights are used to indicate the presence of an error condition in the various units of the system.

Program Register. Indicates the detection of a parity error in the program register.

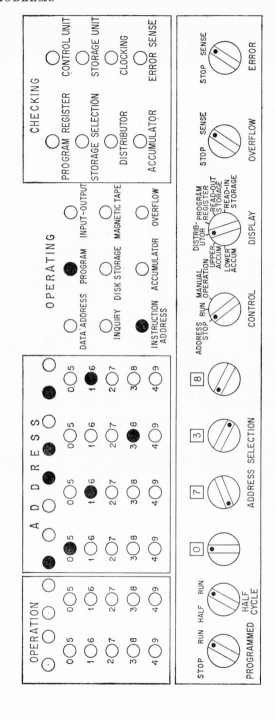

FIGURE 15.11.   Control Panel of IBM 650 Computer and operating description pages 363-365. Reprinted by permission, ©1958 by International Business Machines Corp.

Storage Selection. Can indicate any one of the following error conditions:

1. A read or punch parity error. If this type of error is detected, the input-output light is on, and a valid address appears in the address lights
2. An instruction with an invalid address
3. Information being written in two or more drum locations simultaneously
4. Information not being written in any drum location on a store operation
5. A store operation with a D-address in the 8000 series
6. Attempted manual entry to 800X from the storage-entry switches
7. Not finding an equal or higher value on a TLU operation

Distributor. Indicates the detection of a parity error in the distributor.
Accumulator. Indicates the detection of a parity error in the accumulator.
Clocking. Indicates the detection of an error in the timing circuitry.
Error Sense. Operates in conjunction with the error switch. When this switch is set to sense, the error sense light comes on for one of these conditions:

1. Parity error
2. Clocking error.

The light remains on until the error sense reset switch is pressed.
Control Unit—Storage Unit. The operation of these lights indicates an error in the respective units.

Error Sensing and Stopping

Inherent in the design of the 650 System is a series of checks that assure correct processing of data. If an error should occur, it is signaled on the console and can be corrected manually or automatically.

Unconditional Error Stops. Some error conditions, by their nature, are not correctable by automatic machine procedure. Therefore, they always result in stopping program execution. These errors are:

1. Read parity check
2. Punch parity check
3. Invalid address (Storage Selection)
4. Invalid OP Code
5. Divide overflow.

Conditional Error Stops. Some other error conditions can, when they occur, cause program execution to stop, or programmed error-correction routines to take place. The error switch controls which of these two possibilities is used. These are under control of the error switch:

1. Program register parity error
2. Distributor parity error
3. Accumulator parity error
4. Clocking.

With the error switch set to STOP, any of the preceding errors halt program execution. The location of the error is signaled by the corresponding checking light.

With the switch set to SENSE, any of these errors cause program execution to be momentarily stopped while an automatic computer-reset operation is performed.

Overflow Sensing and Stopping

In the arithmetic operations of many problems, if the capacity of the accumulator is exceeded (overflow), some error has occurred that may require manual handling. In other problems the overflow indicates that a specific point in the problem has been reached, and that a different branch of the program is to be used.

The effect of an accumulator overflow on machine operation is controlled by the overflow switch. When the switch is set at STOP, any overflow causes program execution to stop at the end of the execute cycle during which the overflow occurred. The overflow light indicates the cause of the stop. When the switch is set at SENSE, any overflow except one caused by improper division, lights the overflow light and sets up an internal overflow condition.

This internal overflow condition can be interrogated using the 47 BOV (Branch on Overflow) operation code, which also turns out the overflow light.

Control Keys

Transfer. This key functions only when the control switch is set to manual operation. When operative, pressing this key transfers the number set up in the address selection switches to the address register.

Program Start. This key is used to initiate program execution. The starting point is determined by the setting of the program control and the content of the operation and address registers.

Program Stop. This key is used to halt program execution. It stops at the completion of the cycle during which the key is pressed.

Program Reset. This key resets the program register to zeros, and sets program control to the fetch cycle. Also, it resets the error circuits that have been activated by a program register parity check, storage selection error, or a clocking error. Its effect upon the operation and address registers is determined by the setting of the control switch.

Computer Reset. This key resets all error circuits and sets the program register, distributor, and accumulator to zeros. Also, it sets the program control to the fetch cycle. Its effect on the operation and address registers is identical to the program reset key.

Accumulator Reset. This key resets the distributor and accumulator to zeros. It also resets error circuits that have been activated by an overflow, accumulator parity check, distributor parity check, clocking error, or storage-selection error other than that caused by an invalid address. It has no effect on the contents of the program, operation, and address registers.

Error Reset. This key resets the error circuits activated by a clocking error or a storage selection error other than that caused by an invalid address. It also resets an overflow condition if both the overflow and error switches are set to STOP.

Error Sense Reset. This key resets the error-sense circuit and turns out the error-sense light. It is effective only when the error switch is set to SENSE.

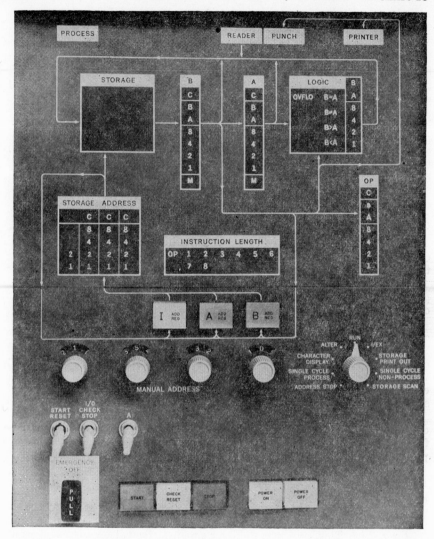

FIGURE 15.12.   Control panel of IBM 1401 data processing system.   Courtesy of International Business Machines Co., Inc.

IBM 1401 CONTROL PANEL DESCRIPTION

Power On. Controls the main power supply for the entire system. Pressing it causes POWER ON key to light.

Power Off. Turns off the main power supply.

Start. This key is used to initiate or resume machine operation after a stop: manual, programmed or automatic. Similar keys are found on each of the other units in the system. Operation of this key is conditioned by the setting of the mode switch.

a. During a normal *run* mode, the system can be started by pressing the start key on any of the units.

b. During a *single cycle* process mode, any of the start keys can cause the system to advance through the program, except on an input-output execution cycle. The start key at the input-output unit must be pressed for this operation.

c. To restart following an error indication, the *check reset* key must be pressed prior to the operation of the start key.

d. Following a card jam or misfeed in either the reader or the punch, the cards in the associated feed must be run out by means of the *non-process-runout* key for that feed, and its hopper must be reloaded before the start key is pressed.

Start Reset. This switch is used to reset the system (except for the data in storage) so that the operator can restart the operation.

Stop. This is a lighted key, and is used to stop processing in the system. It is not effective until the instruction being executed is completed. Similar stop keys (without lights) are provided on each of the other units within the system.

Emergency Off. This is a *pull* switch, located on the console. In an emergency, pulling this switch disconnects all the power to the entire system. This switch should be manually reset by a customer engineer before power is restored to the system.

Check Reset. An error detected by the checking circuits causes this key to light. It must be pressed following a 1401 Processing Unit error, and the system is restarted by pressing the start key.

Checking Lights

Four lights are provided at the top of the console panel, representing the Processing Unit, Reader, Punch, and Printer. When the machine is operating normally, these lights appear as white areas with black lettering. When the machine stops, requiring operator attendance at one of the four units, the appropriate light glows red, indicating an error. The light is extinguished when proper action is performed by the operator.

Storage. The storage light is red when an error at the input to storage is detected by a parity check.

B-light. The B-light comes on when a B register parity check error occurs. The lights underneath display the BCD coding check-bit status, and the word mark status of the character in the B register.

A-light. The A-light comes on when an A register parity check error occurs. The lights below indicate the coded character, check-bit status, and word mark status of the character in the A register.

Logic Block Lights

O-flo. Lights when an overflow condition exists.

B $\neq$ A. Is on when an unequal-compare condition exists after a compare instruction. Additional lights are provided for high-low-equal compare when this optional feature is included in the system.

Bit Display. Shows the bit configuration of the sum of the characters being processed in an arithmetic operation.

Register Lights

OP Register. The *Op* light is red when an incorrect operation code exists in the op register, or if the code is incorrectly interpreted. The lights below indicate the coded character and the check-bit status of the character in the op register.

Instruction Length Lights. Indicate the number of characters in the instruction.

Storage-Address Light. Red when an address register parity check occurs. The lights below, displaying the address, can be checked for the error condition.

Storage Address Display. A group of storage address lights display the storage address (in binary-coded-decimal form) contained in the address register indicated by one of three key-lights:

I Address Register. Glows when the I address is in the storage address display.

A Address Register. Glows when the A address is in the display.

B Address Register. Glows when the B address is displayed.

Stopping the machine and holding down one of these keys causes the contents of the associated register to be displayed in the storage-address lights. When the key is released the storage-address display lights return to their former status, if the mode switch is on RUN.

I/O Check Stop Switch

When in the ON position (up), the machine stops at completion of an I/O operation if an error occurs during that operation. In the OFF position (down), the machine does not stop if it detects a hole count check in the Card Reader or Card Punch, a validity for the Card Reader, or a Print Check. With the switch in the OFF position, error detection must be accomplished by programming.

Manual Address Switches

The four dial switches labeled *Manual Address* are used to select the address to be entered in the storage-address register. These work in conjunction with the address register key-lights and the storage-address display lights.

For example, set the contents of the A address register to 1200.

1. Set the mode switch to ALTER.
2. Set the manual address switches to 1200.
3. Press the A address register key.
4. Press the start key.

The storage-display lights then show the bit configurations for this address (1200).

The manual address switches are also used to select a storage location for a display or alteration, without disturbing the contents of the address registers.

Sense Switches

Seven sense switches can be included in the 1401 Processing Unit. The manual toggle switches that control them are located on the console. Switch A is used to control last card operations by making the TEST AND BRANCH SENSE SWITCH ON instruction effective only when the last card in the reader has passed the second reading brushes. Switch A is standard in all systems except Model D. Six additional sense switches (B, C, D, E, F, and G) are optional features.

The B (I) d TEST AND BRANCH SENSE SWITCH ON instruction can be used to interrogate the setting of the switch specified by the d-character, at any time during processing, and causes a branch to the (I) address if the switch is ON.

Mode Switch

The nine *modes* of machine operation are selected by the *Mode Switch:*

1. RUN. When the mode switch is set to RUN, the system is under control of the stored program.

2. *I/Ex (Instruction/Execution)*. When the mode switch is set to I/EX, the first time the start key is pressed, the machine reads one complete instruction from storage and stops. This is called the *instruction phase*.

The next time the start key is pressed, the machine executes that instruction. This is called the *execution phase*.

Subsequent pressing of the start key results in alternate instruction and execution phases.

3. *Single-Cycle Process*. Each time the start key is pressed, one .012 millisecond storage cycle is taken when the machine is in the *single-cycle process mode*. Console indicating lights display the contents of the OP, I Address, A Address, B Address, A and B registers, and the logic unit.

4. *Single Cycle-Non Process*. This is similar to the single-cycle-process mode, except that no data enters storage from the A register or the logic unit. Data always enters storage from the B register only. This mode permits observing the results of arithmetic operations, one character at a time, in the logic display, without destroying the original B field data.

5. *Character Display*. When the machine is operating in this mode, the start key is pressed to cause the character at the address selected by the manual-address switches to be displayed in the B register.

6. *Storage Print Out*. This mode of operation permits any 100-character block of storage to be printed. The hundreds and thousands manual address switches are used to select the desired block of storage.

Example: 12xx is set in the manual address switches and the start key is pressed. The 100 characters in the selected block 1201-1300 are printed automatically in print positions 1 through 100. Another automatic print cycle causes the word marks for that block to be indicated by printing 1's in their corresponding print positions on the second line. This feature is used to great advantage in program testing, because the contents of a block in core storage is printed and can be easily examined by the programmer. Thus, this feature serves to increase both processing and programming efficiency.

7. *Alter.* The operator can manually change the contents of any address register or storage location if the mode switch is set to ALTER. For example, to change the contents of address registers:

> set the manual address switches at the desired location;
> press the appropriate address register key-light;
> press the START key;
> the selected address register is set with the new address.

To change the contents of a storage location:

> set the manual address switches to the desired location;
> select the bit-structure of the character to be entered, by setting the eight
>   BIT-switches located on the auxiliary console;
> press the ENTER key (also on the auxiliary console).

8. *Storage Scan.* When the mode switch is set to STORAGE SCAN, pressing the start key causes the 1401 to start reading out of storage beginning at the address set in the manual-address switches. If an error condition is detected that had been previously set by an input-output device the machine stops, and the check light with the corresponding unit is turned on; and the location of the card column or print position in error is shown in the storage address display unit. The B-register contains the storage position in which the error was detected, the actual location in storage can be corrected by using the BIT-switches and ENTER key as described under the ALTER mode.

After the error condition is corrected, the MODE switch is again set to STORAGE SCAN and the START key is pressed to cause a read out of storage starting from the address set in the manual address switches. This mode is used as a service aid to insure that all positions of storage are correct.

9. *Address Stop.* When the mode switch is set to ADDRESS STOP, pressing the start key starts the program and the machine stops at the address selected by the manual address switches.

S I X T E E N

A PROBLEM

16.1. INTRODUCTION

Programming is a plan for the solution of a problem. A complete program includes plans for transcription of data, coding for the computer, and plans for the absorption of the results into the system. Programming has been discussed earlier, and the preparation required before the computer can start working on a problem was given preliminary attention. This discussion will assume that a computer has been selected and built. The code for this computer is available and known to the programmer. The computer is functioning properly and computer time is available for the solution of the problem.

The problem for solution is also familiar to the programmer, and he understands the formulas which relate the output to the input information. The form of the data is also known; this includes the range of numbers in both the input and output data, the number of times the routine is repeated as one or more of the parameters in the formulas are varied, the number of significant figures in the input data, and the accuracy required in the solution.

The steps to be taken to solve a problem are now enumerated.

Numerical Solution

A digital computer is only able to perform directly the processes of arithmetic. Any equation or transcendental function must be converted

371

into a numerical approximation. Thus, if the sine of an angle is required somewhere in the problem, an arithmetic method must be used to obtain a trigonometric approximation. The method that you and I use, going to a set of tables, can be incorporated into the computer solution provided enough storage space is available for the computer to "memorize" the function table. Another method that we might use is to expand sin X into a rapidly converging series and substitute the values of X into this expression. This eliminates storing a table within the computer memory but requires the use of a subroutine.

Other problems solved by numerical approximations in this way are differential and integral equations and a variety of transcendental functions.

Analysis into Subproblems

The programmer will find certain sections of a solution, such as finding the sine or the square root of a variable, to be subroutines with which he is familiar. When he recognizes the subroutines, he can consider them as subproblems. This is demonstrated in our sample problem discussed below. Usually the interrelation of certain steps is obvious, and the problem subdivision can follow a natural course.

Layout of Data and Program within the Memory

The number of words of input and output data should be determined as closely as possible. Position of these data in the memory can then be assigned, as long as sufficient space is reserved for the program and certain storage locations are kept free to contain intermediate results and constants.

Flow Chart

The programmer now determines into what subproblems the problem may be divided. He should then know whether subroutines are available for subproblems and where he can locate the subroutines. Each subprogram is flow-charted where a subroutine does not already exist. The flow of information for each section of the problem is laid out in a chart, as previously discussed, and as in the sample problem below. Each of the boxes in the flow chart is assigned a number which is useful when relative coding is done.

Relative coding uses labels to identify storage locations for instructions with respect to their order of appearance in the subroutine, rather than the actual address in memory which will later be assigned to the instruction. Relative coding allows the programmer to refer to data and instructions as operands in the coding before he has determined what their best location is within the memory. This method is demonstrated in the illustrative problem.

Coding

From the flow chart a program can be easily devised, using relative coding.

Integrating the Coding

Once the subproblems have been coded, it is necessary to make a full coding of the problem, working the subproblem codings together. At this point the coding is converted from relative coding to absolute coding. This means that specific addresses in the memory are now assigned to the labels which have been used in the relative coding. At this time break-points are inserted into the coding. A **breakpoint** at one of the steps in the coding will cause the computer to stop there if it is so directed by the operator by means of the control console. The breakpoint allows the operator to obtain intermediate results to see if the solution of the problem is proceeding as planned. A few preliminary results are made by some other method, such as a hand calculator, and these results are compared with the answers the computer produces when it stops at the breakpoint.

Debugging

Now the programming is almost complete. It remains only to be checked. Special simplified data, such as trivial solutions or hand-calculated intermediate answers to one of the sets of actual problems for computer solution, can be used to check out the computer. The data and program codes are entered into the computer memory. The computer is started, and when it comes to a breakpoint, the operator checks the results. If they don't check, the operator and/or the programmer must determine what is wrong. Once the program has been checked out completely in this fashion, the programmer can have confidence in the results for other problem data submitted to the computer.

Running and Interpretation

The set of problems in its entirety is now submitted to the computer. The results obtained may require the placing of titles along the top or side margin or other similar frills, so that the customer can understand the results. Usually the programmer must also examine the results and determine their significance. Unless the customer is a scientist or technician, the interpretation of the results is often left to the programmer.

16.2. ILLUSTRATIVE PROBLEM

To show how these principles are applied, a problem has been chosen which, although fairly simple, requires an analysis following the above description.

The problem is to determine the similarity of certain input waveforms. Suppose that there are 20 of these waveforms labeled X_0 to X_{19}.*

Each of these waveforms is sampled at 18 points. The first sample of the first waveform X_0 is labeled $x_{0,0}$; the second sample is labeled $x_{0,1}$; ... ; the eighteenth sample is labeled $x_{0,17}$.

Similarly, picking X_i as a general waveform, its first sample is labeled $x_{i,0}$, its second is labeled $x_{i,1}$; ... ; its eighteenth sample is labeled $x_{i,17}$. The samples of the waveforms produce a 20×18 matrix, as shown in Figure 16.2.1. The general sample is called $x_{i,a}$, where i is the number of

$i \diagdown a$	0	1	2	... 17
0	$x_{0,0}$	$x_{0,1}$	$x_{0,2}$	... $x_{0,17}$
1	$x_{1,0}$	$x_{1,1}$	$x_{2,2}$	... $x_{1,17}$
2	$x_{2,0}$	$x_{2,1}$	$x_{2,2}$	... $x_{2,17}$
.	.	.	.	.
.	.	.	.	.
.	.	.	.	.
19	$x_{19,0}$	$x_{19,1}$	$x_{19,2}$	... $x_{19,17}$

$i \diagdown j$	0	1	2	... 19
0	$\phi_{0,0}$	$\phi_{0,1}$	$\phi_{0,2}$	... $\phi_{0,19}$
1	$\phi_{1,0}$	$\phi_{1,1}$	$\phi_{1,2}$	... $\phi_{1,19}$
2	$\phi_{2,0}$	$\phi_{2,1}$	$\phi_{2,2}$	... $\phi_{2,19}$
.	.	.	.	.
.	.	.	.	.
.	.	.	.	.
19	$\phi_{19,0}$	$\phi_{19,1}$	$\phi_{19,2}$	... $\phi_{19,19}$

FIGURE 16.2.1. Matrix of sample points of given waveforms.

FIGURE 16.2.2. Matrix of correlation coefficients.

the waveform and a is the number of the sample within that waveform. Let us suppose that the following relationship holds.

$$0 \leqslant |x_{ia}| \leqslant 9.99 \qquad (16.2.1)$$

That is to say, the absolute value of any sample point is less than 10. The

---

* It is often convenient to start the numbering of variables from 0 rather than 1. If the reader will refer to the chapter on coding, he will note that cycling is simple when the initial value of the variable is labeled 0.

correlation coefficient between two waveforms is defined by

$$\phi_{ij} = \frac{\sum\limits_{a=0}^{17} x_{ia}x_{ja}}{\sqrt{\sum\limits_{a=0}^{17} x_{ia}^2 \sum\limits_{a=0}^{17} x_{ja}^2}} \qquad (16.2.2)$$

Here i and j are the numbers of the waveform and a refers to the sample point of each waveform.

The source of (16.2.2) is found in information theory. In the continuous case this would take the form

$$\phi_{ij} = \frac{\int_0^T X_i(t)X_j(t)dt}{\sqrt{\int_0^T X_i^2(t)dt \int_0^T X_j^2(t)dt}} \qquad (16.2.3)$$

The terms in the denominator are the RMS power of the respective waveforms. These are powers needed to normalize these waveforms—the power of each waveform is set equal to unity. The numerator then represents the sum of point products of the waveforms. It can be shown that this is maximum when the X_i and X_j are identical. In that case ϕ_{ii} is 1.

A similar formula arises in statistics where the correlation coefficient of two random variables is called r_{ij} and is defined by

$$r_{ij} = \frac{\sigma_{ij}^2}{\sigma_{ii}\sigma_{jj}} \qquad (16.2.4)$$

where σ_{ij}^2 is the covariance and σ_{ii}^2 and σ_{jj}^2 are the variances with respect to each variable. Upon expansion this is found to be identical with (16.2.2).

The correlation coefficient is a measure of the similarity between two waveforms. When the waveforms correspond exactly with respect to each sample point, the correlation coefficient between them is 1; if the waveforms are mirror images of each other, if each value in one is the negative of the value in the other, the correlation coefficient between them is exactly -1; all other cases result in a correlation coefficient between -1 and $+1$. There is the least similarity between two waveforms when the correlation coefficient between them is 0.

Results

The result of correlating this set of waveforms is a correlation coefficient ϕ_{ij} for every combination of i and j. Since there are 20 i's and 20 j's, there are a total of 400 correlation coefficients. These form a matrix of answers as in Figure 16.2.2. Each of these coefficients is a number between -1 and $+1$. Since the input data is significant to three digits, we cannot expect any greater accuracy in the correlation coefficients.

The problem as stated above makes it clear that the input consists of 360 words and the output consists of 400 words.

16.3. SUBDIVISION OF THE PROBLEM

There are no exponential or transcendental functions encountered in the statement of the problem. The only notable feature is the need to obtain the square root of an expression. Let us assume that this procedure already has been coded as a subroutine and that the coding is readily available to be incorporated into the problem.

In order to facilitate further analysis of the problem, the following simplification is made.

$$y_{ij}^2 = \sum_{a=0}^{17} x_{ia}x_{ja} \tag{16.3.1}$$

and
$$y_{ii} = \sqrt{\sum_{a=0}^{17} x_{ia}x_{ia}} \tag{16.3.2}$$

so that
$$\phi_{ij} = \frac{y_{ij}^2}{y_{ii}y_{jj}} \tag{16.3.3}$$

This notation immediately poses a subdivision to the problem: first, the y_{ij}^2's are calculated; then the square roots of the variables y_{ii}^2 (y_{ij}^2 with

FIGURE 16.3.1. Subdivision of the correlation problem into five major jobs.

$j = i$) are taken to yield y_{ii}; finally, the correlation coefficients are calculated.

The problem then can be divided into five parts as shown in Figure 16.3.1. Here the first and the last parts consist of entering the information and coding into the computer and removing the results from the computer.

We have sufficient information to allocate addresses in memory. This is done, for the most part, arbitrarily. The first computer instruction is best entered at 000 since the computer can be automatically started from this step. The first 200 addresses, 000 to 199, are left for the program, as in Figure 16.3.2. Addresses 200 to 239 are spares. The data occupy posi-

	000 to 099	100 to 199	200 to 299	300 to 399	400 to 499	500 to 599	600 to 699	700 to 799	800 to 899	900 to 999
00's			Spare							
10's										
20's			y_{ii}'s						ϕ's	
30's					x_{ia}'s				Answers	
40's	Program									
50's	and			Data						
60's	Spares									
70's										
80's										
90's										

FIGURE 16.3.2.   Memory map, correlation problem.

tions 240 to 599. The output information, the correlation coefficients, are assigned the spaces 600 to 999.

16.4. MORE INFORMATION ABOUT THE POLYVAC

We are going to do this problem on the Polyvac, so we should learn a few more details about the computer. It is a drum-type computer and the drum rotates at 6000 revolutions per minute. This amounts to 100 revolutions per second, or 10 milliseconds per revolution. The maximum access time for the computer is 10 milliseconds, and the average access time is 5 milliseconds. Let us say that the computer can do an addition in 100 microseconds. Each addition requires the moving of one word, or ten characters. Then each character must be moved in 10 microseconds, so that the character time is 10 microseconds. This requires a basic pulse repetition rate of 100 kilocycles.

The Polyvac has paper tape input and output. Unlike many computers, the Polyvac matches the speed of these devices so that it can accept information at 300 characters per second and punch out information at 300 characters per second. This is well within the state of the art, although the output paper tape punch is more expensive than the input paper tape reader.

More Instructions for the Polyvac*

LOD. In order to load information into the computer, this instruction is given. It may be stated symbolically as

$$\text{LOD:} \quad (PT) \longrightarrow M; \quad (PT) \longrightarrow M + 1; \quad \ldots; \quad (PT) \longrightarrow 999;$$
$$\Rightarrow 000$$

The first complete word is read from the paper tape and inserted into the memory address MMM; the next complete word is read from the paper tape and stored in the succeeding memory address. The process continues until the word read is placed into location 999. After that point no further words are read from paper tape but the next instruction word is taken from the memory address 000 and acted upon.

ULD. To unload information from the memory, the unload order is given.

$$\text{ULD:} \quad (M) \longrightarrow PT; \quad (M + 1) \longrightarrow PT; \quad \ldots; \quad (999) \longrightarrow PT;$$
$$\Rightarrow I + 1$$

The word at address MMM is entered into the paper tape punch and punched onto the paper tape. The words at the succeeding addresses in the memory are punched onto the paper tape similarly. After the word at location 999 is punched onto the paper tape, the computer takes its next instruction from $I + 1$.

RED. This is the instruction to read a single word with the paper tape reader:

$$\text{RED:} \quad (PT) \longrightarrow M$$

The word read from the paper tape is entered into the memory location MMM. The computer takes its next instruction from $I + 1$.

PUN. This order is given to read out or punch a single datum. The word at location MMM is punched into the paper tape and the computer finds its next instruction at $I + 1$.

$$\text{PUN:} \quad (M) \longrightarrow PT$$

Breakpoints

Letters specify the use of one or more characters in the computer instruction word. The computer instruction word now looks like this:

$$\text{PROMMMCB} \times \times$$

where B stands for the breakpoint. It is specified in the form of one of the

*The complete Polyvac code is found in Figure 5.7.

first ten letters of the alphabet. Thus, the Polyvac has ten breakpoints available. The programmer can specify a breakpoint in the program by placing a letter at the position indicated above by B in the instruction word. To use this breakpoint, the operator must throw the breakpoint switch corresponding to the letter in the instruction word. Thus, if the instruction at position 137 is

$$137: \quad ADD \quad 239 \quad 3 \quad A$$

then the computer will stop after completing instruction 137 if the breakpoint switch labeled A has been put in the "on" position by the operator; otherwise, it will disregard the breakpoint letter.

16.5. CORRELATION PROBLEM—FIND y_{ij}^2

For each i and each j there is a y_{ij}^2. Since there are 20 i's and 20 j's, there will be 400 y_{ij}^2's. Remember there are 400 correlation coefficients using the same subscripts. Why not place the y's where the ϕ's will go? These values will then go in one of the storage locations between 600 and 999.

Now, how do we assign a location to y_{ij}^2? Let us start with the very first value, $y_{0,0}^2$, and assign it to the address 600; assign $y_{0,1}^2$ to 601, and so on; then $y_{0,19}^2$ will go into 619. Let us next change i, which was formerly 0, to 1 and place the next values in succeeding locations. Then $y_{1,0}$ goes into 620; $y_{1,1}$ goes into 621, and so on. In general the y_{ij} is assigned to $600 + 20i + j$ so that

$$[y_{ij}] = 600 + 20i + j \tag{16.5.1}$$

At what address is the general x_{ia} stored? Well, the first value, $x_{0,0}$ is assigned to 240; $x_{0,17}$ is found in 257; $x_{1,0}$ is found in 258; and in general

$$[x_{ia}] = 240 + 18i + a \tag{16.5.2}$$

Now that we know where the results and input data are, let us recall the formula relating them (16.3.1), restated here,

$$y_{ij}^2 = \sum_{a=0}^{17} x_{ia} x_{ja} \tag{16.5.3}$$

This is the sum of products. Each product has a fixed i and j and differs only in a. To determine the y_{ij}^2's, we

1. fix i and j and vary a systematically;
2. change j systematically, then varying a again;
3. change i systematically, varying j, then varying a.

Since we have cycle registers available, the variation of a may be made by varying the cycle register. From (16.5.2) it can be seen that varying a varies x_{ia} and x_{ja} simultaneously as desired. If we start with the largest value of a and tally down, we can automatically determine when we have formed the required number of products $x_{ia}x_{ja}$.

We cannot use a cycle register for obtaining the next i or j address because they differ by 18; that is,

$$[x_{i+i,a}] - [x_{i,a}] = 18 = d \tag{16.5.4}$$

This difference, d, of 18, however, can be used to alter i and j by conventional address modification.

Another use of a cycle register is to keep track of the address of the result. If we let

$$b = 20i + j \tag{16.5.5}$$

then $[y_{ij}^2]$ is formed from (16.5.1) by simply adding b to 600. The initial value for b is 0 ($i = 0, j = 0$) and this is established in box 20 of Figure 16.5.1. Setting in this initial value is called **initializing.**

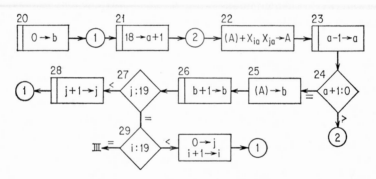

FIGURE 16.5.1. Flow chart of job II: find y_{ij}^2.

Box 21 initializes the cycle index labeled a to 18, because there are 18 different values which a may assume. We are going to form y by working backwards using the last sample of each waveform first. We start with the last sample of the first waveform, $x_{0,17}$ located at 257 and work back to the first sample of the first waveform, $x_{0,0}$ at 240.

The method adds the contents of one of the cycle registers (CY1) to a "fixed" address. "Fixed" is in quotes because it will be modified by the number d discussed above. The first time around, the cycle register is set so that the sum of the fixed address and the cycle index is 257. Just before the cycle index is tallied down to 0, the last product using (240) is formed. Then the *fixed address +1* (the cycle index is 1 before tallying down to 0) must equal 240. Hence, the fixed address is 239. The first value needed is 257, or 239 + 18; hence, the cycle index is initially 18. We knew this before because, since there are 18 sample values, there must be 18 in the cycle index (a rule of thumb).

In box 22 the product of corresponding sample points in two waveforms is added to the sum of the products so far accumulated, and this sum is returned to the A register. In box 23, the a index is tallied down. As long as a is greater than 0, there are more terms to be calculated and added. Box 24 compares a to 0 and loops back via circle 2 to box 22 as long as a is greater than 0. When a is equal to 0, the A register contains the value y_{ij}^2. This value is stored at the b address in box 25, formed by adding b of (16.5.5) to 600. In box 26, b is tallied up to get the *next* address for y_{ij}^2. In box 27, j is compared with 19. If all the possible waveforms have been correlated with *this* waveform (labeled i), if i is now 19, then we proceed to box 29. Otherwise, we can correlate the *next* $(j + 1)$ waveform with *this* (i). Box 28 increases j to $j + 1$.

Box 29 compares the number of this waveform (i) with 19. If they are equal, we are done with this subproblem and go on to subproblem III. Otherwise, in box 30 the index j, which we found to be 19 in box 27, is changed to 0, and the index i is increased by 1.

Coding

In coding this section of the problem, relative coding is done; the complete coding is found in Figure 16.5.2 at the end of the section. Each instruction is numbered according to the box to which it corresponds, rather than the actual location of the instruction in storage. This will be changed when the absolute coding is made up.

First, we initialize b; we set 0 into the cycle register assigned to b, CY2.

Step	PRO	MMM	C	Remarks
20.1	XP2	000		$0 \longrightarrow b$

Next, we set cycle index 1 assigned to a to 18.

21.1	XP1	018		$18 \longrightarrow a + 1$

The next three orders form the partial product. Add it to the partial sum and return the partial sum to A.

22.1	XML	$\underline{239}$	1	$x_{ia} \longrightarrow L$
22.2	MUL	$\underline{239}$	1	$(A) + x_{ia}x_{ja} \longrightarrow L$
22.3	XMA	$\overline{00L}$		$\Sigma\, x_{ia}x_{ja} \longrightarrow A$

Notice that both 239's are underlined. Address modification will be accomplished by actually changing the operand address in the instruction.

This method is required because the address increment in this case is 18 and not 1 and does not lend itself to a simple cycle index method.

Notice that step 22.2 determines the address of x_{ja} by adding (CY1) to 239 the first time; each successive time it is used, the 239 is *adjusted* by adding 18 to get a *new* value of j. In step 22.1 the changes in the operand address are due to the formation of new i values.

Now we tally down the cycle index a and test it to see if the sum of the products is complete—to see if all the a's have been used. If it is not, another product is formed and added by returning to Step 22.1.

Step	PRO	MMM	C	Remarks
23,24	TM1	22.1		$a - 1 \longrightarrow a$

Note that this instruction performs the duties of the two boxes, 23 and 24 and is labeled accordingly. The completed sum is now stored at the b address.

Step	PRO	MMM	C	Remarks
25	XAM	600	2	$y_{ij}^2 \longrightarrow 600 + b$

The b cycle register is increased by 1,

Step	PRO	MMM	C	Remarks
26	TP2	27.1		$b + 1 \longrightarrow b$

Here no decision is required. The next address MMM is filled in as 27.1 so that the next order 27.1 will always be done next.

The j index is checked by taking the command referred to as 22.2 and comparing it with a dummy command stored at [19] to check whether all the values of j have been used. The dummy at [19] will be identical to 22.2 only when $j = 19$.

27.1	XMA	22.2
27.2	CMP	[19] $\Big\}$ $j:19$
27.3	JOE	29.1

If j has not yet reached 19, it is increased by 1 by increasing the operand address in the multiplication order (22.2) by $d = 18$. The next sum of products may then be calculated by returning to Step 22.1.

28.1	ADD	[d]
28.2	XAM	22.2 $\Big\}$ $j + 1 \longrightarrow j$
28.3	UCJ	22.1

If the j values have been exhausted, the i value is next checked. If the i values have been exhausted, this subroutine is completed and we go to III,

29.1	XMA	22.1
29.2	CMP	[19] $\Big\}$ $i:19$
29.3	JOE	III

Otherwise the i value is increased by 1 [adding 18 (d) to the operand address of 22.1].

Step	PRO	MMM	C	Remarks
30.1	ADD	d		$i + 1 \longrightarrow i$
30.2	XAM	22.1		

The j value must also be reset to 0. This is done by replacing the already altered step 22.2 by a prestored copy of the original. We then return to box 21.

Step	PRO	MMM	C	Remarks
30.3	XMA	[New 22.2]		$0 \longrightarrow j$
30.4	XAM	22.2		$\Rightarrow 21.1$
30.5	UCJ	21.1		

This completes the subroutine, presented in full in Figure 16.5.2.

Step	P	R	O	M	M	M	C	Remarks
20.1	X	P	2	0	0	0		$0 \longrightarrow b$
21.1	X	P	1	0	1	8		$18 \longrightarrow a + 1$
22.1	X	M	L	2	3	9	1	$x_{ia} \longrightarrow L$
22.2	M	U	L	$\underline{2}$	$\underline{3}$	$\underline{9}$	1	$(A) + x_{ia}x_{ja} \longrightarrow A$
22.3	X	M	A	$\underline{0}$	$\underline{0}$	$\underline{L}$		
23,24	T	M	1	22.1				$a - 1 \longrightarrow a$
25	X	A	M	6	0	0	2	$y_{ij} \longrightarrow [\phi_{ij}]$
26	T	P	2	27.1				$b + 1 \longrightarrow b$
27.1	X	M	A	22.1				$j:19$
27.2	C	M	P	[19]*				
27.3	J	O	E	29.1				
28.1	A	D	D	[18]***				$j + 1 \longrightarrow j$
28.2	X	A	M	22.2				
28.3	U	C	J	21.1				
29.1	X	M	A	22.1				$i:19$
29.2	C	M	P	[19]**				
29.3	J	O	E	III				
30.1	A	D	D	[18]***				$i + 1 \longrightarrow i$
30.2	X	A	M	22.1				
30.3	X	M	A	[New 22.2]				$0 \longrightarrow j$
30.4	X	A	M	22.2				
30.5	U	C	J	22.1				

These dummies are different

*M U	L	5	7	9	1	0	0	0
**X M	L	5	7	9	1	0	0	0
***0 0	0	0	1	8	0	0	0	0

FIGURE 16.5.2.   Subprogram to find y_{ij}^{2} (II).

16.6. THE SQUARE ROOT SUBROUTINE

This section is not devoted to discussing the square root subroutine itself, but rather how access may be gained to a subroutine from any given point in a program.

The values for which the square root must be found are the 20 y_{ii}^2's. The flow chart for doing this is found in Figure 16.6.1. In box 40 the

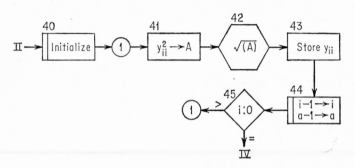

FIGURE 16.6.1.   Flow chart of job III of the correlation problem.

i index is initialized so that $y_{19,19}$ is called for first. In box 41 the quantity for which the square root is to be found, y_{ii}^2, is obtained from the memory and placed into the A register. Box 42 is the square root subroutine. Box 43 stores the square root in the assigned working storage location. Box 44 decreases the cycle index i by 1. Box 45 checks the cycle index i; if all the values y_{ii} have not yet been found, return to box 41 via circle 1.

Each of the answers obtained by taking the square root is stored at the working storage location allocated as

$$[y_{ii}] = 220 + i \qquad (16.6.1)$$

The addresses of the values for which the square root is to be found are given by

$$y_{ii}^2 = 600 + 20i + i = 600 + 21i \qquad (16.6.2)$$

These addresses differ by 21. Successive operands are found by subtracting 21 from the previous operand address in order to procure the next number y_{ii}^2. We start with $y_{19,19}^2$ which is found at 999; the next square root operand, $y_{18,18}$, is found at $999 - 21 = 978$, and so forth.

Coding

The operand address is to be found using (16.6.2). We wish to start with the operand at 999. We find successive operands by successive subtractions of 21. This is stated as

$$[y_{ii}] = 999 - f(19 - i) \qquad (16.6.3)$$

where $f = 21$, or

$$[y_{ii}] = 600 + e - f(19 - i) \qquad (16.6.4)$$

where $e = 399$.

We can get $600 + e$ by storing e in a cycle register and adding it to a command with operand address 600. To get the next operand, subtract f from the cycle register before using.

Successive addresses of y_{ii} differ by 1 so that they can be found by tallying down a cycle index.

The i is kept track of in cycle register 1; the operand increment f ($= 21$) is stored in cycle register 2; the augmented address modifier e is stored in cycle register 3. Then to initialize we have

Step	PRO	MMM	C	Remarks
40.1	XP1	020		$20 \longrightarrow i$
40.2	XP2	021		$21 \longrightarrow f$
40.3	XP3	399		$399 \longrightarrow e$

The value for which the square root is to be taken is entered into the A register.

| 41.1 | XMA | 600 | 3 | $y_{ii}^2 \longrightarrow$ A |

Preparation is made to return to this step in the program by storing the address to which return must be made when the subroutine is completed in cycle register 4.

| 41.2 | XP4 | 43.1 | | $43.1 \longrightarrow$ CY4 |

Now we jump to the square root subroutine which is stored in steps 42.1 to 42.19, say,

| 41.3 | UCJ | 42.1 | | $\Rightarrow \sqrt{}$ |

The last step after the step in the square root subroutine is set up so that a return is made to the proper point in the current routine to pick up where we left off,

| 42.20 | UCJ | 000 | 4 | $\Rightarrow 43.1$ |

The square root is in the A register. It is to be transferred to one of the locations 220 to 239. The proper location is obtained by adding the contents of the cycle register 1 to 219,

| 43.1 | XAM | 219 | 1 | $y_{ii} \longrightarrow [y_{ii}]$ |

The address of the next value for which the square root is to be found is determined by subtracting f from e, which is in cycle register 3. This requires three steps.

Step	PRO	MMM	C		Remarks
44.1	XMA	CY3	$e \longrightarrow$ A		
44.2	SUB	CY2	$e - f \longrightarrow$ A	$\left.\begin{array}{c} \\ \\ \\ \end{array}\right\}$	$e - f \longrightarrow e$
44.3	XAM	CY3	(A) $\longrightarrow$ CY3		

Now we tally down; and at the same time we check to determine if all the square roots have been taken; if not, we return to step 41.1.

45	TMI	41.1	$i + 1 \longrightarrow i$

The access subroutine for the square root subroutine appears below in Figure 16.6.2.

Step	P R O	M M M C	Remarks
40.1	X P 1	0 2 0	$20 \longrightarrow i$
40.2	X P 2	0 2 1	$21 \longrightarrow f$
40.3	X P 3	3 9 9	$399 \longrightarrow e$
41.1	X M A 6	0 0 3	$y_{ii}^2 \longrightarrow$ A
41.2	X C A	43.1	[43.1] $\longrightarrow$ CY4
41.3	U C J	42.1	$\Rightarrow \sqrt{\;}$
42.1			
...	$\left.\begin{array}{c} \\ \\ \end{array}\right\} \sqrt{\;}$		
42.20	U C J	0 0 0 4	$\Rightarrow 43.1$
43.1	X A M 2	1 9 1	$y_{ii} \longrightarrow [y_{ii}]$
44.1	X M A	C Y 3	$\left.\begin{array}{c} \\ \\ \\ \end{array}\right\} e - f \longrightarrow e$
44.2	S U B	C Y 2	
44.3	X A M	C Y 3	
45	T M 1	41.1	$i - 1 \longrightarrow i$
	IV		

FIGURE 16.6.2.   Coding, Part III, correlation problem.

16.7. CALCULATION OF THE PHI'S

The phi's are determined by the formula (16.3.3).

$$\phi_{ij} = \frac{y_{ij}^2}{y_{ii}^2 y_{jj}^2}$$

Flow Chart

The first task is to get a sequence in which to find the ϕ's. Tallying down is our best bet. We start with the largest values of i and j; after each value of ϕ is found, we reduce j by 1, holding i fixed; j is reduced until it becomes 0. We start on another set of ϕ's by reducing i by 1 and using the largest value of j; this requires that j be restored; we then begin reducing j again. We are done when i is reduced to 0.

The place from which y_{ij}^2 is obtained and to which the corresponding ϕ is returned is to be found. The address to be used first for $y_{19,19}^2$ is 999; successive addresses are obtained by subtracting 1. The address of the ϕ's is in the form

$$\phi_{ij} = B + b \qquad (16.7.1)$$

where B is a constant and b is successively reduced by 1.

The flow chart for this is found in Figure 16.7.1. Box 60 is for initializing. In box 61 the product $y_{ii}y_{jj}$ is formed. In box 62 the product formed

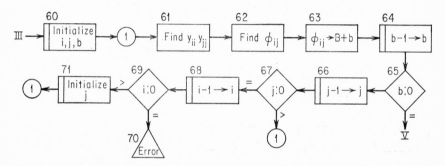

FIGURE 16.7.1.   Flow chart of job IV of the correlation problem.

in box 61 is divided into the corresponding y^2 value, y_{ij}^2, forming ϕ. This value is stored at the address labeled $B + b$ in box 63. The b index is tallied down in box 64 and compared to 0 in box 65. If b is 0, all the ϕ's have been calculated and we go to subroutine V. Otherwise, the j index is reduced by 1, box 66, and checked to see if it has reached zero in box 67. If not, the new ϕ value is found by re-entering box 61. When j is equal to 0, the i index must be reduced by 1 in box 68 and it is compared with 0 as a double check in box 69. If it is equal to 0, an error has been made and the machine stops—box 70. Otherwise, the j index must be reset to 20, box 71, and return made to box 61.

Coding

The coding for part IV is presented in Figure 16.7.2. The reader should now be able to follow the coding with the help of the remarks in the column so headed and with the aid of a few additional notes.

The stumbling blocks to beware of are the initializing and the setting of the operand addresses to be modified. There are 20 each of i and j values and a total of 400 b values; the operand addresses in steps 61.1

Step	P	R	O	M	M	M	C	Remarks
60.1	X	P	1	4	0	0		$400 \longrightarrow b$
60.2	X	P	2	0	2	0		$19 \longrightarrow i$
60.3, 70	X	P	3	0	2	0		$19 \longrightarrow j$
61.1	X	M	L	2	1	9	2	$y_{ii} \longrightarrow L$
61.2	M	U	L	2	1	9	3	$y_{ii}y_{jj} \longrightarrow L$
62.1	X	M	A	5	9	9	1	$y_{ij}^2 \longrightarrow A$
62.2	D	I	V	O	O	L		$\phi_{ij} \longrightarrow Q$
63.1	X	Q	M	5	9	9	1	$\phi_{ij} \longrightarrow B + b$
64, 65	T	M	1	66.0				$b - 1 \longrightarrow b$
		V						
66, 67	T	M	3	61.1				$j - 1 \longrightarrow j$
68, 69	T	M	2	60.3				$i - 1 \longrightarrow i$
71	S	T	P	—				$i = 0$

FIGURE 16.7.2.   Coding, Part IV, correlation problem.

and 61.2 are found by subtracting 20 from $[y_{19,19}]$; that used in both 62.1 and 63.1 is found by subtracting 400 from $[y_{19,19}^2]$.

16.8.   ENTERING AND REMOVING INFORMATION FROM THE COMPUTER

Loading the Computer (I)

The content of the memory has been laid out earlier in Section 16.3. The entire content of the memory, since it is known, is entered into paper tape by a typist from the copy given her by the programmer. The full 1000 words must then be entered from the paper tape into the computer memory.

The paper tape is placed in reading position in the paper tape reader. The operator then sets an order into the control register by means of the operator's console. The order he enters there is

LOD   000

This order causes all the information to be read from the tape into the memory. The computer will then choose its next instruction from the address 000.

Unloading the Computer (*V*)

After the results have been stored in the output section of the memory, one simple order will transfer all the results into punched paper tape. This order is

ULD   600

Reloading the Computer

It is possible to enter a new set of data for calculation by following the unload order by another load order which will cause further information to be entered from paper tape, beginning with the first datum location, 240; the computer will start again from the initial location 000. This is done by placing the new data tape into the input unit and entering on the console the order

LOD   240

16.9. FULL ROUTINE

We shall now take the five subroutines of the problem just devised and integrate them into one coded routine. In so doing, the relative coding is replaced by absolute coding.

The original loading order, as mentioned in Section 16.8 will be entered into the console and is not part of the coding. The first order to be performed by the computer, located at the address 000, is the first order of subroutine II.

The coding of the full routine appears as Figure 16.9. The first steps are a duplicate of those of Figure 16.5.2. The difference is that the location numbers are now absolute; the first one is at 000. Notice that the operand locations can now be filled in while the program is being written in absolute form. Let's examine the first occurrence of this process. Step 005 in the full coding requires that an absolute address be used for its operand. Examining Figure 16.5.2, we notice that this step, which is numbered 23,24, uses as an operand the step numbered 22.1. Its absolute address is determined by returning to Figure 16.9, where we find that the order originally called step 22.1 is here called step 003. All operand locations relatively coded are converted in this manner. When the address called for is one not yet coded, we leave it blank. When the last coding step has been noted, we can return and fill in the blanks.

In Figure 16.5.2, step 27.2, comparison is made and the operand for this comparison is a dummy. The dummy is listed next to the asterisk in that figure. A location has not been assigned to it. We shall work back-

Step	P R O	M M M	CY	BP	Remarks
000	X P 2	0 0 0			$0 \rightarrow b$
001	X P 1	0 1 8	1		$17 \rightarrow a$
002	X M L	2 3 9	1		$x_{ia} \rightarrow L$
003	M U L	2 3 9			$\Big\{\ (A) + x_{ia}x_{ia}$
004	X M A	L 0 0		A	$\rightarrow A$
005	T M 1	0 0 3			$a - 1 \rightarrow a$
006	X A M	6 0 0	1		$y^2_{ij}\ [\phi_{ij}]$
007	T P 2	0 0 8			$b + 1 \rightarrow b$
008	X M A	0 0 4			
009	C M P	2 1 9			$j : 19$
010	J O E	0 1 4			
011	A D D	2 1 8			$j + 1 \rightarrow j$
012	X A M	0 0 4			
013	U C J	0 0 3			
014	X M A	0 0 3			$i : 19$
015	C M P	2 1 7			
016	J O E	0 2 2			
017	A D D	2 1 8			$i + 1 \rightarrow i$
018	X A M	0 0 3			
019	X A M	2 1 6			
020	U C J	0 0 4			$0 \rightarrow j$
021	X P 1	0 0 3			
022	X P 2	0 2 0			$\Big\}$ Initialize
023	X P 3	0 2 1			
024	X M A	3 9 9			
025	X P 4	6 0 0	3		$y^2_{ii} \rightarrow A$
026	U C J	0 2 8			$\Big\}$ Loop to $\sqrt{\ }$
027	X A M	1 8 0			
028	X A M	2 1 9			Store y_{ii}
029	X M A	C Y 3	1		
030	S U B	C Y 2		B	$\Big\}$ $e - f \rightarrow e$
031	X A M	C Y 3			
032	T M 1	0 0 2			$i - 1 \rightarrow i$
033	X P 1	4 0 0			$400 \rightarrow b$
034	X P 2	0 2 0			$19 \rightarrow i$
035	X P 3	0 2 0			$19 \rightarrow j$
036	X M L	2 1 9	2		$x_{ii} \rightarrow L$
037	M U L	2 1 9	3		$x_{ii}x_{ij} \rightarrow L$
038	X M A	5 9 9	1		$y^2_{ij} \rightarrow A$
039	D I V	0 0 L		C	$\phi_{ij} \rightarrow Q$
040	X Q M	5 9 9	1		$\phi_{ij} \rightarrow B + b$
041	T M 1	0 4 5			$b - 1 \rightarrow b$
042	U N D	6 0 0			$\Big\}$ Stop and unload
043	S T P	0 4 4			
044	L O D	2 4 0			Reload
045	T M 3	0 3 6			$j - 1 \rightarrow j$
046	T M 2	0 3 6			$i - 1 \rightarrow i$
047	S T P	0 0 0			Error stop
		Words of 0's to 179			
180 to 199		$\Big\}$ Square Root Coding			
		Words of 0's to 215			
216	M U L	2 3 9	1000		New Order 003
217	X M L	5 7 9	1000		Dummy [19]
218	0 0 0	0 1 8	0000		Tally [18]
219	M U L	5 7 9	1000		Dummy [19]

wards within the spare locations and assign location 219 to this dummy. In the final coding step 009 specifies 219 as its operand for this reason. In a similar manner, the operand in step 015 is specified as 218.

As in Figure 16.5.2, step 29.3 requires a jump-on-equal to III. The operand address of subroutine III is left blank until its place in the absolute program is determined. The second subsection of the problem can be entered in the first 22 locations of memory which ends with location 021. Therefore, the third subsection of the problem will start at step 022. As we start the third subsection, the location 022 can be entered in the blank space of step 016.

The coding continues, now using the steps of Figure 16.6.2.

The next novel situation encountered occurs when the square root routine is called for. Let us assume that the steps for this routine, previously available, can be stored in the locations 180 to 198. When we reach step 027, the location to which the jump should be made is 180. The step to which we wish to return after using the square root routine is that which is after 027, and hence the number is 028. This is the number to be entered into cycle register 4, step 026. Notice that the step following the square root routine, numbered 199, specifies a jump to 000 plus the content of the cycle register. This will cause a return to the main routine at step 028.

The fourth subsection of the program is added in final coding form by simple substitutions using the coding of Figure 16.7.2 as a basis. When unloading is called for, it is specified at step 042 as discussed in the last section. Notice that a stop is called for at step 043 and that the operand address for the stop is 044. This means that if the restart button is pressed, the computer will begin with step 044. Step 044 is a load order. It will load the computer from the punched paper tape input, starting at position 240. This position is where the first input datum is stored. Thus the program will remain untouched and new data will be entered into the computer to be worked on. After the computer is loaded, it will take its next instruction from location 000. This procedure obviates the need for rewriting the program each time new data is to be run.

Breakpoints

One more item which is included in the final program is the breakpoint designation. The first breakpoint appears at step 006. It causes the computer to stop after the first value for y_{ij}^2 has been found and stored. This is the first point at which the programmer can check functioning of his program. The first time around the operator will find $y_{0,0}^2$ in the A register after this order.

The next breakpoint is at step 028, just after y_{ii} has been stored. The first time around, the value of $y_{0,0}$ will be found in the A register, thus providing the second check on the program. If desired y_{ii} may be checked for all values of i at this breakpoint.

The third breakpoint at step 039 occurs after the first answer is obtained. The first time around, this is $\phi_{0,0}$ which should be 1, as the reader can check for himself. Further breakpoints may be added if difficulty should arise in checking out the program.

16.10. PREPARATION AND RUNNING OF THE PROBLEM

Copy Preparation

The final coding of Figure 16.9 is translated for the typist into hard copy, which also includes the input data. Typical copy will appear as in Figure 16.10. In that figure no step number or location need accompany the coding. In fact, it must *not* be present. The copy will be read one word at a time in order into successive memory locations. On the other hand, zeros have been added where previously they were not required in the final coding. This is because each word must have ten characters. If characters are lacking from *this* word, part of the *next* word would be read as belonging to this word.

Notice also that where there are words missing in the program, such as between step 48 and step 180, words or zeros must be filled in. This is for the same reason—if words are omitted, consecutive words on the tape will occupy consecutive positions in the memory. The 220th word of the hard copy is the first word of the input data. Data words are visually distinguished by the presence of a sign in the left-hand position. Notice again that all the words from 600 on consist of ten characters, or zeros. The tape typist receives 1000 words of ten characters each to type. The input tape of 1000 words is prepared from this hard copy.

Running the Problem

After the paper tape has been punched and when time is available on the computer, the tape is loaded into the paper tape reader. The proper switches on the computer are set so that it is supplied with full power and ready to go. The load instruction is entered into the control register. The breakpoint switch is set to A. The start button is pressed.

The computer takes off, and when the first breakpoint answer is ready, it stops. The operator checks the answer with that produced by a hand calculation. If the answer is wrong, he must set about checking his program. He sets the operation switch on the operator's console to one-step operation. He presses the start-at-zero button and examines the content of each register as each step is performed at his instigation. Further

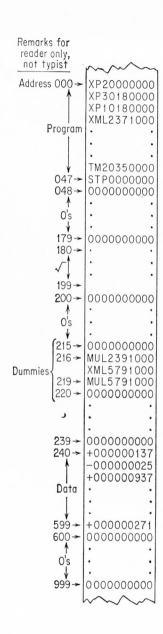

FIGURE 16.10.   Copy for typist, correlation problem.

details of the debugging process can only be gained through experience. Each program has its own eccentricities.

Once the program is checked out, all the breakpoint switches are turned off and the program is run from the beginning. The paper tape punch will start operating as a finale to the program. The paper tape thus produced is entered into the output equipment—in this case a tape-reading typewriter. The typewriter will print out columns of 10-digit numbers. The operator labels these columns to coincide with the answers.

It is usually the job of the programmer to interpret the results. In this case he would examine each of the correlation coefficients to determine which of these was equal to or close to 1 in value. These would indicate waveforms which were similar. Naturally, the correlation coefficient between a waveform and itself should be 1. Hence he would disregard these correlation coefficients, using them only as a check of the authenticity of the program.

PROBLEMS

1. Using the coding of Problem 4 of Chapter 5, write a relative coding for the square root by the Newton-Raphson method. Incorporate this into the routine of Figure 16.9.
2. Start with a table of 100 values of Y, where $Y_i = Y(X_i)$ with the X_i at uniform intervals. Given 75 X_j's set up a program to interpolate to find the Y_j's and then the Z_j's where

$$Z = A_n Y^n + A_{n-1} Y^{n-1} + \ldots + A_1 Y + A_0$$

with $n = 11$. Lay out the complete program together with a special print-out when X_j lies outside the range of the table. Include the in/out procedures.
3. Look up the formula for the solution of a cubic equation. Use for an iteration formula for the cube root

$$Z_{i+1} = Z_i + \frac{1}{3}\left(\frac{X}{Z_i^2} - Z_i\right)$$

Make up a complete program for the solution of sixty cubics.
4. Devise a complete statistical program so that, given corresponding values of two variables as X_i and Y_i, it will find

$$\bar{X} = \frac{\Sigma X_i}{N} \qquad \bar{Y} = \frac{\Sigma Y_i}{N}$$

$$\mu_1 = \frac{\Sigma X_i^2}{N} \qquad \mu_2 = \frac{\Sigma Y_i^2}{N} \qquad \mu_{12} = \Sigma X_i Y_i/N$$

$$\sigma_1 = \sqrt{\mu_1 - \bar{X}^2} \qquad \sigma_2 = \sqrt{\mu_2 - \bar{Y}^2} \qquad \sigma_{12} = \sqrt{\mu_{12} - \bar{X}\bar{Y}}$$

$$\rho = \frac{\sigma_{12}^2}{\sigma_1 \sigma_2}$$

APPENDIX A

GLOSSARY

This glossary was compiled from several current glossaries. Many definitions were added by the author, most of which apply to words defined in the text but missing from the other glossaries. A number of definitions from other glossaries were "adapted." This is my way of saying that I have changed a few words here and there to make the definition read, in my way of thinking, a little more smoothly or accurately.

Each definition is followed by a parenthetical letter indicating its source. These are listed below. When any major change was made, the author takes the full blame; where just a word or two are changed, it is not noted and the original source is given.

DEFINITION SOURCES

A. "Glossary of Computer Engineering and Programming Terminology," Aberdeen Proving Grounds, BRL Report No. 1010. This appeared in several installments in issues of the *Communications of the Association for Computing Machinery* during 1958. It incorporates many definitions from other assorted glossaries.

C. "Glossary of Terms in the Field of Computers and Automation," *Computers and Automation*, October 1958.

I. "IRE Standards on Computers," *Proceedings of the IRE*, September 1956. This is a small list and is for the most part included in (A) and (C) above.

M. "IRE Standards on Static Magnetic Storage: Definitions of Terms 1959," *Proceedings of the IRE*, March 1959.

F. The author's definitions or the author's changes of other definitions.

A

-ac. A suffix meaning "automatic computer," as in Eniac, Seac, Polyvac. (F)

access, arbitrary. Access to storage under conditions in which the next position from which information is to be obtained is in no way dependent on the previous one. (A)

access, random. See *access, arbitrary*.

access time. The time interval between the instant at which the arithmetic unit calls for information from the memory unit and the instant at which the information is delivered from storage to the arithmetic unit. The time interval between the instant at which the arithmetic unit starts to send information to the memory unit and the instant at which the storage of the information in the memory unit is completed. In analog computers, the value at time t of each dependent variable represented in the problem is usually immediately accessible when the value of the independent variable is at time t, and otherwise not accessible. (C)

accumulator. The register and associated equipment in the arithmetic unit in which are formed sums and other arithmetical and logical results; a unit in a digital computer where numbers are totaled, i.e., accumulated. Often the accumulator stores one quantity and upon receipt of any second quantity, it forms and stores the sum of the first and second quantities. (A)

accuracy. Freedom from error. Accuracy contrasts with precision; e.g., a four-place table, correctly computed, is accurate; a six-place table containing an error is more precise, but not accurate. (A)

adder. A device capable of forming the sum of two or more quantities. (A)

adder, full. A functional unit which produces outputs corresponding to the sum and carry of binary addition for inputs corresponding to the addend, augend carry-in bits. (F)

address. A set of characters which identifies either a register, a location in storage, or a device in which information is stored; a label, usually in the form of numerical coordinates. (F)

address, absolute. The label(s) assigned by the machine designer to a particular storage location; specific address.

address part. In an instruction code the part that specifies an address. See *code, instruction*. (F)

address, relative. A label used to identify a word in a routine or subroutine with respect to its position in that routine or subroutine. Relative addresses are translated into absolute addresses by the addition of some specific "reference" address, usually that at which the first word of the routine is stored; e.g., if a relative address instruction specifies an address and the address of the first word of the routine is k, then the absolute address is $n + k$. (A)

address, symbolic. A label chosen to identify a particular word, function, or other information in a routine, independent of the location of the information within the routine; floating address. (A)

allocate. To assign storage locations to the main routines and subroutines, thereby fixing the absolute values of any symbolic addresses. In some cases allocation may require segmentation. (A)

amplifier. A device for increasing the amplitude of electric waves by the control exercised by the input over the power supplied to the output of the amplifier. See also *amplifier, buffer* and *amplifier, torque.* (C)

amplifier, buffer. An amplifier used to isolate the output of any device, e.g., oscillator, from the effects produced by changes in voltage or loading in subsequent circuits. (A)

amplifier, torque. A device which produces an output turning moment in proportion to the input moment, wherein the output moment and associated power is supplied by the device, and the device requires an input moment and power smaller than the output moment and power. (A)

analog. The representation of numerical quantities by means of physical variables, e.g., translation, rotation, voltage, resistance; contrasted with "digital." (A)

analyzer, differential. An analog computer designed and used primarily for solving differential equations. (A)

and. A logical operator which has the property that for two statements P and Q, the statement "P and Q" is true or false according to the following table:

P	Q	P and Q
false	false	false
false	true	false
true	false	false
true	true	true

The *and* operator is represented by a centered dot ($\cdot$), or by no sign as in $P \cdot Q$ or PQ. (A)

and-gate. See *gate.*

arithmetic unit. That portion of the hardware of an automatic computer in which arithmetical and editing operations are performed. (A)

assemble. To integrate subroutines (supplied, selected, or generated) into the main routine, by adapting, or specializing to the task at hand by means of preset parameters, by adapting, or changing relative and symbolic addresses to absolute form, or incorporating, or placing in storage. (A)

asynchronous. See *computer, asynchronous.*

attenuate. To obtain a fractional part or reduce in amplitude an action or signal. (A)

automatic controller. A device which controls a process by (1) automatically receiving measurements of one or more physical variables of the process, (2) automatically performing a calculation, and (3) automatically issuing suitably varied actions, such as the relative movement of a valve, so that the process is controlled as desired; for example, a flyball governor on a steam engine; an automatic pilot. (C)

automation. Process or result of rendering machines self-acting or self-moving; rendering automatic. Theory, art, or technique of making a device, machine, or an industrial process more automatic. Making automatic the process of moving pieces of work from one machine tool to the next. (C)

B

base. A number base; a quantity used implicitly to define some system of representing numbers by positional notation; radix. (A)

beam, holding. A diffused beam of electrons used for regenerating the charges stored on the screen of a cathode ray storage tube. (A)

bias. The average d-c voltage maintained between the cathode and control grid of a vacuum tube. (A)

binary. A characteristic or property involving a selection, choice, or condition in which there are but two alternatives. (A)

binary-coded decimal notation. One of many systems of writing numbers in which each decimal digit of the number is expressed by a different code written in binary digits. For example, the decimal digit 0 may be represented by the code 0011, the decimal digit 1 may be represented by the code 0100, etc. (C)

binary digit. A digit in the binary scale of notation. This digit may be only 0 (zero) or 1 (one). It is equivalent to an "on" condition or an "off" condition, a "yes" or a "no," etc. (C)

binary notation. The writing of numbers in the scale of two. The first dozen numbers zero to eleven are written 0, 1, 10, 11, 100, 101, 110, 111, 1000, 1001, 1010, 1011. The positions of the digits designate powers of two; thus 1010 means 1 times two cubed or eight, 0 times two squared or four, 1 times two to the first power or two, and 0 times two to the zero power or one; this is equal to one eight plus no fours plus one two plus no ones, which is ten. (C) Also called natural binary. (F)

binary number. A number written in binary notation. (C)

binary point. In a binary number, the point which marks the place between integral powers of two and fractional powers of two, analogous to the decimal point in a decimal number. Thus, 10.101 means four, one half, and one eighth. (C)

binary-to-decimal conversion. Converting a number written in binary notation to one written in decimal notation. (C)

biquinary notation. A scale of notation in which the base is alternately 2 and 5. For example, the number 3671 in decimal notation is 03 11 12 01 in biquinary notation; the first of each pair of digits counts 0 or 1 units of five, and the second counts 0, 1, 2, 3, or 4 units. For comparison, the same number in Roman numerals is MMMDCLXXI. Biquinary notation expresses the representation of numbers by the abacus, and by the two hands and five fingers of man; and has been used in some automatic computers. (C)

bit. A binary digit; a smallest unit of information; a "yes" or a "no"; a single pulse position in a group of possible pulse positions. (F)

block. A group of consecutive machine words considered or transferred as a unit, particularly with reference to input and output. In a programming flow chart, an assembly of boxes, each box representing a logical unit of computer programming (see "box"). (C)

bobbin core. See *tape-wound core.*

Boolean algebra. An algebra dealing with classes, propositions, on-off circuit elements, etc., associated by operators AND, OR, NOT, EXCEPT, IF ... THEN, etc. (C)

Boolean calculus. Boolean algebra modified to include time, thereby providing an algebra or calculus for: states and events; additional operators such as AFTER, WHILE, HAPPEN, DELAY, BEFORE; classes whose members change over time; circuit elements whose on-off state changes from time to time such as delay lines, flip-flops, and sequential circuits; so-called step-functions, and their combinations, etc. (C)

Boolean function. A mathematical function in Boolean algebra; examples of common functions are $c = a$ OR $b = a \lor b$, $c = a$ AND $b = a \cdot b$, $c =$ NOT-$a = a'$, $c = a$ EXCEPT $b = a \cdot b'$, $c =$ NEITHER a NOR $b = a' \cdot b'$. (C)

bootstrap. In a programming flow chart, a logical unit of computer programming surrounded by a rectangle and treated as a unit. Often identified by requiring transfer of the instructions referred to therein into and out of the rapid memory of the computer. (C)

breakpoint. A point in a routine at which the computer, under the control of a manually set switch, will stop for an operator's check of the progress of the routine. (C)

branch. See *conditional jump*.

buffer. Storage between the input/output equipment and the computer where information is assembled in easily absorbed units: storage between the main memory and the computer where information is rapidly accessible. (F)

bus. A path over which information is transferred, from any of several sources to any of several destinations. An electrical conductor capable of carrying a large current; a trunk; a heavy wire, line, or lead. (C)

C

call in. To transfer control of a digital computer temporarily from a main routine to a subroutine, which is inserted in the sequence of calculating operations temporarily to fulfill a subsidiary purpose. (C)

call number. A set of characters identifying a subroutine, and containing information concerning parameters to be inserted in the subroutine, or information to be used in generating the subroutine, or information related to the operands. (C)

call word. A call-number which fills exactly one machine word. (C)

capacity. The number of digits or characters which may regularly be processed in a computer, as in "the capacity is ten decimal digit numbers." The upper and lower limits of the numbers which may regularly be handled in a computer, as "the capacity of the computer is $+.00000\ 00001$ to $.99999\ 99999$." Quantities which are beyond the capacity of the computer usually interrupt its operation in some way. (C)

capstan. The rotating shaft on a magnetic tape recording and/or reading device which is used to impart uniform motion to the magnetic tape on command. (F)

card. A document of constant size, thickness, and shape adapted for punching in a pattern which has meaning. The punched holes are sensed electrically by wire brushes, mechanically by metal fingers, or photoelectrically. Also called "punch card." Punch cards are $7\frac{3}{8}''$ long and $3\frac{1}{4}''$ wide and contain 80 or 90 columns in each of which any one or more of several hole sites may be punched. (F)

card column. One of a number of columns (45, 80, or 90) in a punch card into which information is entered by punches. (C)

card feed. A mechanism which moves cards one by one into a machine. (C)

card field. A set of card columns fixed as to number and position, into which the same item of information is regularly entered; for example, purchase order numbers of five decimal digits might be punched regularly into the card field consisting of card columns 11 to 15. (C)

card punch. A mechanism which punches cards, or a machine which punches cards according to a program. (C)

card reader. A mechanism that causes the information in punch cards to be read, usually by passing them under copper wire brushes or across metal fingers. (C)

card stacker. A mechanism that stacks cards in a pocket or bin after they have passed through a machine. Sometimes called "card hopper." (C)

carriage, automatic. A typewriting paper guiding or holding device which is automatically controlled by a program so as to feed forms or continuous paper to a set of impression keys and to provide the necessary space, skip, eject, tabulate, and other operations. (C)

carry. A signal or expression, produced as a result of an arithmetic operation on one digit place of two or more numbers expressed in Positional Notation and transferred to the next higher place for processing there. A signal or expression as defined in (1) above which arises in adding, when the sum of two digits in the same digit place equals or exceeds the base of the number system in use. If a carry into a digit place will result in a carry-out of the same digit place, and if the normal adding circuit is bypassed when generating this new carry, it is called a High-Speed Carry, or *Standing-on-Nines Carry*. If the normal adding circuit is used in such a case, the carry is called a *Cascaded Carry*. If a carry resulting from the addition of carries *is not* allowed to propagate (e.g., when forming the partial product in one step of a multiplication process) the process is called a *Partial Carry*. If it *is* allowed to propagate the process is called a *Complete Carry*. If a carry generated in the most significant digit place is sent directly to the least significant place (e.g., when subtracting numbers using 9's complements addition), that carry is called *End-Around Carry*. In direct subtraction, a signal or expression as defined in (1) above which arises when the difference between the digits is less than zero. Such a carry is frequently called a *Borrow*. The action of forwarding a carry. The command directing a carry to be forwarded. (A)

cascade control. An automatic control system in which control units are associated in a sequence, where each control unit regulates the operation of the next control unit in the sequence. (C)

cathode ray tube. A large electronic vacuum tube with a screen for visual plot or display of output in graphic form by means of a proportionally deflected beam of electrons. A large electronic vacuum tube containing a screen on which information, expressed in pulses in a beam of electrons from the cathode, is stored by means of the presence or absence of spots bearing electrostatic charges. This capacity usually is from 256 to 1024 spots. (C)

cell. Storage for one unit of information, as one bit, one character, or one machine word. More specific terms ("column, location, block") are preferable since there is little uniformity in the use of the term "cell." (C)

centralized control. A computer for which all processing is controlled by a single operational unit is said to have *centralized control*. Otherwise, the computer has *decentralized control*, in which case requests for processing are issued by the *main control unit* to *auxiliary control units*, each of which assumes control of a portion of the processing and surrenders control to the main unit on completion of the auxiliary task. (F)

channel. See *drum, magnetic storage.*

character. A decimal digit 0 to 9, or a letter A to Z, either capital or lower case, or a punctuation symbol, or any other single symbol (such as appear on the keys of a typewriter) which a machine may take in, store, or put out. Representation of such a symbol in a pattern of ones and zeros representing a pattern of positive and negative pulses or states is called a *character code.* (C)

check. A means of verification of information. (A)

check, built-in or automatic. Any provision constructed in hardware for verifying the accuracy of information transmitted, manipulated, or stored by any unit or device in a computer. Extent of automatic checking is the relative proportion of machine processes which are checked or the relative proportion of machine hardware devoted to checking. (A)

check, duplication. A check which requires that the results of two independent performances (either concurrently on duplicate equipment or at a later time on the same equipment) of the same operation be identical. (A)

check, forbidden combination. A check (usually an automatic check) which tests for the occurrence of a non-permissible code expression. A *self-checking code* (or error-detecting code) uses code expressions such that one (or more) error(s) in a code expression produces a forbidden combination. A *parity check* makes use of a self-checking code employing binary digits in which the total number of ones (or zeros) in each permissible code expression is always even or always odd. A check may be made for either even parity or odd parity. A *redundant check* employs a self-checking code which makes use of redundant digits called check digits. (A)

check, mathematical or arithmetical. A check making use of mathematical identities or other properties, frequently with some degree of discrepancy being acceptable; e.g., checking multiplication by verifying that $A \cdot B = B \cdot A$, checking a tabulated function by differencing, etc. (A)

check, modulo N. A form of check digit, such that the sum of the digits in each number A operated upon is compared with a check digit B, carried along with A and equal to the remainder of A when divided by N, e.g., in a "modulo 4 check," the check number will be 0, 1, 2, or 3 and the remainder of A when divided by 4 must equal the reported check number B, or else an error or malfunction has occurred; a method of verification by congruences, e.g. casting out nines. (A)

check, odd-even. See *check, parity.*

check, parity. A summation check in which the binary digits, in a character or word, are added (modulo 2) and the sum checked against a single, previously computed parity digit; i.e., a check which tests whether the number of ones is odd or even. (C)

check, programmed. A system of determining the correct program and machine functioning either by running a sample problem with similar programming and known answer, including mathematical or logical checks such as comparing A times B with B times A and usually where reliance is placed on a high probability of correctness rather than built-in error-detection circuits or by building a checking system into the actual program being run and utilized for checking during the actual running of the problem. (A)

check, redundant. A check which uses extra digits, short of complete duplication, to help detect malfunctions and mistakes. (A)

check, summation. A redundant check in which groups of digits are summed, usually without regard for overflow, and that sum checked against a previously computed sum to verify accuracy. (A)

check, transfer. Verification of transmitted information by temporary storing, re-transmitting and comparing. (A)

check, twin. A continuous duplication check achieved by duplication of hardware and automatic comparison. (A)

checking, marginal. To determine computer circuit weaknesses and incipient malfunctions by varying the power applied to various circuits, usually by a lowering of the d-c supply or filament voltages. (A)

clear. To make all bits zero (or sometimes one) in a storage device. (F)

clock, master. The source of standard timing signals required for sequencing computer operation, usually consisting of a timing pulse generator, a cycling unit, and sets of special pulses that occur at given intervals of time. Usually in synchronous machines the basic frequency utilized is the clocking pulse. (A)

closed shop. A computing installation in which programs and routines are written only by the professional staff of programmers. (F)

code. The machine-language representation of a character. The *instruction code* is the set of symbols which conveys to the computer the operation which it is to perform. The instruction code always specifies a process; it usually specifies one or more operand addresses; it may specify the address of the next order; it may specify additional information such as a cycle index or breakpoint. The *coded instruction code* or machine-language operation code may sometimes be referred to as a code. (F)

code, excess-three. A binary-coded notation for decimal digits which represents each decimal digit as the corresponding binary number plus three; e.g., the decimal digits 0, 1, 7, 9 are represented as 0011, 0100, 1010, 1100, respectively. In this notation, the 9's complement of the decimal digit is equal to the 1's complement of the corresponding four binary digits. (A)

code, instruction. The set of symbols which conveys to the computer the operation which the programmer desires it to perform. The instruction code always specifies a process; it may specify operand addresses; it may specify the address of the next order; it may specify auxiliary information, such as a cycle index register or a breakpoint; see *code, multiple-address.* (F)

code, interpreter. A code which is acceptable to an interpretive routine. (A)

code, multiple-address. When the instruction code specifies no operands nor the next instruction address, since these are implicit in the order structure, the code is called a *zero address code.* The number of operand or result addresses specified in the code may be used to describe it; thus, a *two address code* is one where two operand addresses are specified. If the address of the next instruction is part of the code, the phrase "plus one" is added to the description. Thus, a *one-plus-one address code* specifies one operand address and the address of the next instruction. (F)

code, natural binary. A machine language wherein the code corresponds exactly to the binary numbers used in counting. (F)

code, natural-binary coded decimal. Sometimes *NBCD* or *8421.* A code which uses the four-bit binary number to represent each decimal digit, thus:

0—0000	1—0100	8—1000	F—1100
1—0001	5—0101	9—1001	F—1101
2—0010	6—0110	F—1010	F—1110
3—0011	7—0111	F—1011	F—1111

where F is a forbidden combination. (F)

code, operational. That part of an instruction which designates the operation to be performed. (A)

code, self-complementing. A machine language for which the code of the complement of a digit is the complement of the code of the digit. (F)

coder. A person who translates a sequence of instructions for an automatic computer to solve a problem into the code acceptable to that machine. (C)

coding. The list, in computer code or in pseudo-code, of the successive computer operations required to solve a given problem. (A)

coding, absolute, relative, or symbolic. Coding in which one uses absolute, relative, or symbolic addresses, respectively; coding in which all addresses refer to an arbitrarily selected position, or in which all addresses are represented symbolically. (A)

coding, alphabetic. A system of abbreviation used in preparing information for input into a computer such that information is reported in the form of letters, e.g., New York as NY, carriage return as CN, etc. (A)

coding, automatic. Any technique in which a computer is used to help bridge the gap between some "easiest" form, intellectually and manually, of describing the steps to be followed in solving a given problem and some "most efficient" final coding of the same problem for a given computer; two basic forms are defined under *routine, compiler* and *routine, interpretive.* (A)

coding, minimum latency. See *minimum-access programming*.

coding, numeric. A system of abbreviation used in the preparation of information for machine acceptance by reducing all information to numerical quantities; in contrast to alphabetic coding. (A)

coercive force, H_c. The magnetizing force at which the magnetic flux density is zero when the material is in a *symmetrically cyclically magnetized condition*. [*Note:* Coercive force is not a unique property of a magnetic material, but is dependent upon the conditions of measurement.] (M)

coercivity. The property of a magnetic material measured by the *coercive force* corresponding to the *saturation induction* for the material. [*Note:* This is a quasi-static property only.] (M)

coincident-current selection. The selection of a magnetic cell for reading or writing, by the simultaneous application of two or more currents. (M)

collate. To combine two sequences of items of information in any way such that the same sequence is observed in the combined sequence. For example, sequence 12, 29, 42 and sequence 23, 24, 48 may be collated into 12, 23, 24, 29, 42, 48. More generally, to combine two or more similarly ordered sets of items to produce another ordered set composed of information from the original sets. Both the number of items and the size of the individual items in the resulting set may differ from those of either of the original sets and of their sum. (C)

collator. A machine which has input card feeds, output card pockets, and stations at which a card may be compared or sequenced with regard to other cards, so as to determine the pocket into which it is to be placed. The machine is particularly useful for matching detail cards with master cards, for merging cards in proper sequence into a file of cards, etc. (C)

column. The place or position of a character or a digit in a word or other unit of information. One of the characters or digit positions in a positional-notation representation of a unit of information. Columns are usually numbered from right to left, zero being the rightmost column if there is no decimal (or binary, or other) point, or the column immediately to the left of the point if there is one. A position or place in a number, such as 3876, written in a scale of notation, corresponding to a given power of the radix. The digit located in any particular column is the coefficient of the corresponding power of the radix; thus, 8 in the foregoing example is the coefficient of 10^2. (C)

command. See *instruction*.

comparand. One of the words which the computer compares when executing a given comparison order. (F)

comparator. (1) A circuit which compares two stored codes and supplies an indication of agreement or disagreement; or a mechanism by means of which two items of information may be compared in certain respects, and a signal given depending on whether they are equal or unequal. (2) A device for comparing two different transcriptions of the same information to verify agreement or determine disagreement. (C)

compare. To determine the relative order of two computer words or sets of symbols by some predetermined criteria. The result of such a comparison is equality if the comparands are identical or greater than or less than according to whether the first comparand precedes or follows the second comparand in the predetermined ordering. (F)

compiler. A program-making routine, which produces a specific program for a particular problem by the following process: (1) determining the intended meaning of an element of information expressed in pseudo-code; (2) selecting or generating (i.e., calculating from parameters and skeleton instructions) the required subroutine; (3) transforming the subroutine into specific coding for the specific problem, assigning specific memory registers, etc., and entering it as an element of the problem program; (4) maintaining a record of the subroutines used and their position in the problem program; and (5) continuing to the next element of information in pseudo-code. (C)

complement. A quantity which is derived from a given quantity, expressed in notation to the base n, by one of the following rules. (a) Complement on n: subtract each digit of the given quantity from $n - 1$, add unity to the rightmost digit, and perform all resultant carries. For example, the 2's complement of binary 11010 is 00110; the 10's complement of decimal 679 is 321. (b) Complement on $n - 1$: subtract each digit of the given quantity from $n - 1$. For example, the 1's complement of binary 11010 is 00101; the 9's complement of decimal 679 is 320. The complement is frequently employed in computers to represent the negative of the given quantity. (C)

complete operation. A calculating operation which includes (1) obtaining all the operands out of memory, (2) making a calculation or editing operation, (3) returning the result to memory, and (4) obtaining the next instruction. (F)

computer. A machine which is able to perform sequences of arithmetic and logical operations upon information. (F)

computer, analog. A computer which calculates by using physical analogs of the variables. A one-to-one correspondence exists between each numerical variable occurring in the problem and a varying physical measurement in the analog computer. (C)

computer, asynchronous. A calculating device in which the performance of any operation starts as a result of a signal that the previous operation has been completed; contrasted with synchronous computer. (A)

computer, automatic. A calculating device which handles long sequences of operations without human intervention. (A)

computer, digital. A calculating device using integers to express all the variables and quantities of a problem. (F)

computer, synchronous. A calculating device in which the performance of all operations is controlled with equally spaced signals from a master clock. (A)

conditional. Subject to the result of a comparison made during computation. (C)

conditional breakpoint instruction. A conditional jump instruction which, if some specified switch is set, will cause the computer to stop, after which either the routine may be continued as coded or a jump to another routine may be directed. (C)

conditional transfer of control. A computer instruction which when reached in the course of a program will cause the computer either to continue with the next instruction in the original sequence or to transfer control to another stated instruction, depending on a condition which has then been determined. (C)

content. The information stored in any part of the computer memory. The symbol "(. . .)" is often used to indicate "the content of . . .": for example, (m) indicates the content of the storage location whose address is m. (C)

control. Those parts of a digital computer which effect the carrying out of instructions in proper sequence, the interpretation of each instruction, and the application of the proper signals to the arithmetic unit and other parts in accordance with this interpretation. The components in any mechanism responsible for interpreting and carrying out manually-initiated directions. Sometimes called manual control. In some business applications of mathematics, a mathematical check. (C)

control, cascade. An automatic control system in which various control units are linked in sequence, each control unit regulating the operation of the next control unit in line. (A)

control sequence. The normal order of selection of instructions for execution. In some computers, one of the addresses in each instruction specifies the control sequence. In most other computers the sequence is consecutive except where a jump occurs. (C)

control, sequential. A manner of operation of a computer such that instructions are fed in a given order to the computer during the solution of a problem. (C)

control unit. That portion of the hardware of an automatic digital computer which directs the sequence of operations, interprets the coded instructions, and initiates the proper commands to the computer circuits to execute the instructions. (C)

control unit, auxiliary. See *centralized control.*

control unit, main. See *centralized control.*

convert. To change numerical information from one number base to another (e.g., decimal to binary) and/or from some form of fixed-point to some form of floating-point representation, or vice versa. (A)

converter. A unit which changes the language of information from one form to another so as to make it available or acceptable to another machine, e.g., a unit which changes information punched on cards to information recorded on magnetic tape, possibly including editing facilities. (A)

copy. To reproduce information in a new location replacing whatever was previously stored there and leaving the source of the information unchanged. (A)

core, magnetic. A magnetic material capable of assuming and remaining at one of two or more conditions of magnetization, thus capable of providing storage, gating, or switching functions, usually of toroidal shape and pulsed or polarized by electric currents carried on wire wound around the material. (A)

counter. A device, register, or storage location for storing integers, permitting these integers to be increased or decreased by unity or by an arbitrary integer, and capable of being reset to zero or to an arbitrary integer. (A)

counter, control. A device which records the storage location of the instruction word which is to be obtained next. The control counter selects storage locations in sequence unless otherwise directed. Also *program counter*. (F)

counter, ring. A loop of interconnected bistable elements such that one and only one is in a specified state at any given time and such that, as input signals are counted, the position of the one specified state moves in an ordered sequence around the loop. (A)

CRT. Cathode ray tube; a device yielding a visual plot of the variation of several parameters by means of a proportionally deflected beam of electrons. (A)

cycle. A set of operations repeated as a unit; a nonarithmetic shift in which the digits dropped off at one end of a word are returned at the other end in circular fashion; cycle right and cycle left. To repeat a set of operations a prescribed number of times including, when required, supplying necessary address changes by arithmetic processes or by means of a hardware device such as a *B-box* or *cycle-counter*. (A)

cycle count. To increase or decrease the cycle index by unity or by a selected integer. (A)

cycle criterion. The total number of times the cycle is to be repeated; the register which stores that number. (A)

cycle index. The number of times a cycle has been executed; or the difference, or the negative of the difference, between that number and the number of repetitions desired. (A)

cycle, major. The maximum access time of a recirculating serial storage element; the time for one rotation, e.g., of a magnetic drum or of pulses in an acoustic delay line; a whole number of minor cycles. (A)

cycle, minor. The word time of a serial computer, including the spacing between words. (A)

cycle reset. To return a cycle index to its initial value. (A)

cyclically magnetized condition. A condition of a magnetic material when it has been under the influence of a magnetizing force varying between two specific limits until, for each increasing (or decreasing) value of the magnetizing force, the magnetic flux density has the same value in successive cycles. (M)

D

damping. A characteristic built into electrical circuits and mechanical systems to prevent rapid or excessive corrections which may lead to instability or oscillatory conditions, e.g., connecting a resistor on the terminals of a pulse transformer to remove natural oscillations; placing a moving element in oil or sluggish grease to prevent overshoot. (A)

data. Facts or information taken in, operated on, or put out by a computer or other machine for handling information. (C)

data reduction. Transforming masses of raw test or experimentally obtained data, usually gathered by instrumentation, into useful, ordered, or simplified intelligence. (A)

data reduction, on-line. The processing of information as rapidly as the information is received by the computing system. (A)

datum. One computer word. (F)

decimal point. In a decimal number, the point that marks the place between positive and negative powers of ten. (A)

decimal-to-binary conversion. Converting a number in the scale of ten into the scale of two. (C)

debug. To isolate and remove malfunctions from a computer or mistakes from a routine. (A)

decade. A group or assembly of ten units; e.g., a decade counter counts to ten in one column; a decade resistor box inserts resistance quantities in multiples of powers of ten. (A)

decentralized control. See *centralized control.*

decode. To ascertain the intended meaning of the individual characters or groups of characters in the pseudo-coded program. (A) To activate a corresponding output line when input lines are activated in accordance with the code for that character. (F)

decoder. A logical block which produces an output on one and only one line when one or more input lines are energized; the decoder is used to determine the digit in a given number system to which an indicated code is assigned. (F)

delay element. An element whose output substantially resembles its input except that there is a time displacement between the two; also *delay-line.* (F)

delay-line, electric. A transmission line of lumped or distributed capacitive and inductive elements in which the velocity of propagation of electromagnetic energy is small compared with the velocity of light. Storage is accomplished by recirculation of wave patterns containing information, usually in binary form. (A)

delay-line, magnetic. A metallic medium along which the velocity of propagation of magnetic energy is small relative to the speed of light. Storage is accomplished by recirculation of wave patterns containing information, usually in binary form. (A)

delay-line, mercury or quartz. A sonic or acoustic delay-line in which mercury or quartz is used as the medium of sound transmission. See *delay-line, sonic or acoustic.* (A)

delay-line, sonic or acoustic. A device capable of transmitting retarded sound pulses, transmission being accomplished by wave patterns of elastic deformation. Storage is accomplished by recirculation of wave patterns containing information, usually in binary form. (A)

delta. See *coincident-current selection.*

density, packing. The number of units of useful information contained within a given linear dimension, usually expressed in units per inch, e.g., the number of binary digit magnetic pulses stored on tape or drum per linear inch on a single track by a single head. (A)

design, logical. The planning of a computer or data-processing system prior to its detailed engineering design. The synthesizing of a network of logical elements to perform a specified function. The result of both the above, frequently called the logic of the system, machine, or network. (A)

detector. A functional element which produces an output only when inputs corresponding to a sample code or character are present. (F)

diagram. A schematic representation of a sequence of subroutines designed to solve a problem; a coarser and less symbolic representation than a flow chart, frequently including descriptions in English words; a schematic or logical drawing showing the electrical circuit or logical arrangements within a component. (A)

diagram, logical. A diagram representing the logical elements and their interconnections without construction or engineering details. (A)

differentiator. A device whose output function in proportion to a derivative of its input function with respect to one or more variables. (A)

digit. One of the n symbols of integral value ranging from 0 to $n - 1$ inclusive in a scale of numbering of base n, e.g., one of the ten decimal digits, 0, 1, 2, 3, 4, 5, 6, 7, 8, 9. (A)

digital. Using integers to represent all the quantities that occur in a problem or calculation. (A)

digit, binary. A whole number in the binary scale of notation; this digit may be only 0 (zero) or 1 (one). It may be equivalent to an "on" or "off" condition, a "yes" or a "no," etc. (A)

digit, binary-coded decimal. See *binary-coded decimal*.

digitize. To render an analog measurement into digital form. (F)

digits, check. In a character or word, one or more redundant digits which depends upon the remaining digits in such a fashion that if a digit is corrupted, the malfunction is detectable, e.g., a given digit may be zero if the sum of other digits in the word is odd, and this (check) digit may be one if the sum of other digits in the word is even. (A)

digits, equivalent binary. The number of binary digits required to express a number in another base with the same precision; e.g., approximately $3\frac{1}{3}$ times the number of decimal digits is required to express a decimal number in binary form. For the case of coded decimal notation, the number of binary digits required is 4 times the number of decimal digits. (A)

disturb current cycle. The application of 0 current to all freshly written cores in order to reduce the noise current generated on the next readout cycle. (F)

disturbed-one output. See *coincident-current selection*.

disturbed-zero output. See *coincident-current selection*.

downtime. The period during which a computer is malfunctioning or not operating correctly due to machine failures; contrasted with available time, idle time, or standby time. (A)

drive pulse. A pulsed magnetomotive force applied to a magnetic cell from one or more sources. (M)

drum, magnetic storage. A rotating cylinder, made of or coated with magnetizable material, which may store information by the direction of magnetization that exists at fixed referenced sites. Information is entered by passing current of the proper direction through the *drum writing heads;* it is withdrawn without affecting the information storage by examining the voltage appearing at the *drum reading heads*. A single head may be used for both purposes. The portion of the drum which passes beneath a given head is called a *track;* the tracks which are used to store a complete computer word comprise a *channel;* the portion of channel which holds a complete word is called a *sector*. A channel used as a buffer and shared by the I/O unit with the computer is called a *revolver*. (F)

dummy. An artificial address, instruction, or unit of information. (F)

dump. To withdraw all power accidentally or intentionally. To transfer all or part of the contents of one section of computer memory into another section. (C)

dump check. A check which usually consists of adding all the digits during dumping, and verifying the sum when retransferring. (C)

E

Eccles-Jordan trigger. See *multivibrator*.

echo checking. A system of seeking accuracy in data transmission by reflecting the transmitter and comparing the reflected information with that which was transmitted. (F)

edit. The process of removing or inserting information as a record is passed through the computer. (F)

electronic calculating punch. A punch card machine which in each fraction of a second reads a punch card passing through the machine, performs a number of sequential operations, and punches a result on the punch card. (C)

encoder. A logical block which produces outputs on one or more output lines when only one input line is energized. An encoder is used to produce the binary code corresponding to the digit from another number system. (F)

erase. To replace all the binary digits in a storage device by binary zeros. In a binary computer, *erasing* is equivalent to clearing, while in a coded decimal computer where the pulse code for decimal zero may contain binary ones, *clearing* leaves decimal zero while *erasing* leaves all-zero pulse codes. (A)

error. The loss of precision in a quantity; the difference between an accurate quantity and its calculated approximation. *Errors* occur in numerical methods; *mistakes* occur in programming, coding, data transcription, and operating; *malfunctions* occur in computers and are due to physical limitations on the properties of materials. The differential margin by which a controlled unit deviates from its target value. (A)

error, inherited. The error in the initial values; especially the error inherited from the previous steps in the step-by-step integration. (A)

error, rounding. The error resulting from deleting the less significant digits of a quantity and applying some rule of correction to the part retained. A common round-off rule is to take the quantity to the nearest digit. Thus, pi, 3.14159265..., rounded to four decimals is 3.1416. [*Note:* Alston S. Householder suggests the following terms: "initial errors," "generated errors," "propagated errors" and "residual errors." If x is the true value of the argument, and x^* the quantity used in computation, then, assuming one wishes $f(x)$, $x - x^*$ is the initial error; $f(x) - f(x^*)$ is the propagated error. If $f.$ is the Taylor, or other, approximation utilized, then $f(x^*) - f.(x^*)$ is the residual error. If f^* is the actual result then $f. - f^*$ is the generated error, and this is what builds up as a result of rounding. (A)

error, truncation. The error resulting from the use of only a finite number of terms of an infinite series, or from the approximation of operations in the infinitesimal calculus by operations in the calculus of finite differences. (A)

exchange. To interchange the contents of two storage devices or locations. (C)

execute. The performance of a complete instruction except for a fetch cycle (which see). (F)

extract. To obtain certain digits from a machine word as may be specified. For example, if the ten-digit number 0000011100 is stored in a machine register, the computer can be instructed to "extract" the eighth digit from the left (in this case a 1) and correspondingly perform a certain action. To replace the contents of specific columns of one machine word by the contents of the corresponding columns of another machine word, depending on the instruction. To remove from a set of items of information all those items that meet some arbitrary condition. (C)

F

factor scale. One or more coefficients used to multiply or divide quantities in a problem in order to convert them so as to have them lie in a given range of magnitude, e.g., plus one to minus one. (A)

feedback. The returning of a fraction of the output of a machine, system, or process to the input, to which the fraction is added or subtracted. If increase of input is associated with increase of output, subtracting the returned fraction (negative feedback) results in self-correction or control of the process, while adding it (positive feedback) results in a runaway or out-of-control process. (C)

feed, card. A mechanism which moves cards serially into a machine. (A)

ferroelectric. A phenomenon exhibited by materials within which permanent electric dipoles exist and a residual displacement in the D-E plane occurs. (A)

fetch. The portion of a computer cycle during which the location of the forthcoming instruction is determined, the instruction obtained and modified if necessary, and the instruction entered into the control register. (F)

field. A set of one or more characters (not necessarily all lying on the same word) which is treated as a whole; a set of one or more columns on a punched card consistently used to record similar information. (A)

file. A set of items. (A)

fixed-point calculation. Calculation using or assuming a fixed or constant location of the decimal point or the binary point in each number. (C)

fixed-point representation. An arithmetical notation in which all numerical quantities are expressed by the same specified number of digits, with the point implicitly located at the same specified position. (C)

flip-flop. See *multivibrator*.

floating-point calculation. Calculation taking into account varying location of the decimal point (if base 10) or binary point (if base 2), and consisting of writing each number by specifying separately its sign, its coefficient, and its exponent affecting the base. For example, in floating-point calculation, the decimal number $-638,020,000$ might be reported as $-6.3802,8$, since it is equal to -6.3802×10^8. (C)

flow chart. A graphical representation of a sequence of programming operations, using symbols to represent operations such as COMPUTE, SUBSTITUTE, COMPARE, JUMP, COPY, READ, WRITE, etc. A flow chart is a more detailed representation than a *diagram*, which see. (C)

forbidden combination. Combinations in a given code for which no digit corresponds are called *forbidden combinations*, e.g., 1011 in natural binary coded decimal is a *forbidden combination*. (F)

force (verb). To intervene manually in a program and cause the computer to execute a jump instruction. (C)

frequency response. A measure of the ability of a device to take into account, follow, or act upon a rapidly varying input condition; for example, in the case of amplifiers, the frequency at which the gain has fallen to one-half of the power factor, or to 0.707 of the voltage gain factor; in the case of a mechanical automatic controller, the maximum rate at which changes in the input condition can be followed and acted upon. (C)

function generator. A device which produces a given function of the independent variable. (C)

function table. (1) A tabulation of the values of a mathematical function for a set of values of the independent variables. (2) A device of hardware or a program or a subroutine which translates from one representation or coding of information to another representation or coding. (3) Logic. A dictionary. (C)

functional unit. A combination of logical elements, simple or compound, and delay elements which performs an elementary computer function; the hardware to do this; e.g., comparitor, encoder, pulse generator. (F)

G

gate. A circuit which has the ability to produce an output which is dependent upon a logical function of the input, e.g., an *and* gate has an output pulse when there is time coincidence of all inputs. An *or* gate—or preferably *mixer*— has an output when any one or any combination of input pulses occurs in time coincidence. Any gate may contain any number of inhibits in which there is no output under any condition of input if there is time coincidence with the inhibit signal. (F)

generate. To produce a subroutine from parameters and skeletal coding. (A)

generator. A program for a computer which generates the coding of a problem; a mechanical device which produces an electrical output. (A)

generator, pulse train. A functional unit which generates, in response to an input pulse, a fixed number of equally spaced equal amplitude pulses on one line and one post-train pulse on another line a short time thereafter. (F)

H

half adder. A circuit having two output points, S and C, and two input points, A and B, such that the output is related to the input according to the following table:

INPUT		OUTPUT	
A	B	S	C
0	0	0	0
0	1	1	0
1	0	1	0
1	1	0	1

where
A and B are arbitrary input pulses, and S and C are "sum without carry" and "carry," respectively. (A)

hardware. The mechanical, magnetic, electronic, and electrical devices from which a computer is fabricated; the assembly of material forming a computer. (A)

head. A device which reads, records, or erases information in a storage medium, usually a small electromagnet used to read, write, or erase information on a magnetic drum or tape or the set of perforating or reading fingers and block assembly for punching or reading holes in paper tape. (A)

hold. The function of retaining information in one storage device after transferring it to another device; in contrast to *clear*. (A)

hole site. The place on a punched card or punched paper tape where a hole may or may not appear. This site represents a bit of information. A hole represents a "1" and the absence of a hole (the presence of paper) represents a "0" (sometimes contrariwise). (F)

hunting. A continuous attempt on the part of an automatically controlled system to seek a desired equilibrium condition. (A)

hysteresis loop. For a magnetic material in a *cyclically magnetized condition*, a curve (usually with rectangular coordinates) showing, for each value of the magnetizing force, two values of the magnetic flux density—one when the magnetizing force is increasing, the other when it is decreasing. (M)

I

ignore. A character code indicating that no action whatsoever be taken. (In Teletype or Flexowriter code, all holes punched is an ignore.) An instruction requiring nonperformance of what normally might be executed; not to be executed. (A)

impedance, characteristic. The ratio of voltage to current at every point along a transmission line on which there are no standing waves; the square root of the product of the open and short circuit impedance of the line. (A)

information. Knowledge or intelligence produced, processed, or cognized by the computer. (F)

inhibit pulse. A *pulse* that prevents flux reversal of a magnetic cell by certain specified *drive pulses*. (M)

input. Information received by the computer or its storage device from the outside. (F)

input block. A section of internal storage of a computer generally reserved for the receiving and processing of input information. (C)

input equipment. The equipment used for taking information into a computer. (C)

input/output buffer. An autonomous storage unit which accumulates blocks of information from the I/O unit (usually several words) for distribution to the computer and consisting of control, storage, and an I/O unit. (F)

input/output equipment. Sometimes *"I/O equipment."* The devices which are used for entering and obtaining information from the computer. (F)

input/output mechanism. The mechanism for transmitting information between an intermediate medium and the computer; includes storage only as suggested by the manufacturer. (F)

input/output unit. The I/O unit consists of three sections—the I/O mechanism, storage to accumulate a convenient amount of information and control logic. The latter supervises the accumulation and distribution of information from the intermediate medium and the computer or awaiting storage devices. (F)

instruction. A set of characters which defines a computer operation, together with one or more addresses (or no addresses) referring to the location of the operands and/or results, and which as a unit causes the computer to operate upon the indicated quantities at the indicated or implied location. [*Note:* the term *instruction* is preferred by many to the term *command* or *order*. *Command* is sometimes reserved for electronic signals; *order* is sometimes reserved to mean sequence, as in "the order of the characters." (F)

instruction, breakpoint. An instruction which, if some specified switch is set, will cause the computer to stop. (A)

instruction, breakpoint, conditional. A conditional jump instruction which, if some specified switch is set, will cause the computer to stop, after which either the routine may be continued as coded or a jump may be forced. (A)

instruction, multiple-address. See *code, multiple-address.*

instruction, one-address. An instruction consisting of an operation and exactly one address. The instruction code of a single-address computer may include both zero- and multi-address instructions as special cases. (A)

instruction, one-plus-one or three-plus-one address. A two- or four-address instruction, respectively, in which one of the addresses always specifies the location of the next instruction to be performed. (A)

instruction, transfer. A computer operation which specifies the location of the next operation to be performed and directs the computer to that operation (or instruction). (A)

instruction, zero-address. An instruction specifying an operation in which the locations of the operands are defined by the computer code, so that no address need be given explicitly. (A)

integrator. A device whose output is proportional to the integral with respect to the input variable. (A)

interblock space. A portion of the magnetic tape between blocks of information on which nothing is written. This allows time for the tape to be stopped and brought up to reading speed again between blocks. (F)

interlace. To assign successive storage locations to physically separated storage positions, e.g. on a magnetic drum or tape, usually for the express purpose of reducing access time. (A)

internal memory. The total memory or storage which is accessible automatically to the computer. This equipment is part of and directly controlled by the computer. (C)

internal storage. Same as *internal memory.* (C)

interpreter. A card-handling device which prints upon a card the information appearing in the card in the form of punched holes. See also *routine, interpretive.* (C)

interpreter code. A code acceptable to an *interpretive routine* which see. (F)

item. A set of fields containing related information; a unit of information relating to a single person or object; the content of a single message. (A)

intrinsic induction—B_i. In a magnetic material for a given value of the magnetizing force, the excess of the normal flux density over the flux density in vacuum. The equation for *intrinsic induction* is

$$B_i = B - \mu_v H$$

where μ_v is the factor that expresses the ratio of magnetic flux density to magnetizing force in vacuum. (M)

J

jump. An instruction or signal which, conditionally or unconditionally, specifies the location of the next instruction and directs the computer to that instruction. A jump is used to alter the normal sequence control of the computer. Under certain special conditions, a jump may be forced by manual intervention; in other words a transfer of control is made to a specified instruction. (A)

jump, conditional. An instruction which will cause the proper one of two (or more) addresses to be used in obtaining the next instruction, depending upon some property of one or more numerical expressions or other conditions. (A)

K

key. A group of characters usually forming a field, utilized in the identification or location of an item; a marked lever manually operated for copying a character, e.g. typewriter, paper tape perforator, card punch manual keyboard, digitizer, or manual word generator. (A)

L

lag. A relative measure of the time delay between two events, states, or mechanisms. (A)

language. The form or means by which information is communicated within or between the computer or within or between the computer's auxiliary devices and in the outside world. (F)

language, human. Information in a form readily understood by an informed native, e.g., English-language typing (in the U.S.A.). (F)

language, intermediate. The language in which information may be stored between the time at which it is obtained from a human source and the time at which it is entered into the computer, e.g., punch cards or magnetic tape codes. (F)

language, machine. The code used by the computer for communication among its related parts or in which the computer performs arithmetic and editing. (F)

latency. In a serial or serial-parallel storage system, the access time less the word time, e.g., the time spent waiting for the desired location to appear under the drum heads or at the end of an acoustic tank. (A)

leap frog test. A program to test the internal operation of a computer which performs a series of arithmetic or logical operations on one section of memory location, then transfers to another section, checks to see that the transfer is correct and then begins the series of operations over again. Eventually the checking program will have occupied every possible position in the memory and begins again. The term *leap frog* comes from the jump seen on a monitoring cathode ray tube during transfer. (F)

library. A collection of standard and fully tested programs, routines, and subroutines, by means of which many types of problems and parts of problems can be solved. (C)

line-printing. Printing an entire line of characters across a page as the paper feeds in one direction past a type bar or cylinder bearing all characters on a single element. (A)

line, transmission. Any conductor or system of conductors used to carry electrical energy from its source to a load. (A)

load (unload). To enter (remove) information en masse into (from) the computer from (into) the input (output) unit. (F)

location. A storage position holding one computer word, designated as a specific address or a specific register. The symbol "[X]" is used to indicate "the location at which X is stored." (F)

location hole. A hole punched in paper tape every time a punch magnet is energized or the tape is advanced and by which the tape may be moved mechanically both for punching and reading. (F)

logger. A device which automatically records physical processes and events, usually with respect to time. (A)

logic. The science that deals with the principles and criteria of validity in thought and demonstration; the science of the principles of exact and careful reasoning. the basic principles and applications of truth tables, the relations of propositions, the interconnection of on-off circuit elements, etc., for mathematical computation in a computer. In the phrase "logic of the computer," same as "*logical design,*" which see. (A)

logic, symbolic. The study of the rules governing the composition of propositions using logical elements and symbols, where the symbols represent elementary statements or quantities. (F)

logical comparison. The operation of comparing A and B; the result is 1 or yes if A is the same as B and 0 or no if A is not the same as B (or vice versa). (C)

logical design. That phase of the computer design which combines operational units, functional units, logical elements, and delay elements into an integrated whole supposedly capable, upon realization in hardware, of performing as a computer or computerlike device. (F)

logical element, compound. A function of several variables which uniquely defines the output as either 0 or 1 for all possible combinations of 0 and 1 for each of the inputs; the circuitry to realize the above, e.g. multiple-input &-gate. (F)

logical element, simple, also **logical unit.** A function c of two variables a and b which uniquely defines c as either 0 or 1 for all possible combinations of 0 or 1 for each of a and b; also the circuitry which realizes this performance, e.g. two-input and-gate for $c = a \& b$. (F)

logical unit. See *logical element.*

loop. Repetition of a group of instructions in a routine. See *cycle.* (C)

M

machine-available time. Time during which a computer has the power turned on, is not being maintained, and is known or believed to be operating correctly. (C)

machine cycle. The smallest period of time or complete process of action that repeats itself in order. In some computers, "minor cycles" and "major cycles" are distinguished. (C)

machine language. See *language, machine.*

malfunction. A failure in the operation of the hardware of a computer. (C)

matrix. A set of quantities in a specified array, subject to mathematical operations such as addition, multiplication, inversion, etc., according to specified rules. An array of circuit elements, such as diodes, wires, magnetic cores, relays, etc., arranged and designed to perform a specific function, for example, conversion from one numerical system to another. (C)

memorize. The process of setting one or more words into the computer memory. (F)

memory. A device into which information can be introduced and then extracted at a considerably later time. (F)

memory capacity. The amount of information which a memory unit can store. It is often measured in the number of decimal digits or the number of binary digits which the memory unit can store. Other measures of memory capacity have also been defined. (C)

memory, fast-access. In large computers which have two or more sections of memory which differ in access time, the faster (fastest) section. (F)

merge. To produce a single sequence of items, ordered according to some rule (i.e., arranged in some orderly sequence), from two or more sequences previously ordered according to the same rule, without changing the items in size, structure, or total number. Merging is a special case of collating. (C)

message. A group of words, fixed or variable in length, transported as a unit. (C)

microsecond. A millionth of a second. (C)

millisecond. A thousandth of a second. (C)

minimum-access programming. Programming in such a way that minimum waiting time is required to obtain information out of the memory. Also called *minimum latency programming* or *forced coding*. (C)

mistake. A human error which results in an incorrect instruction in a program or in coding, an incorrect element of information, or an incorrect manual operation. (C)

mixed-base notation. A number system in which a single base, such as 10 in the decimal system, is replaced by two number bases, used alternately, such as 2 and 5. See *biquinary notation*. (C)

mnemonic. Assisting, or intending to assist, remembering; a set of letters, usually three or less, used by the programmer or coder to indicate what transpires during a given instruction and usually differing from the machine code for the instruction. (F)

modifier. A quantity, sometimes the cycle index, used to alter the address of an operand. (C)

modify. (1) To alter in an instruction the address of the operand. (2) To alter a subroutine according to a defined parameter. (C)

multivibrator. An electronic device which may be found in either of two states. It may be observed by examining the state of either of two output connections. There are three kinds of multivibrators: the *bistable multivibrator*, otherwise called *flip-flop, multi* (used here), or *toggle* (predominantly British) has two input leads—a signal on either causes the device to assume the corresponding output state regardless of its previous state; the *monostable multivibrator*, otherwise *uni* (used here), *flip-flip* or delay flip-flop has but one (effective) lead which, when energized, causes the device to assume the corresponding output state (say 1) for a fixed length of time (τ) and then return to the 0 state— depending upon the particular circuit, the *one* may or may not be affected by 1 input signals when in the 1 state; the *astable multivibrator* or *free running multivibrator* has no inputs and alternately assumes its 0 and 1 states, remaining in each for a relatively fixed time τ_0 and τ_1, respectively—when the *multivibrator* is said to have a symmetric output. The *trigger* is a *multi* whose inputs are connected together and which operates so that an input signal causes the device to assume the state complementary to the one it has just occupied. (F)

N

negative feedback. See *feedback.*

network analyzer. An analog computer using electrical circuit elements which simulates and solves (analyzes) problems of the electrical behavior of a network of power lines and electrical loads, and related problems. (C)

nor **element.** An element with an output only when all inputs are absent. (F)

normalize. To change a floating-point result, such as 63.2×10^8, so that the exponent, in this case 8, and the mantissa, in this case 63.2, lie in the prescribed or standard normal range. For example, in this case, the normal or standard result might be 6.32×10^9 or $.632 \times 10^{10}$ depending on the computer's adopted standard. (C)

notation (in the sense "scale of notation"). A systematic method for stating quantities in which any number is represented by a sum of coefficients times multiples of the successive powers of a chosen base number n (sometimes more than one). If a quantity is written in the scale of notation n, then the successive positions of the digits report the powers of n. Thus 379 in the scale of 10 or decimal notation means 3 hundreds, 7 tens, and 9. The number 379 in the scale of 16 (used in some computers) means 3 times sixteen squared, plus 7 times sixteen, plus 9 (which in decimal notation would be 889). 1101 in the scale of two means 1 eight, 1 four, 0 twos, and 1 one (which in decimal notation would be 13). In writing numbers, the base may be indicated by a subscript (expressed always in decimal notation) when there may be doubt about what base is employed. For example, 11.101_2 means two, plus one, plus one half, plus one eighth, but 11.101_3 means three plus one, plus one third, plus one twenty-seventh. Names of scales of notation which have had some significant consideration are:

Base	Name
2	binary
3	ternary
4	quaternary, tetral
5	quinary
8	octal, octonary
10	decimal
12	duodecimal
16	hexadecimal, sexadecimal
32	duotricenary
2, 5	biquinary (C)

number, pseudo random. A set of digits constructed in such a sequence that each excessive digit is equally likely to be any of n digits where the number is written in the base n. (F)

number system. See *notation.*

O

octal digit. See *notation*.

odd-even check. Same as *check, parity*.

off-line operation. See *on-line operation*.

one-address code. See *code, multiple-address*.

one output. See *one state*.

one state. A state of magnetic cell wherein the magnetic flux through a specified cross-sectional area has a positive value, when determined from an arbitrarily specified direction of positive normal to that area. A state wherein the magnetic flux has a negative value, when similarly determined, is a *zero state*.

A *one output* is (1) the voltage response obtained from a magnetic cell in a *one state* by a reading or resetting process or (2) the integrated voltage response obtained from a magnetic cell in a *one state* by a reading or resetting process. A ratio of a *one output* to a *zero output* is a *one-to-zero ratio*.

A pulse—for example, a *drive pulse*—is a *write pulse* if it causes information to be introduced into a magnetic cell or cells, or is a *read pulse* if it causes information to be acquired from a magnetic cell or cells. (M)

one-to-partial-select ratio. See *coincident-current selection*.

one-to-zero ratio. See *one state*.

on-line operation. Copying, translating, editing, and pre- and post-processing work which requires the time of the computer. When computer time is not required, this is called *off-line operation*. (F)

operand. Any one of the quantities entering into or arising from an operation. (F)

operation, arithmetic. An operation in which numerical quantities form the elements of the calculation (e.g., addition, subtraction, multiplication, division). (A)

operation, average-calculating. A common or typical calculating operation longer than an addition and shorter than a multiplication; often taken as the mean of nine addition times and one multiplication time. (A)

operation, complete. An operation which includes (a) obtaining all operands from storage, (b) performing the operation, (c) returning result to storage, and (d) obtaining the next instruction. (A)

operation, computer. The electronic action of hardware resulting from an instruction; in general, computer manipulation required to secure computed results. (A)

operation, fixed-cycle. Computer performance whereby a fixed time is allocated to an operation; synchronous or clocked type arrangement within a computer in which events occur at multiples of fixed time intervals. (F)

operation, logical. An operation in which logical (yes-or-no) quantities form the elements being operated on (e.g., comparison, extraction). A usual requirement is that the value appearing in a given column of the result shall not depend on the values appearing in more than one given column of each of the arguments. (A)

operation number. A number indicating the position of an operation or its equivalent subroutine in the sequence forming a program. When a problem is stated in pseudo-code, each step is assigned an operation number. (C)

operation, red-tape. An operation which does not directly contribute to the result; i.e., arithmetical, logical, and transfer operations used in modifying the address section of other instructions in counting cycles, in rearranging data, etc. (A)

operation, transfer. An operation which moves information from one storage location or one storage medium to another (e.g., read, record). (A)

operation, variable cycle. Computer action in which any cycle of action or operation may be of different lengths. This kind of action takes place in an asynchronous computer. (A)

operational unit. A combination of functional units and logical and delay elements which performs one computer operation or process. One or more functional units, logical elements, or delay elements may be shared by several operational units; the hardware which realizes the above. (F)

operator. The person who manipulates the computer controls, places information media into the input devices, removes the output, presses the start button, and so on; a mathematical symbol which represents a mathematic process to be performed on an associated function. (A)

or-mixer. An electrical or mechanical device which yields an output signal whenever there are one or more inputs on a multi-channel input, e.g., an or-mixer is one in which a pulse output occurs whenever one or more inputs are pulsed; forward merging of pulses simultaneously providing reverse isolation. (F)

or operator. A logical operator which has the property such that if P or Q are two statements, then the statement "P or Q" is true or false precisely according to the following table of possible combinations:

P	Q	P or Q
false	true	true
true	false	true
true	true	true
false	false	false	(A)

order. A defined successive arrangement of elements or events. The word *order* is losing favor as a synonym for instruction, command, or operation, part due to ambiguity. (A)

order, memory reference. An order which includes in its execute portion the obtaining of a datum from memory (e.g., add, transfer). (F)

order, reflexive. An order which requires no data processing but rather alters the behavior of the computer (e.g., jump). (F)

output. Information transmitted by the computer or its storage device to the outside. (F)

output block. A segment of the internal storage reserved for receiving data to be transferred out. (C)

output equipment. The equipment used for transferring information out of a computer. (C)

overflow. In a counter or register, the production of a number which is beyond the capacity of the counter. For example, adding two numbers, each within the capacity of the registers holding them, may result in a sum beyond the capacity of the register that is to hold the sum; overflow. (A)

P

pack. To combine several brief fields of information into one machine word. For example, an employee's pay number, weekly pay rate, and tax exemptions may be stored together in one word, each of these fields being assigned a different set of digit columns. (C)

parallel. Handled at the same time in separate equipment; operating on two or more parts of a word of item simultaneously; contrasted with *serial*. (C)

parallel operation. The flow of information through the computer or any part of it using two or more lines or channels simultaneously. (C)

parameter. In a subroutine, a quantity which may be given different values when the subroutine is used in different main routines or in different parts of one main routine, but which usually remains unchanged throughout any one such use; in a generator, a quantity used to specify input-output devices, to designate subroutines to be included, or otherwise to describe the desired routine to be generated. (A)

parameter, preset. A parameter incorporated into a subroutine during input. (A)

parameter, program. A parameter incorporated into a subroutine during computation. A program parameter frequently comprises a word stored relative to either the subroutine or the entry point and dealt with by the subroutine during each reference. It may be altered by the routine and/or may vary from one point of entry to another. (A)

partial-read pulse. See *coincident-current selection.*

partial-select output. See *coincident-current selection.*

partial-write pulse. See *coincident-current selection.*

patch. Section of coding inserted into a routine to correct a mistake or alter the routine; explicitly transferring control from a routine to a section of coding and back again. (A)

patchboard. Same as *plugboard,* but not restricted to punch card machines. (C)

patchcord. A short connecting wire cord for plugging or patching between terminals in a plugboard or patchboard. (C)

path length. The length of a magnetic flux line in a core. In a toroidal core with nearly equal inside and outside diameters, the value

$$l_m = \frac{\pi}{2}(\text{O.D.} + \text{I.D.})$$

is commonly used. (M)

peak flux density, B_m. The maximum flux density in a magnetic material in a specified *cyclically magnetized condition.* (M)

peak magnetizing force, H_m (*peak field strength*). The upper or lower limiting value of magnetizing force associated with a *cyclically magnetized condition.* (M)

perforation, rate of. Number of characters, rows, or words punched in a paper tape by a device per unit of time. (A)

piezoelectric. Having the property of producing different voltages on different crystal faces when subjected to a stress (compression, tension, twist, and so on) or of producing a stress when subjected to such voltages. (C)

plotter. A visual display in which a dependent variable is graphed by a moving pen or pencil as a function of the independent variable. (C)

plotting board. An output unit which plots the curves of one or more variables as a function of one or more other variables. (C)

plugboard. A removable board holding many hundreds of electric terminals into which short connecting wire cords may be plugged in patterns varying for different programs for the machine. To change the program, one wired-up plugboard is removed and another wired-up plugboard is inserted. A plugboard is equivalent to a program tape which presents all instructions to the machine at one time. It relies on X-punches and other signals in the punch card passing through the machine to cause different selections of instructions in different cases. (C)

plug-in-unit. A subassembly of tubes, resistors, condensers, diodes, and so on, wired together, of a standard type and which as a whole can be plugged in or pulled out easily. (C)

Polyvac. Composite computer used in this book to exemplify existing computers. From polygenic veriform automatic computer.

post mortem. A diagnostic routine which either automatically or when called for prints out information concerning the content of all or a specified part of the registers of the computer, after a problem tape has "died" on the computer. The purpose of a post mortem tape is to assist in the location of an error in coding the problem or in machine function. (C)

precision. The degree of exactness with which a quantity is stated; a relative term often based on the number of significant digits in a measurement. See also *accuracy.* (A)

precision, double. Retention of twice as many digits of a quantity as the computer normally handles, e.g., a computer whose basic word consists of 10 decimal digits is called upon to handle 20-decimal-digit quantities by keeping track of the 10-place fragments. (A)

prestore. To set an initial value for the address of an operand or a cycle index; to store a quantity in an available or convenient location before it is required in a routine. (A)

preventive maintenance. Maintenance of any system which aims to prevent failures ahead of time rather than eliminate failures which have occurred. (C)

printer. An output mechanism which prints or typewrites characters. (C)

process control. Automatic control over industrial processes for manufacturing continuous material or energy, such as refining oil, generating electricity, or making paper. (C)

program. A plan for the solution of a problem. A complete program includes plans for the transcription of data, coding for the computer, and plans for the absorption of the results into the system. The list of coded instructions is called a *routine;* the act of planning a computation or process from the asking of a question to the delivery of the results, including the integration of the operation into an existing system. This programming consists of planning and coding, including numerical analysis, systems analysis, specification of printing formats, and any other functions necessary to the integration of a computer in a system. (A)

programmer. A person who prepares instruction sequences without necessarily converting them into the detailed codes. (A)

programming, automatic. Any technique in which the computer is used to help plan as well as to help code a problem; e.g., compiling routines, interpretive routines. (A)

programming, optimum. See *minimum-access programming.*

programming, random-access. Programming without regard for the time required for access to the storage positions called for in the program; contrast with minimum-access programming. (A)

program register. The register in the control unit of the computer which stores the current instruction of the program and thereby completely controls the operation of the computer during the cycle of execution of that instruction. Same as *control register*. Also called *program counter*. (A)

program-sensitive malfunction. A malfunction which occurs only when some unusual combination of program steps occurs. (A)

program tape. The tape which contains the sequence of instructions to the computer for solving a problem. (A)

pseudo code. An arbitrary code, independent of the hardware of a computer, which must be translated into computer code. (A)

pulse. A change in intensity or level over a relatively short period of time, e.g., a shift in electric potential; i.e., if the voltage level of a point shifts with respect to ground for two microseconds, one says that the point received a two-microsecond pulse. (F)

punch, calculating, electronic. A card-handling machine which reads a punched card, performs a number of sequential operations, and punches the result on a card. (A)

punch, card. A device which perforates or places holes in cards in specific locations designated by a program. (A)

punch, summary. A card-handling machine which may be electrically connected to another machine—e.g., tabulator—and which will punch out on a card the information produced, calculated, or summarized by the other machine. (A)

punched tape. Paper tape punched in a pattern of holes so as to convey information. (C)

punching, rate of. Number per unit time of cards, characters, blocks, fields, or words of information placed in the form of holes on cards, or tape. (A)

punch position. The location of the row in a columniated card; e.g., in an 80-column card the rows or "punch positions" may be 0 to 9 or "X" and "Y" corresponding to positions 11 and 12. (A)

Q

quantity. An *integer* or multiple thereof. *Quantity* is preferred to *number* in referring to numerical data. (F)

quantizer. A device which converts an analog quantity into a digital number. (F)

R

range. All the values which a function may have. (A)

ratio, operating. The ratio obtained by dividing the number of hours of correct machine operation by the total hours of scheduled operation, e.g., on a 168-hour week scheduled operation, if 12 hours of preventive maintenance is required and 4.8 hours of unscheduled downtime occurs, then the operating ratio is $(168 - 16.8)/168$, which is equivalent to a 90 per cent operating ratio. (A)

read. To copy, usually from one form of storage to another, particularly from external or secondary storage to internal storage; to sense information on a recording medium. (F)

read-around ratio. In electrostatic storage tubes, the number of times a specific spot (digit or location) may be consulted before "spill over" will cause a loss of information stored in surrounding spots, immediately prior to which the surrounding information must be restored; read-around number. (A)

read pulse. See *one state.*

reader, card. A mechanism that permits the sensing of information punched on cards by means of wire brushes or metal feelers. (A)

reader, tape, magnetic. A device capable of converting to a train or sequence of electrical pulses, information recorded on a magnetic tape in the form of a series of magnetized spots. (A)

reader, tape, paper. A device capable of converting to a train or sequence of electrical pulses, information punched on a paper tape in the form of a series of holes. (A)

reading, rate of. Number of characters, words, fields, blocks, or cards sensed by an input sensing device per unit of time. (A)

readout, destructive. If the reading of information in a storage medium destroys the information, this is called *destructive readout:* otherwise it is *nondestructive readout.* (F)

real time operation. Solving problems in real time. More precisely, processing data in time with a physical process so that the results of the data-processing are useful in guiding the physical operation. (A)

record. All the information regarding one individual or item pertinent to a given problem or set of problems, usually located on one physical document or consecutive locations on the intermediate medium or in the computer memory. The document upon which the results of the computer appear in human language is sometimes called the *output record.* (F)

red tape operations. Computer operations called for by a program which do not directly contribute to solving the problem; namely, arithmetical, logical, and transfer operations used in modifying the address section of other instructions, in counting cycles, in rearranging data, and so forth. (A)

reel. A spool of tape, generally magnetic. (C)

reference record. An output of a compiler that lists the operations and their position in the final specific routine, and contains information describing the segmentation and storage allocation of the routine. (C)

reference time, T_0. An instant near the beginning of switching chosen as an origin for time measurements. It is variously taken as the first instant at which the instantaneous value of the *drive pulse*, the voltage response of the magnetic cell, or the integrated voltage response reaches a specified fraction of its peak pulse amplitude. (M)

regenerate. In the operation of electrostatic storage, to restore information currently held in a cell on the cathode ray tube screen in order to counteract fading and disturbances. (C)

register. The hardware for storing one computer word. Registers are usually zero-access storage devices. (A)

register, addressable. A register to which there corresponds an address which may be used as the location of the operand in the instruction word. (F)

register, circulating (or memory). A register (or memory) consisting of a means for delaying information and a means for regenerating and reinserting the information into the delaying means. (A)

register, control. The accumulator, register, or storage unit which stores the current instruction governing the computer operation; an instruction register. (A)

register, program. A register in the control unit which stores the current instruction of the program and controls computer operation during the execution of the instruction; control register; program counter. (A)

register, shift. A register within which information may be reoriented by a circular permutation. (F)

remanence, B_d. The magnetic flux density which remains in a magnetic circuit after the removal of an applied magnetomotive force. [*Note:* This should not be confused with *residual flux density*. If the magnetic circuit has an air gap, the *remanence* will be less than the *residual flux density*.] (M)

remember. To obtain information from the computer internal memory without removing the impression of the information from the memory; *remembering* for a destructive read-out memory requires both reading and writing. (F)

repetition rate of pulse. The number of electric pulses per unit of time experienced by a point in a computer, usually the maximum, normal, or standard rate of pulses. (A)

representative circulating time. A method of evaluating the speed performance of a computer. One method is to use one-tenth of the time required to perform nine complete additions and one complete multiplication. A complete addition or a complete multiplication time includes the time required to procure two operands from high-speed storage, perform the operation, and store the result, and the time required to select and execute the required number of instructions to do this. (A)

reproducer. A punch card machine that punches cards to agree as may be specified with other cards. (C)

rerun. To run a program or a portion of it over again on the computer. (C)

rerun point. One of a set of planned-for points in a program such that if an error is detected in between two such points, to rerun the problem it is only necessary to go back to the last rerun point, instead of returning to the start of the problem. Rerun points are often three to five minutes apart so that very little computer time is required for a rerun. All information pertinent to a rerun is available in standby registers during the whole time from one rerun point to the next. (C)

reset. To return a register or device to zero or to a specified initial condition. (C)

reset pulse. A *drive pulse* which tends to reset a magnetic cell. (M)

residual flux density, B_r. The magnetic flux density at which the magnetizing force is zero when the material is in a *symmetrically cyclically magnetized condition.* (M)

resolver. A device which separates or breaks up a quantity, particularly a vector, into constituent parts or elements, e.g., to form the three mutually perpendicular components of a space vector. (A)

restore. To return a cycle index, a variable address, or other computer word to its initial or preselected value; periodic regeneration of charge, especially in volatile, condenser-action storage systems. (A)

retentivity, B_{rs}. The property of a material which is measured by the *residual flux density* corresponding to the *saturation induction* for the material. (M)

return. To go back to a specific, planned point in a program, usually when an error is detected, for the purpose of rerunning the program. (A)

revolver. See *drum, magnetic storage.*

rewind. To return a film or tape to its beginning. (A)

robot. A machine containing sensing instruments, acting mechanisms, and guidance circuits, where the circuits receive signals from the sensing instruments, perform reasonable calculations on those signals, and deliver appropriate signals to the acting mechanisms. A machine that runs by itself; an automaton. A thermostatically controlled automatic oil furnace in an ordinary home is a robot according to both the first and second definitions; a spring-wound clock is a robot by the second definition but not by the first. (C)

roll back. See *rerun*.

roll out. To read out of a register or counter by the following process: add to one digit in each column simultaneously; do this 10 times (for decimal numbers); when the result in each column changes from 9 to 0, issue a signal. (C)

round off. To change a more precise quantity to a less precise one, usually choosing the nearest precise one; see *precision*.

rounding error. The error resulting from dropping certain less significant digits of a quantity, and applying some adjustment to the more significant digits retained. Also called *round-off error*. A common round-off rule is to take the quantity to the nearest digit. Thus pi, 3.14159265 ... , rounded to four decimals is 3.1416. [*Note:* Alston S. Householder suggests the following terms: *initial errors, generated errors, propagated errors*, and *residual errors*. If x is the true value of the argument, and x^* the quantity used in computation, then, assuming one wishes $f(x)$, $x - x^*$ is the initial error and $f(x) - f(x^*)$ the propagated error. If f_a is the Taylor, or other, approximation utilized, then $f(x^*) - f_a(x^*)$ is the residual error. If f^* is the actual result then $f_a - f^*$ is the generated error, and this is what builds up as a result of rounding.] (C)

routine. A sequence of operations for a digital computer to perform. The sequence of instructions determining these operations. A set of coded instructions arranged in proper sequence to direct the computer to perform a desired series of operations. See also *subroutine* and *program*. (C)

routine, compiling. An executive routine which, *before* the desired computation is started, translates a program expressed in pseudo-code into machine code (or into another pseudo-code for further translation by an interpreter). In accomplishing the translation, the compiler is required to decode, convert, select, generate, allocate, adapt, orient, incorporate, or record. (A)

routine, diagnostic. A specific routine designed to locate either a malfunction in the computer or a mistake in coding. (A)

routine, executive. A set of coded instructions designed to process and control other sets of coded instructions; a set of coded instructions used in realizing "automatic coding"; a master set of coded instructions. (A)

routine, floating point. A set of coded instructions arranged in proper sequence to direct the computer to perform a specific set of operations which will permit floating-point operation, e.g., enable the use of a fixed-point machine to handle information on a floating-point basis from an external point of view. Floating-point routines are used in computers which do not have built-in floating-point circuitry. (A)

routine, general. A routine expressed in computer coding designed to solve a class of problems, specializing to a specific problem when appropriate parametric values are supplied. (A)

routine, interpretive. An executive routine which, as the computation progresses, translates a stored program expressed in some machine-like pseudo-code into machine code and performs the indicated operations, by means of subroutines as they are translated. An interpretive routine is essentially a closed subroutine which operates successively on an indefinitely long sequence of program parameters (the pseudo-instructions and operands). It may usually be entered as a closed subroutine and exited by a pseudo-code exit instruction. (A)

routine, minimal latency. Especially in reference to serial storage systems, a routine so coded by judicious arrangement of data and instructions in storage, that the actual latency is appreciably less than the expected random-access latency. Also called *minimum-access routine.* (A)

routine, rerun. A routine designed to be used in the wake of a computer malfunction or a coding or operating mistake to reconstitute a routine from the last previous rerun point; roll-back routine. (A)

routine, sequence checking. A routine which checks every instruction executed, printing certain data, e.g., printing out the coded instruction with addresses, and the content of each of several registers; or it may be designed to print out only selected data, such as transfer instructions and the quantity actually transferred. (A)

routine, service. A routine designed to assist in the actual operation of the computer. Tape comparison block location, certain post mortems, and correction routines fall in this class. (A)

routine, specific. A routine expressed in computer coding designed to solve a particular mathematical, logical, or data-handling problem in which each address refers to explicitly stated registers and locations. (A)

routine, test. A routine designed to show whether or not a computer is functioning properly. (A)

routine, trace. See *routine, sequence checking.*

run. One performance of a program on a computer; performance of one routine, or several routines automatically linked so that they form an operating unit, during which manual manipulations are not required of the computer operator. (A)

S

saturation flux density. See *saturation induction.*

saturation induction, B_s. The maximum *intrinsic induction* possible in a material (see *intrinsic induction*). *Saturation induction* is sometimes loosely referred to as *saturation flux density*. (M)

scale. To alter the units in which all variables are expressed so as to bring all magnitudes within the capacity of the computer or routine at hand. (A)

scale factor. One or more factors used to multiply or divide quantities occurring in a problem and convert them into a desired range, such as the range from plus one to minus one. (C)

scanner. An instrument which automatically samples or interrogates the state of various processes, conditions, or physical states and initiates action in accordance with the information obtained. (A)

sector. See *drum, magnetic storage*.

segment. To divide a routine in parts, each consisting of an integral number of subroutines, each part capable of being completely stored in the internal storage and containing the necessary instructions to jump to other segments; in a routine too long to fit into internal storage, a part short enough to be stored entirely in the internal storage and containing the coding necessary to call in and jump automatically to other segments. Routines which exceed internal storage capacity may be automatically divided into segments by a compiler. (A)

select. To take the alternative A if the report on a condition is of one state, and alternative B if the report on the condition is of another state; to choose a needed subroutine from a file of subroutines. (A)

selection ratio. See *coincident-current selection*.

selector. A device which interrogates a condition and initiates a particular operation according to the interrogation report. (A)

sense. To examine, particularly relative to a criterion; to determine the present arrangement of some element of hardware, especially a manually set switch; to read holes punched in paper. (A)

sentinel. A symbol marking the beginning or the end of some element of information such as a field, item, block, tape, and so forth; a tag. (A)

sequence. To select A if A is greater than or equal to B, and select B if A is less than B, or some variation of this operation. (A)

sequence control tape. Program tape (obsolescent term). (C)

serial. Handled one after the other in a single piece of equipment. (C)

serial operation. The flow of information through the computer or in any part of it using only one line or channel at a time. Contrasted with *parallel operation*. (C)

serial storage. Storage in which time is one of the coordinates used to locate any given bit, character, or (especially) word. Storage in which words, within given groups of several words, appear one after the other in time sequence, and in which access time therefore includes a variable latency or waiting time of zero to many word-times, is said to be serial by word. Storage in which the individual bits comprising a word appear in time sequence is serial by bit. Storage for coded-decimal or other nonbinary numbers in which the characters appear in time sequence is serial by character; for example, magnetic drums are usually serial by word but may be serial by bit, or parallel by bit, or serial by character and parallel by bit, and so forth. (C)

serial transfer. A system of data transfer in which the characters of an element of information are transferred in sequence over a single path in consecutive time positions. (C)

servomechanism. A closed loop system in which the error or deviation from a desired or preset norm is reduced to zero, and one in which mechanical position is usually the controlled variable; e.g., a synchronized drum storage system requires a servomechanism to insure synchronism between a crystal-controlled electronic oscillator and a rotating cylinder; an anti-aircraft fire control gun-positioning system requires a servo to insure that deviations are corrected. (A)

set pulse. A *drive pulse* which tends to set a magnetic cell. (M)

shaper. Unique to this book. A differentiating and clipping circuit which produces a single pulse when a bistable device changes from one state to another, but not when the change of state occurs in the opposite direction. The change in state which causes a pulse is determined by the output of the bistable device to which the shaper is connected—thus, when a shaper is connected to the *one* output of a flip-flop, it produces a pulse when that flip-flop changes from 0 to 1 but produces no pulse when the flip-flop changes from 1 to 0. (F)

shift. To move the characters of a unit of information column-wise right or left. For a number, this is equivalent to multiplying or dividing by a power of the base of notation. (A)

shift, arithmetic. To multiply or divide a quantity by a power of the number base, e.g., binary 1011 represents decimal 11, therefore two arithmetic shifts to the left is binary 101100, which represents decimal 44. (A)

shift, cyclic. A shift in which the digits dropped off at one end of a word are returned at the other in a circular fashion; logical, non-arithmetical, or circular shift. (A)

shift, end around. See *shift, cyclic.* (F)

shift, long. An order which permutes circularly the characters in several registers. (F)

shift out. To cause information to move within a register toward one end, in such a way that as information passes out this end, 0's are entered into the other end. (F)

shift pulse. A *drive pulse* which initiates shifting of characters in a register. (M)

sign digit. A digit, usually 1 or 0, used to designate the algebraic sign of a quantity (plus or minus). (C)

significant digits. Digits appearing in the coefficient of a number when the number is written as a coefficient between 1.000 ... and 9.999 ... times a power of 10 (called scientific normal form); and similarly for any base of notation other than 10. Examples: .000376, which is equal to 3.76 times 10^{-4}, has three significant digits; 12 million, equal to 1.2 times 10^7, has two significant digits; 300,600, equal to 3.006 times 10^5, has four significant digits; in the statement, "J. B. Smith's book had exactly 1000 pages," "1000" has four significant digits, although ordinarily 1000 would have only one significant digit. (C)

simulation. The representation of physical systems and phenomena by computers, models, or other equipment. (C)

simulator. A computer or model which represents a system or phenomenon and which mirrors or maps the effects of various changes in the original, enabling the original to be studied, analyzed, and understood by means of the behavior of the model. (C)

single-address. See *code, multiple-address.*

skip. An instruction to proceed to the next instruction; a "blank" instruction. (C)

slow memory. Sections of the memory from which information may be obtained automatically but not at the fastest rate of the several sections. (C)

solver, equation. An analog calculating device which solves systems of linear simultaneous non-differential equations or determines the roots of polynomials or both. (C)

sort. To arrange items of information by a key contained in the items according to a rule. (F)

sorter. A machine which sorts punched cards. (F)

specific coding. Coding in which all addresses refer to specific registers and locations. (C)

squareness ratio. (1) B_r/B_m. For a material in a *symmetrically cyclically magnetized condition,* the ratio of the flux density at zero magnetizing force to the maximum flux density. (2) R_s. For a material in a *symmetrically cyclically magnetized condition,* the ratio of the flux density when the magnetizing force has changed halfway from zero toward its negative limiting value, to the maximum flux density. [*Note:* Both of these ratios are functions of the maximum magnetizing force.] (M)

stacker, card. A mechanism that accumulates cards in a bin after they have passed through a machine operation; a hopper. (A)

standardize. To adjust the exponent and mantissa of a floating-point result so that the mantissa lies in the prescribed normal range; normalize; see *floating-point calculation.* (A)

step. An indication of the ordinal sequence in which the instructions are stored within the computer memory; to each step there can correspond one and only one instruction—an instruction may be used on none, one, or many steps. (F)

storage. Any device into which information can be copied, which will hold this information and from which the information can be obtained at a later time; the erasable storage in any given computer. (A)

storage, circulating. A device using a delay line, or unit which stores information in a train or pattern of pulses, where the pattern of pulses issuing at the final end is sensed, amplified, reshaped and reinserted in the delay line at the beginning end. (A)

storage, dynamic. Storage such that information at a certain position is moving in time and so is not always available instantly; e.g., acoustic delay line, magnetic drum; circulating or recirculating of information in a medium. (A)

storage, electrostatic. A device possessing the capability of storing changeable information in the form of charged or uncharged areas on the screen of a cathode ray tube. (A)

storage, erasable. Media which may hold information that can be changed; i.e., the media can be reused; e.g., magnetic tape, drum, or core. (A)

storage, external. Storage facilities divorced from the computer itself but holding information in the form prescribed for the computer; e.g., magnetic tapes, magnetic wire, punched cards, and so forth. (A)

storage, magnetic. Any storage system which utilizes the magnetic properties of materials to store information. (A)

storage, mercury. Columns of a liquid mercury medium used as a storage element by the delaying action or time of travel of sonic pulses which are circulated by having electrical amplifier, shaper, and timer circuits complete the loop. (A)

storage, nonerasable. Media used for containing information which cannot be erased and reused, such as punched paper tapes and punched cards. (A)

storage, nonvolatile. Storage media which retain information in the absence of power and which may be made available upon restoration of power; e.g., magnetic tapes, drums, or cores. (A)

storage, parallel. Storage in which all bits, or characters, or (especially) words are essentially equally available in space, without time being one of the coordinates. Parallel storage contrasts with serial storage. When words are in parallel, the storage is said to be *parallel by words.* When characters within words (or binary digits within words or characters) are dealt with simultaneously, not one after the other, the storage is *parallel by characters* (or *parallel by bit* respectively). (A)

storage, secondary. Storage facilities not an integral part of the computer but directly connected to and controlled by the computer; e.g., magnetic drum, magnetic tapes, and so forth. (A)

storage, serial. Storage in which time is one of the coordinates used to locate any given bit, character, or (especially) word. Storage in which words, within given groups of several words, appear one after the other in time sequence, and in which access time therefore includes a variable latency or waiting time of zero to many word-times, is said to be *serial by word*. Storage in which the individual bits comprising a word appear in time sequence is *serial by bit*. Storage for coded-decimal or other non-binary numbers in which the characters appear in time sequence is *serial by character;* e.g., magnetic drums are usually serial by word but may be serial by bit, or parallel by bit, or serial by character and parallel by bit, and so forth. (A)

storage, static. Storage such that information is fixed in space and available at any time; e.g., flip-flop, electrostatic, or coincident-current magnetic-core storage. (A)

storage, temporary. Internal storage locations reserved for intermediate and partial results. (A)

storage, volatile. Storage media such that if the applied power is cut off, the stored information is lost; e.g., acoustic delay lines, electrostatic tubes. (A)

storage, working. A portion of the internal storage reserved for the data upon which operations are being performed. (A)

storage, zero-access. Storage for which the latency (waiting time) is negligible at all times. (A)

store. To transfer an element of information to a device from which the unaltered information can be obtained at a later time. (A)

subroutine. The set of instructions necessary to direct the computer to carry out a well-defined mathematical or logical operation; a subunit of a routine. A subroutine is often written in relative or symbolic coding even when the routine to which it belongs is not. (A)

subroutine, closed. A subroutine not stored in its proper place in the linear operational sequence, but stored away from the routine which refers to it. Such a subroutine is entered by a jump, and provision is made to return, i.e., to jump back to the proper point in the main routine at the end of the subroutine. (A)

subroutine, dynamic. A subroutine which involves parameters, such as decimal point position or item size, from which a relatively coded subroutine is derived. The computer itself is expected to adjust or generate the subroutine according to the parametric values chosen. (A)

subroutine, open. A subroutine inserted directly into the linear operational sequence, not entered by a jump. Such a subroutine must be recopied at each point at which it is needed in a routine. (A)

subroutine, static. A subroutine which involves no parameters other than the addresses of the operands. (A)

substep. Each step of a computer's task in the computer with centralized control is often divided into substeps—a portion of a step. (F)

substitute. To replace an element of information by some other element of information. (A)

switch, function. A circuit having a fixed number of inputs and outputs designed such that the output information is a function of the input information, each expressed in a certain code or signal configuration or pattern. (A)

switching coefficient, S_w. The derivative of applied magnetizing force with respect to the reciprocal of the resultant *switching time*. It is usually determined as the reciprocal of the slope of a curve of reciprocals of *switching times* vs. values of applied magnetizing forces. The magnetizing forces are applied as step functions. (M)

switching time. (1) T_s, the time interval between the *reference time* and the last instant at which the instantaneous voltage response of a magnetic cell reaches a stated fraction of its peak value. (2) T_x, the time interval between the *reference time* and the first instant at which the instantaneous integrated voltage response reaches a stated fraction of its peak value. (M)

symbol, logical. A symbol used to represent a logical element graphically. (A)

symmetrically cyclically magnetized condition. A condition of a magnetic material when it is in a *cyclically magnetized condition* and the limits of the applied magnetizing forces are equal and of opposite sign, so that the limits of flux density are equal and of opposite sign. (M)

synchronous. See *computer, synchronous.*

system, data processing. The assembly of equipment including a computer (if used) and associated processing equipment, the purpose of which is to solve a problem or set of problems. The system often includes the procedural details and computer coding called the *program*. (F)

T

tabulator. A machine which reads information from one medium, e.g., cards, paper tape, magnetic tape, and produces lists, tables, and totals on separate forms or continuous paper. (A)

tag. A unit of information, whose composition differs from that of other members of the set so that it can be used as a marker or label; a sentinel. (A)

tally. To add 1 to or subtract 1 from a quantity, usually to the content of a register; tally *up* is used to indicate addition of a unit, while tally *down* indicates subtraction of a unit. (F)

tank. A unit of acoustic delay line storage, containing a set of channels each forming a separate recirculation path; a circuit consisting of inductance and capacitance used for the purpose of sustaining electrical oscillations. (A)

tape, magnetic. A tape or ribbon with a magnetic surface on which information may be placed as magnetically polarized spots. (A)

tape, program. A tape which contains the sequence of instructions required for solving a problem and which may be read by the computer. (A)

tape reservoir. That part of a magnetic tape recording and/or reproducing system which is used to isolate the inertia of the tape from the drive system. (F)

tape-wound core. A length of ferromagnetic tape coiled about an axis in such a way that one convolution falls directly upon the preceding convolution. The greater of the cross-sectional dimensions of the tape is the *tape width*, and the other is the *tape thickness*. A *wrap* is one convolution of the tape about the axis. *Wrap thickness* is the distance between corresponding points on two consecutive wraps, measured parallel to the *tape thickness*.

A *bobbin core* is a *tape-wound core* in which the ferromagnetic tape has been wrapped on a form or bobbin which supplies mechanical support to the tape. The dimensions of a bobbin are illustrated in Figure 1. The *bobbin I.D.* is the center-hole diameter (D) of the bobbin. The *bobbin O.D.* is the over-all diameter (E) of the bobbin. The *bobbin height* is the over-all axial dimension (F) of the bobbin. The *groove diameter* is the diameter (G) of the center portion of the bobbin on which the first tape *wrap* is placed. The *groove width* is the axial dimension (H) of the bobbin measured inside the groove at the groove diameter. (M)

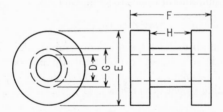

FIGURE 1. Dimensions of a bobbin.

telemeter. To transmit measurements and observations over a distance, as for example by radio transmission from a guided missile to a receiving magnetic tape recorder on the ground. (C)

ternary. Pertaining to the system of notation utilizing the base of 3, employing the characters 0, 1, and 2. (A)

test, crippled leap frog. A variation of the leap frog test, modified so that it repeats its tests from a single set of storage locations rather than a changing set of locations. (A)

test, leap frog. A program designed to discover computer malfunction, which performs a series of arithmetical or logical operations on one group of storage locations, transfers itself to another group of storage locations, checks the correctness of the transfer, then begins the series of operations over again. Eventually, all storage positions will have been occupied and the test will be repeated. (A)

tetrad. A group of four, usually four pulses, in particular, a group of four pulses used to express a digit in the scale of 10 or 16. (A)

thermistor. The thermistor is a solid-state, semiconducting device made by sintering mixtures of the oxide powders of various metals. It is made in many shapes, such as beads, disks, flakes, washers, and rods, to which contact wires are attached. As its temperature is changed, the electrical resistance of the thermistor varies. The associated temperature coefficient of resistance is extremely high, nonlinear, and negative. (A)

thermocouple. A device made of two bi-metal joints (forming a closed loop) so that if the two junctions are at different temperatures, a difference of potential exists between the two junctions. (A)

three-address. See *code, multiple-address.*

threshold field, H_0. The least magnetizing force in a direction which tends to decrease the *remanence,* which, when applied either as a steady field of long duration or as a pulsed field appearing many times, will cause a stated fractional change of *remanence.* (M)

thyratron. A hot-cathode, gas-discharge tube in which one or more electrodes are used to control electrostatically the starting of a unidirectional flow of current. (A)

time, code checking. All time spent checking out a problem on the machine making sure that the problem is set up correctly, and that the code is correct. (A)

time, engineering or servicing. All machine downtime necessary for routine testing, for machine servicing due to breakdowns, or for preventive servicing measures, e.g., block tube changes. Includes all test time following breakdown and subsequent repair or preventive servicing. (A)

time, idle. Time in which machine is believed to be in good operating condition and attended by service engineers but not in use on problems.

time, no charge machine-fault. Unproductive time due to a computer fault such as the following: (1) nonduplication, (2) transcribing error, (3) input/output malfunction, (4) machine malfunction resulting in an incomplete run. (A)

time, no charge non-machine-fault. Unproductive time due to no fault of the computer such as the following: (1) good duplication, (2) error in preparation of input data, (3) error in arranging the program deck, (4) error in operating instructions or misinterpretation of instructions, (5) unscheduled good testing time, run during normal production period when machine malfunction is suspected but is demonstrated not to exist. (A)

time, production. Good computing time, including occasional duplication of one case for a check or rerunning of the test run. Also, duplication requested by the sponsor; any reruns caused by misinformation or bad data supplied by sponsor. Error studies using different intervals, convergence criteria, and so forth. (A)

time, pulse. In a cycle of computer processing, the instant at which information scanned for detection. (F)

time, standby unattended. Time in which the machine is in an unknown condition and not being used to solve problems. Includes time in which machine is known to be defective and work is not being done to restore it to operating condition. Includes breakdowns which render it unavailable due to outside conditions such as power outages. (A)

time, system improvement. All machine downtime needed for the installation and testing of new components, large or small, and machine downtime necessary for modification of existing components. Includes all programmed tests following the above actions to prove machine is operating properly. (A)

toggle. See *multivibrator*.

track. See *drum magnetic storage*.

transcribe. To copy, with or without translating, from one external storage medium to another. (A)

transducer. A device which converts energy from one form to another; e.g., a quartz crystal imbedded in mercury can change electrical energy to sound energy as is done in sonic delay lines in computer storage systems. (A)

transfer. To copy, exchange, read, record, store, transmit, transport, or write data; to change control; to jump to another location. See *jump*. (A)

transfer check. Verification of transmitted information by temporary storing, retransmitting, and comparing. (C)

transfer, parallel. A system of data transfer in which the characters of an element of information are transferred simultaneously over a set of paths. (A)

transfer, serial. A system of data transfer in which the characters of an element of information are transferred in sequence over a single path in consecutive time positions. (A)

transform. To change information in structure or composition without altering the meaning or value; to normalize, edit, or substitute. (A)

transient. A phenomenon experiencing a change as a function of time; something which is temporary; a build-up or breakdown in the intensity of a phenomenon until a steady state condition is reached; an aperiodic phenomenon; the time rate of change of energy is finite and some form of energy storage is usually involved. (A)

translate. To change information (e.g., problem statements in pseudo-code, data, or coding) from one language to another without affecting the meaning. (A)

transmit. To reproduce information in a new location replacing whatever was previously stored and clearing or erasing the source of the information. (A)

transport. To convey as a whole from one storage device to another. (A)

trigger. See *multivibrator.*

trouble-location problem. A test problem whose incorrect solution supplies information on the location of faulty equipment; used after a check problem has shown that a fault exists. (A)

trouble-shoot. To search for a coding mistake or the cause of a computer malfunction in order to remove same. (A)

truncate. To drop digits of a number or terms of a series thus lessening precision. See *precision.* For example, the number pi, 3.14159265 ... , is *truncated* to three figures in 3.14.

truncation error. The error resulting from the use of only a finite number of terms of an infinite series, or from the approximation of operations in the infinitesimal calculus by operations in the calculus of finite differences. (A)

trunk. A path over which information is transferred; a bus. (A)

truth table. A list in tabular form of the output of a logical function or element for all combinations of inputs. (F)

tube, Williams. A cathode ray tube used as an electrostatic storage device of the type designed by F. C. Williams, University of Manchester, England. (A)

two-address code. See *code, multiple-address.*

typewriter. An I/O device used to receive information directly or indirectly from the computer in computer or human language by means of a modified conventional electric typewriter. The computer typewriter is often used to convert language for direct communication with the computer; in combination with a paper tape punch it converts human to intemediate language. (F)

U

ultrasonics. The field of science devoted to frequencies of sound above the human audio range, i.e., above 20 kilocycles per second. (A)

unconditional. Not subject to conditions external to the specific instruction. (A)

undisturbed-one output. See *coincident-current selection.*

undisturbed-zero output. See *coincident-current selection.*

uni. See *multivibrator.*

unload. See *load.*

unpack. To decompose packed information into a sequence of separate words or elements. (A)

unwind. To code explicitly, at length, and in full all the operations of a cycle thus eliminating all red-tape operations in the final problem coding. Unwinding may be performed automatically by the computer during assembly, generation, or compilation. (A)

V

validity. Correctness; especially the degree of closeness by which iterated results approach the correct result. (A)

verifier. (1) A punch card machine operated manually which reports by signals whether punched holes have been inserted in the wrong places in a punch card or have not been inserted at all. (2) An auxiliary device on which a previous manual transcription of data can be verified by comparing a current manual transcription character-by-character during the current process. (C)

volatile. See *storage, volatile.*

W

winding. A conductive path, usually of wire, inductively coupled to a magnetic core or cell. When several windings are employed, they may be designated by the functions performed. Examples are: sense, bias, and drive windings. Drive windings include read, write, inhibit, set, reset, input, shift, and advance windings. (M)

wire, magnetic. Wire made of a magnetic material along small incremental lengths of which magnetic dipoles are placed in accordance with binary information. (A)

word. A set of characters which occupies one storage location and is treated by the computer circuits as a unit and transported as such. Ordinarily a word is treated by the control unit as an instruction, and by the arithmetic unit as a quantity. Word lengths are fixed or variable depending on the particular computer. (A)

word time. The time required to transport one word from one storage device to another. See also *access time.* (A)

wrap. See *tape-wound core.*

write. To record or copy information in reusable form for future reference. (F)

write pulse. See *one state.*

X

XS3. See *code, XS3.* (F)

Z

zero. The computer's conception of zero. [*Note:* the computer may provide for two zeros. Positive binary zero is represented by the absence of digits or pulses in a word. Negative binary zero in a computer operating with 1's complements may be represented by a pulse in every pulse position in a word. In a coded decimal computer, decimal zero and binary zero may not have the same representation. In most computers, there exist distinct and valid representations both for positive and for negative zero.] (C)

zero-access storage. Storage for which the latency or waiting time is negligible. (C)

zero-address instruction. See *code, multiple-address.*

zero output. See *one state.*

zero state. See *one state.*

zero suppression. The elimination of non-significant zeros to the left of the integral part of a quantity before printing is begun. One of the operations in editing is to suppress these zeros. (C)

zone. Any of the three top positions 12, 11, and 0 in an 80-column punch card; in these zone positions a second punch can be inserted, so that with punches in the remaining positions 1 to 9, enough two-punch combinations are obtained to represent alphabetic characters. A portion of internal storage allocated for a particular purpose. (C)

APPENDIX B

ANNOTATED BIBLIOGRAPHY

The purpose of this bibliography is to supply you with a short list of source material in such a way that you will know approximately what you will find when you get a copy of the reference. A good jumping-off place for a concentrated literature search is the bibliography.

1. Netherwood, Douglas B., "Logical Machine Design: A Selected Bibliography," Parts I and II, *IRE Transactions of the Professional Group on Electronic Computers*, Vol. EC7, No. 2, June 1958, pp. 155–178; Vol. EC8, No. 3, Sept. 1959, pp. 367–380.

INTRODUCTORY

There are *many* introductions to the study of digital computers. Usually they don't go into the matter very deeply. My recommendation for a book which will introduce the reader to the *logical block design* of digital computers is (2) below; it should also prove valuable to the reader of *this* volume if he should find the going rough (quite unlikely, of course). I often refer to this book in a friendly, even respectful, manner as the *computer comic book*. It is crammed full of fine drawings which explain, better than many words, the broad principles of block design. It is the basis of a course for training computer technicians and so stresses the practical in contrast to the theoretical.

2. Murphy, John S., *Basics of Digital Computers*. New York: John F. Rider, 1958. 3 Vols.: Vol. 1, 116 pp.; Vol. 2, 133 pp.; Vol. 3, 135 pp.

BOOLEAN LOGIC

Logic is used by many authors to mean the attempt at systematization which relies almost completely upon Boolean equations and algebra to express the interrelations which exist within the computer. To introduce

446

this philosophy, (3) is most valuable. It is written for the engineer who does not have previous logical background. It contains many drawings and illustrative problems. It thoroughly explains the Karnaugh map technique. The address is included below, for the book is most easily obtained directly from the publisher.

3. Beizer, Boris, and Stephen W. Leibholz, *Engineering Applications of Boolean Algebra*. New York: Gage Publishing Co., 1250 Sixth Ave., New York 20, N.Y. 68 pp. $2.00.

The mapping technique was first presented in

4. Veitch, F. W., "A Chart Method for Simplifying Truth Fractions," *Proceedings of the Association for Computing Machinery*, Vol. 5, Feb. 1952.

It was developed into a somewhat more useful form in

5. Karnaugh, M., "Synthesis of Combinational Logic Circuits," *Communications and Electronics*, No. 9, Nov. 1953, pp. 593–599.

A thorough coverage of logic as applied to switching circuits but with slight application to computers is found in

6. Caldwell, Samuel H., *Switching Circuits and Logical Design*. New York: John Wiley, 1958. xvii + 686 pp.

The classical work which applies Boolean algebra to computers is (7). Presented here are models which incorporate a concept of time. This is a pioneering attempt to systematize the computer art; the trouble is, it seems to add little to the one's ability to design a better computer.

7. Phister, Montgomery Jr., *Logical Design of Digital Computers*. New York: John Wiley, 1958. xvi + 408 pp.

Another pioneering work is (8), the first to organize computer art into one comprehensive volume. Many variations of combinations of elementary blocks which do specific tasks are presented. Even in this fast-changing field many useful concepts can be gleaned from

8. Richards, R. K., *Arithmetic Operations in Digital Computers*. Princeton, N.J.: D. Van Nostrand, 1955. vi + 397 pp.

COMPONENT AND CIRCUITS

Excellent detailed descriptions of vacuum tube circuits together with fine explanations of their operation and interconnection are found in

9. Millman, J. and H. Taub, *Pulse and Digital Circuits*. New York: McGraw-Hill, 1956. xvix + 687 pp.

Magnetic components are given especial attention in (10) as are various memory devices. These are combined to form many circuits.

10. Richards, R. K., *Digital Computer Components and Circuits*. Princeton, N.J.: D. Van Nostrand, 1957. vii + 511 pp.

The latest in computer transistor circuits is found in

11. Pressman, A. I., *Design of Transistorized Circuits for Digital Computers*. New York: John F. Rider, 1959.

The reader interested in a family of circuits used in an existing computer will find these described in

12. Booth, G. W., and T. P. Bothwell, "Basic Logic Circuits for Computer Applications," *Electronics*, Vol. 30, March 1957, pp. 196–200.

MAGNETICS AND MEMORIES

Here is a fine discussion about magnetic materials and recording. Starting from fundamentals, the phenomena surrounding magnetic recording are simply explained in

13. Begun, S. J., *Magnetic Recording*. New York: Rinehart, 1949. x + 242 pp. $5.00.

A fine summary of the work done with cores and core-type devices is found in

14. Rajchmain, J. A., "Magnetics for Computers: A Survey of the State of the Art," *RCA Review*, Vol. XX, No. 1, March 1959, pp. 92–135.

Specific problems in storing and retrieving information in core memories are covered in

15. McMahon, Robert E., "Transistorized Core Memory," *IRE Transaction of the Professional Group on Instrumentation*, Vol. 16, No. 2, June 1957, pp. 153–156.

PROGRAMMING

An introductory approach to programming is found in

16. McCracken, D. D., *Digital Computer Programming*. New York: John Wiley, 1957. vii + 253 pp. $7.75.

Many new concepts in programming are described in (17) if the reader is willing to start at the beginning with the author and work up to them. Here is the only place where interpretive, executive, and compiling routines are given a brief explanation.

17. Jeenal, *Jeenel*, Joachim, *Programming for Digital Computers*. New York: McGraw-Hill, 1959. viii + 517 pp. $12.00.

BLOCK LOGICAL DESIGN

You can see how block logical design is applied to specific computers in the following articles:

18. J. C. Alrich, "Engineering Description of the Electro Data Digital Computer," *IRE Transactions of the Prof. Group on Electronic Computers*, Vol. EC4, March 1955, pp. 1–10.

19. Hughes, E. S. Jr., "The IBM Magnetic Drum Calculator Type 650; Engineering and Design Considerations," *Western AIEE-IRE-ACM Computer Conference*, Feb. 1954 at Los Angeles, pp. 140–154.

20. Ross, H. D. Jr., "The Arithmetic Element of the IBM 701 Computer," *Proceedings IRE*, Vol. 41, Dec. 1953, pp. 1287–1294.

21. Bucholtz, W., "System Design of the IBM 701 Computer," *Proceedings IRE*, Vol. 41, Oct. 1953, pp. 1262–1275.

22. Leiner, Notz, Smith, and Weinberger, "System Design of the SEAC & DYSEAC," *Transactions of the Professional Group on Electronic Computers*, Vol. EC3, No. 2, June 1954, pp. 8–22.

23. Banks, A. W., "The Logical Design of an Idealized General Purpose Computer," *Journal of the Franklin Inst.*, March 1956, pp. 297–314; April 1956, pp. 421–436.

24. Astrahan and Rochester, "The Logical Organization of the New IBM Scientific Calculator," *Proceedings of the Association for Computing Machinery*, May 1952.

COMPUTER SPECIFICATION

By now you are probably interested in the properties of available computers. Many texts on computers have an appendix section for this information. I feel that the most complete source on the characteristics of extant computers is (25). Besides the computer description, many installations are catalogued and the full complement of equipment used is itemized. It also includes a most thorough design and application bibliography.

25. Controllership Foundation, *Business Electronics Reference Guide*, Vol. 4. New York: Controllership Foundation, 1959. 602 pp. $15.00.

SYMBOLS

Until the IRE symbols are officially issued and become standard, the many manufacturers will continue to use different symbols. Most of these are gathered together for reference in (26).

26. RCA Service Company, *The Language and Symbology of Digital Computer Systems*. Camden, N.J.: RCA Corporation, 1959. vi + 114 pp.

GENERAL

An interesting collection of articles on computers is

27. *Control Engineering* Staff, *The Use of Digital Computers in Science in Business and Control*. New York: *Control Engineering* Magazine, 1958. 112 pp. $3.00.

PERIODICALS

There are a few publications which appear at regular intervals and which contain contributions in specific areas for computer hardware, system design, and component development. There is:

28. *Transactions of the Professional Group on Electronic Computers*. Quarterly by the Institute of Radio Engineers, New York.

For mathematical analyses, system design, and advanced programming techniques, there is

29. *Transactions of the Association for Computing Machinery*. Quarterly by the ACM, New York.

Professional, company, and equipment news and program applications are reported in

30. *Communications of the Association for Computing Machinery*. Monthly by the ACM, New York.

New papers on various phases of computers appear yearly in

31. *Convention Record of the Institute of Radio Engineers.*

32. *Wescon Record of the Institute of Radio Engineers.*

33. *Proceedings of the Eastern Joint Computer Conference.*

34. *Proceedings of the Western Joint Computer Conference.*

These are available from the IRE headquarters, 1 East 79th Street, New York.

APPENDIX C

SPECIFICATIONS OF THE
POLYVAC

Name: POLYgenic Variform Automatic Computer
Operation: Serial;   Pulse rate: 100 kc
Machine language: NBCD or XS3. 4 bits, per character
Word length: Nine decimal characters plus sign
Instruction type: One address
Memory: 1000 word drum storage;   Average access time: 5 milliseconds
Instruction repertoire: 38 instructions in mnemonic form (see Figure 5.7)
Cycle registers: Nine cycle registers of three characters each, which may
     be tallied up or down
Data: Numeric only
Console with nine breakpoints
Paper tape reader, 300 characters per second
Paper tape punch, 300 characters per second
Typewriter limited to about 10 characters per second
Operates from paper tape or punches paper tape
Addition time: 10 microseconds

INDEX

Multiplication (Continued):
  signed, 229
Multivibrator, 146

Nor, 142
Not, 131
Numbers:
  irrational, 100
  natural, 97
  rational, 100
  real, 99
Number systems, 95

Order:
  specification of, 50
  symbolic description, 51
Off line operation:
  magnetic tape, 359
  off-line processing, 359
  punch cards, 359
  punched paper tape, 359
  verification, 360

Polyvac:
  arithmetic orders, 54
  break points, 378
  chart of commands, 76
  code of, 121
  comparison orders, 66
  cycle index register orders, 72
  description, 377
  end around shift order, 53
  jump orders, 66
  load instructions, 378
  long shift order, 54
  shift out orders, 52
  stop orders, 67
  transfer orders, 52
  unload instructions, 378
Problem:
  analysis, 26
  calculations, 31
  coded routine for, 32
  data flow, 31
  description, 29
  document flow, 29
  initial statement, 26
  preparation for computer, 25
  pre-processing requirements, 26
  systems analysis, 29

Processing:
  description, 5
Programming:
  external, 43
  internal, 44
  permanent, 42
Propositions, 132
Punch card:
  collating, 331
  merging, 331
  punching, 330
  reading, 331
  selecting, 331
  single record processing, 330
  sorting, 330
Punched paper tape input equipment:
  general, 317
  paper tape punch, 324
    control, 327
    punching, 325
    tape feed, 326
  paper tape reader, 319
    optical reading system, 320
    tape feed mechanism, 319
    tape mechanism control, 322

Quinary system, 107

Record keeping, 4
Register, 17, 45
  cycle index, 71
  tally, 202
Remembering, 19
Revolvers, 269

Shaper, 148
Shifting, 46
Shift orders:
  logic, 294
Shift register:
  dynamic, 168
  symbol, 170
  using magnetic core, 165
  with built-in storage, 165
Simplification:
  logical, 131
Simulation:
  nuclear reactor, 3
  real time, 2
  scaled, 2